Coping with family violence.

DATE			

COPING WITH FAMILY VIOLENCE

COPING WITH FAMILY VIOLENCE

RESEARCH AND POLICY PERSPECTIVES

Gerald T. Hotaling
David Finkelhor
John T. Kirkpatrick
Murray A. Straus
editors

SAGE PUBLICATIONS
The Publishers of Professional Social Science
Newbury Park Beverly Hills London New Delhi

For information address:

SAGE Publications, Inc.
2111 West Hillcrest Drive
Newbury Park, California 91320

SAGE Publications Inc.
275 South Beverly Drive
Beverly Hills
California 90212

SAGE Publications Ltd.
28 Banner Street
London EC1Y 8QE
England

SAGE PUBLICATIONS India Pvt. Ltd.
M-32 Market
Greater Kailash I
New Delhi 110 048 India

Printed in the United States of America

Library of Congress Cataloging-in-Publication Data

Main entry under title:

Coping with family violence : research and policy perspectives /
Gerald T. Hotaling . . . [et al.].
p. cm.
Bibliography: p.
ISBN 0-8039-2722-3. ISBN 0-8039-2723-1 (pbk.)
1. Family violence—United States. 2. Family violence—Government policy—United States. I. Hotaling, Gerald T.
HQ809.3.U5C67 1988
362.8′2—dc19 88-1874
CIP

FIRST PRINTING 1988

Contents

Preface

This book grew out of the Second National Conference for Family Violence Research held at the University of New Hampshire. It represents what can happen when academic researchers, service providers, and policymakers come together to work on a common problem. The 21 chapters making up this volume address issues that are in need of answers in order to understand, treat, and ultimately prevent family violence and abuse. This book is dedicated to the idea that research and policy should constantly inform one another. This is not an easy task since these groups have their own agendas and only rarely agree on anything. But the fact that therapists, physicians, government officials, and researchers from psychology, sociology, public health, social work, law, and gerontology could exchange ideas for three days is a noteworthy event.

Several organizations played key roles in promoting the working relationship between research, policy, and treatment at both the conference and in this book. Some of these include the Battered Women's Movement, the Domestic Abuse Project of Minneapolis; EMERGE, Boston; the Sexual Assault Center, Harborview Medical Center, Seattle; Family Service, Madison, Wisconsin; Servicios de la Raza, Denver; the Department of Youth Services, Boston; the Institute for the Black Family, University of Pittsburgh; Children's Hospital Medical Center, Boston; the Texas Council on Family Violence; the American Humane Association; the American Bar Association; the National Committee for the Prevention of Child Abuse; the National Committee for the Prevention of Rape; the National Institute of Justice; the national Center on Child Abuse and Neglect; and the National Institute of Mental Health.

The enormous problems of organizing and planning a large conference and preparing a manuscript for publication could not have been overcome had it not been for Kathy Cole, Sieglinde Fizz, Heidi Gerhardt, Charlene Hodgdon, Ruth Miller, and Donna Wilson.

The financial support of the Undesignated Gifts Fund at the University of New Hampshire is greatly appreciated.

A special word of thanks must go to David Finkelhor. David worked hard to ensure that research on policy, treatment, and prevention issues were represented at the conference and in this book. This is not surprising to anyone familiar with David's own research. His research has always been conducted in such a way to be immediately useful to people who need it the most: those who work directly with abusive offenders and the victims of abusive behavior. In many ways, David's work is an excellent example of how research can be done well and contribute to our knowledge base and at the same time be used to lessen the pain and suffering of the victims of violence and abuse.

Introduction

The papers in this volume are all testimony to the rapid expansion and increasing sophistication of a social system that is taking family violence more seriously and trying, however imperfectly, to deal with it. Ten years ago research was confined largely to describing the extent and the nature of the problem, and to a lesser extent documenting the inadequacy of social responses. Since that time, however, social responses have evolved considerably. They have not reached the level or sophistication that many had hoped, but as these papers show, there is much that is new and interesting, if not effective.

For example, these papers reflect the increasing maturity of the shelter movement, which has consolidated its presence and legitimacy in communities around the country. They report on innovations and experiments within the child welfare system in its response to child abuse. They show a criminal justice system that has adapted in response to many of the criticisms of advocates for battered women.

In fact, the papers reported here are particularly auspicious indicators of this evolution because they are not simply descriptions of services but evaluations and studies of services. When services are tenuous and experimental, it is actually rare that they generate research. It is only after a period of some consolidation that research is accommodated.

Parts I and II provide a background to much of the rest of the volume. In the process of developing social responses, workers in the field of family violence have had to think more critically about the "help-seeking," not to mention the "help-providing" process. An early realization was that when victims and families are offered help—even extremely battered victims and extremely suffering families—they do not necessarily take it. Obviously victims are not "seeing" themselves or their situations in the same way as help providers see them. Why?

Three of the initial chapters in this book address the question of what gets defined and labeled as *abuse, battering,* and *victimization.* The papers make clear that what seems "obvious" to some of those in the family violence field is not so for others. For example, Sharon Herzberger and Howard Tennen (Chapter 1) make clear that among other things, gender, profession, religion, social class, and childhood history may all affect judgments about whether something is abusive. Andrea Sedlak (Chapter 2) confirms what many others have shown: that people who have suffered even very serious forms of violence are less likely to see themselves as "battered" (or by extension abused) unless injury has occurred. And Michele Bograd's (Chapter 3) findings point out how battered women's self-perceptions differ from the kinds of analyses family violence professionals are apt to make of the causes of the violence they suffer.

If victims of violence do not seek or accept help, definitions are only part of the problem. Another important, if not the most important, factor concerns what victims see as their options. From the point of view of service providers, the choice between help and continued victimization would seem so obvious. But considering that many do not seek help, victims must see things differently.

Three more of the initial chapters in this book look at how victims tend to see their own options. One of the points that can be inferred from the work of Lee Bowker (Chapter 4), is that victims who do not seek formal help sources are not necessarily being passive. Victims have their own strategies for ending the violence. However, in many cases they are not effective strategies or they are based on erroneous or wishful views of the situation. Many victims return to their batterers in spite of the counsel they receive from family violence professionals. Both Michael Strube (Chapter 5) and Lewis Okun (Chapter 6) contribute thoughtful chapters toward trying to help the field understand why this occurs.

In Part III, we get into studies of some of the social responses themselves, turning first to shelters and batterers' programs. Battered women's shelters have been the sites of a rapidly increasing number of research studies in recent years, in part because they inspired the imagination and idealism of young researchers and in part because as a new social institution, there was much to be studied. Andrea Sedlak's research (Chapter 7) is representative of the best of these studies.

In contrast with shelters, however, programs for men who batter have been slower to gain legitimacy, subject to many controversies, and not very intensively researched. It has been hard to persuade men to accept treatment in the first place. Second, since the safety and well-being of others are at stake, mistakes are very costly and this has led to reasonable demands for clear proof of effectiveness. But unfortunately, research and evaluation is extremely problematic because of ethical issues, as Daniel Saunders (Chapter 9) points out. Both Saunders and Edward Gondolf (Chapter 8) are leaders in the small but growing field of services for men who batter, and both communicate the complexity of the problem. Gondolf concludes that there is no easy formula for understanding or predicting why men stop abusing.

Evolution toward more effective and sophisticated social responses to family violence has been no more difficult anywhere than in the criminal justice system. Traditional attitudes about women and families were deeply rooted there in the, until recently, all male fraternities of police and courts. These systems, already overburdened, resisted strongly taking on additional responsibilities to deal with what were regarded as low-status, time-consuming, highly sensitive intrafamily victimizations.

In spite of this resistance, however, the criminal justice system has been changed, and changed, many would agree, permanently, as a result of its confrontation with the problem of family violence. The articles in Part IV, are all testimonies in one way or another to these changes, both in-process and completed. Chapters by Barbara Smith (Chapter 12) and by Richard Berk, Sarah Fenstermaker, and Phyllis Newton (Chapter 10) reflect a reassessment of the operation of the criminal justice system in cases of family violence. Smith finds that even when complainants fail to follow up on charges, there is evidence that the criminal justice system served a useful function for them. Berk, Fenstermaker, and Newton judge that while police decisions can be influenced by irrelevant prejudices, they are not the full story. Eve Buzawa (Chapter 11), finding that police are more disposed than many would think to make arrests in domestic violence cases, sees this as evidence that police attitudes have changed. Gamache, Edleson, and Schock (Chapter 13) demonstrate how change can be brought about through imaginative community planning and coordination.

The medical and mental health systems have also resisted accommodating to the challenge of family violence, as many critics have pointed out. Hospitals and doctors have often avoided these problems entirely or looked at them from a narrowly medical angle. The mental health system has had a tendency to treat victims as though they were responsible for their own abuse. Unfortunately, we only have one chapter each reporting on the social response of these institutions. This is, in part, because reports on these institutions are so readily available in other sources. The piece by Robert Hampton and Eli Newberger (Chapter 14) is noteworthy in documenting an allegation long made without good evidence that medical institutions (and the argument could be extended to other institutions as well) have clear social class and racial biases in their management of child abuse situations.

The last few years have seen important changes in the delivery of traditional protective services as well. For one thing, protective services have had to grow quickly to stay abreast of the skyrocketing reports of child abuse and especially sexual abuse. Sexual abuse has posed particular challenges, since these cases have been extremely difficult to investigate and mandate a higher degree of coordination with other agencies, like the police. Protective services have also had to deal with increased public and political scrutiny, both from those who felt they were not doing enough and those who felt they were doing too much.

The papers in Part VI give a window on some of the changes and challenges confronting protective services. Like the medical sector, protective service workers are also influenced by characteristics of the child and circumstances of the abuse that affect their responses. Susan Wells (Chapter 16) highlights and discusses some of the factors that influence the response of the child protection system in dealing with abuse and neglect.

Foster care has always been one of the big bones of contention between those who worry that protective services were doing too much or not enough. Desmond Runyan and Carolyn Gould's (Chapter 15) research gives a balanced picture of foster care that certainly seems to justify its usefulness for cases of severe child abuse. Rosalie Wolf and Karl Pillemer's (Chapter 17) contribution illustrates one of the important changes experienced by protective service; a broad expansion of their mandate to include the situations of maltreated adults, particularly the elderly. Deborah Daro and Ann Cohn (Chapter 18) have findings that suggest some important limitations to the traditional protective service approach; they find in their extensive review that lay counseling and group services including self-help groups may be more effective than traditional casework in reducing the likelihood of abusive parents to continue to maltreat. Sandra Azar's work (Chapter 19) is a fitting summary to this section because it raises a number of important considerations that all efforts to evaluate the effectiveness of protective services must confront.

In Part VII, we turn to a broader perspective on the issue of social responses to family violence—to the issue of prevention. Almost everyone pays lip service to prevention, considering it the far preferable solution. Yet few social agencies, by comparison, devote themselves to the tasks of prevention. Moreover, the concrete work to prevent family violence remains abstract.

The chapters in this section renew in their various ways the argument for prevention as a more central task in the field of family violence. Katherine Christoffel (Chapter 21) confronts us with the need and our simultaneous capacity to prevent one of the most costly forms of family violence: child homicide. In Jon Conte's (Chapter 20) review, we learn about the initial positive results of perhaps one of the most widely and enthusiastically adopted facets of family violence prevention: child sex-abuse education.

The chapters in this volume are illustrative of an important facet about the field of family violence: there is a high level of interdependency and cooperation between researchers, practitioners, and advocates. The relationships are not always congenial and views are not always identical. But more so than in many other fields of social science and social welfare there is an active partnership. This partnership bodes well for future breakthroughs in our efforts to respond ever more effectively and compassionately to this painful social problem.

PART I

Personal Responses to Violence: The Search for Meaning

1

Applying the Label of Physical Abuse

Sharon D. Herzberger
Howard Tennen

Has this child been physically abused? Answering this question has been problematic for researchers, practitioners, and laypeople who attempt to grapple with the phenomenon of violence against children. Whether it be the researcher who decides which children to include in his or her abused sample, the teacher or neighbor who decides whether to involve social service professionals in a family's affairs, or the social worker or doctor who decides whether to call upon the legal system, all must face the problem of determining whether an act of abuse has occurred. The determination is often a difficult one. This chapter reviews the literature on defining child abuse and attempts to identify factors that contribute to decision making in this area. We first examine the definitions that have been used to identify abuse and discuss their limitations. We then discuss differences among observers that may produce variations in their application of the label *abuse* and may impede uniform decision making processes.

Analysis Based upon Actual Parent and Child Behavior

A perusal of the statutory definitions of child abuse immediately demonstrates the difficulty of operationalizing the concept of abuse. Connecticut's statute (Public Act 82-203, Section 17-38B) mandates those in professional contact with children to report physical injuries inflicted

AUTHORS' NOTE: Requests for reprints may be sent to Sharon Herzberger, Department of Psychology, Trinity College, Hartford, CT 06106.

"other than by accidental means" or injuries "at variance with the history given." California's criminal statute permits incarceration of a person who "willfully causes or permits any child to suffer . . . unjustifiable physical pain or mental suffering" (California Penal Code, sec. 273A). In these definitions no elaboration is provided of the meaning of physical injury, physical pain, and mental suffering, nor is there discussion of the term *unjustifiable.* Other state statutes share these problems (see Giovannoni & Becerra, 1979).

Despite the failure of statutes to provide guidance for professionals or researchers, some experts deny the merit of specifying abuse in more concrete terms (see Giovannoni & Becerra, 1979). They believe that interpretations of law must be left to the discretion of the social service or legal professionals who are involved with each particular case. In this way professionals remain free to examine the familial circumstances and cultural or neighborhood mores. Wald (1976), however, is suspect of the ability of professionals to make decisions independent of their own personal biases and in a manner likely to benefit the child. He called upon the scientific community to outline, for legal and social service professionals, the scientific evidence to guide decisions in cases of abuse, particularly in a decision to remove a child from the home.

Most people look beyond the vague state statutes to devise a method of designating cases of abuse. In so doing they take into account parental action, parental intent, and the child's injury. Straus (1978), for example, selected parental actions that were likely to result in serious injury and thus labeled parents as abusive if they had *ever* kicked, bitten, punched, or hit the child with an object, beaten the child, or used a knife or a gun. Designations based solely upon parental behavior are rare, however, since the intention behind an action is deemed important. As Connecticut's statute exemplifies, accidental injury to a child is not labeled abuse, and medical professionals attempt to distinguish between accidental and intentional injury by comparing the child's injury to the parent's account of how the injury occurred. Repeated injuries and those that fail to match the account given by the parent arouse the suspicion of the medical team and are more likely to be labeled as abuse-related (Newberger & Hyde, 1975).

The degree of injury also weighs in the decision. Giovannoni and Becerra (1979) asked attorneys, pediatricians, social workers, and policemen to rate the severity of specific actions by the parent, both independent of and with knowledge of the specific injury sustained by the child. In almost all cases, when the professional considered the nature of the child's injury, the parent's behavior was deemed more serious. For example, hitting the child with a wooden stick received a rating of 4.59 on a 9-point scale; knowing that the child suffered a concussion as a result merited a 7.90 rating.

Spanking the child with a leather strap earned a rating of 4.07; leaving red marks as a result of the spanking earned 5.37. Not all instances of reporting the injurious consequence, however, increased the seriousness rating. Hitting the child in the face with the fist earned a 7.25, whereas reporting that in addition the child suffered a black eye and a cut lip reduced the rating to 6.72. Presumably in such cases the imagined injuries exceeded the actual injuries and resulted in higher ratings.

Intention to perform a physically violent act against a child must also be distinguished from intention to inflict injury, and the distinction may reside in the parent's ability to foresee the injury that would result and the degree of planning involved. It is conceivable, for example, that a punch in the head that results in a concussion would be regarded more seriously than would the same injury sustained when a child accidentally fell against a wall after being slapped by the parent. A broken leg incurred from being thrown down the stairs deliberately may be deemed more abusive than would the broken leg resulting from a fall down the stairs after the parent shakes the child at the top of a stairwell. Although hard evidence in this regard is lacking, Giovannoni and Becerra's (1979) data suggest that the factor of foreseeability may be operating. Some of the most extreme seriousness ratings were attached to parental acts that required planning and led to predictably severe consequences. Burning the child with a cigarette on the buttocks and chest or immersing the child in a tub of hot water received high ratings. Hitting the child with a fist, in contrast, may be perceived to have occurred impulsively and may be seen as an extension of spanking or slapping, disciplinary tools common among parents in most communities (see Gelles & Straus, 1979). Burning with a cigarette or immersing in hot water are more unique, and therefore, raters may see the acts as nonnormative and odd.

It should be noted that almost no research has defined physical abuse by reference to the emotional harm done to the child. Although many investigators (see Martin & Rodeheffer, 1976) have catalogued the emotional consequences of abuse, the application of the "abuse" label to a child has depended for the most part upon physical injury, not emotional injury (see Gelles, 1977, for a possible exception). Yet, many writers (Jayaratne, 1977; Kinard, 1979) have argued that the emotional harm resulting from acts of physical violence may be of equal, if not greater, magnitude than the physical harm, and thus should be assessed simultaneously.

Knowledge of the child's provocation also affects judgments of abuse. Herzberger and Tennen (1982) asked young adults to read descriptions of a disciplinary interaction between parent and child. For some participants the descriptions included presentation of the child's misbehavior; others were not privy to this information. Participants rated the discipline as more severe and less appropriate when the child's misbehavior was described, and overwhelmingly rated the child more responsible for the parent's action. At first glance this result might appear to be understandable. However, one might question whether harsh treatment should be regarded as acceptable or justifiable under any conditions—regardless of the child's provocation—and whether states such as California should include the term *unjustifiable suffering* in their penal code. In this study the findings were particularly alarming since the provocations described were not extreme (spilling grape juice on a rug after being asked several times not to drink it in the living room; smoking a cigarette; refusing to clean up one's room). These are not acts of delinquency or extreme violence that might warrant an extreme parental response. The results suggest that research should examine the extent to which the child's provocation is considered by interventionists when deciding whether a case of abuse has transpired.

Analysis Based upon Characteristics of Parent, Child, and Observer

Apart from considerations of the details of the violent interaction itself, other factors enter into the definitional process. One's perspective on the act is likely to affect the tendency to see the act as abusive. And one's perspective is likely to be affected by professional training and one's own characteristics and upbringing, and the characteristics of individuals involved in the abusive interaction. In the following section we discuss how these factors can influence one's judgments about abuse.

Professional Affiliation

Giovannoni and Becerra (1979) performed the landmark study of professionals' perceptions of abuse (see also Craft, Epley, & Clarkson, 1980). They interviewed attorneys, pediatricians, social workers, and policemen, providing them with descriptions of parental acts and asking them to rate the seriousness of each act. Pediatricians, social workers, and police officers tended to agree on the seriousness of cases of physical abuse. Lawyers rated the incidents as less serious than the others. The patterns of agreement among the professionals may relate to overlapping or nonoverlapping functions. Pediatricians, social workers, and police officers are most interested in protecting individuals from injury; a lawyer is charged with being an advocate for a particular client, regardless of the client's guilt or innocence. In addition, lawyers are less likely than other professionals to see the child immediately following a violent episode.

Giovannoni and Becerra (1979) also compared lay and professional attitudes toward abuse. The concern that professionals may impose the values of middle-class society upon other groups appears unfounded in view of their findings. Laypeople viewed acts of physical abuse as more serious than did professionals, while spanking was regarded by both groups as not serious. Thus it seems unlikely that professional intervention in cases of physical mistreatment would offend the community.

Socioeconomic and Ethnic/Racial Affiliation

Variations in the use and acceptability of various discipline techniques might be expected across ethnic and socioeconomic lines. Despite a wealth of survey and epidemiological studies, however, few concrete conclusions can be drawn. Most of the research has examined ethnic and socioeconomic differences in the use of corporal punishment (see Bronfenbrenner, 1958; Erlanger, 1974). However, spanking for most people is not abuse, and it has not been conclusively demonstrated that spanking connotes a predisposition to engage in violent acts (as Gelles & Straus, 1979, note, upwards of 90% of parents may use physical punishment).

Most researchers (see Garbarino, 1977; Parke & Collmer, 1975; Simons, Downs, Hurster and Archer, 1966), however, report a higher rate of abuse among lower socioeconomic groups and among black and Hispanic families who disproportionately characterize this group. While some authors claim racial/ethnic effects even when reporting bias is controlled, Hampton and Newberger (1984) found that among hospital personnel, socioeconomic and racial factors were *more important* than the severity of the physical injury in deciding whether to report a case of abuse! Externally verified cases of abuse were less likely to be reported when victims were white and came from families with higher incomes. When these findings are considered in the context of evidence that there is less tolerance among racial/ethnic minorities and those with lower incomes for physical violence against children (Giovannoni & Becerra, 1979), a picture emerges in which reporting bias may play a substantial role in establishing the rates of abuse.

Religious Affiliation

Differences in perspective on abuse may be related to religious or cultural orientation (Morris, 1979). Newspapers periodically recount instances of parental refusal to allow medical treatment for seriously ill children. Parental refusal may stem from religious prohibitions against specific forms of treatment, such as blood transfusions, or from a general belief that God's will must be followed. While medical professionals might see such refusal as abusive because it results in unjustifiable physical suffering, parents may see the proffered treatment as the cause of spiritual harm—a more important evil in their eyes. Similarly, clitorectomies and circumcisions, practiced freely among some groups, are seen as abusive among others (see Wallerstein, 1980).

History of Abuse

Substantial speculation, but little empirical examination, is focused on the abusive parent's own history of discipline as a child. For years it was assumed that one of the most important factors contributing to the tendency to engage in abusive interactions was whether the parent had been exposed to such interactions as a child (see Parke & Collmer, 1975). While recent writings have questioned specific aspects of the "cyclical hypothesis" (Jayaratne, 1977; Potts, Herzberger, & Holland, 1979), some research suggests that childhood history of abuse contributes to violence toward children (Kaufman & Zigler, in press). Straus (1978) found that 17.6% of parents who had been abused as children were abusive toward their own children, whereas only 12.5% of parents who had not been abused reported the use of such disciplinary tactics. Herrenkohl, Herrenkohl, and Toedter (1983) found that abuse by one's mother and abuse by both parents were particularly likely to relate to abuse of one's own children.

A history of abuse in childhood may affect one's perspective about currently observed acts of abuse. Straker and Jacobson (1981), for example, have shown that empathy is low among abused children. Similarly, Herzberger and Tennen (1985b) found that people who had experienced abuse were more accepting of comparable treatment of others. In this study, young adults rated disciplinary interactions between a parent and child on a number of dimensions. They were asked to judge the severity and appropriateness of the parental discipline and to note whether the discipline was likely to result in emotional harm or increased misbehavior. They also noted whether the parental act could be termed "abuse" and estimated the proportion of responsibility that could be accorded to the child for the parental act. After reading eight instances of disciplinary interaction (two each of physical and emotional punishment and physical and emotional abuse) and providing the requisite judgments, participants were asked to reread the cases and to note whether they had experienced similar treatment by their parent(s) as a child. The judgments of participants who had experienced similar treatment were compared to those of participants who had not experienced similar treatment. Comparisons demonstrated consistently that similar treatment corresponded with lenience toward the described parental acts. Participants who had experienced similar treatment regarded their treatment as less severe, less "abusive," more appropriate, and more the child's responsibility. Furthermore, these participants believed that the treatment would be less likely to result in emotional harm or to increase the incidence of future misbehavior.

These results, while not directly testing the cyclical hypothesis, certainly suggest a mechanism by which the cyclical process might occur. People who experience harsh treatment may in some cases (see Herzberger, 1983, for suggested exceptions) view it more dispassionately than do others, and thus may be more likely to adopt such treatment when exposed to similar circumstances as a parent. Participants in this study, however, were not parents and one might argue that the results would not generalize to people who have had considerable experience with children. We conducted two studies to assess the external validity of these findings.

First, in a pilot study, we asked 16 parents to rate the same vignettes that had been rated by college students. Although the sample was too small to provide many statistically significant results, the mean ratings were essentially the same as with the college student sample. Parents who had experienced the discipline in question judged it to be less harmful and less severe than had other parents. There was one exception to this general finding: parents who had experienced *emotional* abuse as a child were more rejecting of similar treatment of others. These preliminary findings suggested that the process of defining a specific act as abusive may well depend upon one's personal history of abusive encounters as a child.

The findings of our pilot study led us to conduct a more extensive investigation of how one's own childhood experience with abuse shapes one's definition of abusive treatment (Howe, Herzberger, & Tennen, in press). We asked a large sample of psychologists and counselors who worked regularly with child abuse cases to review a series of vignettes depicting disciplinary exchanges between a parent and child. Unlike the respondents in our lay sample (Herzberger & Tennen, 1985b), those professionals who reported having been abused themselves, viewed the parental acts as more severe and more likely to be harmful than did those with no reported history of abuse. The apparent differences between findings based on lay samples and the findings based on a professional sample underscore the need for further investigation of the role of childhood experiences on when people apply the label of physical abuse. As Kaufman and Zigler (1987) report in their summary of evidence for the intergenerational transmission of abuse, individuals vary substantially in their interpretation and opinions about their own history of abuse and how such variation relates to their current treatment of children.

Parenting Experience

The findings we have reviewed suggest that being a parent per se generally does not affect judgments of severe discipline. Giovannoni and Becerra (1979) also found few significant differences between parents and nonparents in their professional samples in the seriousness ratings of specific acts. When differences occurred, parents and nonparents each rated the act more seriously about half the time. Giovannoni and Becerra (1979) concluded, "Many childless practitioners have doubtless heard the comment . . . 'If you only had children of your own, you would understand and not be so hard on me.' The information gathered on these professionals suggests that that is a vain hope" (p. 144).

Some differences between parents and nonparents have been found, however. Straus, Gelles, and Steinmetz (1980) report that parents are less likely than are childless individuals to see relatively minor corporal punishment (slaps, spankings) as "normal, good, and necessary" (p. 56). They speculate that this difference may result from parents learning first-hand that corporal punishment is ineffective at best and may be imitated by the child. But in our pilot study described earlier, those who spanked viewed it as a more appropriate punishment tool and were more likely to see it as promoting positive emotional development than were those who did not spank. Thus, at least among some parents who use corporal punishment, the technique is viewed as beneficial.

Gender

One factor that has been examined insufficiently in the abuse literature has been gender. Some research (Straus, Gelles, & Steinmetz, 1980) suggests that boys are more likely to be abused than are girls and that mothers are more likely to abuse children than are fathers. However, we know little about how gender contributes to the application of the label of abuse. Although Garrett & Rossi (1978) found no effects of gender, Herzberger and Tennen (1985a) found that discipline directed toward daughters was regarded as more severe, less appropriate, and more emotionally harmful than the same discipline directed at sons (see Fromuth & Burkhart, 1986, for similar findings from self-appraisals of sexually abusive history). Physical discipline of daughters also was more likely to be labeled "abuse." Discipline by fathers was regarded more harshly, particularly when directed toward a daughter. Furthermore, female observers judged disciplinary tactics more harshly than did male observers. Females viewed harsh discipline as more severe, less appropriate, and more likely to result in emotional harm to the child. Female observers regarded as particularly inappropriate physical abuse by the mother, even though they regarded physical abuse by the father to be more severe.

In contrast to these results with laypeople, Giovannoni and Becerra (1979) claimed not to find stereotypical gender differences among the professionals. Although females rated parental acts as more serious than did males in 36% of the situations described, further analyses revealed that in almost all cases social workers rated the incidents as more serious than did either males or females. Giovannoni and Becerra concluded that professional orientation outweighed gender differences. Although professional orientation may be a more important factor, their analysis does not convincingly eliminate gender as a contributor. A more appropriate test would have compared male and female ratings within a given profession. This analysis would have controlled for professional orientation and permitted a test of the effects of gender.

Martin (1983) also found no gender differences in dispositions recommended by social workers. She studied all verified cases of child abuse reported to social service agencies in Wisconsin during 1974-1975, and found that cases involving boys and girls were equivalently referred for court action and boys were as likely to be removed from the home as girls. She also found that mothers and fathers were equally likely to be referred by the social worker for court action. However, a disproportionate number of abusers (13 out of 14) involved with the criminal court were fathers, regardless of similarities to mothers in the degree of injury inflicted upon the child. Hampton and Newberger (1984) also found no differences in the report rate of abuse to boys and girls by medical personnel, but maternal perpetrators were less likely to be reported than were paternal perpetrators. Most recently, however, Howe et al. (in press) found that among social service professionals, female respondents more than males rated descriptions of parental disciplinary actions as more severe and more likely to have a deleterious effect. In addition, mothers' actions were considered less severe than the same behavior by fathers.

In summary, we have found differences in judgments about abuse related to the gender of the child, the parent, and the observer (Herzberger & Tennen, 1985a, 1985b; Howe et al., in press). Giovannoni and Becerra (1979) report no verified gender differences among professional observers. Martin (1983) and Hampton and Newberger (1984) report only differences related to the gender of the parent. It should be noted that our studies used experimentally created descriptions of abusive episodes that varied only the gender of the victim and perpetrator. Martin and Hampton and Newberger studied actual cases of abuse and attempted to examine the role of gender by controlling for the severity of injury. To the extent that judgments of the severity of the injury are tainted by knowledge of the victim's or perpetrator's gender, however, some confounding may occur. Thus it may be necessary to disguise gender when working with nonexperimental methodology. In any case, it is obvious that more research should investigate the dynamics of gender in relation to judgments of abuse. Since a substantial proportion of those who initially identify cases of abuse are laypeople (45% according to a study reported in Giovannoni & Becerra, 1979), research should examine the dynamics in both lay and professional samples.

Implications and Conclusions

We have discussed many of the factors that contribute to judgments about abuse. Some factors relate to the details of the incident: what the child did to provoke a parental response, the parent's reaction, and the nature of the resulting injury. The label "abuse" also depends upon more socially relevant variables that affect one's interpretation of the violent episode. Among the factors that appear to affect one's perspective are the gender of participants and observer, professional affiliation, religion, sociocultural membership, and history of abusive treatment. We are certain that this is not an exhaustive list, and we encourage more investigation in this area.

Individuals vary in how they view specific incidents of harsh treatment of children and it is important to study the ramifications of this variation. Do judgments differ only in relative terms, with people making similar decisions, despite differences in judgments of the severity of the act? Or does one's perspective, background, or gender lead to different decisions about whether abuse has occurred? Much more research is needed before a definitive answer to these questions is found. However, some evidence is available. As noted, our own investigations found that a childhood history of abuse and the gender of the observer, victim, and parent affected the observer's belief that an act of abuse transpired. If the observer were in a position to report the parent, to decide whether to press charges, to incarcerate the parent, or to remove the child from the home, such factors would then be of practical significance. These findings suggest, for example, that fathers may be cited for abuse more frequently when a daughter is involved rather than a son, or that female observers may be more likely to cite the parent than would males. Similarly, Hampton and Newberger (1984) suggest that lower income individuals, racial/ethnic minorities, and fathers may be more likely to be labeled abusive than would their counterparts. Two types of error—overestimating the degree of harm and falsely intervening, and underestimating the harm and failing to intervene—may result from different interpretations of the parent-child interaction. Since the primary concern of most people who work in this area is to protect children, the latter error may be less tolerable. However, falsely disrupting the family and causing unnecessary hardship upon the accused and other family members will result from the former error. Therefore, we need to identify accurately true cases of abuse.

Giovannoni and Becerra's (1979) data underscore further the importance of understanding the conditions under which abuse is identified. They found that lawyers rated parental reactions as less serious than did other professional groups, and that ratings of seriousness related to the dispositions of cases. Parental attitudes affected decisions as well. Parents who indicated that they wanted "emotional help" or wanted to have the child removed from the home were likely to have their wishes counted in the disposition of the case. Serious incidents of abuse often did not result in removal of the child when parents indicated a need for help. These findings suggest that judgments of seriousness and perceived parental attitudes affect case disposition.

Other factors that may affect the disposition are judgments about the appropriateness of the parents' action and beliefs about the behavioral and emotional harm incurred by the child. Because these judgments are a function of one's perspective, it is again critical that the judgments be applied fairly and uniformly.

More than a decade ago Wald (1976) called for more research into how individuals make decisions about alleged cases of child abuse. A start has been made; it is time to heed his call.

References

Bronfenbrenner, U. (1958). Socialization and social class through time and space. In E. C. Maccoby, T. M. Newcomb, & E. L. Hartley (Eds.), *Readings in social psychology* (3rd ed.). New York: Holt, Rinehart & Winston.

Craft, J. L., Epley, S. W., & Clarkson, C. D. (1980). Factors influencing legal decisions in child abuse investigation. *Journal of Social Service Research, 4*, 31-46.

Erlanger, H. S. (1974). Social class differences in parents' use of physical punishment. In S. K. Steinmetz and M. A. Straus (Eds.), *Violence in the family*. New York: Harper & Row.

Fromuth, M. E., & Burkhart, B. R. (1986, August). Childhood sexual victimization among college men: Definitional and methodological issues. Paper presented at the American Psychological Association meetings, Washington DC.

Garbarino, J. (1977). The human ecology of child maltreatment: A conceptual model for research. *Journal of Marriage and the Family, 39*, 721-735.

Garrett, K. A., & Rossi, P. H. (1978). Judging the seriousness of child abuse. *Medical Anthropology, 2*(1).

Gelles, R. J. (1977). Problems in defining and labeling child abuse. Paper presented to the Study Group on Problems in the Prediction of Child Abuse and Neglect. Wilmington, DE.

Gelles, R. J., & Straus, M. A. (1979). Determinants of violence in the family: Toward a theoretical integration. In W. R. Burr, R. Hill, F. I. Nye, & I. L. Reiss (Eds.), *Contemporary theories about the family*. New York: Free Press.

Giovannoni, J. M., & Becerra, R. M. (1979). *Defining child abuse*. New York: Free Press.

Hampton, R. L., & Newberger, E. H. (1984, August). Child abuse incidence and reporting by hospitals: Significance of severity, class, and race. Paper presented at the Second Family Violence Researchers Conference, Durham, NH.

Herrenkohl, E. C., Herrenkohl, R. C., & Toedter, L. J. (1983). Perspectives on the intergenerational transmission of abuse. In D. Finkelhor, R. Gelles, G. T. Hotaling, and M. Straus (Eds.), *The dark side of families: Current family violence research* (pp. 305-316). Beverly Hills, CA: Sage.

Herzberger, S. D. (1983). Social cognition and the transmission of abuse. In D. Finkelhor, R. Gelles, G. T. Hotaling, and M. Straus (Eds.), *The dark side of families: Current family violence research* (pp. 317-329). Beverly Hills, CA: Sage.

Herzberger, S. D., & Tennen, H. (1982, August). The social definition of abuse. Paper presented at the American Psychological Association convention, Washington, DC.

Herzberger, S. D., & Tennen, H. (1985a). Snips and snails and puppy dog tails: Gender of agent, recipient, and observer as determinants of perceptions of discipline. *Sex Roles, 12,* 853-865.

Herzberger, S. D., & Tennen, H. (1985b). The effect of self-relevance on moderate and severe disciplinary encounters. *Journal of Marriage and the Family, 47,* 311-318.

Howe, A., Herzberger, S. D., & Tennen, H. (in press). The influence of personal history of abuse and gender on clinicians' judgments of child abuse. *Journal of Family Violence.*

Jayaratne, S. (1977). Child abusers as parents and children: A review. *Social Work, 22,* 5-9.

Kaufman, J., & Zigler, E. (1987). Do abused children become abusive parents? *American Journal of Orthopsychiatry, 57,* 186-192.

Kaufman, J., & Zigler, E. (in press). The intergenerational transmission of child abuse. In D. Cicchetti and V. Carson (Eds.), *Research in the consequences of child maltreatment*. Cambridge: Cambridge University Press.

Kinard, E. M. (1979). The psychological consequences of abuse for the child. *Journal of Social Issues, 35,* 82-100.

Maccoby, E. E. (1976). Sex differentiation during childhood development. *JSAS Catalog of Selected Documents in Psychology, 6*(4), 97 (ms. 1339).

Martin, H. P., & Rodeheffer, M. A. (1976). The psychological impact of abuse on children. *Journal of Pediatric Psychology, 1,* 12-16.

Martin, J. (1983). *Gender-related behaviors of children in abusive situations*. Saratoga, CA: R & E.

Morris, B., (1979). Value differences in definitions of child abuse and neglect. Jehovah's Witnesses: A case example. *Child Abuse and Neglect, 3,* 651-655.

Newberger, E., & Hyde, J. (1975). Child abuse: Principles and implications of current pediatric practice. *Pediatric Bulletin of North America, 22,* 695-715.

Parke, R. D. and Collmer, C. W. (1975). *Child abuse: An interdisciplinary analysis*. Chicago: University of Chicago Press.

Potts, D. A., Herzberger, S. D., & Holland, A. E. (1979, May). Child abuse: A crossgenerational pattern of child rearing? Paper presented at the annual meetings of the Mid-western Psychological Association, Chicago.

Simons, B., Downs, E. F., Hurster, M. M., & Archer, M. (1966). Child abuse: Epidemiologic study of medically reported cases. *New York State Journal of Medicine, 66,* 2783-2788.

Straker, G., & Jacobson, R. S. (1981). Aggression, emotional maladjustment, and empathy in the abused child. *Developmental Psychology, 17,* 762-765.

Straus, M. A. (1978). Family patterns and child abuse in a nationally representative American sample. Paper presented at the Second International Congress on Child Abuse and Neglect, London.

Straus, M. A., Gelles, R. J., & Steinmetz, S. K. (1980). *Behind closed doors: Violence in the American family.* Garden City, NY: Anchor/Doubleday.

Wald, M. S. (1976). Legal policies affecting children: A lawyer's request for aid. *Child Development, 47,* 1-5.

Wallerstein, E. (1980). *Circumcision: An American health fallacy.* New York: Springer.

2

The Effects of Personal Experiences with Couple Violence on Calling It "Battering" and Allocating Blame

Andrea J. Sedlak

Despite the rapidly growing literature concerned with violence between intimate partners, many questions about how couples construe these events remain unanswered. The study reported here had three main goals: First, it aimed to uncover the dynamics of "labeling" in this context (i.e., when will a person regard a given episode as "battering?"). Little is presently known on this point, yet such labeling may be a critical prerequisite to help seeking. The second aim was to identify how personal experiences with intimate violence may relate to general attitudes on this subject and affect evaluations of specific episodes. While these connections seem plausible enough, there has been little empirical grounding for them to date. Finally, the third goal of the research was to determine how the victim's reactions (nonviolent or violent) to the assault might modify observers' evaluations and perceptions of the episode. Since violent couple relationships typically involve violence by both parties (see Straus, Gelles, & Steinmetz, 1980), this point would appear to be critical to an understanding of how blame is allocated in most circumstances of intimate violence.

AUTHOR'S NOTE: This chapter represents an integration and simplification of two previous reports that adopted different analytic approaches to the same database (see Sedlak, 1984a, 1984b). The study was conducted while the author was Temporary Associate Professor at Iowa State University in Ames, IA. The author is grateful to Sheila A. Frana for helping to administer the questionnaire and to Christine A. Paisley for developing the computer data tapes. Correspondence should be addressed to the author at Westat, Inc., 1650 Research Blvd., Rockville, MD 20850.

Method

Subjects

Undergraduate volunteers from introductory psychology classes at Iowa State University participated for experimental credit. On signing up for the study, subjects were told that they would be asked to complete an anonymous questionnaire on their (1) attitudes, (2) personal experiences, and (3) judgments of case studies regarding both physical aggression between intimates and episodes of forced sex.

The final sample of 125 who completed questionnaires consisted of 68 males (54.4%) and 57 females (45.6%). Participants were largely Caucasian (85.6%), with only small percentages of Black (4%), Oriental (4%), Hispanic (2.4%), and Amerind students (0.8%), (the remaining 3.2% of participants did not indicate any classification).

The age range of 19-20 predominated in the sample (49.6%), with substantial proportions falling in the ranges of 21-22 (34%) and 17-18 (14.4%). Although the average ages for male and female respondents did not differ, the genders were distributed differently, since females tended to be overrepresented in the youngest and oldest groupings, while males predominated in the midranges.

Instrument

Respondents completed a three-part questionnaire that addressed the topic of forced sex as well as battering, but this report focuses only on those questions concerned with violence between intimate partners (a total of 93 multiple-choice and 8 short-answer questions).[1] Part I included the 17-question Battering Empathy Scale given in Table 2.1, which assesses general attitudes about violence between intimates. This scale was developed specifically for the present study and was modeled closely after the Rape Empathy Scale (REB) designed by Deitz, Blackwell, Daley, and Bentley (1982).[2] Part II contained two subsections assessing the respondent's personal history as victim or as actor in physically abusive episodes with an intimate partner. Persons who reported such experiences indicated the nature and length of the relationship and the types of abuse and injury that had occurred. In addition, they rated the extent to which they regarded the behavior as "battering." Part III included a "case study" involving intimate-partner violence. This was a brief hypothetical scenario that systematically varied three dimensions of the situation in eight different versions in a 2 × 2 × 2 design: (1) the introductory instructions (standard versus empathy instructions), (2) the force used by the abusive partner (high versus low), and the victim's physical response to the assault (high versus

TABLE 2.1
Battering Empathy Scale

For Questions 1 through 9, rate the degree to which you *agree* or *disagree* with the statement according to the following scale:

Agree Completely 1 : 2 : 3 : 4 : 5 : 6 : 7 : 8 : 9 *Disagree* Completely

1. In most cases when a woman is physically abused by her mate she was asking for it.
2. Most women are masochistic and secretly desire to be physically abused to some degree.
3. Under certain circumstances, I can understand why a man would use physical force with his partner in an intimate relationship.
4. When a woman acts belligerent and disrespectful toward her partner she must be willing to accept the consequences, including her partner's physical retaliation.
5. It is possible for a woman who is physically attacked by her partner to get psychological satisfaction from the experience of being physically controlled, whether she admits it or not.
6. I can really empathize with the helplessness a person might feel who becomes physically abusive with their partner, since they are at the mercy of forces beyond their control.

*7. I can really empathize with the helplessness a person might feel who is physically abused by their partner, if all their attempts to avoid the abuse have failed.

8. A husband has the right to enforce his wife's obedience, even if this means using physical force to do so.

*9. I can understand a wife's humiliation and anger if her husband used physical force against her.

For Questions 10 through 16, rate the degree to which you would select the *Victim* or the *Abuser* in a situation of physical aggression in an intimate relationship according to the following scale:

Victim 1 : 2 : 3 : 4 : 5 : 6 : 7 : 8 : 9 Abuser
Both Equally

*10. I would find it easier to imagine the feelings of the ______ during a battering episode.

11. The ______ must be held accountable for his/her behavior during an argument.

*12. I would find it easier to empathize with the shame and humiliation the ______ might feel during a courtroom hearing.

13. In deciding whether an assault has occurred, the burden of proof should rest with the ______. [Note: For the Victim, this means it should be assumed that nothing happened unless they can prove it did; for the Abuser, this

(*continued*)

TABLE 2.1 (continued)

means it should be assumed the assault occurred as charged unless they can prove it did not.]

*14. I think the ______ would suffer more emotional torment in dealing with the police.

*15. If a hearing on an assault charge were publicized in the press, I feel the ______ would suffer more emotional trauma from the publicity.

*16. If I were a member of a jury in a trial for assault between intimates, I would probably be more likely to believe the ______'s testimony.

*17. The situation in which a person uses physical force against their partner in an intimate relationship is:

*Un*justifiable under any circumstances	1 : 2 : 3 : 4 : 5 : 6 : 7 : 8 : 9	Justifiable under certain circumstances

*Denotes items requiring reverse scoring.

low resistance). The specific scenario used is given in Figure 2.1 together with the alternative texts used in manipulating these three design factors. Each participant was given only one version of the scenario, with approximately equal numbers of the eight versions distributed among participants of a given gender. Following the scenario in Part III were 24 evaluation, perception, and attribution questions, as discussed in detail in the description of the results.

Results and Discussion

General Limitations of the Study

Two major limitations of the project should be borne in mind throughout this discussion. First, the fact that the sample was self-selected means that frequencies and correlations may not be generalized beyond this group. Moreover, it means that this group (and its subgroups) may have been especially sensitive (or insensitive) to the dimensions varied in the scenario. Second, because the findings reported here are based on questions embedded in a longer questionnaire that also asked about forced sex, and because embedding the violence questions in this context may have influenced responses in indeterminate ways, the findings here should be confirmed by replication in future research that focuses solely on intimate violence.

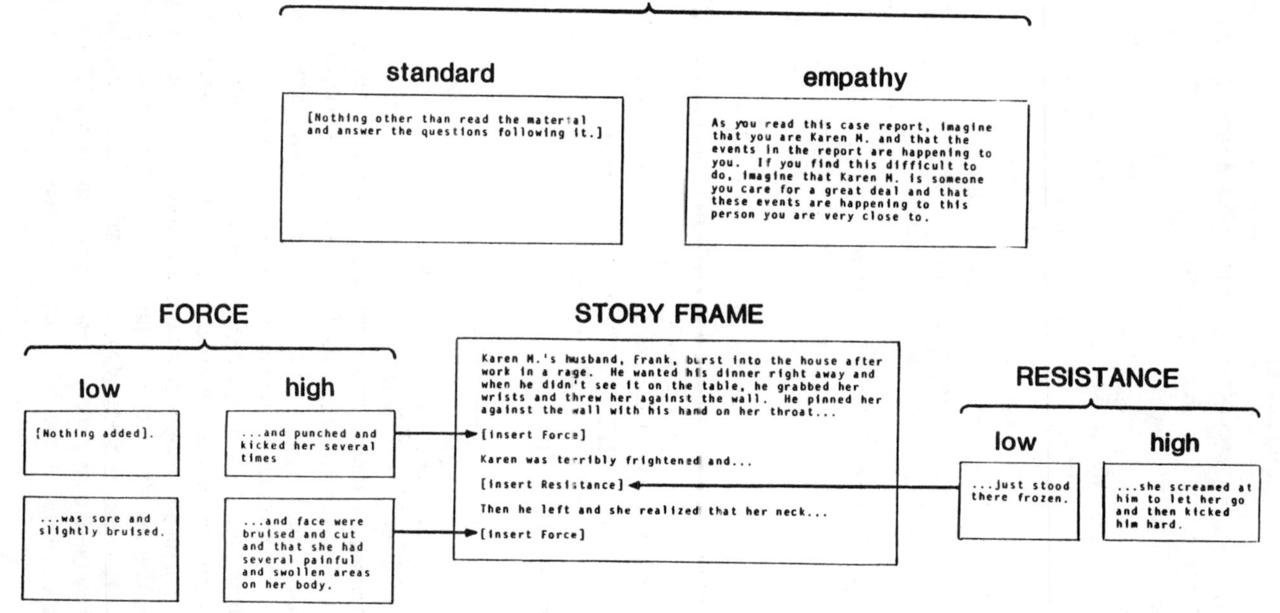

Figure 2.1 Design of the "Case Study" material in Part III of the questionnaire, indicating the Instructions (2) × Force (2), × Resistance (2) manipulations.

Experience With Intimate Violence

Nearly one-fourth (24%) of the sample reported personal experiences with violence in an intimate relationship: 10% solely as victims, 6% solely as abusers, and 8% as both victims and abusers. Although admittedly not based on a representative sample, the prevalence of couple violence here is in the range of that reported for eight other samples using college-student populations (30% = Bernard & Bernard, 1983; 19% = Bogal-Allbritten & Allbritten, 1983; 22% and 25% = Ferraro & Johnson, 1984; 25-30% = Laner & Thompson, 1982; 21% = Makepeace, 1981; 10% victims and 11% aggressors = Makepeace, 1983; 23% = Matthews, 1984). At the same time, it is above the level found in one investigation (14% = Makepeace, 1984) and notably below that found in five other samples (52% = Comins, 1984; 37% and 41% = Ferraro & Johnson, 1984; 40% = Murphy, 1984; 48 to 59% = Sigelman, Berry, & Wiles, 1983). At present, the reasons for these similarities and differences in prevalence rates are not apparent, but the set of studies did use widely varying methods of sample selection and questionnaire structure.

In the sample here, females were more frequently victims (16% of females, 6% of males), whereas greater proportions of males were abusers (7% males versus 4% females) or both victim and abuser (13% males versus 2% females). The types of violence reported by respondents with violent experiences are given in Table 2.2. Reflecting the young, independent, and predominantly unmarried status of the respondents, the great majority of those who experienced intimate violence did so in dating relationships (80%), as opposed to relationships with cohabiting partners (7%), spouses (3%), ex-spouses (3%), or parents (7%).

Although many of those who had experiences with both victim and abuser roles had evidently been involved in reciprocal physical abuse with a single partner, some reported their victim experiences in connection with one relationship and their abuser experiences in another. For this reason, it was necessary to distinguish between the reports given by Both-role respondents regarding their victim experiences (Both/V), and those associated with their abuser experiences (Both/A).

Overall, one-third (33%) who had experiences with violence were still in the abusive relationship, although this proportion varied markedly depending on the respondent's role in the violence: only 8% of Victim, and 29% of Abuser, but 70% of Both/V and 56% of Both/A relationships were ongoing at the time of the study. Not only were Victims and Abusers less likely to still be in their violent relationships, but their relationships were also shorter in duration and the violence occurred less frequently than for respondents with Both role experiences. The majority of Victims (69%) and

TABLE 2.2
Types of Violence Reported by Respondents with Violent Relationships

Type of Violence	% Who Reported It
Smashed, hit, kicked something in anger, while partner was there	80
Threw something in anger while partner was there, but not at the partner	70
Pushed, shoved partner	77
Grabbed, shook partner	73
Slapped partner with open hand	60
Threw something at partner with anger	27
Clawed, scratched, bit partner	27
Threw partner bodily	27
Kicked, punched, hit partner with fist	23
Hit partner with object	10
Smothered, strangled, choked partner	10
Threatened partner with weapon	10
Other (physical restraint)	3

Abusers (100%) had violent relationships of less than a year in duration, whereas greater proportions of those with Both experiences continued their relationships longer (60% of Both/V relationships and 67% of Both/A relationships were a year or longer in duration). Moreover, Victims and Abusers typically experienced the violence only once (54% and 71%, respectively), whereas a greater proportion of those with a history of Both roles experienced violence more frequently ("every few months" typified 56% of the Both/A reports, and 50% of Both/V reports indicated that violent episodes occurred at least monthly).

The most serious injury a respondent reported suffering (as victim) or inflicting (as abuser) was classified into one of four categories: none, objects only (torn clothing, broken glasses), minor personal injuries (scrapes, splinters, small bruises), and moderate personal injuries (medium bruises, cuts, twisted wrists). Although large proportions of all groups denied there was any injury as a result of the violence, some intergroup differences were apparent. Most abusers denied inflicting any injury, whereas the *only* reports of moderate levels of personal injury occurred in accounts of a respondent's own victimization (i.e., Victim and Both/V reports).

In summary, a substantial minority of participants reported personal experiences of violence in dating relationships, and subgrouping the respondents based on their roles in the violence revealed both qualitative and quantitative differences among them in other respects. Specifically, respondents who had been *both* victim and abuser tended to have longer violent relationships, were more likely to still be in their violent relationships, and reported more frequent occurrences of violent episodes compared with persons who had been only victims or only abusers. Reports of the maximum injury inflicted or received differed along the abuser/victim dimension, with only victims reporting moderately serious consequences, and abusers more frequently denying any injurious results of their actions.

Attitudes About Couple Violence

Simple totals were obtained on the 17-item Battering Empathy Scale (BES), (with reverse scores used on the items indicated in Table 2.1), so scores could theoretically range from 17 to 153. The actual scores obtained by this group of participants represented a broad spectrum of the potential spread, ranging from 70 to 150 points. Coefficient alpha (Cronbach, 1951) was .796 for the item set, demonstrating an acceptable degree of internal consistency for the BES. Item-total correlations further showed that all items should be retained in the instrument.

Because a Sex × Battering Experiences classification of respondents resulted in a design with only one individual in the Female/Both-roles cell, the effects of these two factors on Battering Empathy were assessed in separate ANOVAs. Females were found to have significantly higher BES scores than had males ($\overline{X}_f = 123.3$, $\overline{X}_m = 116.1$; $F(1,123) = 5.784$, $p < .05$). Comparisons on individual scale items revealed that these differences derived primarily from females' significantly higher empathy on items 1, 2, 8, 10, and 17.

The four subject groupings with different experiences with violence differed significantly in overall Battering Empathy scores ($F(3,121) = 4.998$, $p < .01$). Scheffé tests of pairwise differences revealed that respondents who had experienced Both roles were significantly less empathetic than were each of the other three groups on total BES scores, but that there were no significant differences in empathy among Victims, Abusers, or those with no experiences with intimate violence.

Comparisons of the groups on individual scale items revealed that this difference in overall BES derived primarily from answers to a single item ($F(3,121) = 6.815$, $p < .001$). This question (number 10) asked respondents to indicate whether they "would find it easier to imagine the feelings of the [Victim or the Abuser] during a battering episode."Again, Scheffé tests of pairwise differences indicated that the ratings of those who had experienced Both roles differed from those of the other respondents but that the remaining three groups did not differ among themselves. Specifically, those with Both experiences felt they could equally imagine the feelings of Victim and Abuser ($\overline{X}_B = 5.1$), whereas all the other respondent groups more easily imagined the Victim's feelings ($\overline{X}_N = 2.94$, $\overline{X}_V = 1.62$, $\overline{X}_A = 1.86$).

Thus the group differences in battering empathy were a mix of expected and surprising findings. The fact that females obtained higher BES scores parallels the pattern of sex differences on Deitz et al.'s RES (1982), after which the present scale was patterned. However, the relationship that emerged between battering empathy and personal experiences with violence was not entirely anticipated. One might have expected that persons with experiences as Victims in situations of intimate violence would evidence greater empathy on the BES than would those with no experiences of this sort or those whose experiences had been as Abusers. Clearly the present findings did not bear this out. Indeed, those who had been Abusers were as empathetic toward a hypothetical victim as were those who had themselves been victims of an intimate partner. At the same time, respondents who had reported backgrounds in Both roles emerged as significantly lower in victim-empathy than the remainder of the sample. Recall that this group was also distinguished by a deeper involvement in intimate violence in that their violent relationships tended to be ongoing, of longer duration, and were associated with more frequent experiences of violence. Interestingly, this pattern is the *reverse* of the one that prevails with rape empathy, in which persons who have been personally victimized or who have resisted an assailant are more empathetic with victims than are those with less personal involvement (see Deitz et al., 1982). At the same time, it is not an altogether surprising result when one recognizes that those who were more involved had had a dual role in the violence in the present sample, that is, those with experience in Both roles found it equally easy to imagine the feelings of hypothetical victims and abusers alike.

Calling One's Own Experiences "Battering"

Respondents who reported personal experiences with violence in their romantic relationships were asked to rate the extent to which they considered these events "battering" on a 9-point scale. Most declined to apply the "battering" label to their own experiences: only 21% rated their experiences above the midpoint toward the "battering" pole, whereas 68% gave ratings below the midpoint, thereby not regarding their experiences as battering, and 11% were noncommittal (at the midpoint).

The three groups with personal violent experiences did not differ in their ratings, and analyses uncovered only one significant correlate of their self-labeling decisions: these decisions were related to the degree of maximum injury suffered by those in victim roles (i.e., Victims and Both/V respondents: $\underline{r}_V = .620$, $p < .025$; $\underline{r}_{B/V} = .679$, $p < .025$), but labeling decisions were not related to the severity of injuries reportedly inflicted by respondents in abuser roles (Abusers and Both/A respondents).

Table 2.3 presents the results of a content analysis of short-answer explanations for the decision about calling one's own experiences "battering." (Since a respondent's explanation was included in any and all applicable explanation categories, the table total exceeds 100%.) The results confirm the importance of physical injury as a criterion for applying the "battering" label. Also important among the labeling criteria mentioned were characteristics of the physical abuse itself (particularly its duration and repetitiveness), the underlying motives for the abuse whether the intention was to physically harm the partner, whether the abuser's anger was understandable, and the emotional context of the relationship in general.

In summary, respondents declined to use the term *battering* in referring to themselves, and their willingness to use it depended on the seriousness of the injuries suffered by those who were the victims of their partners' abuse.

Reactions to the Case Study

Method of analysis. Recall that the hypothetical "case study" scenario in Part III of the questionnaire occurred in eight different versions according to a 3-way Instructions (2) × Force (2) × Resistance (2) design. In addition to expecting that these stimulus dimensions might affect evaluations and perceptions, one might also expect that sex or background experiences with violence would condition responses.

Because a Sex × Experience classification of respondents could not be analyzed (as it resulted in a cell with only one respondent), separate series of analyses were necessary to assess the influences of these characteristics. The first series, reported in Sedlak (1984a), analyzed the reaction data according to a 5-way design: Battering Empathy (2) × Sex (2) × Instructions (2) × Force (2) × Resistance (2). The second series of analyses, detailed in Sedlak (1984b), focused on the effects of personal experiences with violence in relation to the different story dimensions. Again, it was necessary to adapt to the limits of the respondent sample, which led to empty (and nearly empty) cells in the 4-way classification of Experience (4) × Instructions (2) × Force (2) × Resistance (2). As a result, three separate 2-way ANOVAs were necessary: Experience (4) × Instructions (2), Experience (4) × Force (2), and Experience (4) × Resistance (2).[3] All dependent measures reflected respondents' ratings on 9-point scales.

Because of greatly differing n's within the cells of the design, it was necessary to use a method of analysis appropriate for this situation. The method used was computationally straightforward, treating cell means as

TABLE 2.3
Reasons for Calling/Not Calling Own Experience "Battering"

Reason	% Who Gave It
Severity of the physical consequence (or lack of it)	47
Frequency, repetitiveness, duration (or insufficiency)	17
Mere use of physical force	10
Emotional closeness of the relationship in general	10
Intention to hurt (or its absence)	7
Justifiability/understandability of the abuser's anger	7
Controllability of the abuser's actions (lack of)	3
(No explanation offered for labeling decision)	23

single observations and adjusting the error mean square by a correction factor (see Edwards, 1968). Caution is urged in considering the results, since this method yields only approximate results. Since the likelihood of a Type I error was inflated by the number of tests performed here, the alpha level was adjusted by requiring that an effect attain what would ordinarily be the .001 level in order to be regarded as significant in the present context.[4]

In discussing the case study reactions, those that relate to empathy and labeling decisions will be treated first, followed by the results for other perceptions and evaluations.

Identification with Victim and Abuser. Recall that, on the BES responses reported earlier, Both-role persons could equally imagine the feelings of both parties, whereas the three other groups did not differ—Victims, Abusers, and those with No Experiences of couple violence more readily imagined the victim's emotions. Responses to the different versions of the case study provide further insights into this pattern, revealing that experiences do, in fact, have a greater effect on identification with the different parties than the general form of inquiry on the BES could reveal.

Respondents rated their feelings of similarity relative to the victim and to the abuser in two separate questions. The experience groups differed in both cases (for victim-similarity: $F(3,117) = 7.76$; for abuser-similarity: $F(3,117) = 9.36$. Consistent with the BES pattern, persons who had experienced Both roles offered the lowest average ratings of victim similarity ($\bar{X} = 2.2$), and the highest abuser similarity ratings ($\bar{X} = 3.8$) across the four experience groups. Also, as one might have expected, those with no personal experiences of violence offered moderately low victim-similarity ratings ($\bar{X} = 3.6$), and the lowest average abuser-similarity ratings ($\bar{X} = 1.8$). What came as a surprise, however, was the relatively high victim identification expressed by Abusers ($\overline{X}$ = 5.0, very close to that of Victims themselves, $\overline{X}$ = 4.9), and the relatively high abuser-similarity of the Victims ($\overline{X}$ = 3.1, which is higher than the average ratings of the Abusers, $\overline{X}$ = 2.4). In both cases, however, an interaction between the effects of Experience and the victim's Resistance in the case study provide some insight into these results.

According to this interaction on victim identification (F(3,117) = 14.76), which is graphed in Figure 2.2, Abusers departed markedly from the pattern exhibited by the other experience groups: whereas other respondents felt more similar to the victim when she did *not* offer high physical resistance, Abusers felt far more similar to her when she did. Thus Abusers identified more with the victim when her behavior most closely matched their own, that is, when she herself used physical force (albeit in response to her partner's abuse). This intriguing finding suggests that these Abusers may have regarded their own use of physical force as having been a *response* to some nonphysical "attack" by their partner.

Similarly, the overall higher abuser identification of the Victim group can be understood in light of the Experience × Resistance interaction on that measure (F(3,117) = 5.87). Figure 2.3, which graphs this interaction, reveals that the Victim group identified most with the abuser when the case study victim had offered high resistance, that is, when this hypothetical abuser was himself "victimized." An unstated assumption may prevail among these participants that they had somehow triggered or evoked their partner's violence and that this violence was essentially a *response* to their own (albeit nonviolent) behavior.

In general, one can summarize these results by saying that Victims and Abusers were differentially affected by the victim's resistance. Abusers showed greater levels of victim identification when the victim resisted and (as they had done) used physical violence with her partner, whereas Victims showed greater levels of identification with the case study abuser when his experiences were most similar to their own and he was the recipient of violence because the victim resisted and used physical violence against him.

Calling the case study "battering." Respondents rated the extent to which they considered the incident described in the case study to be "battering" on a 1 ("not at all") to 9 ("completely") scale. Only the two-way Experience × Resistance effect attained the .001 level on this question (F(3,117) = 17.36). As Figure 2.4 shows, the victim's Resistance made no difference to the labeling decisions of respondents with no experiences of intimate violence and had little impact on those who had been solely Abusers. On the other hand, those who had been Victims themselves and those with experiences in Both roles were influenced in opposite ways: Victims were less likely to call it battering when the hypothetical victim

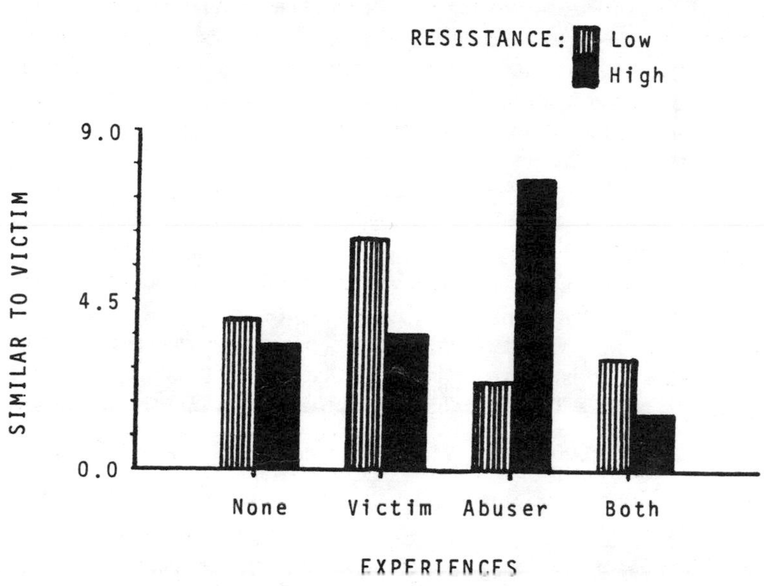

Figure 2.2 **Ratings of respondents' feelings of similarity to the victim as a function of victim's resistance and respondents' personal experiences with couple violence.**

physically resisted her abuser, whereas those with Both types of experience were less likely to consider it "battering" when she did *not* physically respond to her partner's assault. It is interesting that these are the respondent groups with personal experiences as victims and that their labeling decisions regarding the case study tended to reject the "battering" term for response patterns that *departed* from their own typical reactions to their partners (Victims having not reported themselves as violent in response, but Both-role respondents often describing reciprocal violence in their backgrounds).

Punishing the Abuser. The extent to which the abuser should be punished was indicated on a 1 ("not at all") to 9 ("a great deal") scale. Responses to this question revealed only a main effect of Force: more punishment was recommended when the abuser used high Force ($\overline{X} = 8.4$) than when he used low Force ($\overline{X} = 6.4$), $F(1,116) = 14.93$. As will be seen, this is one of the few main effects to emerge in this study, and the only main effect that remains unqualified by interactions. This underscores the importance of the degree of violence (and severity of consequences, with

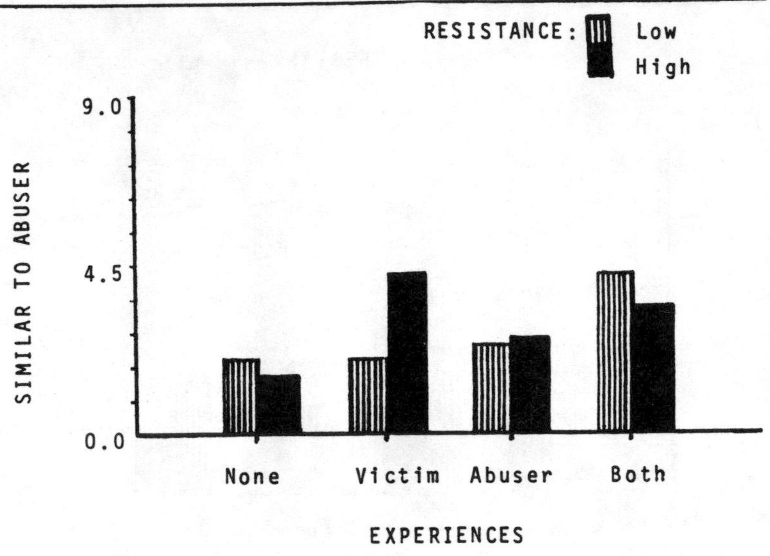

Figure 2.3 **Ratings of respondents' feelings of similarity to the abuser as a function of victim's resistance and respondents' personal experiences with couple violence.**

which it was associated in this study) in evaluations of episodes of intimate-partner violence.

Blame and responsibility. There were four questions about blame and responsibility—two concerning how responsible the victim and the abuser had been for the incident, and two regarding the extent to which each should be blamed for the incident. In all four cases, similar effects characterized the data.[5] The pattern of results for judgments of the victim's responsibility is given in Figure 2.5, ($F(3,117) = 11.19$). As can be seen, the level of the victim's Resistance made virtually no difference to the decisions of those with no experiences of intimate violence, but the different violence experienced groups varied in their judgments. Those who had been Victims assigned far more responsibility to the case study victim when she responded to her abuser violently than when she was passive in response, whereas those who had been Abusers and those who have been Both victims and abusers saw slightly *less* victim responsibility for the incident when she responded with high Resistance. The victim-blame decisions followed a very similar pattern ($F(3,117) = 19.62$).

It is interesting that these victim-responsibility and victim-blame decisions related systematically to the respondents' own behavior patterns.

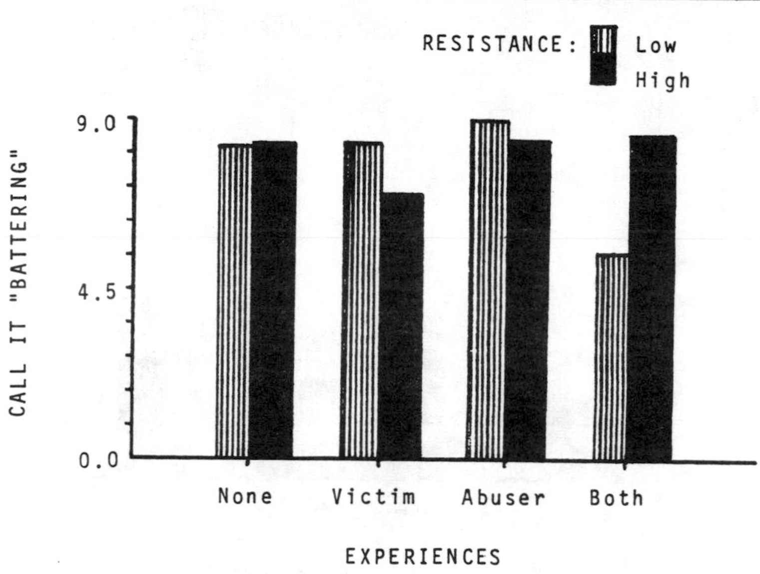

Figure 2.4 **Ratings of respondents' willingness to call it "battering" as a function of victim's resistence and respondents' personal experience with couple violence.**

Respondents absolved the case study victim of responsibility and blame when her behavior with her partner matched their own behavior in intimate interactions, and they conferred relatively higher levels of blame and responsibility on her when her actions departed from a response pattern that was familiar to them.

Abuser-responsibility judgments ($F(3,117) = 15.80$) and abuser-blame decisions ($F(3,117) = 19.83$) were essentially mirror images of this pattern: That is, the victim's resistance again had no effect on those with no violent experiences, but Abusers and those with Both role experiences gave the abuser *greater* responsibility and blame when his victim resisted him, and Victims *absolved* him of responsibility and blame when she resisted.

It would appear that Victims consider violent resistance on the part of a victim to be a circumstance that *mitigates* the abuser's accountability in the situation (as it accentuates her own). Those who have themselves been physically violent toward an intimate partner regard the victim's violent response quite differently. Perhaps they consider her reactions as *consequences* that must be weighed in determining blame and responsibility and thus the stronger her reactions the more severe these judgments must be. In

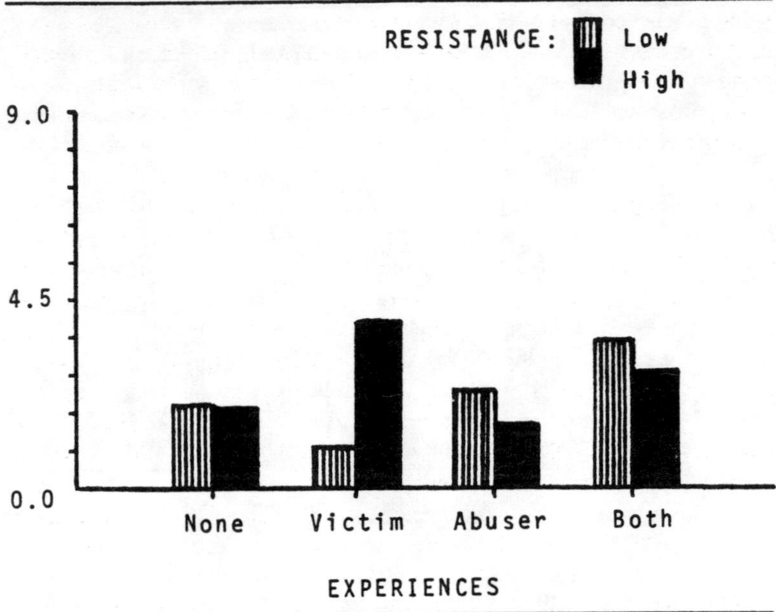

Figure 2.5 Ratings of victim's responsibility as a function of victim's resistance and respondents' personal experiences with couple violence.

any event, while these interpretations are consistent with the results, they are admittedly speculative at this point.

Abuser's and Victim's control. Ratings of how much control each protagonist had in the situation again yielded significant Experience × Resistance interactions and mirror-image patterns for the means in each case. Average ratings of the victim's control in the different Resistance conditions for the four experience groups are shown in Figure 2.6 ($F(3,117) = 25.25$). The inverse pattern described the means for ratings of the abuser's control in the situation ($F(3,117) = 29.05$). Resistance made essentially no difference in the ratings of those with no violent experiences or of those who had been Abusers, but differently affected the judgments of Victims and those who had experiences in Both roles. Victims saw the case study victim as having far more control in the situation when she resisted her assailant violently than when she responded passively. Certainly, this active response style contradicts their own typical reaction to their abusive partners. Perhaps they expected that such an actively responding victim would thereby *gain* more control over the situation, unlike their own typical feelings and experiences with their abusive partners. Alternatively, they may have believed that such a victim would necessarily have had more control over the situation *to begin with* in order to have had the option to respond in such an active way—a way so alien to their own experiences. In contrast, those who had experienced Both roles ascribed greater control to the passive victim. The reasons for this are not intuitively obvious. One possibility is that they, like the victims, believed that a person who responded *dis*similarly to themselves would gain the control that had eluded them in their personal encounters. Another, less probable, explanation is that they (unlike all other respondents here) interpreted the question as referring to "self-control" and thus rated the victim as possessing more when she was passive than when she reacted violently. In any event, these interpretations remain conjectures at present and their validity must be assessed in future research.

Victim's characteristics. Respondents were asked to indicate how intelligent and how respectable the victim was, and in both cases a significant Experience × Resistance effect emerged.

Figure 2.7 graphs this interaction for ratings of the victim's intelligence ($F(3,117) = 8.04$). Note that this figure approximates a mirror image of the means graphed in Figure 2.5, concerning her responsibility for the incident. Apparently, the more responsibility she was considered to have, the less intelligent she was deemed to be. Her level of Resistance was of only slight concern to respondents with no violent background, and to those who had been Abusers, or who had experiences as Both abuser and victim. In all three groups, the case study victim was viewed as slightly more intelligent when she strongly resisted than when she reacted passively. The Victim group, however, was again strikingly affected by her Resistance level. They perceived her to be a markedly less intelligent person when she reacted violently to her abuser's assault. Recall that, besides being related to victim's responsibility, this same overall pattern of group differences also characterized ratings of the degree to which the victim's personality causally contributed to the incident and of the degree to which the victim was careless. Here, again, the Victim respondent group judged their hypothetical counterpart especially severely when her behavior departed from their own reportedly passive responses to their abusive partners.

The degree to which the participant groups saw the victim as respectable under the different Resistance conditions is shown in Figure 2.8 ($F(3,116) = 7.00$). The pattern in the figure is quite clear and rather unlike any encountered thus far. Here, the groups appear to fall into response patterns primarily on the basis of their *degree* of involvement in intimate battering. The case study victim's resistance made no detectable difference to those with virtually no experiences of this sort. Victims and Abusers had some personal exposure to violent interactions with an intimate partner, but

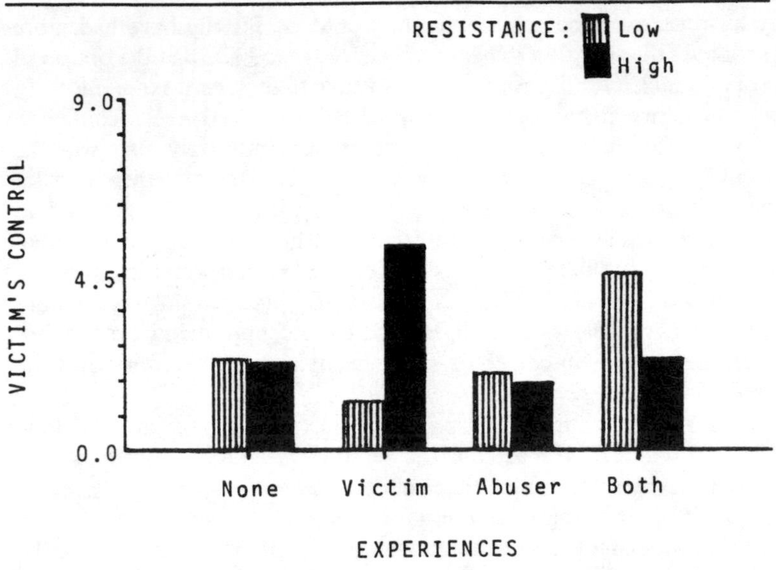

Figure 2.6 Ratings of victim's control as a function of victim's resistance and respondents' personal experiences with couple violence.

these had been relatively infrequent; their relationships had been generally of short duration, and most had been dissolved prior to the time of this study. These groups regarded the victim who resisted strongly as comparatively less respectable than one who responded passively. In contrast, respondents who had reported experiences as Both victims and abusers had had much greater personal involvement in violence with their intimate partners. Recall that these participants had reported relatively frequent episodes of violence and that their relationships tended to be of longer duration and were generally still ongoing at the time of their participation in the study. These respondents viewed the passive victim as *less* respectable than the active victim.

Apart from interpreting the Figure 2.8 pattern as deriving from differences in level of personal involvement by the different groups, one might alternatively regard it as reflecting the connection between the type of violent experience one has had and one's beliefs about what "appropriate" victim's behaviors are in such a situation. Victims and Abusers were most familiar with the circumstance of *one-sided* violence, in which only the abuser acted violently. These groups saw the victim who departed from a passive behavior pattern as less respectable. Respondents with Both experiences were generally more familiar with interactions in which *both*

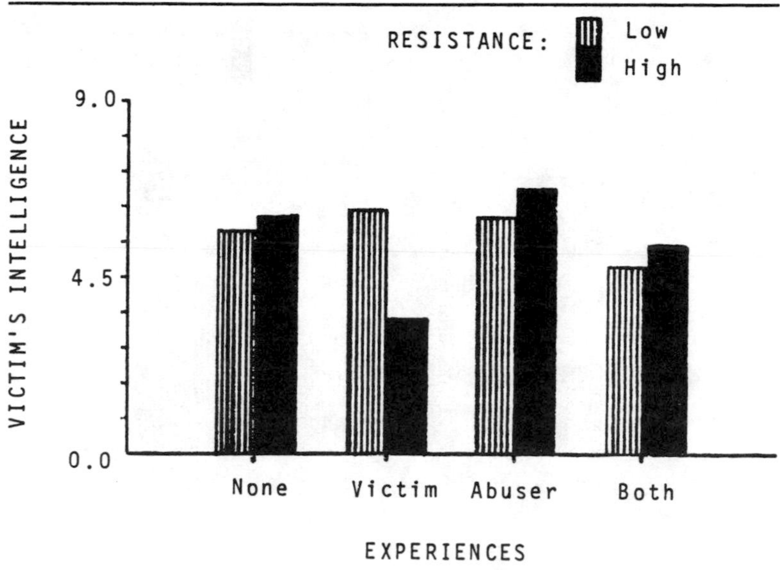

Figure 2.7 Ratings of victim's intelligence as a function of victim's resistance and respondents' personal experiences with couple violence.

partners behaved violently, and they considered a passive victim to be less respectable than one who responded violently to her partner's abuse.

Abuser's characteristics. Of four questions pertaining to the abuser's traits, only one emerged with significant effects in this study. In contrast to the findings for the victim's characteristics, ratings of the abuser's intelligence and of the abuser's respectability were *un*affected by any of the factors examined here. Nor were there any effects associated with ratings of the abuser's immorality.

Only judgments of the extent to which the abuser was mentally ill exhibited significant results. These decisions varied as a function of both respondents' experiences and victim's level of resistance ($F(3,117) = 8.16$), as depicted in Figure 2.9. Note that this pattern resembles that shown in Figure 2.8 regarding the victim's respectability, except for the fact that the Abuser group tended to give lower overall ratings here, denying that their hypothetical counterpart was mentally ill. That this configuration does parallel the Figure 2.8 ratings suggests that these decisions about the abuser's mental illness might similarly be explained as deriving from the respondents' level of involvement in intimate violence, or from their views about "appropriate" victim behaviors in such interactions.

Thus, for respondents who had only moderate levels of personal

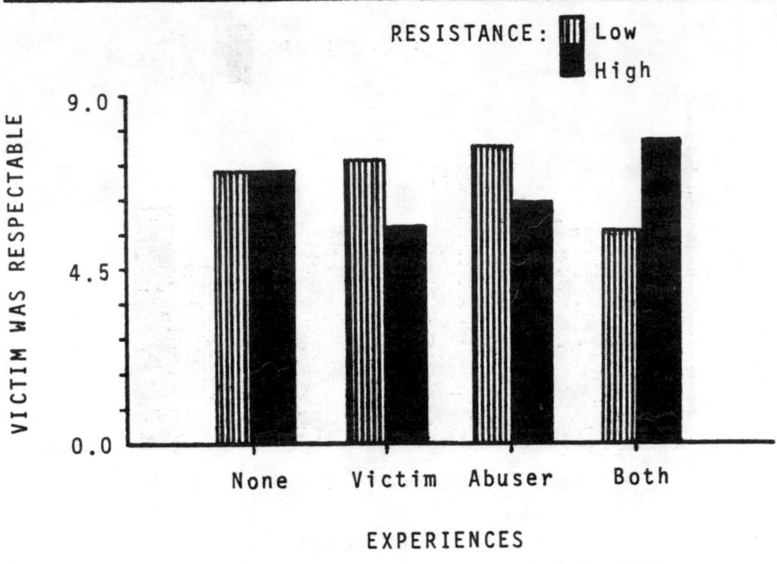

Figure 2.8 Ratings of victim's respectability as a function of victim's resistance and respondents' personal experiences with couple violence.

involvement in violence with a partner or who were personally most familiar with situations in which the victim reacted passively (i.e., Victims and Abusers), strong resistance on the victim's part weakened impressions of the abuser's psychopathology. On the other hand, for respondents who had deeper levels of personal involvement in intimate violence, or who were personally most familiar with situations in which the victim reacted violently in turn (i.e., Both-role respondents), it was passivity on the part of the victim that interfered with perceiving the abuser to be mentally ill. It would appear, then, that the more a respondent regards the victim's response as comprehensible, familiar, or appropriate, the more he or she is willing to consider the abuser to be mentally ill, and vice versa.

Motives of the Abuser and Victim. Three questions related to the motives of the protagonists in the case study, two of which revealed significant effects in this analysis. No findings emerged here in connection with a question that asked subjects to rate the extent to which the abuser had "a need to prove his manhood."

Judgments of the extent to which the abuser was "motivated by a desire for violence" yielded two significant interactions. The Experience × Force effect ($F(3,113) = 7.66$) is shown in Figure 2.10, which indicates that while the abuser's Force made little difference to respondents who had no violent

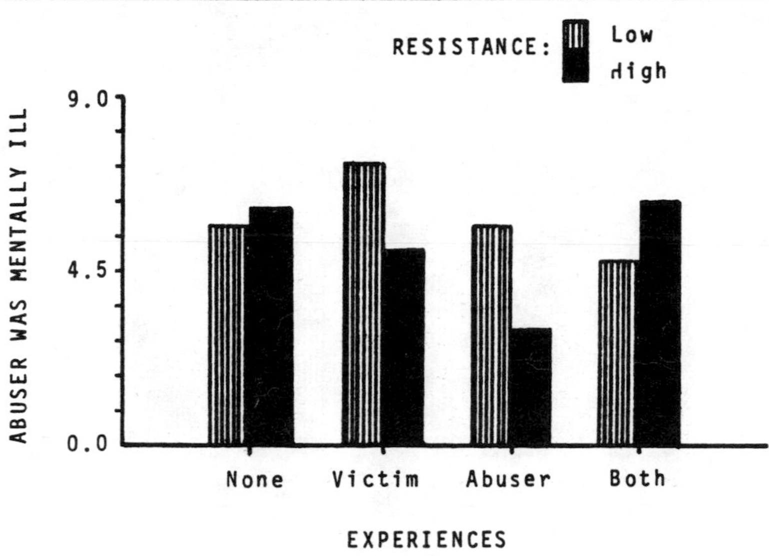

Figure 2.9 Ratings of extent to which abuser was mentally ill as a function of victim's resistance and respondents' personal experiences with couple violence.

backgrounds, the decisions of the groups with violent experiences were differently affected by this factor. Victims saw him as far more strongly motivated by a desire for violence when he used a high level of force, whereas the two respondent groups with experiences in the abuser role (Abusers and Both) saw him as actually wanting the violence *less* in the high Force case. A possible (admittedly speculative) explanation for this pattern is that the two abuser groups perceived the highly forceful abuser as "out of control" and hence as being less directed by specific motives and deliberate choices than the abuser who used a lower level of force.

The Experience × Resistance effect on attributions of the abuser's violence motive is given in Figure 2.11 (F(3,113) = 8.78). Very clearly, the victim's resistance affected these judgments *only* among Abusers, who substantially underrated the abuser's motive for violence when his victim reacted violently in return. In this connection, it is interesting to note that the Abuser respondent group was most personally familiar with passive victims. One wonders how stronger reactions by their partners would have affected their own desire for violence.

Ratings of the extent to which the victim had "a desire to be beaten or hit" revealed a main effect of Experience (F(3,117) = 6.99), which was

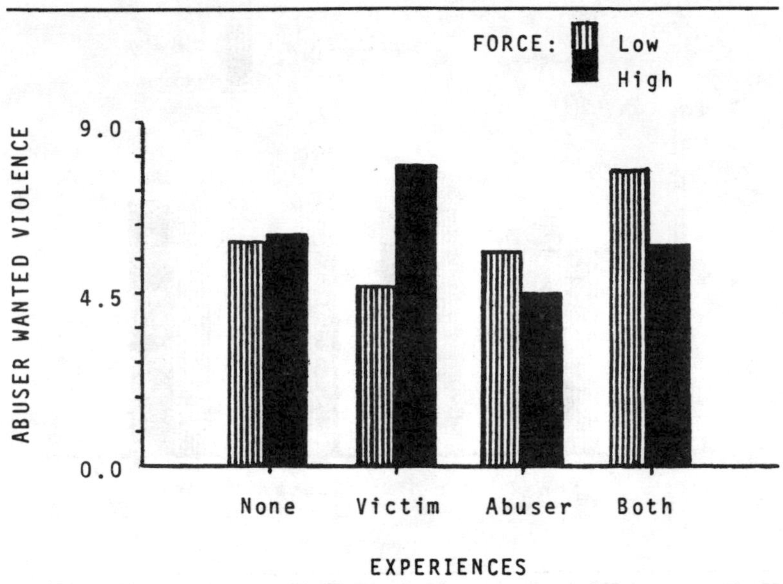

Figure 2.10 Ratings of abuser's desire for violence as a function of his use of force and respondents' personal experiences with couple violence.

qualified by two significant interactions. Overall, Victims and those with Both experiences gave ratings near the midpoint ($\overline{X}_B = 5.4$, $\overline{X}_V = 4.8$), while Abusers and those with no experiences of violence thought the victim had somewhat less desire for the abuse ($\overline{X}_N = 3.0$, $\overline{X}_A = 2.8$).

A separate graph is not provided here for the Experience × Resistance interaction on perceptions of the victim's masochism ($F(3,117) = 19.19$), since the means for this effect approximated the pattern shown in Figure 2.5, which indicates the victim's responsibility.

The Experience × Force interaction ($F(3,117) = 12.01$) for ratings of the victim's masochism, shown in Figure 2.12, indicates that the Abuser's force made no difference to the judgments of those with no experiences of violence, but that the other three groups differed depending on their level of personal involvement. Victims and Abusers, who had personally had relatively moderate involvement in intimate abuse, saw the victim as wanting abuse *less* when it was more serious and its consequences were more severe. In contrast, those whose own personal experience had been more extensive and serious (i.e., those who had experienced Both roles) saw the victim as wanting her abuse *more* when it was described as more serious and its consequences were more severe. Ironically, it seems that a

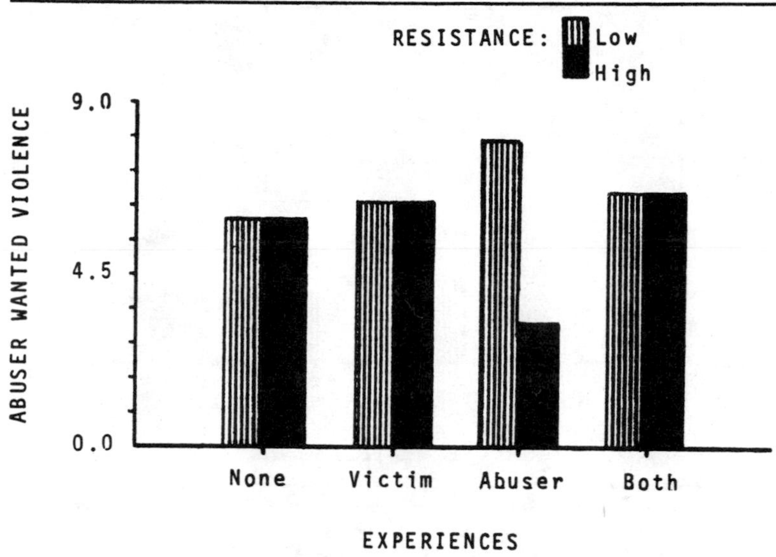

Figure 2.11 Ratings of abuser's desire for violence as a function of victim's resistance and respondents' personal experiences with couple violence.

hypothetical victim is viewed as wanting her abuse more the more closely the seriousness of her circumstance conforms to an observer's own exposure to violence with an intimate partner.

Summary

This section will focus on the central questions that guided the research, which were introduced briefly at the outset of this report.

Relation of personal experiences to general attitudes and evaluations. The respondent sample included subgroups with personal experiences in violent relationships, and dividing them on the basis of their roles in the violence revealed both qualitative and quantitative differences among them in other respects. On the one hand, general attitude measures about intimate violence revealed that individuals who had had experiences in both victim and abuser roles had lower victim empathy than did other respondents, and indicated that they could more equally imagine the feelings of both victim and abuser during a battering episode. This group was also distinguished by a deeper involvement in their violent relationships in that these tended to be ongoing, be of longer duration, and involve more frequent violent episodes. On the other hand, more complex differences

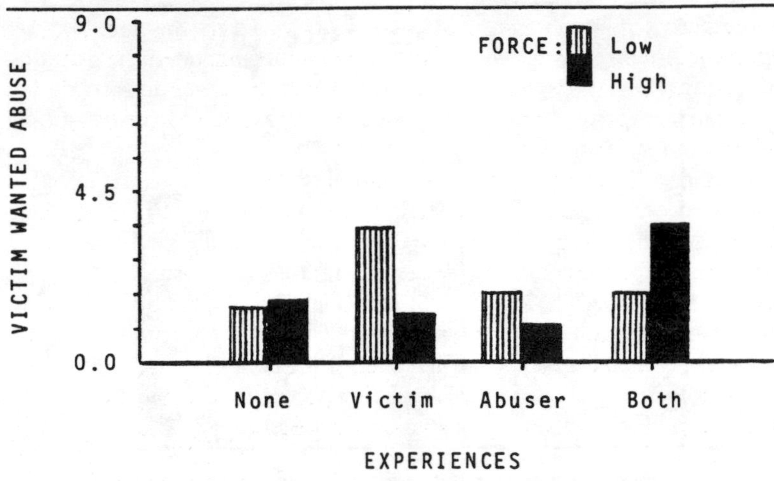

Figure 2.12 Ratings of victim's desire for abuse as a function of abuser's level of force and respondents' personal experiences with couple violence.

among the groups were uncovered in their sensitivity to the dimensions of the case study episode, particularly in their reactions to variations in the level of physical resistance offered by the victim. These are discussed more fully below.

Calling it "battering." One of the major purposes of this research was to explore the dynamics that govern a person's willingness to term an event or series of events "battering." Three aspects of the findings reported here bear on this question. First, ratings by those with personal experiences of intimate violence concerning their willingness to call their own experience "battering" are an important resource, together with the correlates of these willingness ratings. As noted earlier, most respondents who had themselves had violent experiences declined to call these "battering," and groups who differed in the types of experiences they had (victim, abuser, both roles) did not differ overall in their rated willingness to apply the term "battering" to themselves. Analyses have succeeded in identifying only one significant correlate of the labeling decision: the degree of maximum injury suffered by participants who had been victims. Thus the more serious the consequence to oneself, the more willing one was to call a personal experience "battering." It was interesting that those in the abuser role were not analogously influenced to call themselves "batterers" on the basis of the seriousness of the injuries they had inflicted.

Second, respondents' verbal explanations of their decisions about considering themselves to be "battered" or "batterers" confirmed the importance of physical injury as a criterion for using this label. Other important criteria mentioned in these explanations included the duration and repetitiveness of the physical abuse, whether there was an intention to harm, whether the abuser's anger was understandable, and the emotional closeness of the relationship apart from the violence.

The third and final source of information on the labeling issue were the factors that were found to affect respondents' willingness to call the case study episode "battering." Both past experiences and the victim's level of resistance proved to be important determinants in this regard. Respondents with no experiences of violence and those who had been only abusers in their personal histories were relatively unaffected by the victim's resistance when making their decisions about labeling the case "battering." However, those who had had experiences as victims were affected by the victim's resistance in different ways, depending on whether they had been only victims or had also been abusive themselves. That is, these respondents rejected the term "battering" in relation to victim's responses that departed from their own typical reactions—violent victims were not considered "battered" by those who had only been victims (and not themselves abusive), while passive victims were less likely to be termed "battered" by those who had themselves been violent.

Effects of Victim's reactions on evaluations and perceptions. Whether the victim responded passively or was violent in return had far-reaching effects on respondents' evaluations of the case study, although the specific form of the effect in each case depended on the nature of the respondent's own experiences with intimate violence. The findings associated with the decision to label the case study "battering" have been summarized above, but this factor was also found to be the basis of most of the remaining results described in this report:

(1) Identification with the victim and with the abuser were not affected by the victim's resistance for respondents with no violent experiences or for those whose experiences had encompassed both victim and abuser roles. However, participants who had been only victims and those who had been only abusers were affected by the victim's resistance when responding to the role that was not familiar to them: Abusers identified more with the victim when she strongly resisted and was violent (as they had been), while victims identified more with the abuser when he was strongly resisted by his victim (and was himself assaulted, as they had been).

(2) Respondents absolved the case study victim of responsibility and blame when her behavior matched their own (i.e., the passive victim was absolved by those who had themselves been passive victims, while the violent victim was absolved to some degree by those who had themselves acted violently). Decisions about the abuser's responsibility and blame were

essentially mirror images of this pattern.[6]

(3) The victim's resistance affected decisions about the abuser's and victim's control in the situation, but the exact nature of the effect depended on whether the respondents had themselves been passive (victim only) or violent in turn (both victim and abuser). In both cases, more control was accorded a victim who *departed* from the respondent's own familiar method of response. The degree of control accorded the abuser was essentially a mirror image of that attributed to the victim.

(4) Ideas about the victim's respectability followed a different pattern, with those who had had a single role in their past (victim or abuser) seeing strong resistance as less respectable, and those who had experienced both roles, feeling the more strongly resisting victim was more respectable. It is unclear whether this result relates to the differences among these groups in their level of involvement in violent relationships or whether it relates to their ideas about what types of responses are "appropriate" for a victim of partner violence. In any event, it is clear that the groups do judge the victim's respectability differently, depending on her reactions and on their own backgrounds.

(5) Ideas about the abuser's characteristics were largely unaffected by the factors examined here, with one exception. Judgments about whether the abuser was mentally ill tended to parallel decisions about the victim's respectability. The more a respondent considered the victim's response to be comprehensible, familiar, or appropriate, the more he or she was willing to regard the abuser as mentally ill. When the victim's response departed from what the respondent was familiar with in terms of victim behavior, however, ratings of the abuser's psychopathology showed that he was given the benefit of the doubt.

(6) Results for decisions about the abuser's motive for violence were consistent with the idea that those who had themselves been violent toward a partner regarded him as more "out of control" and hence as less directed by specific motives and deliberate choices when he used high force, whereas those whose experience had been only as victims saw the abuser as more strongly motivated by a desire for violence when he used a high level of force. Curiously, only those who had been abusers (and only abusers) were affected by the victim's resistance when deciding on the abuser's desire for violence. They tended to underrate his motive for violence when the victim responded violently (i.e., in a manner alien to their own experiences with passive partners).

(7) Judgments of the victim's desire to be beaten or hit (masochism) also followed ratings of the degree to which her behaviors had causally contributed to the incident in that the different subject groupings were differently affected by the victim's resistance according to the same pattern.

At the same time, however, the abuser's use of force also affected judgments of masochism. Those whose personal experiences with abuse had been moderate (abusers only and victims only) saw the victim as desiring the abuse less when it was more serious and had more severe consequences. In contrast, those with more extensive personal experiences of intimate violence (in both victim and abuser roles) concluded the opposite—that she wanted it more the more serious and forceful it had been.

Thus the nature of the victim's reaction in an abusive episode has pervasive effects on evaluations and perceptions of the circumstance. Even more importantly, the exact nature of these effects is not the same for all observers, but depends critically on the nature of the observer's own personal history of violent interactions with an intimate partner. This study provides a beginning in the effort to uncover some of the complexities involved in this link between personal backgrounds and judgments regarding couple violence.

Notes

1. A report on the forced-sex data was presented in Sedlak (1985).

2. It primarily differs from Deitz et al.'s (1982) scale in its simplification of the attitude questions into single statements. Deitz et al.'s measure presents two polar positions for each question, and requires the respondents to rate their own position on a scale defined by these poles.

3. The 3-way Instructions (2) × Force (2) × Resistance (2) interaction, together with its component 2-ways, were treated in the larger 5-way ANOVAs.

4. Only one of the effects from the first completed series of analyses (largely given in Sedlak, 1984a) met this stringent test, and this result appears among the findings presented here (see the main effect of Force on recommended punishment for the abuser). Thus neither sex nor battering empathy as measured by the BES (alone or in conjunction with the story dimensions), and none of the interactive effects of the story dimensions, were notable according to the present criterion.

5. Three other questions relating to the victim's causal involvement also yielded very similar results. That is, Experience × Resistance interactions of very similar forms emerged for ratings concerning how careless the victim was ($F(3,117) = 30.07$), how much her personality characteristics caused the incident in the case study ($F(3,117) = 14.52$), and the degree to which her behaviors were causally involved ($F(3,117) = 11.57$). These results are not graphed separately in this report. It was noteworthy that neither of the remaining questions concerning causality yielded significant findings in this study—one concerning the abuser's personality characteristics and another concerning the role of chance factors in precipitating the episode.

6. Impressions about the victim's causal contributions to the violent episode essentially paralleled the results about her responsibility, and were reflected in ratings of her carelessness, and of the causal contribution exerted by her personality characteristics and by her behaviors. Surprisingly there was no parallel pattern for ratings of the abuser's personality characteristics, which were not similar to judgments of his responsibility. Perceptions of the victim's

intelligence were mirror images of the ratings of her carelessness and responsibility—the more careless and responsible she was considered, the less intelligent she was thought to be.

References

Bernard, M. L., & Bernard, J. L. (1983). Violent intimacy: The family as a model for love relationships. *Family Relations, 32*, 283-286.

Bogal-Allbritten, R., & Allbritten, B. (1983, August). *The hidden victims: Premarital abuse among college students.* Paper presented at the 91st Meeting of the American Psychological Association, Anaheim, CA.

Cate, R. M., Henton, J. M., Koval, J., Christopher, F. S., & Lloyd, S. (1982). Premarital abuse: A social psychological perspective. *Journal of Family Issues, 3,* 79-91.

Comins, C. A. (1983, March). *Violence between college dating partners: Preliminary findings.* Paper presented at the meeting of the Southeastern Psychological Association, Atlanta, GA.

Comins, C. A. (1984, August). *Courtship violence: A recent study and its implications for future research.* Paper presented at the Second National Conference for Family Violence Researchers, Durham, NH.

Cronbach, L. J. (1951). Coefficient alpha and the internal structure of tests. *Psychometrika, 16*, 297-334.

Deitz, S. R., Blackwell, K. T., Daley, P. C., and Bentley, B. J. (1982). Measurement of empathy toward rape victims and rapists. *Journal of Personality and Social Psychology, 43*, 372-384.

Edwards, A. L. (1968). *Experimental design in psychological research* (3rd ed.). New York: Holt, Rinehart & Winston.

Ferraro, J., & Johnson, M. (1984, August). *The meanings of courtship violence.* Paper presented at the Second National Conference for Family Violence Researchers, Durham, NH.

Krulewitz, J. E., & Nash, J. E. (1979). Effects of rape victim resistance, assault outcome, and sex of observer on attributions about rape. *Journal of Personality, 47*, 557-574.

Laner, M. R., & Thompson, J. (1982). Abuse and aggression in courting couples. *Deviant Behavior, 3,* 229-244.

Makepeace, J. M. (1981). Courtship violence among college students. *Family Relations*, 30, 97-102.

Makepeace, J. M. (1983). Life events stress and courtship violence. *Family Relations, 32,* 101-109.

Makepeace, J. M. (1984, August). *The severity of courtship violence injuries and individual precautionary measures.* Paper presented at the Second National Conference for Family Violence Researchers, Durham, NH.

Matthews, W. J. (1984). Violence in college couples. *College Student Journal, 18*, 150-158.

Murphy, J. E. (1984, August). *Date abuse and forced intercourse among college students.* Paper presented at the Second National Conference for Family Violence Researchers, Durham, NH.

Sedlak, A. J. (1984a, August). *Violence between intimate partners: Calling it "battering" and allocating blame.* Paper presented at the Second National Conference for Family Violence Researchers, Durham, NH.

Sedlak, A. J. (1984b, August). *Understanding violence between intimate partners: The effects of personal experience and victim reactions on labeling it "battering" and allocating blame.* Paper presented at the 92nd Annual Convention of the American Psychological Association, Toronto, Canada.

Sedlak, A. J. (1985, March). *Forced sex by acquaintances and strangers: Calling it rape and evaluating the aggressor.* Paper presented at the Association for Women in Psychology conference, New York, NY.

Sigelman, C. K., Berry, C. J., & Wiles, K. A. (1983, March). *Violence in college students' relationships.* Paper presented at the meeting of the Southeastern Psychological Association, Atlanta, GA.

Straus, M. A., Gelles, R., and Steinmetz, S. K. (1980). *Behind closed doors: Violence in the American family.* Garden City, NY: Anchor/Doubleday.

3

How Battered Women and Abusive Men Account for Domestic Violence: Excuses, Justifications, or Explanations?

Michele Bograd

Violence between spouses, or domestic violence, has recently become an area of social and academic concern. Current theoretical approaches minimize the intervening subjective meanings of participants and observers regarding domestic violence. In distinction, this research assumed that domestic violence is a socially constructed activity that is imbued with meaning by actors and observers alike. This exploratory study was one of the first studies to systematically examine how battered women and abusive men perceive, define, and evaluate acts of physical force in their marriages, and to assess whether their perceptions differ from those of nonviolent men and women.

Theoretical Approach of the Study

The theoretical approach employed in this study has been labeled the "interpretive paradigm" (Wilson, 1970). In this paradigm, meaning is viewed as a critical component of social action. Through language or speech acts, individuals construct specific meanings for specific situations that may differ significantly from abstract cultural meanings (Berger & Luckman, 1967; Brittan, 1973; Cicourel, 1967, 1974; Douglas, 1970; Harre & Secord, 1973; Scott & Douglas, 1972; Spradley, 1972). Investigators focus on persons' common sense understandings of everyday life and on

AUTHOR'S NOTE: Address comments and correspondence to Michele Bograd, 33 Paulina Street, Somerville, MA 02144 contextual meanings of actions, in order to understand how persons attribute meaning to particular activities.

Imagine two men hitting each other until one, bloodied and bruised, falls to the ground. Now think of a boxing match. For many people, their initial reactions of horror change. The action becomes understandable and, to some, is no longer considered violent. A pacifist may still believe there is nothing in the situation that warrants the conduct of the fighters. But the boxers view their behavior as appropriate and normal given their definition of the circumstances.

This suggests that research into domestic violence should assume that battered women and abusive men are "normal" rather than bad, mad, or deviant (Chatterdon, 1976), in order to focus on the understandings reflected through their use of force on others.

Review and Critique of Current Theoretical Frameworks

In both theoretical and empirical works, the three current major approaches to domestic violence tend to deemphasize the importance of how battered women, abusive men and other people interpret the use of physical force in marriage. In the psychopathology model, theorists assume that violence occurs in marriages when either or both of the partners exhibit incomplete psychosexual development or poor psychological adjustment (Ball, 1977; Halleck, 1976; Hanks & Rosenbaum, 1977; Kutash, 1978; Lesse, 1974; Reynolds & Siegle, 1959; Schultz, 1960; Snell, Rosenwald, & Robey, 1964; Toby, 1966). In the social structural model of domestic violence, theorists do not examine social meanings but focus on observable rates of domestic violence and their association with relatively stable, enduring, supraindividual dimensions of society such as class, education, and race (Bandura, 1973, 1978; Farrington, 1980; Gelles, 1976, 1979; Owens & Straus, 1975; Steinmetz, 1977a, 1977b; Straus, Gelles, & Steinmetz, 1980; Straus & Hotaling, 1980). In distinction to structural theorists, other authors place emphasis on some types of social meanings, such as norms and values that specify who can hit whom and under what circumstances (Foss, 1980; Gelles, 1972; Goode, 1971; Harrington, 1972; Hotaling, 1980; Straus, 1976, 1977, 1977-78). The norms and value model of domestic violence is exemplified in the subculture theory of violence (Wolfgang, 1958, Wolfgang & Ferracuti, 1967): violence is sanctioned by the values of a distinct group that stands apart from the dominant (and presumably nonviolent) culture.

Each of these models attempts to reduce the complexity of domestic violence to several discrete variables. High levels of inference are used to abstract traits or typical norms as causes of domestic violence. Authors rarely provide a link between a general norm and a specific violent action because they assume that members of a group share a relatively stable system of symbols and meanings that are self-evident and consistently organized (Collett, 1977). In contrast, the interpretive model states that social meanings are often implicit, vague, and inconsistent. Their application is not automatic, but must be constantly renegotiated in situations of their use.

Several other problems exist in these models. "Violence" may not mean the same things to participants as to researchers. Physical acts are a unique kind of social behavior because their "brutishness" or existence cannot be denied (Pearce & Cronen, 1980; Searle, 1969). Yet physical force alone, however destructive it may be, does not constitute violence until it is imbued with social meaning (Marsh, Rosser, & Harre, 1978). That a man hits his wife is undeniable; whether the act is violent or not, good or bad, normal or deviant, is open to social interpretation.

The Study of Social Meanings Through Accounts

The kinds of social meanings imputed to domestic violence were explored in this study through the analysis of *accounts*. When action falls outside the bounds of expectation, people offer accounts, or interpret their actions to make them more understandable or acceptable to themselves or to others (Blum & McHugh, 1971; Burke, 1945; Horai, 1977; McCaghy, 1968; Marsden, 1978; Mills, 1940; Scott & Lyman, 1970; Taylor, 1972, 1979). Although accounts are everyday rudimentary theories of social action, they are not simply explanations. The study of accounts is based on a model of man-as-rhetorician: The purpose of accounts is persuasive, not merely descriptive. By bridging action and expectation, they function to neutralize potentially deviant behavior. Within this frame of reference, the importance of accounts is assessed by their social function, not by their validity. While the study of accounts is not intended to provide a comprehensive explanation of domestic violence, the description of understandings of domestic violence provides an explanation of social phenomena on one level of analysis.

Review of Empirical Literature on Accounts of Domestic Violence

There are few systematic empirical studies about how violent and nonviolent men and women think about domestic violence. Based on ethnographic or clinical interviews, it has been suggested that battered women normalize, rationalize, or justify their husbands' behavior on the grounds that he is under stress, mentally ill, under the influence of drugs or alcohol; that husbands have the right to hit their wives; or that the woman deserved the abuse because she was provocative (Hilberman, 1980; Hilberman & Munson, 1977-78; Pagelow, 1981). Abusive men rarely define their violence as deviant behavior and attempt to rationalize their behaviors through minimization (I didn't hurt her that bad); denial of intention (I didn't mean to hurt her); confusion (I don't know what happened); outright denial; intoxication; loss of control; and projection of blame onto the woman (Adams & McCormack, 1982; Dobash & Dobash, 1977-1978; Straus, 1980). Greenblatt (1983) suggests that accounts such as excusing the husband because of his drinking are evidence of implicit tolerance of domestic violence.

The manner in which conclusions are drawn from clinical and ethnographic articles is often unclear. Findings are based on data generated in unstructured interviews with small select samples; comparison groups are rarely used and statistical analyses are nonexistent. Only one study provides an in-depth empirical analysis of causal statements of battered women. Using an attribution theory framework, Frieze (1979) found self-blame of battered women tended to decrease over time. Because of the nature of the coding scheme, the actual content of the accounts was not documented, though Frieze stresses the importance of cognitive factors in understanding domestic violence.

In summary, these studies suggest that battered women and abusive men provide a range of accounts and that sex differences are likely, though no study has directly compared the perceptions of battered women and abusive men. However, these studies lack explicit conceptualization and careful operational definitions of accounts. There is little systematic comparison between violent and nonviolent samples.

Major Research Questions

Using the theoretical framework of accounts, this study focused on investigation of the following questions: (1) How do battered women and abusive men account for domestic violence? (2) Do accounts function to excuse or to justify domestic violence?

Accounts of battered women and abusive men. The basic research task was to establish the range and empirical distribution of the verbal strategies typically employed by battered women and abusive men to account for concrete instances of husband-to-wife violence. More attention is paid to what accounts *do* than to what they *are* in the theoretical literature. Accounts were operationally defined as: (1) the reasons why an incident of domestic violence occurred; (2) attributions about the husbands' intentions;

(3) definitions of incidents as violent or not. Although intention seems to be a critical dimension of accounts (Collett, 1977; McHugh, 1970), accounts analysts have not directly examined how participants in domestic violence attribute intention to the abusive husband. A similar problem exists regarding definitions of violence. Violence is not an intrinsic quality of an act: it is a property of participants' perceptions of the event (Chandler, 1973). Little research exists on what is defined as violence by participants, though Gelles (1972) developed a typology of the "meanings of violence" characterized by three dimensions: legitimate/nonlegitimate; intentional/nonintentional; victim precipitated/nonvictim precipitated.

Verbal strategies as excuses or justifications. Accounts are generally defined as neutralizing deviant behavior in two ways: (1) through *excuses* that admit that an act is inappropriate but mitigate the actor's responsibility; (2) through *justifications* that accept responsibility but reduce the act's pejorative qualities by denial of its negative or deviant consequences (Scott & Lyman, 1968, 1970; Sykes & Matza, 1957). While theorists make assumptions about whether battered women and abusive men excuse or justify domestic violence, they have rarely asked participants about *their* assessments of violent incidents. The second task of this research was to document whether certain kinds of verbal strategies function either to excuse or justify domestic violence from the respondents' frames of reference.

The Sample

The complete sample consisted of 30 men and women. The domestic violence sample was composed of 15 men and 15 women in a marital or cohabiting relationship of at least six months' duration, who had experienced two or more incidents of husband-to-wife violence in the year preceding the research interview.

Over half of the respondents were not related to each other as it proved difficult to interview both spouses of a couple, particularly for the domestic violence sample. The respondents were white Irish-Catholic working-class adults who had been married or cohabiting on an average of three years; the majority were less than 35 years old.

Nine battered women and ten abusive men were interviewed from the Family Service Unit, a social service/criminal justice agency providing services only to domestic violence cases; six battered women were interviewed from DOVE, a shelter for battered women; five abusive men were interviewed from Emerge, a nonsexist all-male collective that counsels only abusive husbands.

Procedures

The interviews were conducted between November, 1981, and July, 1982, in Boston. Each interview, except one, was conducted by the author in a single meeting that lasted an average of two hours. The Family Service Unit respondents were interviewed at the agency; the DOVE women in the shelter; the Emerge men in the author's private office. With the respondents' permission, all interviews were audiotaped and transcribed by the author. During five interviews for which permission to tape was not obtained, extensive verbatim notes were taken.

To ensure that the goals of the research could be accomplished without compromising the immediate personal needs of the domestic violence sample, respondents met with the author after an initial meeting with a caseworker who provided crisis intervention, and were then referred back to their caseworker for follow-up and/or treatment. Before the research interview, counselors had met on the average of once with battered women and twice with abusive men.

The interviews took place in a context in which men and women who had been abusive were talking with a person they perceived as a mental health professional, as a highly educated investigator, or as a representative of society who was trying to better understand domestic violence but did not condone it. For many of the domestic violence respondents, the interview was the first time they had accounted for their behavior in detail. The process of the interview led to self-reflection for respondents of the entire sample. Accounts may have been altered accordingly. This, however, is not a flaw of the research but is at its very heart: the description of the interviewing process acknowledges that accounts must be examined with a clear understanding of the context of their use.

Description of the Interview

To collect accounts from the domestic violence sample, respondents described three incidents of domestic violence that had occurred in their marriages: (1) the first or earliest remembered; (2) the most recent; (3) the worst. A set of open-ended questions was administered to ensure that major areas of research interest were explored: (1) What do you think are the reasons for the incident? (2) Did the husband mean to hurt his wife? What was he trying to accomplish through his use of physical force? (3) Was the incident violent? Why or why not? (4) Was the incident justified? Why or why not? A set of nondirective probes were used so that sufficiently detailed descriptions of the incidents were obtained.

Data Analysis

Analysis of qualitative data. The qualitative data consisted of 38 accounts of battered women and 40 accounts of abusive men; and responses to the open-ended questions for the entire sample. A coding scheme was constructed based on categories that were inductively derived with a minimal amount of inference from content analysis of the transcribed texts of the interviews. For each question of the research, every interview was coded on a present/absent basis for each category, since there is not a clear association between frequencies of categories and their importance to respondents (Krippendorf, 1980). (A description of incidents and coding procedures is available from the author.)

For the statistical analyses of accounts, chi-squares were calculated over the 78 accounts to test the null hypothesis that a given category was present with equal frequency in the accounts of battered women or abusive men. Examination of the data had revealed that respondents did not tend to use identical content categories in their accounts, which suggests that there was little interdependence among categories in the accounts of any given respondent.

For certain analyses of the accounts, the incidents were divided into more than two subgroups. If the overall chi-square was significant at the .05 level or better, post hoc analyses were conducted through nonindependent partitioning, since there were few theoretical or empirical bases for combining any of the subgroups prior to the analyses. If a subgroup contained less than eight accounts, it was excluded from the statistical analyses. For post hoc analyses, the chi-squares were calculated according to a conservative formula that corrects for nonindependent partitioning (Everitt, 1977).

Reliability. Coding reliability was established for each research question using two independent ratings of 20 randomly selected accounts and 30 randomly selected protocols of the questions posed to the entire sample. The formula for calculating reliability (Krippendorf, 1980) controlled both for small sample size and for the frequency with which a given category was used. Reliability between the two raters ranged from .82 for coding of why a given incident was justified to .94 for whether husband-to-wife violence is appropriate.

Validity. Since content analyses in exploratory studies are unique, it is not possible to gather data to examine convergent or predictive validity (Krippendorf, 1980). Instead, several methods were used to examine independent confirmations and conformity to established theory. First, the accounts of the domestic violence sample were compared to reports provided by police and intake workers. Given the high correspondence between these sources, it appeared that respondents' accounts were not significantly modified in these different contexts, nor did they change over one to two months duration. Second, the content areas emerging from the data reflected the range of perceptions the author had observed in other contexts through providing therapy to battered women and abusive men or training seminars to the community. Last, the major categories of the coding scheme were consonant with those discussed in the theoretical and clinical literature (Frieze, 1979; Gelles, 1972; Greenblatt, 1983; Hilberman & Munson, 1977-78).

Another dimension of validity is the generalizability of findings. The entire sample was rather homogeneous in terms of age, ethnicity, and social class; the domestic violence group was composed of self-identified battered women and abusive men. Because a wide range of accounting strategies were used, it is likely that the categories emerging from the data are representative of the understandings of domestic violence by men and women in this society. Further studies with representative samples are necessary to explore the influence of such variables as age or social class on the frequencies of categories found in this study.

Results and Discussion

The results of the data analysis will be summarized through a focus on the major trends relevant to each of the questions of primary interest to this research.

The accounts of battered women and abusive men. The results of this study indicated that battered women and abusive men do *not* share similar perceptions or understandings of domestic violence.

Reasons for the domestic violence incident. Battered women and abusive men offered a relatively limited set of reasons for why a violent incident occurred (see Table 3.1) that conform with those described in the domestic violence literature (Dobash & Dobash, 1977-1978; Greenblatt, 1983; Martin, 1976; Roy, 1977; Walker, 1979). While battered women more often perceived their husbands as suffering from chronic emotional problems, both battered women and abusive men perceived domestic violence as resulting from factors that temporarily reduce the husband's capacity for self control: transient physical states owing to alcohol or drugs, transient psychological states such as loss of control, and external stresses such as job problems.

Since violence was viewed as the result of transient factors, the abusive man was rarely labeled as responsible for the abuse. More than half of the abusive husbands named the woman as the primary reason for the incident,

TABLE 3.1
Reasons Offered for Why Domestic Violence Incidents Occur in Accounts of Domestic Violence Group

Reason	Battered Women %	Abusive Men %	Effect
Psychological characteristics of man			
insecure personality	34	18	
emotional problems	58	13	$\chi^2 = 17.74$***
transient physical state (alcohol or drugs)	26	40	
transient pyschological state (internal pressure)	42	33	
Circumstance			
external stress	24	35	
no options perceived for expression of anger	8	18	
Partner responsible for incident			
man	11	3	
woman is physically or verbally aggressive	3	28	$\chi^2 = 9.26$**
woman fails to fulfill obligations of a good wife	13	58	$\chi^2 = 16.65$***
Total number of incidents	38	40	

** $p < .01$; ***$p < .001$

most often for her failure to meet the man's expectation of "the good wife." Contrary to the findings of some previous studies (Gelles, 1972; Greenblatt, 1983; Hilberman, 1980; Hilberman & Munson, 1977-1978), few battered women stated that they deserved or provoked the abuse. This may be a function of the social-historical context of the research, since recent media coverage has emphasized that women are not responsible for battering. Sample differences may also have influenced this result as women who seek help from domestic violence agencies, rather than from mental health clinics, may evidence low incidence of self-blame (Frieze, 1979).

Intent of the abusive husband. More battered women than abusive men stated that the husband had intended to hurt his wife (see Table 3.2). When asked what the husband was trying to accomplish through physical force, the husband was not perceived as having a goal in one-third of the accounts because he was out of control or had no other options with which to express his anger. Neither of these responses was associated with whether or not the husband was perceived as intending to hurt his wife, which is not consistent with the common assumption that these statements denote lack of intention (Gelles, 1972). In approximately half of the accounts, the domestic violence sample stated that husbands had employed physical force in order to control or influence their wives. For battered women, this was perceived as coercive or hostile; this purpose tended to be associated with the women's perception that their husbands had meant to hurt them. In contrast, abusive men stated they had been trying to accomplish a positive or beneficial end, such as facilitating communication or stopping the fight, which was associated with the men's beliefs that they had not intended to hurt their wives.

Though Greenblatt (1983) found that few of her respondents stated that abusive husbands employ physical force in order to dominate their wives, her study has serious methodological limitations. In contrast, the findings of the current study lend support to the analysis that abusive men use physical force as a means of dominating their wives and of conveying rules to regulate "proper" female behavior (Dobash & Dobash, 1977-1978).

Is the incident perceived as violent? Battered women more frequently defined the incident as violent than did abusive men. Battered women and abusive men who labeled the act as violent did so on the basis that the act was severe in nature or that the husband was out of control (see Table 3.3). Of this subsample, battered women were more likely to state that their husbands had intended to hurt them. Men who denied that the act was violent explained that the acts had not been severe. Though battered women were more likely to describe the act itself as more severe in form (i.e., beating) and in consequence than were abusive men, definitions of the act as violent were relatively independent of the actual physical dimensions and consequences of the incident. This provides support for a social-meaning approach to domestic violence.

These results are not consistent with a typology of violence developed by Gelles (1972), which may be a function of the level of inference employed in the data analysis. His dimensions seem more reflective of the mind of a sociologist than of a battered woman. Based on the findings of the current study, it appears that different dimensions are employed by battered women and abusive men in their definitions of acts as violent.

Summary. The analysis of accounts clearly indicated that there are important differences between how battered women and abusive men perceive domestic violence. This may be a function of actor/observer differences (Jones & Nisbett, 1971). Though some of the findings of the current study conform to this pattern, actor/observer differences cannot explain the range of differences that emerged in the accounts. Even if actor/observer differences *are* located, Orvis, Kelley, & Butler (1976)

TABLE 3.2A

Perceptions of Husband's Intention to Harm Wife Across Individuals of Domestic Violence Group

Intent to harm present in account	Battered Women N = 15	(%)	Abusive Men N = 15	(%)	P
Intended to harm wife					
over zero or one account	10	(67)	9	(60)	.03
over two or three accounts	5	(33)	6	(40)	

NOTE: Individuals were grouped for statistical comparison according to the median number of accounts in which the husband was perceived as intending to hurt his wife.

TABLE 3.2B

Perceptions of Husband's Purpose in Using Physical Force Across Individuals of Domestic Violence Groups

Purpose present in account	Battered Women N = 15	(5)	Abusive Men N = 15	(%)	P
Explicit purposes:					
to influence or control woman	11	(73)	9	(60)	NS
to achieve a positive or beneficial end (stop fight, aid communication)	3	(20	12	(80)	.001
retaliation	3	(2)	3	(20	NS
No purposes perceived:					
man is out of control	8	(53)	7	(47)	NS
no other options to express anger	3	(2)	3	(20)	NS

NOTE: Each respondent gave accounts of two or three incidents of husband-to-wife violence. A given response category was coded on a present/absent basis if it appeared in at least one of the accounts.

suggest that the *process* underlying the attributions is different from that defined by attributional theorists. Abusive men and battered women are not simply passive information processors who infer different causes for domestic violence on the basis of limited information: They are partners in an intimate relationship, who are negotiating their understandings of threatening physical force. Second, the differences in the accounts may be a function of sample selection. It is possible that battered women turned to

TABLE 3.3
Whether Act of Physical Force Defined as Violent Across Individuals of Domestic Violence Group

	Battered Women N = 15	(%)	Abusive Men N = 15	(%)	P
Act of physical force defined as violent					
over zero or one account	2	(13)	11	(73)	.001
over two or three accounts	13	(87)	4	(27)	

NOTE: Each respondent gave two or three accounts of husband-to-wife violence. For statistical comparison, individuals were grouped according to the median number of accounts in which they defined the physical force as violent.

the domestic violence agencies because they had already defined their husbands' actions as intentional, controlling, or violent; and not because the men perceived their actions as wrong or violent. But the sample of the current study was representative of the population that seeks help from domestic violence agencies (Roy, 1982). Therefore, it is possible that even greater differences between battered women and abusive men would emerge from a randomly selected sample of participants in violent marriages.

The Function of Accounts as Excuses or Justifications

Given the differences between perceptions of battered women and abusive men, this section explores the possible *function* of accounts as excuses or justifications. This entire section is limited by the fact that too few women justified the incidents to be included in the analysis.

Significantly more abusive men than battered women justified the incidents (see Table 3.4). Abusive men justified their actions on grounds that: (1) the wife deserved the abuse because she either failed to meet the husband's expectations or was verbally or physically aggressive with him; (2) the husband perceived no other way to handle the marital conflict (see Table 3.5). But these accounts have been defined as *excuses* in the theoretical literature (Henslin, 1970; Scott & Lyman, 1968). In contrast, battered women and abusive men who did not justify the incidents stated: (1) the act was not right; (2) the woman's actions did not warrant a violent response; (3) the husband *did* have other behavioral options. Abusive men also stated that the act was not justified because they had been out of control, though battered women did not use this rationale.

TABLE 3.4
Whether Act of Physical Force Is Justified Across Individuals of Domestic Violence Group

	Battered Women N = 15	(%)	Abusive Men N = 15	(%)	P
Act of physical force is justified					
never	9	(60)	3	(20)	.002
in one to three accounts	6	(40)	12	(80)	

NOTE: Each respondent gave two or three accounts of husband-to-wife violence. For statistical comparison, individuals were grouped according to the median number of accounts justified by the domestic violence group.

In response to an explicit question about the justifiability of domestic violence, statements given to justify or not justify the acts tended to be mutually exclusive and limited in range. It is possible, however, that evaluations of whether or not the act is justified are associated with the reasons people offer to account for why the incident occurred, attributions of intent and purpose of husband, and definitions of the act as violent. But analysis of the data revealed no clear-cut evidence that verbal strategies functioned as excuses or justifications. In fact, there were *no* differences between abusive men who did and those who did not justify their actions on any of these dimensions. Some differences were found between those battered women or abusive men who did not justify the incidents, which may be a matter of chance given the number of analyses. Battered women were more likely to state that their husbands had emotional problems and that the act was violent and less likely to state that they deserved the abuse. Abusive men were more likely to state that the woman deserved the abuse; that the men had been trying to accomplish a positive end; or that the act had not been violent because the act wasn't severe, or because the men had not meant to hurt their wives.

Summary. These findings do not provide strong evidence that certain accounts are employed to excuse or justify domestic violence. In fact, men who did *not* justify their actions employed accounts that are defined as *justifications* in the theoretical literature, such as hoping to achieve a positive end (Scott & Lyman, 1968). This may be a result of the methodological decision to divide the sample according to whether or not the respondents justified the act. If respondents denied that the act was justified in response to an explicit question, correlations between the accounts and justifications would not then be expected. Yet this method did ensure that the accounts were evaluated from the respondents' perspectives.

It is more likely that the conceptual distinctions between excuses and justifications that are typically drawn in the accounts literature are not relevant to how verbal strategies are employed by persons in everyday contexts. Wootten (1976) criticizes accounts analysts for their lack of theoretical and methodological clarity regarding what kinds of accounts function as excuses or justifications. While the analysis of accounts is based on the often implicit assumption that accounts are consistent and function unambiguously as excuses or justifications, the results of the current study suggested that different kinds of statements are given in response to different eliciting questions and that statements in a single account can seem contradictory. For example, men who did not justify the incident never blamed their wives when asked whether the incident was justified; yet a small percentage of these same men in the same account *did* blame their wives when asked why the act occurred. This suggests that accounts of domestic violence do not function clearly as excuses or justifications.

This study was the first to systematically explore the meanings attributed to the use of physical force in marriages by battered women, abusive men, and nonviolent persons. It demonstrated that it is possible to empirically document how people perceive and understand domestic violence. Acts of physical force, however chaotic and irrational they seem to external observers, are rendered intelligible by the accounts of battered women and abusive men. Domestic violence is not defined simply by brute physical reality, but through the interpretive meaning systems of participants and observers. The results of this study suggested that (1) there are important and significant differences between how battered women and abusive men construe acts of physical force in marriage; (2) battered women and abusive men employ different explanatory frameworks to account for personal experiences with domestic violence and for why domestic violence occurs in general.

The conclusions of this study have a number of important implications. First, the findings of this study challenge current theoretical approaches to domestic violence and suggest that an integrative model of domestic violence must include the component of social meaning. Second, findings did not support the distinction between excuses and justifications, indicating that the analysis of accounts requires conceptual clarification and careful operationalization of major constructs.

There are a number of directions for future research. First, it will be important to explore accounts in a more immediate and interactive context since, in the current study, accounts were retrospective and were offered in the relatively static context of a single interview. Second, research can explore the developmental course of perceptions of domestic violence; it is likely that battered women and abusive men have different understandings and definitions of domestic violence over time. Third, this research examined perceptions of domestic violence alone. Although there is an increasing consensus that cognitive factors are important mediating variables in the maintenance or perpetuation of domestic violence, future research can clarify the association between thought and action in domestic violence.

References

Adams, D., & McCormack, A. (1982). Men unlearning violence: A group approach based on a collective model. In M. Roy (Ed.), *The abusive partner: An analysis of domestic battering.* New York: Van Nostrand Reinhold.

Ball, B. (1977). Issues of violence in family casework. *Social Casework, 58,* 3-12.

Bandura, A. (1973). *Aggression: A social learning analysis.* Englewood Cliffs, NJ: Prentice-Hall.

Bandura, A. (1978). Learning and behavioral theories of aggression. In J. Kutash, S. Kutash, L. Schlesinger & Associates (Eds.), *Perspectives on murder and aggression.* San Francisco: Jossey-Bass.

Berger, P., & Luckman, J. (1967). *The social construction of reality.* Middlesex, England: Penguin.

Blum, A., & McHugh, P. (1971). The social ascription of motives. *American Sociological Review, 36,* 98-109.

Brittan, A. (1973). *Meanings and situations.* Boston: Routledge & Kegan Paul.

Burke, K. (1945). *The grammar of motives.* Englewood Cliffs, NJ: Prentice-Hall.

Chandler, D. B. (1973). Toward a classification of violence. *Sociological Symposium, 9,* 69-83.

Chatterdon, M. (1976). The social contexts of violence. In M. Borland (Ed.), *Violence in the family.* Manchester, England: Manchester University Press.

Cicourel, A. V. (1967). Fertility, family planning and the social organization of family life: Some methodological issues. *Journal of Social Issues, 23,* 57-81.

Cicourel, A. V. (1974). *Cognitive sociology.* New York: Free Press.

Collett, P. (1977). (Ed.), *Social rules and social behavior,* Totowa, NJ: Rowman and Littlefield.

Dobash, R. E., & Dobash, R. P. (1977-1978). Wives: The "appropriate victims of marital violence." *Victimology: An International Journal, 2,* 426-442.

Douglas, J. (Ed.). (1970). *Deviance and respectability: The social construction of moral meanings.* New York: Basic Books.

Everitt, B. S. (1977). *The analysis of contingency tables.* New York: John Wiley.

Farrington, K. M. (1980). Stress and family violence. In M. A. Straus & G. T. Hotaling (Eds.), *The social causes of husband-wife violence.* Minneapolis: University of Minnesota Press.

Foss, E. (1980). The paradoxical nature of family relationships and family conflict. In M. A. Straus & G. T. Hotaling (Eds.), *The social causes of husband-wife violence.* Minneapolis: University of Minnesota Press.

Frieze, I. H. (1979). Perceptions of battered wives. In I. H. Frieze, D. Bar-Tal, & J. S. Carroll (Eds.), *New approaches to social problems.* San Francisco: Jossey-Bass.

Gelles, R. J. (1972). *The violent home: A study of physical aggression between husbands and wives.* Beverly Hills: Sage.

Gelles, R. J. (1976). Abused wives: Why do they stay? *Journal of Marriage and the Family, 38,* 659-668.

Gelles, R. J. (1979). *Family violence.* Beverly Hills: Sage.

Goode, W. J. (1971). Force and violence in the family. *Journal of Marriage and the Family, 33,* 524-636.

Greenblatt, C. S. (1983). A hit is a hit is a hit. Or is it? Approval and tolerance of the use of physical force by spouses. In D. Finkelhor, R. Gelles, G. Hotaling, & M. Straus (Eds.), *The dark side of families: Current family violence research.* Beverly Hills: Sage.

Halleck, S. (1976). Psychodynamic aspects of violence. *Bulletin of the American Academy of Psychiatry and Law, 4,* 328-336.

Hanks, S. E., & Rosenbaum, C. (1977). Battered women: A study of women who live with violent and alcohol-abusing men. *American Journal of Orthopsychiatry, 47,* 291-306.

Harre, R., & Secord, P. (1973). *The explanation of social behavior.* Totowa, NJ: Littlefield, Adams.

Harrington, J. A. (1972). Violence: A clinical viewpoint. *British Medical Journal, 1,* 228-231.

Henslin, J. M. (1970). Guilt and guilt neutralization. In J. Douglas (Ed.), *Deviance and respectability: The social construction of moral meanings.* New York: Basic Books.

Hilberman, E. (1980). Overview: The "wife-beater's wife" reconsidered. *American Journal of Psychiatry, 137,* 1336-1347.

Hilberman, E., & Munson, K. (1977-1978). Sixty battered women. *Victimology, 2,* 460-470.

Horai, J. (1977). Attributional conflict. *Journal of Social Issues, 33,* 88-101.

Hotaling, G. T. (1980). Attribution processes in husband-wife violence. In M. A. Straus & G. T. Hotaling (Eds.), *The social causes of husband-wife violence.* Minneapolis: University of Minnesota Press.

Jones, E., & Nisbett, R. (1971). *The actor and the observer: Divergent perceptions of the causes of behavior.* New York: General Learning Press.

Krippendorf, K. (1980). *Content analysis: An introduction to its methodology.* Beverly Hills, CA: Sage.

Kutash, S. B. (1978). Psychoanalytic theories of aggression. In I. Kutash, S. Kutash, L. Schlesinger, & Associates (Eds.), *Violence: Perspectives on murder and aggression.* San Francisco: Jossey-Bass.

Leiter, K. (1980). *A primer on ethnomethodology.* New York: Oxford University Press.

Lesse, S. (1974). The status of violence against women: Past, present and future factors. *American Journal of Psychotherapy, 33,* 190-200.

Lincoln, A. L. (1973). Justification and condemnations of violence: A typology of responses and a research review. *Sociological Symposium, 9,* 51-68.

Marsden, D. (1978). Sociological perspectives on family violence. In J. P. Martin (Ed.), *Violence and the family.* New York: John Wiley.

Marsh, P., Rosser, E., & Harre, R. (1978). *Rules of disorder.* London: Routledge and Kegan Paul.

Martin, D. (1976). *Battered wives.* New York: Pocket Books.

McCaghy, C. H. (1968). Drinking and deviance disavowal: The case of child molesters. *Social Problems, 16,* 43-49.

Mills, C. W. (1940). Situated actions and vocabularies of motive. *American Sociological Review, 5,* 904-913.

Orvis, B., Kelley, H., & Butler, D. (1976). Attributional conflict in young couples. In J. Harvey, W. Ickes, & R. Kidd (Eds.), *New directions in attribution research* (Vol. 1). Hillsdale, NJ: Lawrence Erlbaum.

Osgood, C., Suci, G., & Tannenbaum, P. (1957). *The management of meaning.* Urbana: University of Illinois Press.

Owens, D., & Straus, M. (1975). The social structure of violence in childhood and approval of violence as an adult. *Aggressive Behavior, 1,* 193-211.

Pagelow, M. (1981). *Woman-battering: Victims and their experiences.* Beverly Hills: Sage.

Pearce, W. B., & Cronen, V. E. (1980). *Communication, action, and meaning: The creation of social realities.* New York: Praeger.

Reynolds, R., & Siegle, E. (1959). A study of casework with sado-masochistic marriage partners. *Social Casework, 40,* 545-551.

Roy, M. (1982). Four thousand partners in violence: A trend analysis. In M. Roy (Ed.), *The abusive partner: An analysis of domestic battering.* New York: Van Nostrand Reinhold.

Roy, M. (1977). A current survey of 150 cases. In M. Roy (Ed.), *Battered women: A psychosociological study of domestic violence.* New York: Van Nostrand Reinhold.

Rubington, E., & Weinberg, M. (1968). *Deviance: The interactionist perspective.* New York: Macmillan.

Schultz, L. (1960). The wife-assaulter: One type observed and treated in a probation agency. *Journal of Social Therapy, 6,* 103-111.

Scott, M., & Lyman, S. (1968). Accounts. *American Sociological Review, 33,* 42-62.

Scott, M., & Lyman, S. (1970). Accounts, deviance and social order. In J. Douglas (Ed.), *Deviance and respectability: The social construction of moral meanings.* New York: Basic Books.

Scott, R., & Douglas, J. (1972). *Theoretical perspectives on deviance.* New York: Basic Books.

Searle, J. (1969). *Speech acts.* London: Cambridge University Press.

Snell, J., Rosenwald, R., & Robey, A. (1964). The wifebeater's wife: A study of family interaction. *Archives of General Psychiatry, 11,* 107-112.

Spradley, J. (Ed.). (1972). *Culture and cognition: Rules, maps, and plans.* San Francisco: Chandler.

Steinmetz, S. (1977a). *The cycle of violence: Assertive, aggressive and abusive family interaction.* New York: Praeger.

Steinmetz, S. K. (1977b). The use of force for resolving family conflict: The training ground for abuse. *Family Coordinator, 26,* 19-26.

Straus, M. (1980). Victims and aggressors in marital violence. *American Behavioral Scientist, 23,* 681-704.

Straus, M. A. (1977-1978). Wife-beating: How common and why? *Victimology: An International Journal, 2,* 443-458.

Straus, M. A. (1977). A sociological perspective on the prevention and treatment of wifebeating. In M. Roy (Ed.), *Battered women: A psychosociological study of domestic violence.* New York: Van Nostrand Reinhold.

Straus, M. A. (1976). Sexual inequality, cultural norms, and wife-beating. *Victimology: An International Journal, 1,* 54-76.

Straus, M. A., Gelles, R., & Steinmetz, S. (1980). *Behind closed doors: Violence in the American family.* Garden City, NY: Anchor/Doubleday.

Straus, M. A., & Hotaling, G. T. (Eds.). (1980). *The social causes of husband-wife violence.* Minneapolis: University of Minnesota Press.

Sykes, G., & Matza, D. (1957). Techniques of neutralization: A theory of delinquency. *American Sociological Review, 22,* 664-670.

Taylor, L. (1979). Vocabularies, rhetorics and grammar: Problems in the sociology of motivation. In D. Downes & P. Rock (Eds.), *Deviant interpretations.* New York: Barnes & Noble.

Taylor, L. (1972). The significance and interpretation to motivational questions: The case of sex offenders. *Sociology, 6,* 23-39.

Toby, J. (1966). Violence and the masculine ideal: Some qualitative data. *Annals of the American Academy of Political and Social Science, 364,* 19-28.

Walker, L. (1979). *The battered woman.* New York: Harper & Row.

Wilson, T. P. (1970). Normative and interpretive paradigms in sociology. In J. Douglas (Ed.), *Understanding everyday life.* New York: Aldine.

Wolfgang, M. E. (1958). *Patterns in criminal homicide.* Philadelphia: University of Pennsylvania Press.

Wolfgang, M. E., & Ferracuti, F. (1967). *The subculture of violence.* London: Tavistock.

Wootten, A. (1976). *Dilemmas of discourse: Controversies about the sociological interpretation of language.* New York: Holmes & Meier.

PART II

Taking Action: Decisions to Deal with Violence

4

The Effect of Methodology on Subjective Estimates of the Differential Effectiveness of Personal Strategies and Help Sources Used by Battered Women

Lee H. Bowker

What do we mean when we say that a given personal strategy (avoidance, running and hiding, counterviolence, talking, promising, nonviolent threatening, and passive defense), informal help source (family, friends, in-laws, and neighbors) or formal help source (police, physicians and nurses, the clergy, lawyers, district attorneys, social service and counseling agencies, women's groups, and battered women's shelters) is effective in decreasing or ending wife beating? It is evident that different people mean quite different things when they talk about the effectiveness of these strategies and help sources. For example, there are issues such as direct versus indirect effects, long-term versus short-term effects, and the quality, length, and timing of the intervention.

Some of these differences in meaning are related to the positions held by the opinion makers. Police officers may define effectiveness in terms of law enforcement goals, the clergy with respect to religious precepts, and counselors with an eye to personal development and responsible choice. Other differences are related to the ideological beliefs and private experiences of the opinion makers. Political conservatives are unlikely to define effectiveness in the same way as liberals, and wife beaters certainly

AUTHOR'S NOTE: Some of the data reported in this study were collected under National Institute of Mental Health grant number 1 RO1 MH33649. Many thanks to Jeffrey Koob and Lorie Maurer for their assistance in data analysis and to Coleen Seagren for her aid in the development of this manuscript.

would see things differently than would battered wives.

The research reported in this chapter is oriented toward victims as consumers of help offered by informal and formal sources. The victims' perspectives are taken as reasonable approximations to empirical reality. More importantly, their definitions of the situation are assumed to be more important than the definitions held by any other class of individuals, including social scientists. If the phenomenological experience of a battered wife leads her to conclude that something works in terminating the violence, it is difficult to see why we should reject her definition unless there is overwhelming evidence against her.

In the process of data aggregation, socially defined categories of experience, action, and opinion acquire a facade of standardization that they never have in the private lives of the people who contribute the data. Effectiveness means different things to different battered wives. To tease out a typology of the shades of meaning with respect to effectiveness in violence diminution and cessation would be a study in itself. We currently have no data with which we could make intelligent assumptions about the distribution of meanings of effectiveness in the sample or any other group of battered wives. We are forced to accept a functional equality of meaning by default. At the same time, the way we measure this meaning is dependent upon the uses we wish to make of the data thus created (Kaplan, 1964).

If meanings both complex and diverse are reduced through methodological conventions to an imposed and artificial unity, then it makes sense to assume that the apparent meaning of quantitative variables will vary with different ways of measuring these variables. Following this line of reasoning, comparisons among variables (in this case personal strategies and help sources) are also likely to vary according to methodology employed. There is no single methodology or standard operational definition of variables in the study of family violence. Furthermore, there probably never will be because of the logical structure of scientific investigation. Lastrucci (1963) summed up the situation as follows.

> Measurement . . . can be employed only with operational definitions. The initial problem, therefore, requires the translation of theoretical concepts into operational equivalents . . . there is *no* purely *logical* way of doing this. Achieving a satisfactory operational definition of a theoretical concept is a matter of *consensus*, not of demonstrable logical equivalence. (p. 167)

With the possible exception of the Conflict Tactics Scale (Straus, Gelles, & Steinmetz, 1980), no such theoretical or methodological consensus has yet been established in the area of family violence.

Previous Research on the Effectiveness of Personal Strategies and Help Sources

There is no dearth of published research on wife battering (see Bowker, 1983a, for a brief summary of this literature), but few studies have included information on comparative use and effectiveness of help sources. Three early exceptions to this are the work of Schulman (1979), Pagelow (1981a, 1981b), and Frieze, Knoble, Washburn, and Zomnir (1980). Frieze et al. found that members of the wife's family were more likely to be sought out for help to end the battering than was any other informal help source. The use of help sources by violent families in their sample was 55% for family members, 52% for friends, 43% for social service agencies, 42% for therapists, and 39% for priests. The police were more likely to be approached than were any of these help sources, having been contacted by nearly two-thirds of the battered women. The battered wives found all help sources except the police to be of approximately equal helpfulness in ending their victimization. The police received significantly lower ratings than did other help sources, and were as likely to make things worse as to help.

Overall, 55% of Pagelow's sample of clients from battered women's shelters used the police, higher than utilization rates for lawyers and other legal agents (44%), psychiatrists and psychologists (28%), the clergy (22%), and marriage counselors (15%). Lawyers and marriage counselors were found to be more helpful than psychologists, psychiatrists, and the clergy. The police were heavily criticized for their inadequate service delivery to the battered women.

Schulman used one of the few random samples in the literature on family violence to identify a representative group of battered wives in the state of Kentucky. These victimized women expressed a much higher level of satisfaction with police services than did the women studied by Pagelow. Satisfaction was not reported for all help sources, but Schulman found that the battered women were most likely to have discussed the batterings with family members (61%) or friends (49%). Formal help sources such as the clergy (14%) and therapists or agency workers (19%) were much less likely to be contacted than informal help sources.

The first comprehensive analysis of the use and effectiveness of help sources was carried out by Bowker (1982a, 1982b, 1983b, 1983c, 1984a, 1984b; Donato & Bowker, 1984) with a volunteer sample of 146 women from southeastern Wisconsin, all of whom had been free of violence for at least a year before the interview. Family members and friends were found to be more helpful to the once-battered wives than were neighbors and in-laws. Among formal sources of help, women's groups were particularly successful and police notably unsuccessful in helping the women. Nonviolent threatening showed promise as a personal strategy for ending the battering, presumably because of its tie to public exposure and possible criminal prosecution. According to the respondents, the batterers were most likely to react positively to interventions by lawyers and district attorneys, social service agencies, and family members.

Methodology

This chapter summarizes the experiences of 1,000 battered women recruited through an advertisement in *Woman's Day* magazine and a variety of media solicitations in southeastern Wisconsin. The 146 Wisconsin women were interviewed in depth, whereas the *Woman's Day* respondents were sent a questionnaire (six pages in length). The first 854 returned questionnaires were added to the interview data and coded in the same format to make up the 1,000 case data set. The response rate on the mailed questionnaires was 87%. Topics covered in the interviews and questionnaires included the characteristics of husband, wife, and family, the nature and extent of the violence, and the use and effectiveness of various personal strategies and help sources. Because of this mode of data collection, the results of the study cannot be generalized to any identifiable population of battered wives. They should be taken as no more than indicative of what might be the case among battered wives in America.

In view of the nonrepresentativeness of the sample, it is desirable to briefly characterize the respondents. All of the women cohabited at length with their batterers, but only 906 were legally married to them. Education was relatively high among the women in the sample, with 112 having graduated from college, and only 253 having failed to graduate from high school. The women were overwhelmingly white (906), had an average of two children with the batterer, and reported a mean annual family income of $16,200 in 1982. The average income was depressed by the fact that half of the women were no longer living with the batterer by 1982.

The sample appears to be solidly middle class. A total of 38% of the men and 43% of the women were professionals or white-collar workers other than clericals, and an additional 26% of the men and 40% of the women were blue-collar workers or clericals. Six out of every ten couples purchased at least one of the homes they lived in during their relationship.

As might be expected, these were rather unhappy marriages. The women were generally dominated by their husbands, winning only 3% of the arguments in their first year together and 12% in their most recent year together. Despite this degree of dominance by the batterers, 13% of the women reported being very satisfied with their marital relations, apart from the batterings. An additional 24% indicated that they were somewhat satisfied. The violence was frequent and severe in all but a few of the families. Weapons involvement occurred in 406 families, child abuse in 543, marital rape in 562, assaults while pregnant in 479, and miscarriages resulting from the batterings in 72. In all, 49% of the women were still living with the batterer (or ex-batterer) at the time they participated in the study.

There is no suggestion in these data that the violent families in the sample were unusually poor or transient. We have every reason to believe that most of the families appeared to outsiders as stable, solid, and productive in the years during which the batterings occurred.

Findings

There are at least four ways of examining the question of how best to combat wife beating at the family level within the limitations of the data collected in the *Woman's Day* survey. These are: (a) a review of the wives' reports of the differential effectiveness of the various personal strategies and help sources, (b) the advice offered by the battered women based on their own experiences, (c) the wives' opinions of what worked best for them in decreasing or ending the violence, and (d) empirical correlates of battering cessation in the sample. Each has its advantages and disadvantages as a method of evaluating what works in ending the violent behavior of abusive husbands.

The Differential Effectiveness of Personal Strategies and Help Sources

According to the battered wives, personal strategies for reducing or ending the battering were less effective than informal help sources, which in turn were less effective than formal help sources. Among the personal strategies, "hiding and running away" was the most effective, rated as very or somewhat effective by 36% of the battered wives who tried it. Avoiding the husband when he was in a violent mood was almost as effective (34%), and other relatively effective personal strategies were threatening to call the police or file for divorce (29%), talking the husband out of further violence (23%), and engaging in counterviolence (18%). There was considerable risk in using a number of the personal strategies. A total of 58% of those who tried counterviolence found that it resulted in increased violence against them, as it did with 29% of the women who threatened to call the police or file for a divorce and 23% of the women who hid or ran away from their husbands.

Informal help sources were slightly more effective than personal strategies, but they were considerably less likely to cause increased violence. Help from the wife's own family was rated as very or somewhat effective by 38% of the women who received family help, and help from friends was right behind the family at 37%. Help from in-laws (24%) and neighbors (30%) was less likely to be effective than was help from family and friends. Increased violence as a result of using help sources occurred for 11% of the women who used family help, 13% who received help from friends, 14% for neighbors' help, and 18% for in-laws' help.

Formal help sources, much the same as informal help sources and personal strategies, vary greatly in their effectiveness. The proportion of women using a formal help source who rated it as very or somewhat effective in reducing or ending the violence ranges from 31% for those using physicians and nurses to 60% for those using women's groups. Other help sources receiving high ratings were battered women's shelters (56% very or somewhat effective), lawyers (50%), and social service or counseling agencies (47%). The police (39% very or somewhat effective), district attorneys (38%) and the clergy (34%) were rated below the more effective help sources, but above physicians and nurses. Only three formal sources of help caused increased violence for more than 10% of the women who used them—the police (19%), district attorneys (17%) and lawyers (11%). Women's groups (5%), battered women's shelters (7%) and the clergy (7%) were the safest of the formal help sources.

Advice from Battered Wives

The *Woman's Day* questionnaire asked the battered wives if they had any general advice for other battered women. The 853 answers received were coded using content analysis. Even though many of these women were still being battered by their husbands, they felt they had learned something through their careers as victims that might be useful to other battered wives.

The most common advice offered by the battered wives was to separate from the batterer, see a lawyer, and obtain a divorce. This was mentioned by 441 women. Seeking out counseling for self and/or husband was recommended by 238 women; 164 advised that help should be sought as soon as the batterings begin in order to block the establishment of a violent pattern; and 152 said that battered women must raise their self-esteem and become more independent. Other commonly mentioned pieces of advice were: tell others, keep no secrets (99 women); be firm (67 women); call the police, file charges, and have the batterer arrested (59 women); ask friends or neighbors for help (58 women); go to a battered women's shelter (54 women); and go to the women's groups or a feminist therapist (46 women).

Three of the less commonly given recommendations were passive rather than active in intent, and one was violent. The passive recommendations made by the battered wives were to pray, contact the clergy and read the Bible (35 women), to try to understand the batterer (30 women), and to give in and do everything the batterer wants (21 women). The only violent recommendation, "to assault, kill, or disable the batterer," was made by 17 women. Except for the single woman who recommended a change of environment, the proviolence advice was the least commonly mentioned of all the actions recommended by the respondents.

The Wives' Opinions of What Worked Best for Them

Of all the personal strategies and help sources examined in the questionnaire, which did the battered women find to be most effective? Leaving the batterer was rated as the most effective action by 30% of respondents. It was the most commonly cited factor despite the fact that it was, in essence, a write-in vote. That is to say, leaving the batterer was not a strategy that was formally included in the questionnaire. In the terms used in the questionnaire, leaving the batterer would be an extreme case of the avoidance strategy. Some of the women who cited this factor probably meant leaving the batterer to go to a shelter, so this response is also related to the use of battered women's shelters.

No other strategy or help source was rated as working best for more than 7% of the battered wives. The most frequently chosen categories were: social service or counseling agencies (7%), the police (7%), threatening to call the police or obtain a divorce (7%), going to a battered women's shelter (5%) and counterviolence (4%).

Empirical Correlates of Battering Cessation

For 240 of the women in the study, the batterings were still occurring. Although the cross-sectional design of the survey and the nonrandom nature of the sample do not allow us to control variation well enough to make strong statements about causal relationships, it is useful to compare the correlations between the use of the various help sources and personal strategies and the cessation of the violence in order to obtain hints about the differential effectiveness of these help sources and strategies.

None of the correlations between a utilization variable and cessation rises above ±.06. Correlations involving effectiveness rather than utilization are somewhat stronger, but only four of them are above ±.10. These are for the relationships between cessation and the effectiveness of women's groups (tau b = .19), battered women's shelters (tau b = .18), lawyers (tau b = .17) and social service or counseling agencies (tau b = .13). All four of these effectiveness variables refer to formal help sources.

The weakness of these sets of correlations stimulates us to look elsewhere for factors that might be related to cessation in the sample. Correlations with personal and family characteristics are very weak, most less than ±.06. The three strongest relationships with cessation are found in the wife's occupational status (tau b = .11), annual family income (tau b = –.16) and the degree of husband-dominance in solving family problems and settling arguments during the couple's most recent year together (tau b = –.11). Cessation is most likely to be found in families with low incomes in which husbands are less dominating, and wives have relatively high status occupations. However, the relationship to income is misleading. Income is depressed when a couple permanently separates or divorces, because the batterer's income is no longer counted as part of the family income. Since the battering usually ceases when the marriage breaks up (tau b = .41), the apparent relationship between income and cessation is spurious.

Following convention rather than technical statistical assumptions, one can use a standard difference of means test to compare currently violent marriages with those in which the violence has ceased. All of the variables for which correlations are listed in this section differentiate between current violence and terminated violence at the .01 level of statistical significance or better. Other variables differentiating between current violence and terminated violence at the .01 level or better are: husband's participation in violent sports, wife's church attendance, number of marital separations because of the batterings, the effectiveness of help from both family and friends, the wife's use of counterviolence, the frequency with which the violence occurred, and whether or not the husband sought help to end the violence.

How did advice from the wives who became free of the battering differ from the advice of currently battered women? It is reasonable to assume that violence-free women might have learned something that is not yet known to the currently battered women. The correlations between cessation and the major categories of advice yield nothing higher than ±.11. The highest correlations are with advice to be independent and raise one's self-esteem (tau b =.11), and to get help immediately (tau b = .10). The means of these two variables for the currently victimized and violence-free groups differ at the .01 level of statistical significance.

Table 4.1 illustrates a multivariate approach to the same problem using stepwise discriminate function analysis (Klecka, 1980). Use, effectiveness, demographic, violence, and advice variables having the highest correlations were included in the analysis. To simplify the analysis, use categories were collapsed into groups: (a) medical, social service and counseling, women's groups, shelters, (b) criminal justice and lawyers, (c) informal help sources, (d) counterviolence, (e) active nonviolent personal strategies, and (f) passive personal strategies. Overall, 16 variables met the statistical criteria for inclusion. The highest lambdas were calculated for the advice to be independent and raise self-esteem, lawyers' effectiveness, family income, counterviolence, and the use category combining medical, social service and counseling, women's groups, and battered women's shelters. Using this analysis, it was possible to classify 73% of the current violence cases and 63% of the cessation cases correctly. This rather low classification accuracy attests to the limited differences found between the currently battered and violence-free respondents in the *Woman's Day* sample.

Discussion

Table 4.2 summarizes the most successful factors in violence cessation using four different measurement methodologies. These are effectiveness ratings, advice from battered wives, wives' opinions of what worked best in ending the violence, and empirical correlates of cessation. Additional measurement methodologies could have been used had the batterers also participated in the study or if third-party reports had been collected from the helping professionals who intervened in these violent families.

The only help source appearing in the results using three of the four measurement methodologies is lawyers. Women's groups, battered women's shelters, social service and counseling agencies, and separation/divorce appear twice, and two pieces of advice appear once: to seek help immediately and to raise one's self-esteem while becoming more independent. There is no common factor found using all four methodologies. The conclusion drawn from these diverse findings is that different methodologies produce different results, even with the same set of questionnaire data.

Although the 1,000-woman sample produced the data set used in all four methodological strategies, it would not be accurate to say that exactly the same women were studied using each methodological strategy. The effectiveness ratings were completed only by those women who actually used each help source and then chose to rate that help source on the questionnaire. In the *Woman's Day* study, the range of cases for formal help source use was from 119 for district attorneys to 537 for both the police and social service/counseling agencies. These subgroups are statistically

TABLE 4.1
Discriminant Function Analysis of Wife-Beating Cessation

Variable	Wilkes's Lambda	Statistical Significance	Standardized Canonical D.F. Coefficients
Advice—be independent, raise self-esteem	.936	.001	–.661
Lawyers' effectiveness	.924	.001	–.223
Family income	.914	.001	.318
Counterviolence use	.907	.001	.148
Medical, counseling, women's resource use	.901	.001	–1.202
Active nonviolent strategies use	.892	.001	.977
Husband in combat	.886	.001	.196
Husband dominance, recent year	.883	.001	.180
Advice—get help immediately	.880	.001	–.144
Husband played violent sports	.878	.001	.162
Frequency of violence	.875	.001	.147
Informal help-source use	.874	.001	.251
Family effectiveness	.872	.001	–.161
Criminal justice system use	.870	.001	–.752
Advice—women's groups	.867	.001	–.701
Battered women's shelter effectiveness	.866	.001	.132

NOTE: N = 993

distinct from each other, although substantive differences between the subgroups are modest. For example, police usage by sample women was associated with factors such as lower status occupations for husband and wife, high frequency and severity of violence, alcohol as a causal factor in the violence, low marital stability, and wife's low marital satisfaction, when compared with the violent families with which the police did not become involved.

It is evident that the largest discrepancy among effectiveness estimates occurs between the two estimates developed from precoded multiple response items and the two developed from open-ended questions that were later coded using content analysis. One of the two open-ended questions, a direct query about what worked best, referred to the precoded categories used earlier in the questionnaire, but many of the respondents ignored the directions and made up their own categories. The precoded category answers were limited by the researcher's concept of the varieties of personal strategies and help sources, while the open-ended questions permitted the women to be more creative in their personal responses. Our understanding

TABLE 4.2
Summary of Successful Factors in Violence Cessation Using Four Different Measurement Methodologies

Factors	Effectiveness Ratings[a]	Advice from Battered Wives[b]	What Worked Best[b]	Correlates of Cessation[c]
Women's groups	X			X
Battered women's shelters	X			X
Lawyers	X	X		X
Social service/counseling agencies	X	X		
Separation/divorce		X	X	
Seek help immediately		X		
Raise self-esteem, be more independent		X		

a. More than 40% very or somewhat effective
b. Mentioned by more than 100 women (10% of the sample)
c. Correlations above ±.15, not spurious

of the effectiveness of the personal strategies and help sources would have been sadly attenuated had we used only one of the four methods described in this analysis, particularly if that one used precoded categories reflecting the theoretical biases of the researcher. Our understanding is still seriously deficient because of our necessary reliance on the perceptiveness, accurate memory, and other characteristics of the respondents, to say nothing of the biases structured into the sample when volunteer recruitment is the method of sample selection.

Summary

Questionnaire data from a national volunteer sample of currently and previously battered wives were added to an existing data set derived from in-depth interviews with 146 previously battered wives in southeastern Wisconsin to constitute a 1,000-case sample for the purpose of increasing our understanding of what works for battered wives who are struggling to free themselves from the felonious violence directed toward them by their husbands. The differential effectiveness of the personal strategies, informal help sources, and formal help sources in ending wife beating was estimated using four methodologies: wives' reports of the effectiveness of each strategy and help source rated separately from other strategies and help sources; wives' opinions of what worked best in decreasing or ending the violence; wives' advice to other battered wives; and empirical correlates of cessation in the sample. These methodologies produced very different configurations of factors that were effective.

The four most effective help sources based on direct effectiveness ratings were women's groups, battered women's shelters, lawyers, and social service/counseling agencies. When asked to give advice to other battered wives, the respondents cited two formal help sources (lawyers and social service/counseling agencies) and three personal strategies (separating and obtaining a divorce, seeking help immediately, and raising self-esteem while increasing independence) as the most effective factors in combating their husbands' violence. The single dominating factor in the women's opinions about what worked best was "separation and divorce." Finally, the three help sources most strongly correlated with cessation in violent families were women's groups, battered women's shelters and lawyers.

It is clear from these findings that one's answer as to what works best in alleviating assaultive spousal victimization has a great deal to do with how one asks the question. In the *Woman's Day* study, the greatest discrepancies occurred between open-ended questions coded through content analysis and precoded, forced-choice questions. This analysis demonstrates the close link between methodology and conclusion in applied social science research, a correspondence that may in some cases be stronger than the relationship between ultimate empirical reality and published research findings.

References

Bowker, L. (1982a). Battered women and the clergy: An evaluation. *Journal of Pastoral Care, 36,* 226-234.

Bowker, L. (1982b). Police services to battered women: Bad or not so bad? *Criminal Justice and Behavior, 9,* 476-494.

Bowker, L. (1983a). *Beating wife-beating.* Lexington, MA: D.C. Heath.

Bowker, L. (1983b). Marital rape: A distinct syndrome? *Social Casework, 64,* 347-352.

Bowker, L. (1983c). Battered wives, lawyers and district attorneys: An examination of law in action. *Journal of Criminal Justice, 11,* 403-412.

Bowker, L. (1984a). Coping with wife abuse: Personal and social networks. In A. Roberts (Ed.), *Battered women and their families* (pp. 168-191). New York: Springer.

Bowker, L. (1984b). Battered wives and the police: A national study of usage and effectiveness. *Police Studies, 7,* 84-93.

Donato, K., & Bowker, L. (1984). Understanding the helpseeking behavior of battered women: A comparison of traditional social service agencies and women's groups. *International Journal of Women's Studies, 7,* 99-109.

Frieze, I., Knoble, J., Washburn, C., & G. Zomnir (1980). *Characteristics of battered women and their marriages.* Final Report of NIMH grant #RO1 MH 30913 (in part). Pittsburgh: University of Pittsburgh Press.

Kaplan, A. (1964). *The conduct of inquiry.* San Francisco: Chandler.
Klecka, W. (1980). *Discriminant analysis.* Beverly Hills, CA: Sage.
Lastrucci, C. (1963). *The scientific approach.* Cambridge, MA: Schenkman.
Pagelow, M. (1981a). *Woman-battering: Victims and their experiences.* Beverly Hills, CA: Sage.
Pagelow, M. (1981b). *Secondary battering and alternatives of female victims to spouse abuse.* In L. Bowker (Ed.), *Women and crime in America* (pp. 277-300). New York: Macmillan.
Schulman, M. (1979). *A survey of spousal violence against women in Kentucky.* Washington DC: Government Printing Office.
Straus, M., Gelles, R., & Steinmetz, S. (1980). *Behind closed doors: Violence in the American family.* Garden City, NY: Anchor/Doubleday.

5

The Decision to Leave an Abusive Relationship

Michael J Strube

Concern over the widespread incidence of wife abuse has led to increased efforts among social scientists to uncover the determinants of this ubiquitous problem (e.g., Gelles, 1979; Giles-Sims, 1983; Hilberman, 1980; Martin, 1977; Roy, 1977; Straus, 1978; Straus & Hotaling, 1980). Prevalence data indicate that as many as 1.8 million women are beaten by their husbands each year (Straus, 1978), and nearly 30% of all couples report experiencing at least one violent episode during their marriages. One particularly alarming aspect of wife abuse is that many women choose to remain in their violent relationships, even though they may risk severe injury or death. Understanding this decision process is crucial to the understanding of wife abuse in general. The major purposes of this chapter are (a) to review critically the available empirical research that has addressed the decision to leave an abusive relationship, and (b) to examine several theoretical models that provide potentially useful frameworks within which this decision process can be understood.

Empirical Research

Because much research on wife abuse is conducted with women seeking counseling or aid at shelters, one piece of information that is sometimes obtained is relationship status at various time points after the women are discharged. Studies reporting this information (e.g., Giles-Sims, 1983—42%; Hilberman & Munson, 1978—53%; Korlath, 1979—50%; Labell,

AUTHOR'S NOTE: Address correspondence to Michael J Strube, Department of Psychology, Washington University, St. Louis, MO 63130. A more extensive version of this review can be found in *Psychological Bulletin, 104* (Strube, 1988).

1979—28%; Pfouts, 1978—57%; Rounsaville, 1978—68%; Snyder & Fruchtman, 1981—60%; Walker, 1983—24%) provide one means of estimating the magnitude of the problem. Although reported percentages vary, it appears that about half of all women who seek some form of aid for spouse abuse can be expected to return to their partners. This return rate is staggering in light of the fact that women are typically reluctant to seek aid for their abuse and do so only when it becomes life threatening. That approximately half of these women then return to such a dangerous environment suggests that powerful forces are operating to keep them in a cycle of continuous abuse. Although these studies are informative regarding the rate at which women return to their abusive partners, they typically were not designed with the intent of identifying the concomitants of the decision to leave the relationship. Accordingly, these studies provide relatively little information concerning the dynamics of this decision process (for exceptions, see Rounsaville, 1978; Snyder & Fruchtman, 1981). By contrast, four studies have been conducted in which the primary purpose has been identifying factors related to the decision to leave an abusive relationship.

The earliest was conducted by Gelles (1976) who examined the modes of intervention (e.g., called police, separation or divorce, went to an agency) used by women from 41 abusive relationships. Overall, 78% of the women were still living with their assailants at the time of the interview. The more severe the abuse, however, the more likely that women had sought some form of intervention, with divorce or separation being most likely (as opposed to calling police or going to an agency). Frequency of abuse was also related to type of intervention, but in a complex fashion. Women who were hit frequently (weekly to daily) most often called police to intervene, whereas women hit less frequently (at least once a month) opted for divorce or separation. As Gelles suggests, perhaps women who are hit frequently desire immediate intervention. It's also possible that women hit less often but more severely find the unpredictable events more traumatic and seek a permanent solution.

Gelles found very little evidence for a relationship between experience or exposure to violence in one's family of origin and mode of intervention. There was a slight tendency for divorced or separated women to be more likely to report having observed their parents exhibit violent behavior toward each other, but no apparent effect of having been a victim of violence as a child. There was also no evidence that women who left the relationship were more likely to be better educated, be employed, or have fewer children than were those women who remained. However, as Gelles notes, there is no way to determine when the women in his sample obtained employment (i.e., before versus after separation or divorce) making the results less clear.

A more recent study, conducted by Snyder and Scheer (1981), attempted to predict relationship disposition following a brief stay at a shelter. While in residence at the shelter, women were administered a questionnaire that measured basic sociodemographic information, domestic violence history, current medical status, and length of residence. Two months following discharge the women were contacted to determine their current relationship status. Overall, 55% of the 74 women contacted were living with their assailants. Women who returned to their assailants differed reliably from those who left in that they more often sought admission to the shelter to allow a short-term separation from their abusers, or sought conjoint marital counseling. Women who returned were also more likely to be married to their assailants, and to be members of longer-term relationships, compared to women who were not living with their abusive partners. Finally, women who returned were more likely to be affiliated with the Roman Catholic religion, less likely to have had previous separations, had spent less time at the shelter, and were more likely to say they intended to return to their partners when interviewed at discharge. A discriminant analysis indicated that three of these variables contributed independently and significantly to relationship status (in order of importance): length of relationship, previous separations, and religious affiliation. Contrary to the results reported by Gelles (1976), Snyder and Scheer did not find severity or frequency of abuse to be related to relationship status.

In a more recent study, Strube and Barbour (1983) focused on two variables hypothesized to affect relationship decisions: psychological commitment and economic dependence. Strube and Barbour argued that the more committed a woman is to the relationship the harder it is to justify psychologically that leaving is the best decision. Moreover, the longer a woman has been a member of a relationship, the more committed she becomes, and the more likely she will become "entrapped" in the relationship. With respect to economic dependence, Strube and Barbour followed previous researchers in hypothesizing that the lack of independent employment outside the home makes it difficult for the woman to leave. During an intake interview at a counseling unit women were questioned about these two variables, with both objective and subjective measures collected. The objective measures were the length of relationship and the presence or absence of employment. The subjective measures were the women's self-generated reasons for staying with their partners at intake. These were categorized into seven types of reasons including "love" and "economic hardship."

Strube and Barbour found that 38% of the 98 women returned to live with their assailants, and that psychological commitment and economic dependence were independent predictors of relationship status at follow-up. Women who were unemployed, and women who were members of relatively long-term relationships, were less likely to leave their assailants. Furthermore, women who were still living with their partners at follow-up were more likely to have said at intake that they were staying because of love, or economic hardship.

Strube and Barbour (1984) conducted a second study that attempted to replicate their initial results, and investigated additional variables that might predict relationship decisions. Overall, 29.5% of the 251 women contacted returned to live with their assailants. Replicating their first study, Strube and Barbour found that length of relationship, employment status, and the subjective measures of love and economic hardship were reliably related to relationship status. It was also found that women who left the relationship were more likely than were those who remained to have brought assault charges against their partners, or to have obtained a protection order. They were also less likely to have said at intake that they were staying because they had nowhere else to go. A multiple regression analysis found that independent predictors of relationship status were (in order of importance): employment status, length of relationship, economic hardship (subjective), love (subjective), ethnicity (Caucasians more likely to stay), and having nowhere else to go (subjective). Of note here are variables that did not discriminate women who left the relationship from women who remained: marital status, number of children, presence of child abuse, presence of alcohol as a precipitating event, number of previous abusive relationships, and presence of social support.

Summary

Before turning to a summary of the conclusions suggested by the above research, it is necessary to note the methodological problems inherent in that research. Any conclusions from this research are ultimately limited by the validity of the methods used, and the conduct of future research may profit from an explication of these limitations.

One of the most common problems with research in this area is the selective nature of the samples. None of the studies previously mentioned used a random sampling procedure and thus the representativeness of the samples is unknown. Indeed, most of the studies examined women who initially sought aid at a shelter, and these women may differ in important ways from those who never appear at shelters.

A second problem is the retrospective nature of research in this area. The antecedents of the decision to leave an abusive relationship can be identified only by using time-based research designs. Accordingly, it is also critical to consider the length of time between the initial interview and the follow-up interview(s). Much of the variability in relationship decisions, and in identification of antecedent factors, may stem from the wide variability in the time frames used. Future research needs to control or measure this factor carefully because the decision to leave or remain with an abuser may be unstable and change over time (e.g., Snyder & Scheer, 1981; Snyder & Fruchtman, 1981), and may itself be an important outcome variable to assess. Finally, careful attention must be given to differential attrition and the variety of other artifacts that can confound time-based research (Cook & Campbell, 1979).

A third problem with previous research is an overreliance on self-report data. One solution is to attempt to collect both objective and subjective measures of the same underlying variable or process (e.g., Kalmuss & Straus, 1982; Strube & Barbour, 1983, 1984). Although this procedure is not without its own interpretive difficulties (see Strube & Barbour, 1983), it does provide an additional source of data that may clarify relationship decision antecedents. A second "solution" is for researchers to have a more healthy respect for the biases and distortions that may plague self-report data, particularly when the topic is very sensitive. Obviously, in this latter regard, some types of data (e.g., reports on the partner's history of violence, abuse of alcohol) must be considered less reliable and valid than other types of data (e.g., number of previous separations).

Finally, the studies reviewed above differ widely in the number and type of variables that are measured. These variables differ in their distribution characteristics that can affect the statistical conclusions reached when they are related to each other or to relationship status. Because of the complex interrelationships among these variables, a lack of commonality across studies makes interpretation and comparison difficult. For any reasonable attempt at future integration of research in this area, it will be necessary for researchers to design their studies in light of, not in spite of, past research, and be attentive to the statistical features of their data that affect their conclusions.

With these limitations in mind, the research reviewed previously does provide several insights into the dynamics of leaving an abusive relationship, and indicates several consistencies that should be highlighted. First, four studies implicate relationship length, marital status, or commitment as an important determinant of relationship decisions (e.g., Snyder & Fruchtman, 1981; Snyder & Scheer, 1981; Strube & Barbour, 1983, 1984); women more committed to their relationships are less likely to leave. Second, at least three studies (Pfouts, 1978; Strube & Barbour, 1983, 1984) have found that women who lack the economic means to establish an independent living arrangement are likely to remain with their partners. Finally, at least two studies have found that compared to women who leave their assailants, women who remain have suffered less severe abuse (Gelles, 1976; Rounsaville, 1978; but see also Snyder & Fruchtman, 1981), are less likely to report child abuse (Rounsaville, 1978; Snyder & Fruchtman, 1981), have separated from their abusers less often (Snyder & Fruchtman, 1981; Snyder & Scheer, 1981), are less likely to have taken legal action against their abusers (Rounsaville, 1978; Strube & Barbour, 1984), and are more likely to say they intend to return to the abuser when interviewed at discharge from a shelter (Snyder & Fruchtman, 1981; Snyder & Scheer, 1981). Overall, these studies paint a picture of women who lack the economic means to leave an abusive relationship, are willing to tolerate abuse so long as it does not become too severe or involve the children, and who appear to be very committed to making their relationships last.

Future research that avoids the methodological problems outlined previously will add measurably to our understanding of this decision process. These empirical efforts alone, however, will not provide a complete description of the causal dynamics underlying the decision to leave an abusive relationship. It will also be necessary to ground such research in theory that allows clear guidance for variable selection, and interpretation of results.

Theoretical Issues

A basic assumption inherent in the discussion to follow is that the decision to leave an abusive relationship is a "rational" decision when considered from the perspective of the decision maker. The decision is based on an analysis of available "data" and follows predictable "decision rules." The outcome may be considered abnormal by normative standards (i.e., who in one's right mind would choose to remain in an abusive relationship?), but the process is not pathological. With these comments in mind we turn to a discussion of three theoretical models that show promise for guiding the study of relationship decisions. The following three models do not, of course, exhaust the available theoretical frameworks but do represent models that have been given some attention by family violence researchers.

Psychological Entrapment

The idea that battered women can become "entrapped" in abusive relationships is a popular one (e.g., see Gelles, 1976). The terminology is, however, unfortunate because contrary to the general use of the term, entrapment also refers to a specific psychological decision process.

Psychological entrapment was first described by Rubin and Brockner (1975) and refers to investment decision situations in which an escalating conflict between goal attainment likelihood and investments may lead individuals to perceive that they have "too much invested to quit" (Teger, 1980). The typical consequence of psychological entrapment is continued investment, even though costs may far exceed the worth of the final goal. Essentially, psychological entrapment is based on the idea that individuals feel compelled to justify resources they have spent in pursuit of some goal (see cognitive dissonance theory in Festinger, 1957, and Wicklund & Brehm, 1976), and continue to invest resources in pursuit of the goal to justify past expenses (to give up without achieving success would mean admitting the investment had been wasted).

In a general sense, the decision to remain in an abusive relationship can be thought of as effort justification. Initially the woman exerts effort to make the relationship work, but as with most abusive relationships, these efforts fail and the abuse continues. Feeling compelled to justify these past efforts the woman continues to try and salvage the relationship under the belief that if she tries hard enough her efforts will succeed. This belief is engendered, of course, by the cultural norm that it is the woman's responsibility to make the relationship run smoothly, and that if the relationship is failing, she must not be trying hard enough. The more time and effort the woman invests, the harder it becomes to give up without success, and the less likely that a battered woman will leave the relationship (see Strube & Barbour, 1983, 1984).

Rubin and Brockner and their colleagues (e.g., Brockner, Rubin, Fine, Hamilton, Thomas, & Turetsky, 1982; Brockner, Rubin, & Lang, 1981; Brockner, Shaw, & Rubin, 1979) have uncovered a variety of antecedent conditions that enhance the likelihood of psychological entrapment, all of which appear to be present in the abusive relationship. First, the investments (e.g., time, effort, money) must be viewed as irretrievable expenses. Women who tolerate abuse invest considerable time, effort, and emotional involvement (Foss, 1980) and forego many personal, educational, and economic opportunities. Second, the individual must believe that she had a choice in entering into the situation. Again, few women marry against their will. Third, the individual must believe that the goal may never be attained, or if certain to be attained, will require investments disproportionate with available resources. The battered woman who commits herself to the relationship probably feels she will eventually succeed, but it may take a very long time. Fourth, entrapment is most pronounced when the salience of the costs or investments is low (Rubin & Brockner, 1975), and the continued investment is a passive decision (Brockner et al., 1979). The intermittent nature of abuse, which produces relatively longer periods of harmony between the explosive episodes (see Walker, 1979), may serve to reduce the salience of costs. Also many of the costs of abuse accrue gradually (e.g., lower employment salability) which can further reduce their salience, and enhance the temptation to continue investing (Rubin & Brockner, 1975). That relationship maintenance is the status quo (it takes an *active* effort to end a relationship) suggests it is a passive decision. Finally, entrapment is most likely if the behavior being performed is viewed as socially appropriate (Brockner et al., 1981; Teger, 1980). As mentioned previously, relationship harmony is viewed as the prevalent norm and women may persist in their efforts to achieve that norm.

Overall, the psychological entrapment model provides a very intriguing framework within which relationship decisions can be examined. It is a ubiquitous decision process with antecedents that are clearly identifiable in abusive relationships. The full utility of the entrapment model, however, must await future empirical test. In particular, it is essential that the antecedent conditions be investigated, and also crucial that the time course of psychological entrapment in abusive relationships be charted. At what critical time point does a person become "entrapped" rather than exiting early from the relationship? As will be noted below, Pfouts's cost/benefit model provides one possible answer to this question. Despite the relative lack of research that has investigated entrapment in abusive relationships, the entrapment model provides a framework of great promise, particularly when combined with the learned-helplessness model.

Learned Helplessness

Walker (1978, 1983) has suggested that battered women can be characterized as exhibiting learned helplessness (Seligman, 1975). Learned helplessness arises as a result of a perceived noncontingency between responses and outcomes, and typically has three major consequences. First, there is a motivational deficit characterized by the inability to initiate responses that could remove the individual from the helplessness-inducing situation. Second, there is a cognitive deficit characterized by the inability to learn that responses and outcomes are contingent, should the situation change. Finally, there is an affective deficit characterized by severe depression and self-blame. Together these three deficits conspire to create a self-perpetuating cycle of helplessness. The belief that responses have no impact on outcomes reduces the likelihood that new responses (that could end the helplessness) will be initiated. Even if new responses are initiated, and have some impact, they may not be recognized as such. On a descriptive level, the learned-helplessness model provides a compelling account of the battered woman syndrome, although direct empirical support is scarce.

The learned-helplessness model holds promise for helping us understand why some women remain in abusive relationships. However, it is evident that not all women remain with their abusers; some decide to terminate the relationship and apparently break out of the learned-helplessness cycle. A truly useful learned-helplessness account must be able to explain why some, but not all, women are at risk for continued abuse. Fortunately, recent advances in learned-helplessness theory provide a possible resolution.

Abramson, Seligman, and Teasdale (1978; see also Abramson, Garber, & Seligman, 1980) have proposed an attributional reformulation of the learned-helplessness model. Quite simply, this reformulation states that experience with noncontingency between responses and outcomes is not sufficient by itself to produce the deficits associated with learned helplessness. There is, in addition, an intermediate attribution stage that also influences the response to noncontingency. According to Abramson et al., when confronted with noncontingency individuals make causal attributions that can be conceptualized along three dimensions: internality, stability, and globality. Classic learned helplessness occurs when the noncontingency between responses and negative outcomes is attributed to internal, stable, and global causes. Under these circumstances, individuals blame themselves for their negative outcomes, and expect them to persist over time, and to extend into other domains of their lives. In other words, the helplessness experience is profound, chronic, and general. On the other hand, helplessness will not be accompanied by self-blame if an external attribution is made; will only be temporary if an unstable attribution is made; and have only a narrow range of impact if a specific attribution is made. Of importance for our purposes here is the proposition that people vary in their attributional styles. That is, some people are more predisposed to making the internal, stable, and global attributions for negative outcomes that enhance the likelihood of learned helplessness (Miller & Seligman, 1982; Peterson & Seligman, 1984). In light of this attributional reformulation it becomes clear that the learned-helplessness model could provide an explanation for why some, but not all, women remain in abusive relationships. It could be that women who remain have the attributional style that makes learned helplessness more likely.

An obvious question concerns how the learned-helplessness and entrapment explanations can both provide accounts of relationship decisions. One model proposes that women are passive participants in their relationships (i.e., learned helplessness) whereas the other suggests a more active effortful role (i.e., entrapment). One resolution is to suggest a two-stage process of entrapment followed by learned helplessness. Initially women exert great effort to get their relationships to work, and may persist in these efforts partly to justify past investment. Eventually, however, the women reach a point at which it is evident that their responses have no impact (i.e., noncontingency). Depending on the attributions made for this failure, some women will leave the relationship, whereas others will succumb to the self-perpetuating cycle of learned helplessness. [Note that this sequence is very similar to the integration of reactance theory and learned helplessness proposed by Wortman and Brehm (1975), and verified by Pittman and Pittman (1979).] This integration of the entrapment and learned-helplessness models suggests an exciting area for future research, but one that will require careful charting of responses to violence over time, measurement of attributional styles, and assessment of the key parameters specified by both models.

Relative Costs and Benefits

A third conceptual model that can be used to examine relationship decisions derives from exchange theory (e.g., Kelley & Thibaut, 1978; Thibaut & Kelley, 1959) and is based on the premise that relationship decisions follow from an analysis of costs and benefits of current relationships in comparison to alternative relationships. Within the spouse abuse literature this type of model has been articulated by Pfouts (1979) who follows Thibaut and Kelley (1959) in suggesting a two-stage decision process. First, the battered woman decides whether the total benefits of the relationship are greater than the total costs of the relationship, arriving at a subjective estimate of satisfaction. Second, satisfaction with the current relationship is compared to estimated satisfaction with alternatives to the relationship (should she decide to leave). Thus rewards can be greater than or less than costs in the current relationship; and rewards can be greater than or less than costs in the alternative relationships. This gives rise to four possible situations or coping strategies. According to Pfouts, when costs are greater than rewards in both the current and alternative relationships the typical coping behavior is the "self-punishing response." In this situation, "the wife blames herself for being trapped in a violent marriage in which she can neither change her husband's behavior nor find nonviolent alternatives for herself or her children" (p. 103, Pfouts, 1979). A second situation, also likely to keep a woman in an abusive relationship, occurs when the rewards exceed costs in the current relationship, but costs exceed rewards in alternative relationships. In this instance, an "aggressive response" is likely whereby "the wife responds to violence with violence, sometimes against her husband but more often against her children, or she takes her anger into another violent relationship." (p. 103, Pfouts, 1979). By contrast, when the rewards of alternative relationships exceed costs, the woman is likely to leave the abusive relationship. The timing of the departure, however, depends on the payoffs in the current relationship. When costs exceed rewards in the abusive relationship, the "early disengagement response" is likely whereby "because she has viable alternatives, the wife either moves quickly out of the marriage or forces the husband to give up abusive behavior" (p. 103, Pfouts, 1979). On the other hand, when rewards exceed costs in the abusive relationship, the "reluctant mid-life disengagement response" is more likely whereby "because she has devoted many years to 'saving' the marriage, the wife moves reluctantly into a nonviolent alternative when she finally becomes convinced that the abuse is too high a price to her and her children" (p. 103, Pfouts, 1979).

The cost/benefit analysis provided by Pfouts is very useful in identifying multiple responses to abusive relationships (see Snyder & Fruchtman, 1981). It also provides an explanation for women who don't become entrapped in continuous abuse (i.e., early disengagement response) and thus provides a nice complement to the entrapment and learned-helplessness models. Thus far, however, Pfouts's model has only been tested indirectly.

A similar model, and onc with more empirical backing (though not in the spouse abuse domain), has been proposed by Rusbult (Rusbult, 1980, 1983; Rusbult, Zembrodt, & Gunn, 1982). She suggests that commitment to a relationship (generally defined) is determined by three factors: (a) the outcome value of the present relationship, (b) the outcome value of the most attractive alternative relationship, and (c) the amount and importance of resources invested in the current relationship. The first two factors operate in a manner similar to those in Pfouts's model. The investment factor is important in that Rusbult claims that commitment increases with investment (consistent with the entrapment model), and could conceivably override the effects of the other two factors. Recently, Rusbult et al. (1982) have more fully articulated the responses to relationship dissatisfaction, identifying four strategies: (a) leaving the relationship, (b) active attempts at improvement of the relationship, (c) neglect of the relationship, and (d) loyalty or passive waiting for the relationship to improve. Rusbult et al. (1982) have found that the type of response chosen depends on prior satisfaction with the relationship, past investments, and (to a lesser extent) quality of alternatives. Though not yet applied specifically to abusive relationships, Rusbult's conceptual model and methodology are sufficiently well-developed to make such application highly desirable. The commonality between the response typologies proposed by Pfouts and Rusbult will also need to be examined.

Although the exchange theory approach to relationship decisions is very attractive, there are limitations to current applications that need to be recognized. First, exchange theories propose that the analysis of relationship costs and benefits is a complex, reciprocal, dyadic process (indeed, it is an "exchange" process). The dynamics of relationship maintenance and satisfaction can be understood only when the perceptions of both participants are considered. (This criticism applies to all models discussed, but is more apparent here). Second, it is insufficient to designate a priori the costs and benefits that apply to all relationships. Some account must be taken of idiosyncratic payoffs demanding some recourse to an ideographic approach. Finally, the quantity and quality of costs, benefits, and investments will shift over time. The impact of these shifts on relationship status (and vice versa) needs to be addressed.

Summary and Conclusions

This chapter has attempted to review the current state of affairs, both empirical and theoretical, with respect to the decision to leave an abusive relationship. The goal has been to highlight stable empirical findings, outline methodological problems, and examine theoretical issues, in the hope that future research in this area will proceed more smoothly and productively. Although a fair amount of knowledge has accumulated regarding relationship decisions, our understanding of the dynamics of this decision process is still weak. It is hoped that the concurrent development of sounder methods and theory will produce the level of knowledge that will aid effective intervention and spare many women needless and senseless suffering.

References

Abramson, L. Y., Garber, J., & Seligman, M.E.P. (1980). Learned helplessness in humans: An attributional analysis. In J. Garber & M.E.P. Seligman (Eds.), *Human helplessness: Theory and applications*. New York: Academic Press.

Abramson, L. Y., Seligman, M.E.P., & Teasdale, J. (1978). Learned helplessness in humans: Critique and reformulation. *Journal of Abnormal Psychology, 87*, 49-74.

Brockner, J., Rubin, J. Z., Fine, J., Hamilton, T., Thomas, B., & Turetsky, B. (1982). Factors affecting entrapment in escalating conflicts: The importance of timing. *Journal of Research in Personality, 16*, 247-266.

Brockner, J., Rubin, J. Z., & Lang, E. (1981). Face-saving and entrapment. *Journal of Experimental Social Psychology, 17*, 68-79.

Brockner, J., Shaw, M. C., & Rubin, J. Z. (1979). Factors affecting withdrawal from an escalating conflict: Quitting before its too late. *Journal of Experimental Social Psychology, 15*, 492-503.

Cook, T. D., & Campbell, D. T. (1979). *Quasi-experimentation: Design and analysis issues for field settings*. Chicago: Rand McNally.

Festinger, L. (1957). *A theory of cognitive dissonance*. Stanford, CA: Stanford University Press.

Foss, J. E. (1980). The paradoxical nature of family relationships and family conflict. In M. A. Straus & G. T. Hotaling (Eds.), *The social causes of husband-wife violence*. Minneapolis, MN: University of Minnesota Press.

Gelles, R. J. (1976). Abused wives: Why do they stay? *Journal of Marriage and the Family, 38*, 659-668.

Gelles, R. J. (1979). *Family violence*. Beverly Hills, CA: Sage.

Giles-Sims, J. (1983). *Wife battering: A systems theory approach*. New York: Guilford.

Hilberman, E. (1980). Overview: The "wife-beater's wife" reconsidered. *American Journal of Psychiatry, 137*, 1336-1347.

Hilberman, E., & Munson, K. (1978). Sixty battered women. *Victimology: An International Journal, 2*, 460-470.

Kalmuss, D. S., & Straus, M. A. (1982). Wife's marital dependency and wife abuse. *Journal of Marriage and the Family, 44*, 277-286.

Kelley, H. H., & Thibaut, J. W. (1978). *Interpersonal relations: A theory of interdependence*. New York: Wiley.

Korlath, M. J. (1979). Alcoholism in battered women: A report of advocacy services to clients in a detoxification facility. *Victimology: An International Journal, 4*, 292-299.

Labell, L. S. (1979). Wife abuse: A sociological study of battered women and their mates. *Victimology: An International Journal, 4*, 258-267.

Martin, D. (1977). *Battered wives*. New York: Pocket Books.

Miller, S. M., & Seligman, M.E.P. (1982). The reformulated model of helplessness and depression: Evidence and theory. In R. J. Neufeld (Ed.), *Psychological stress and psychopathology*. New York: McGraw-Hill.

Peterson, C., & Seligman, M.E.P. (1984). Causal explanations as a risk factor for depression: Theory and evidence. *Psychological Review, 91*, 347-374.

Pfouts, J. H. (1978). Violent families: Coping responses of abused wives. *Child Welfare, 57*, 101-111.

Pittman, N. L., & Pittman, T. S. (1979). Effects of amount of helplessness training and internal-external locus of control on mood and performance. *Journal of Personality and Social Psychology, 37*, 39-47.

Rounsaville, B. J. (1978). Theories in marital violence: Evidence from a study of battered women. *Victimology: An International Journal, 3*, 11-31.

Roy, M. (Ed.) (1977). *Battered women: A psychosociological study of domestic violence*. New York: Van Nostrand Reinhold.

Rubin, J. Z., & Brockner, J. (1975). Factors affecting entrapment in waiting situations: The Rosencrantz and Guildenstern effect. *Journal of Personality and Social Psychology, 31*, 1054-1063.

Rusbult, C. E. (1980). Commitment and satisfaction in romantic associations: A test of the investment model. *Journal of Experimental Social Psychology, 16*, 172-186.

Rusbult, C. E. (1983). A longitudinal test of the investment model: The development (and deterioration) of satisfaction and commitment in heterosexual involvements. *Journal of Personality and Social Psychology, 45*, 101-117.

Rusbult, C. E., Zembrodt, I. M., & Gunn, L. K. (1982). Exit, voice, loyalty, and neglect: Responses to dissatisfaction in romantic involvements. *Journal of Personality and Social Psychology, 43*, 1230-1242.

Seligman, M.E.P. (1975). *Helplessness: On depression, development, and death*. San Francisco: Freeman.

Snyder, D. K., & Fruchtman, L. A. (1981). Differential patterns of wife abuse: A data-based typology. *Journal of Consulting and Clinical Psychology, 49*, 878-885.

Snyder, D. K., & Scheer, N. S. (1981). Predicting disposition following brief residence at a shelter for battered women. *American Journal of Community Psychology, 9,* 559-566.

Straus, M. A. (1978). Wife beating: How common and why? *Victimology: An International Journal, 2,* 443-458.

Straus, M. A., Gelles, R. J., & Steinmetz, S. K. (1980). *Behind closed doors: Violence in the American family*. Garden City, NY: Anchor Books.

Straus, M. A., & Hotaling, G. T. (Eds.) (1980). *The social causes of husband-wife violence.* Minneapolis, MN: University of Minnesota Press.

Strube, M. J., & Barbour, L. S. (1983). The decision to leave an abusive relationship: Economic dependence and psychological commitment. *Journal of Marriage and the Family, 45*, 785-793.

Strube, M. J., & Barbour, L. S. (1984). Factors related to the decision to leave an abusive relationship. *Journal of Marriage and the Family, 46,* 837-844.

Teger, A. I. (1980). *Too much invested to quit*. New York: Pergamon.

Thibaut, J. W., & Kelley, H. H. (1959). *The social psychology of groups*. New York: Wiley.

Walker, L. E. (1978). Battered women and learned helplessness. *Victimology: An International Journal, 2,* 525-534.

Walker, L. E. (1979). *The battered woman*. New York: Harper & Row.

Walker, L. E. (1983). Victimology and the psychological perspective of battered women. *Victimology: An International Journal, 8,* 82-104.

Wicklund, R. A., & Brehm, J. W. (1976). *Perspectives on cognitive dissonance*. Hillsdale, NJ: Lawrence Erlbaum.

Wortman, C. B., & Brehm, J. W. (1975). Responses to uncontrollable outcomes: An integration of reactance theory and the learned helplessness model. In L. Berkowitz (Ed.), *Advances in experimental social psychology*, Vol. 8. New York: Academic Press.

6

Termination or Resumption of Cohabitation in Woman Battering Relationships: A Statistical Study

Lewis Okun

Probably the most frequently asked question about battered women is why they continue cohabiting with their violent male partners. Typically this question is phrased simply as "Why does she stay?" Despite the popularity and persistence of this question, research on this topic has barely even begun. I shall present here the findings of a study of whether certain factors were statistically related to the outcomes of the relationships of a group of battered women taking refuge in a women's shelter. Before turning to the methods and results of the study, however, it is necessary to comment further on the question, "Why does she stay?"

In the first place, let's look at why we ask this particular question about woman battering. Historically, this question has been posed in order to imply that battered women are deviant—particularly, that they provoke violence in order to gain some sort of masochistic satisfaction from being assaulted (Snell, Rosenwald, & Robey, 1964; Reynolds & Siegle, 1959). As such, the question has been consistent with the traditional tendency to hold the battered woman responsible for the violence inflicted upon her. "Why does she stay?" also has been asked in order to imply that battered women have an ethical obligation to leave their abusers. This amounts to an

AUTHOR'S NOTE: The material in this chapter is presented more fully in *Woman Abuse: Facts Replacing Myths* (Okun, 1986). The data and results described in this chapter originally appeared in a different form in "A Study of Woman Abuse: 300 Battered Women Taking Shelter, 119 Woman-Batterers in Counseling" (Okun, 1983), a dissertation submitted in partial fulfillment of the requirements for the degree of Doctor of Philosophy in the University of Michigan.

expectation that battered women must prove themselves "worthy victims" in order to be deserving of assistance or even of sympathy (Eisenberg & Micklow, 1975, 1977).

Researchers have another motive to focus upon battered women rather than abusers, which is that battered women are much easier to study than are woman batterers. At least two studies that set out to study women and men equally have been obliged to content themselves with sets of subjects that were overwhelmingly female (Gelles, 1972; Snell et al., 1964). I have shown elsewhere that woman batterers are unreliable reporters of the violence that they have committed (Okun, 1983, 1986). Finally, battered women are also much more accessible to researchers because they are much more likely than are woman batterers to seek intervention: thus it is far easier to find populations of battered women than to locate abusers for study.

The question "Why does she stay?" assumes that most battered women do remain with their abusive mates. This assumption is still unproven, however, and potentially could be disproven by future research. Many who ask "Why does she stay?" overlook the complete lack of safe alternative shelter for battered women prior to the mid-1970s, and the continued insufficiency of shelter space to meet the needs of all battered women. "Why does she stay?" usually implies that leaving is the safer alternative for all battered women. This is not necessarily the case. Often the battered woman's fear that her mate will kill her if she tries to leave turns out to be tragically realistic. Thus the question tends to overestimate greatly both the safety of attempting to break up with a batterer, and the ease of finding a safe alternative dwelling.

"Why does she stay?" also tends to ignore the fact that it is not entirely up to the battered woman whether or not she continues to cohabit with the batterer. Often batterers will reestablish cohabitation by force. This is done by intruding into the woman's home, by outright abduction, by coercive threats of violence, or by violent—often life-threatening—acts of coercion. In such instances, since there is usually not adequate legal protection for the battered woman, she literally has no realistic choice but to comply with the batterer and resume cohabitation.

The preoccupation of both the public and the literature on woman battering with "Why does she stay?" can mislead us into believing that this is indeed the most important question for researchers studying woman abuse. In fact, it is not. Historically, the most important research was that which established a point we now know very well, that woman battering is a lethal problem of epidemic proportions. In my opinion (and perhaps I betray my clinical bias here), the most important type of contemporary research investigates what sorts of interventions and social changes are most effective in halting or preventing battering. The first study comparing different police strategies of intervention and their relative effectiveness in preventing repeated episodes of battering set a very healthy example for us in this respect (Berk, Berk, & Newton, 1984; Sherman & Berk, 1984).

To recapitulate, the question "Why does she stay?" deserves the following terse retorts: "Who says she does stay? Where do you suggest she go? Who says she has to leave? Often it isn't a matter of her not leaving, but of him continuing to show up on her doorstep. And, by the way, why do you ask this particular question about battered women?"

Given the preceding, why have I chosen the present topic instead of one more oriented toward intervention? A major reason is that, as a worker in a domestic violence program, I have been in a uniquely good position to study the outcomes of shelter residents' relationships. Furthermore, taking the above cautionary discussion into account, there are still some good reasons to study the factors which affect battered women in their decisions whether or not to attempt to terminate their violent relationships. Since ending a battering relationship in general maximizes the opportunity for a battered woman to avoid violence for the rest of her life, it is worthwhile to discover what factors tend either to facilitate or to obstruct her decision to try to dissolve her relationship with the batterer. This is not to say that battered women are ethically obliged to attempt to end their violent relationships, because I do not believe that they are. Rather, my intent here is to recognize that there are powerful influences that restrict battered women's choices. Factors which limit the battered woman's options take her decisions about her marriage/relationship out of the context of her absolute preferences, and instead place her in a context of enforced restriction of choice (Waites, 1978). Discovering influences that are crucial to battered women's decision making about the termination of their relationships can help us make constructive social changes that best promote women's freedom. Findings of this sort should also inform the approaches taken by shelter programs, counselors, and therapists. Finally, when I undertook this study, I hoped to be able to derive data contradictory to the popular fallacy that few or no battered women ever do leave their abusive relationships.

This latter approach to studying the termination of woman-battering relationships demands a restructuring of the inquiry. Pfouts (1978) describes the real context of this issue very well:

> Given that most coping decisions are made in the grip of self-doubt and terror, on inadequate information and insufficient community support, it is surprising, not that many of these decisions fail to solve the problem, but that some of them do. (p. 110)

Consequently, I would argue that when we do investigate the subject of the termination of battered women's conjugal relationships, we need to rephrase "Why does she stay?," to something more along the lines of "How can she get out?," or perhaps, "What facilitates freer choice for her?" I have used this latter perspective in the present study.

Method

The present study involves a sample composed of residents of SAFE House, the battered women's shelter in Washtenaw County, Michigan. The sample consists of 300 consecutive residents who took refuge at the shelter between September 1978, and October 1980, and who were battered by their male conjugal partners. Women taking shelter from other sorts of violence were not included in the study sample. For the women who were sheltered at SAFE House on multiple occasions during the period studied, only data regarding the woman's first shelter stay were included.

The data used here come from three sources: (1) SAFE House intake forms; (2) a questionnaire distributed to shelter workers and ex-shelter workers; and (3) public divorce records available at the Washtenaw County Clerk's office. Data was gathered from shelter intake forms concerning 36 variables. Also, each of 21 shelter workers was sent an outcomes questionnaire regarding all battered women who had been in SAFE House concurrently with the worker's employment there. The shelter workers were asked to indicate to the best of their knowledge whether or not each battered woman had resumed cohabiting with her abusive partner within one year of exit from SAFE House, or whether this information was unknown. Of the 21 workers, 19 returned the completed questionnaire, a response rate of 90.5%.

In order to determine whether cohabitation resumed or was terminated after the residents left SAFE House, the following standards were used. Cohabitation was rated as having terminated under the following circumstances: if two or more shelter workers unanimously agreed that the given woman had not resumed cohabiting with her abuser; if at least two-thirds of a group of at least four shelter workers agreed that the woman had not resumed cohabiting with her original partner; if less than a two-thirds majority of workers were corroborated by objective proof that cohabiting had not resumed; or if there was clear documentation that cohabiting had not resumed, regardless of shelter worker judgments on this issue. The same criteria were applied in reverse for rating cohabitation as having resumed after the woman left SAFE House: unanimous agreement by at least two shelter workers that cohabiting had resumed; or two-thirds agreement among at least four workers; or a simple majority of workers corroborated by objective proof; or irrefutable objective documentation that cohabiting had resumed.

In some cases, it became clear that a woman had resumed cohabiting with her abusive partner, but had later separated from him for at least one year prior to the administration of the outcomes questionnaire. For these cases a third outcomes category was added, "cohabitation currently terminated for over a year, after a period of recohabitation." In other cases, it was clear that the cohabitation had ended for at least one year prior to the outcomes investigation, but it was unknown whether there had been any intervening period of resumed cohabiting between the woman's exit from the shelter and the outcome investigation: this type of outcome formed a fourth category. If none of the above criteria applied, or if the woman came from a noncohabitant relationship, then the outcome of the relationship could not be assigned to any of the preceding four categories, and the outcome was therefore considered unknown. To repeat, the four scoreable categories of the outcomes variable thus derived were: (1) no resumption of cohabitation; (2) cohabitation resumed; (3) cohabitation resumed for a time, but has since terminated for at least one year; and (4) cohabitation terminated, but not known if there was a period of resumed cohabitation after the woman left the shelter. From the original four-category outcomes variable just described were derived the two outcomes variables of interest to the present study. The first variable recorded whether or not there was any resumption of cohabiting after each woman left the shelter. The other outcomes variable reflected whether or not cohabitation was terminated for a year or longer by the time of the study's outcomes investigation. Criteria for considering an outcome to be unknown were identical for all outcomes variables.

Using the above method, outcomes could be rated for 187 shelter residents' conjugal relationships (62.3% of the sample), leaving the outcome unknown in 113 cases. In 85.9% of their individual judgments on outcomes, the shelter workers' ratings were the same as the final outcome rating for the given woman's relationship. This represents high reliability for the outcomes ratings. Overall, 30.5% of the women were rated as having never resumed cohabitation with the abuser from whom they had fled to the shelter, and over 43% of the women eventually terminated cohabitation with the batterer.

It was not entirely a matter of each shelter resident's preference whether cohabitation resumed or ended after she left the shelter. Many of the relationship outcomes are directly attributable to the actions of the male partners. Frequently a man would forcibly intrude into his partner's new home and establish cohabitation with her in this way, regardless of her preference. In a few cases, batterers refused to recohabit with women who were willing to do so.

It is also important to note some possible confounds in the outcomes definitions. First, the criterion for considering cohabitation terminated—one year without resuming cohabitation—fails to exclude a few relationships in which cohabitation will resume after separations of a year or longer. Second, it is certain that some women categorized in this study as having resumed cohabitation actually had their relationships eventually terminate after one period of resumed cohabitation. There are also probably some cases of cohabitation here considered terminated, in which the couple have in fact resumed cohabiting. Despite these problems with the accuracy of the scoring of outcomes, I believe that the following analyses of statistical relationships between the outcomes and other factors remain valuable, and statistically representative of the actual experiences of the shelter residents studied.

For purposes of semantic convenience, I will use the following terminology in discussing outcomes categories. If a woman never resumed cohabiting with her assailant partner after she left the shelter, the outcome will be referred to as "terminated immediately." If cohabitation had terminated for at least one year by the time of the study after an intervening period of resumed cohabitation, the outcome will be referred to as "terminated eventually." The outcomes for 11 women known to have terminated cohabitation for at least one year by the time of the study, but for whom it is not known whether they had earlier resumed cohabiting or not, will also be referred to as "terminated eventually."

Results

A very strong relationship was derived between the outcome of the shelter residents' relationships and the relative economic position of the battered woman and her violent mate. Looking at the employment status of each shelter resident and her mate, and at the woman's welfare-recipient status, it was obvious that in 33 couples, the battered woman was producing more income than was the batterer. Among these 33 couples, the rate of immediate termination of cohabitation was 54.5%, compared to a rate of 27.7% among couples in which the batterer was an equal or greater income producer than was the battered woman. That is, couples in which the battered woman was unambiguously the main producer of income were twice as likely to break up immediately, as were couples in which the batterer was producing an income nearly equal, equal, or greater than that produced by the battered woman. Statistically, this difference in rates of immediate termination is very significant ($\chi^2 = 8.78$, df = 1, $p < .005$).

The same statistical relationship applies at a near-significant level to the eventual termination of cohabitation ($\chi^2 = 3.8$, df = 1, $p < .053$). Couples in which the battered woman was the main income producer were about one and a half times more likely to break up eventually than were couples in which the batterer was an equivalent or greater income producer than was the shelter resident. The rates of eventual termination of cohabitation were 57.6% among couples in which the shelter resident was the main income earner, compared to 39.1% among the rest of the relationships.

Another strong statistical relationship was found to obtain between outcomes and the batterer's employment status. For 50 assailants without gainful employment—men whose job status was given as not employed, disabled, retired, or student—the rate of immediate termination of cohabitation was 48%, compared to a 26.6% rate of breakup for couples involving assailant partners who were listed as full-time or self-employed ($\chi^2 = 7.4$, df = 1, $p < .01$). Similarly, a one-way analysis of variance showed significant differences in the rate of immediate breakup across the five categories of assailant job status (not employed, self-employed, full-time employed, disabled/retired, student, $p < .03$). The above significant relationships between the assailants' employment status and the rate of immediate termination of cohabitation do not hold true for the relationship between assailant employment status and an outcome of eventual termination. This may be a result of fluctuations in assailant job status over time that are not available in the present data.

Since higher education is associated with greater material resources, I am regarding education here as an economic variable. The data show a significant difference between the average educational levels of batterers who continued cohabiting and those whose cohabitation terminated immediately (11.4 versus 10.6 years, respectively; $t = 1.861$, df = 142, $p < .04$, one-tailed). This effect does not hold true between the batterer's educational level and the eventual termination of cohabitation, however.

There was also a near-significant trend for welfare recipients to be more likely than were nonrecipients to terminate cohabitation immediately ($\chi^2 = 2.596$, df = 1, $p < .11$). The strength of this tendency did not persist in relation to the eventual termination of cohabitation, although welfare recipients were insignificantly more likely to have cohabitation eventually end (50% of the welfare recipients versus 40.7% of non-welfare recipients, $p = .25$).

The average number of previous separations among women who resumed cohabiting with the batterer was 2.42, compared to 5.07 among shelter residents who never resumed cohabiting after they left the shelter.

This difference is statistically significant ($t = 1.85$, $df = 163$, $p < .05$, one-tailed). Women who had experienced one or no separations previous to entering SAFE House were only about half as likely as those who had experienced two or more prior separations to terminate cohabitation immediately (23% versus 44.6%).

Women who terminated cohabitation immediately had on the average experienced significantly more recent separations previous to taking shelter than had women who later recohabited with their partners (10.6 months versus 20.2 months since the last separation, $t = 2.1$, $df = 97$, $p < .02$, one-tailed). This effect also applied significantly to the difference between women whose cohabitation terminated eventually and those women who continued cohabiting (20.9 months average among recohabiting women versus 11.2 among eventual terminators, $t = 2.35$, $df = 104$, $p < .02$, one-tailed).

Turning to the duration of the last conjugal separation prior to each woman's entry into SAFE House, women who immediately terminated cohabitation averaged significantly longer prior separations than women who resumed cohabitation with their mates (124 days versus 63 days, $t = 1.95$, $df = 97$, $p < .03$, one-tailed). This significant effect also extends to the difference in the average length of separation between shelter residents eventually terminating cohabitation and those resuming cohabitation (114 days' duration versus 63 days, $t = 1.74$, $df = 103$, $p < .05$).

The following variables showed no significant statistical relationship to the outcomes variables:

> age of the battered woman, and of her assailant partner; age difference between mates; race of the woman, and of the batterer; racial composition of the couple; number of children; age of the youngest child; age of the eldest child; the batterer's class status; marital status; whether the battered woman had had previous counseling or psychotherapy; whether or not the woman tended to retaliate physically in self-defense; the number, frequency, and behavioral severity of assaults reported by the battered woman; concomitant child abuse by the woman batterer; concomitant alcohol abuse by the batterer; the woman's employment status; whether the batterer attended batterers' counseling; whether the woman had psychoactive prescriptions; the length of the relationship; the time elapsed since the first conjugal assault; whether the battered woman had been abused as a child; whether the woman was the daughter of a battered woman.

The apparent unimportance of the level of violence experienced by the women to the probability that cohabitation terminated is probably related to the crudeness of the measures used for determining the level of violence. Also, there is a distinct possibility that there is a curvilinear relationship between violence severity and the termination/resumption of cohabitation (Okun, 1983, 1986). Since only linear statistical analyses are here being discussed, curvilinear relationships cannot be proven or disproven at this time.

There were two variables that showed tendencies that were not statistically significant, but still have some interesting clinical implications for therapists. Pearson χ^2 analysis reveals that there was a near-significant tendency ($p < .08$) for cohabitation to be more likely to resume if the batterer entered counseling at DVP (a program of batterers' counseling affiliated with SAFE House). Although 65% of batterers not entering counseling resumed cohabitation, 83% of those in counseling at DVP experienced the resumption of cohabitation with their wives/partners. The tendency for cohabitation to terminate eventually remained smaller for those couples in which the batterer sought counseling at DVP (37.5%), than for those in which the batterer did not receive batterers' counseling (44.2%), but this result is statistically insignificant ($p > .50$).

Shelter residents taking prescribed psychoactive medications (not including the major tranquilizers) were more likely to resume cohabiting with their abusers than were battered women not taking this sort of medication, to a substantial but not statistically significant degree. Overall, 79% of the women with psychoactive prescriptions in the shelter resumed cohabiting with their abusers, compared to 64.5% of shelter residents without psychoactive prescriptions ($\chi^2 = 1.96$, $df = 1$, $p < .20$). Women with psychoactive prescriptions were also less likely to have cohabitation terminate eventually than were those women without such prescriptions (34.6% versus 44.5%), but this latter difference is statistically trivial ($p > .33$).

While the data show no important difference between the mean lengths of the marriage/relationship for shelter residents terminating cohabitation and those resuming cohabitation with their partners ($p > .50$), the data do indicate that the peak likelihood of immediate termination occurs among relationships of between five and seven years (39%). The rate of immediate termination rises steadily as the relationship gets longer, up until five to seven years' duration, and then the likelihoods decrease again. Shelter residents with relationships of less than one year are less than half as likely to experience the immediate termination of cohabitation as are women from lengthier relationships (14% versus 31%).

Women who entered the shelter within one year of the first assault in their relationship had above-average rates of both immediate and eventual termination of cohabitation (38% and 52% respectively, versus overall rates of 33% immediately and 43% eventually terminating). Women who had survived in the same battering relationship for over a decade had the lowest rates of both immediate and eventual termination (23.5% and 29.5%) among any of the categories of elapsed time since the initial battering. Peak rates of termination—both immediate and eventual—were recorded for shelter residents who had endured from four to five years of battering.

In the shelter sample, a little more than two out of every seven women considered themselves to be daughters of battered women. These shelter residents who were daughters of battered women were slightly more likely than were the other shelter residents to terminate cohabitation immediately (38.6% versus 31.8%, $p < .40$), and were also more likely to experience the eventual termination of cohabitation (52% versus 40.4%). This latter statistical effect approaches significance enough to be termed a substantial trend ($\chi^2 = 1.88$, $p < .18$).

Discussion

A common analysis, which I term *feminist resource theory,* predicts that battered women will be more likely to terminate relationships with men who provide fewer material resources, and that the more independent economic resources that a battered woman has, the more likely she will be to dissolve her relationship. This line of thinking would also predict that the greater the relative economic contribution of the woman to the relationship, the more likely her attempt to leave the batterer permanently.

The study results clearly demonstrate the importance of economic considerations in the shelter residents' decisions whether or not to terminate their conjugal relationships. In general, the data show that the greater the woman's own independent economic resources were relative to her mate's income, the greater the likelihood was of cohabitation terminating (presumably at the woman's instigation). Couples in which the battered woman was unambiguously the main income producer were twice as likely to experience immediate breakups as the rest of the shelter sample. In fact, a majority (54.5%) of the couples primarily supported by the battered woman's income broke up immediately.

Of the couples in the shelter sample in which the batterer was not employed, almost half (48%) broke up immediately, a significantly higher termination rate than the rate among couples in which the batterer had a job. Among the relationships terminating immediately, the abusers had a significantly lower mean educational level than had the batterers from relationships in which cohabitation resumed after the woman left SAFE House. Since more education is positively correlated with earning more income, the above result concerning the batterers' education can be interpreted as reflecting the relative income production of the two groups of woman batterers. The study results also show a trend for shelter residents who receive an independent income by virtue of being welfare recipients to be more likely to break off cohabitation, and a very slight tendency for battered women having a job outside the home to be more likely to terminate cohabitation.

The demonstrated tendency for battered women with greater independent economic resources to be more likely to terminate their battering relationships is very important. In light of these results, women having equal access to the paid work force and receiving equal pay for comparable work as men, can be seen as not only a fundamental matter of gender justice, but also as a source of leverage to stop woman battering. Job training, career counseling, and job placement programs designed wholly or largely for women—for example, displaced homemaker programs, educational programs for nontraditional students—should function similarly to reduce the prevalence and perpetuation of battering relationships.

As suggested in the existing literature, previous behavior regarding conjugal separations was a strong predictor of the termination or resumption of cohabitation after the shelter stay. On the average, shelter residents who ended cohabitation had experienced just over five previous conjugal separations, significantly more than the average number of previous separations among women who recohabited. This figure is also very close to that predicted by Walker and by Hilberman and Munson for battered women sundering their marriages/relationships (Hilberman & Munson, 1978; Walker, 1979). Women terminating cohabitation had also experienced conjugal separations prior to the shelter stay that were significantly more recent, and significantly longer, on the average, than those experienced by women resuming cohabitation. The women's relationships reached their peak likelihood of termination at five to seven years' duration, or after four to five years had elapsed since the first assault on the woman by her partner.

These findings suggest that, of battered women who experience repeated conjugal separations and recohabitations, many—if not most—are experiencing a process in which they become progressively more likely to end their conjugal relationships. For many—probably most, perhaps all—battered women who use conjugal separation as a coping strategy, the process of leaving their abusers and then returning to them is not an endless treadmill. Rather, it is a progressive process in which women exert increasing leverage upon their violent mates to change, while the women simultaneously become more familiar and more competent with living separately from their mates. Successive separations may also afford the battered woman opportunities to build up her resources—financial, educational, and occupational—in order to effect eventually a successful termination of her violent relationship. Often battered women are unwilling to relinquish right away their hopes and dreams of conjugal happiness in their current relationship, as indicated by the peak likelihood of divorce or breakup occurring after five to seven years' duration of the relationship (or after four to five years have elapsed since the initial battering incident). This fact should not surprise us, however, nor should it be morally repellent, as if people are ethically obliged to terminate their conjugal relationship should their mate assault them.

To reiterate, the study findings indicate that the process of separating and recohabiting by battered women is not an endless back-and-forth shuttle in static equilibrium, but a progressive process toward change in the violent relationship, including the termination of that relationship. The view supported by the data is very much at odds with a commonly held public attitude that there is little point in sheltering battered women since they just go back home anyway. The current study demonstrates, however, that battered women in fact do experience permanent breakups from their abusers with some regularity: over 30% terminated their relationships beginning directly with the shelter stay studied, and over 43% within two years of that shelter stay. Thus battered women do tend to leave their abusers on a permanent basis, they tend to go through several temporary conjugal separations before making a permanent conjugal break, and they are not obliged in the first place to prove themselves worthy victims by breaking off their violent conjugal relationships.

Various theoretical arguments can be made in order to support the hypothesis that daughters of battered women will be more likely to remain in violent relationships than will daughters of women who were not battered. Some theoretical processes that support the above expectation are: learning by vicarious reinforcement, or modeling; unconscious identification or transference; acceptance of conjugal violence as normal, or tolerable, or inevitable; assimilation of values that dictate preserving marriage at great cost, or at all costs; membership in an undifferentiated family of origin, and so on. Gelles, however, found a statistically insignificant tendency for battered women who had observed spouse abuse between their own parents to be more likely to divorce their husbands than would battered wives who were daughters of conjugally nonviolent couples (Gelles, 1976). The present findings similarly weigh against the notion that battered women who are daughters of battered women would be less likely to stop cohabitation with their violent partners.

As a batterers' counselor, I am concerned with the possible effect on battered women's decision making of the availability of specialized counseling for woman abusers. Since hope that the man will reform his behavior is a major motive for women who choose to recohabit with the batterer (Gayford, 1975; Roy, 1977; Pagelow, 1981), we might well expect a greater tendency for women to resume cohabiting with batterers who attend counseling. The current study supports this expectation, although it also indicates that in the long run counseling for batterers may not have any overall impact on the probability of termination of cohabitation in a violent relationship. In any case, this is an important issue to consider for organizations developing counseling programs for woman abusers.

The results of this study of course apply reliably only to the population of battered women taking refuge at SAFE House. How well the results generalize to women using other battered women's shelters, or to those battered women who do not use shelters, is unknown. Further research will be necessary in order to determine whether the effects derived here extend to other populations of battered women, or to battered women in general.

References

Berk, R. A., Berk, S. F., & Newton, P. J. (1984, August). *An empirical analysis of police responses to incidents of wife battery.* Paper presented at the second National Conference for Family Violence Researchers, Durham, NH.

Eisenberg, S., & Micklow, P. (1975). *The assaulted wife: "Catch-22" revisited.* Unpublished manuscript, Domestic Violence Project, Ann Arbor, MI. (Revised and edited version published in *Women's Rights Law Reporter,* Spring/Summer 1977.)

Gayford, J. J. (1975). Wife battering: A preliminary survey of 100 cases. *British Medical Journal, 1,* 194-197.

Gelles, R. J. (1972). *The violent home.* Beverly Hills, CA: Sage.

Gelles, R. J. (1976). Abused wives: Why do they stay? *Journal of Marriage and the Family, 38*(4), 659-666.

Hilberman, E. C., and Munson, K. (1978). Sixty battered women. *Victimology, 2*(3-4), 460-471.

Okun, L. (1983). A study of woman abuse: 300 battered women taking shelter, 119 woman-batterers in counseling. *Dissertation Abstracts International, 44*(6). (University Microfilms No. DA83-24,256).

Okun, L. (1986). *Woman abuse: Facts replacing myths.* Albany: SUNY Press.

Pagelow, M. D. (1981). *Woman-battering: Victims and their experiences.* Beverly Hills, CA: Sage.

Pfouts, J. (1978). Violent families: Coping responses of abused wives. *Child Welfare, 57*(2), 101-111.

Reynolds, R., & Siegle, E. (1959). A study of casework with sado-masochistic marriage partners. *Social Casework, 40,* 545-551.

Roy, M. (1977). A current survey of 150 cases. In M. Roy (Ed.), *Battered women* (pp. 25-44). New York: Van Nostrand Reinhold.

Sherman, L., & Berk, R. A. (1984). *The Minneapolis domestic violence experience* (Police Foundation Reports, April 1984). Washington, DC: Police Foundation.

Snell, J., Rosenwald, R., & Robey, A. (1964). The wife-beater's wife. *Archives of General Psychiatry, 11,* 107-112.

Waites, E. A. (1978). Female masochism and the enforced restriction of choice. *Victimology, 2*(3-4), 535-544.

Walker, L. (1979). *The battered woman.* New York: Harper/Colophon.

PART III

Seeking Help: The Use of Shelters and Programs for Men Who Batter

7

The Use and Psychosocial Impact of a Battered Women's Shelter

Andrea J. Sedlak

In the last several years, spouse abuse has emerged into public awareness as a significant social problem. Shelters for battered women are the cornerstone of efforts to combat wife beating, but evaluations of the impact of these programs are still in the most elementary stages (Colorado Association for Aid to Battered Women, 1979).

One purpose was to explore the factors affecting a woman's use of a shelter by examining how different demographic characteristics and life circumstances related to how long a woman eventually stayed in the shelter. The second aim was to attack a serious gap in existing research by demonstrating some of the cognitive and emotional effects of staying in a shelter.

The significance of this second goal deserves comment. Researchers have sometimes inferred the importance of shelters by pointing to findings that anywhere from half to two-thirds or more of the women who use shelters do not return to their batterers (Colorado Association for Aid to Battered Women, 1979; Doherty, 1981; Labell, 1979; Menzies, 1978; Snyder & Scheer, 1980; Walker, 1978).[1] In fact, nonreturn rates have been the most accessible and most frequently reported outcome measure in studies on battered women's shelters. But as an indicator of shelter impact, they are inadequate in two respects: First, they are severely limited, and in focusing on them, we ignore other important benefits of a shelter. Even those women who do return to their battering partners may have

AUTHOR'S NOTE: This chapter is based on a paper presented at the Annual Meeting of the American Psychological Association, 1983. Correspondence should be addressed to the author at Westat, Inc., 1650 Research Blvd., Rockville, MD 20850.

psychologically progressed toward a more permanent separation in the future or may substantially alter their relationships as a result of their shelter stay (Colorado Association for Aid to Battered Women, 1979; Ridington, 1977-1978; Seward, 1980; Snyder & Scheer, 1980; Vaughan, 1979; Walker, 1978). Second, while we generally assume that shelters induce various social and psychological changes in a client and that these changes in turn affect the likelihood that the woman will return to her abuser, the existing evidence does not even support a correlation between shelter stay and nonreturn likelihood, let alone a causal link as our reasoning would suggest. This is so because the comparison groups needed to show that *un*sheltered women return to their abusers at *different* rates are virtually always lacking.[2] As a result, it is not clear that residence in a shelter per se is associated with any difference in likelihood of returning to the abuser. Notice that both of these criticisms of the reliance on nonreturn rates hinge on the assumption that shelters have a variety of psychological effects on their clients, but to date there is little evidence on this score.

To summarize then, this project had two major goals: (1) to uncover the correlates of different lengths of stay in a shelter, and (2) to evaluate the psychosocial impact of shelter residence on women who stay for a nontrivial period of time.

Goal I: Length of Shelter Stay Correlates

First, regarding the correlates of length of shelter stay: Subjects for this part of the study were all the women (a total of 59) who entered the New Haven Shelter for Battered Women (Connecticut) during a four-month period. For this part of the project, shelter records for the women were examined and the association with length of stay was analyzed for any characteristic for which information could be had on 70% or more of the women.

Length of stay turned out *not* to be related to a woman's age, race, education, the length of her abusive relationship, number or ages of her children, or her current pregnancy status.

Length of stay *was*, however, related to both the nature of her relationship with her partner and to her destination on leaving the shelter. Women abused by their husbands were more than twice as likely as others (81% versus 39%) to leave in their first week. This may be because they were more likely to return to their partners but we do not really know this because clients who departed early most often had unknown destinations (which is the second characteristic relating to length of stay). It does seem to be a reasonable conjecture, though, especially in view of the fact that the staff in this shelter conveyed their disapproval of impulsive returns to a violent partner in no uncertain terms, so many of the women with unknown destinations in week 1 may have returned to their partners but were too embarrassed to let this fact be known.

As I just mentioned, a woman's length of stay in the shelter was also related to her ultimate destination, with 42% of those who left in their first 2 days having unknown destinations as compared with only 14% of those leaving later. Also, in this regard the likelihood of *not* returning to the violent partner was an increasing function of length of stay: 33% of the women who left in week 1 did *not* return to their partners, 55.6% in week 2, 66.7% in weeks 3 or 4, and 88% in weeks 5 or later. This pattern may reflect the shelter's impact on the women, or it may merely indicate that women who intend to not return avail themselves of the shelter for longer periods. In any event, it does document a clear association between length of time in the shelter and likelihood of returning to an abusive relationship.

Goal II: Psychosocial Effects of Shelter Residence

Regarding the second goal—the shelter's psychological and social effects on its residents: Subjects for this part of the study were all the women in the four-month period who stayed long enough to complete their scheduled interviews—a total of 20 clients. A quasi-experimental design was used.[3] Women were randomly (and secretly) assigned to pretest and posttest groups at the time they entered the shelter. Pretest women were interviewed during their first week, whereas posttest women were interviewed in their third week. The interview consisted of a structured series of more than 400 questions, assessing seven major areas of social and psychological functioning with both standardized measures and open-ended questions, and requiring about two to two and a half hours to complete.

The analyses began with a comparison of the women who were lost to the interview part of the study and those who successfully completed their interviews. This comparison showed no sample bias resulting from selection or mortality on any of the women's known characteristics (such as their age, race, nature or length of relationship, children, return likelihood). Women were lost to the interview part of the study primarily because they left the shelter very soon after their arrival (lost women had an average stay of only 4 days compared with an average stay of 28 days for those who completed their interviews, $p = .001$). Not surprisingly then, there are also differences between the women lost and the women interviewed in their destinations (see Table 7.1). Like most women leaving early, those lost to the study more often had unknown destinations, whereas those who were

TABLE 7.1

Destinations of Women Interviewed Versus Those Lost

	% Interviewed	% Lost
Returned to abuser	33	25
Did not return	67	39
Unknown destination	0	36

TABLE 7.2

Depression and Hopelessness

Scale	Pretest Mean	Posttest Mean	F[c]	p
CES-D[a]	30.18	23.56	7.23	.017
Beck Hopelessness[b]	5.00	5.56	8.07	.013

a. Score range: 0—60; high score signifies depression.
b. Score range: 0—7; high score signifies hopefulness.
c. df = 1, 17.

interviewed resembled most women who stayed longer in that they were more likely to *not* return to their violent partners. Because the interview data are extensive, I will discuss only three aspects of the findings that emerged in preliminary analyses.

(1) Depression. Two measures of depression were used in the interview, the Center for Epidemiological Studies Depression Scale (CES-D) and an abbreviated version of the Beck Hopelessness Scale. The posttest women (in their third week of stay) were less depressed on the CES-D and more hopeful on the Beck (see Table 7.2).[4]

(2) Self-Esteem and Feelings of Efficacy. The Coopersmith Self-Esteem Inventory and Levenson's Tridimensional Locus of Control Scale were used to gauge these dimensions. Levenson's scale includes an Internal scale (which measures a person's belief in her own causal efficacy), a Powerful Others scale (which indexes her feelings of being subject to the control exerted by others), and a Chance scale (which reflects the degree of credence she gives to luck or fate). Posttest women were expected to have higher scores on the Coopersmith and on Levenson's Internal scale and lower scores on the Powerful Others and Chance scales. The prediction regarding their feelings of personal power was the only one supported by the interview data (see Table 7.3).

TABEL 7.3

Self-Esteem and Feelings of Efficacy

Scale	Pretest Mean	Posttest Mean	F[e]	p
Coopersmith[a]	13.82	13.62	.004	n.s.
Internal Scale[b]	33.54	40.38	13.673	.004
Powerful Others[c]	17.18	25.62	2.723	.118
Chance[d]	24.46	24.00	.005	.942

a. score range: 0—24; high score signifies high self-esteem.
b. score range: 0—48; high score signifies high self-efficacy.
c. score range: 0—48; high score signifies belief in other's control over self.
d. score range: 0—48; high score signifies belief in luck or fate.
e. df = 1, 17.

TABLE 7.4

Psychological Dependence on Partner

Measure	Pretest Mean	Posttest Mean	F[c]	p
Predicted chances of return to partner[a]	1.88	1.50	3.960	.062
Gain in friendships since entering shelter[b]	2.00	2.67	10.079	.009

a. score range: 1-5; high score signifies high likelihood of return.
b. score range: 1-3; high score signifies greater gain.
c. df = 1, 13.

(3) Psychological Independence from the Abuser. Two questions germane to this were analyzed: a woman's assessment of the likelihood she would return to her partner and her gain in friendships with people unconnected with her partner since she entered the shelter. In both cases, there were substantial pretest-posttest group differences in the directions we would expect.[5] (See Table 7.4.)

Like most studies in the shelter context, a number of compromises from what would be ideal were necessary in this case. In looking at the results I have reported, one should keep in mind at least four things that could interfere with our detecting the shelter's actual benefits. First, the interview sample is extremely small, only 20 women, and a much larger *n* might be needed to demonstrate significant patterns. Second, the pretest was delayed up to a week after a woman entered the shelter, and it is possible that the shelter had already exerted most of its effects by the time of the pretest interviews. Third, the pretest and posttest groups differed in their stay only an average of two weeks at the time of their interviews, and a longer interval might be needed for the shelter's benefits to be detectable. And fourth, I might have just not happened to select measures for this preliminary analysis that optimally displayed the shelter's impact. Overall, however, the fact that evidence for the shelter's benefits was found in each of the three areas examined here suggests that a shelter can have powerful effects robust enough to override these various limits and interferences. To be sure, the fact that this study did not have an unsheltered control group for comparison means that we cannot definitely conclude that the shelter was causally involved in the group differences we see. For example, the differences may reflect a spontaneous recovery that would have occurred in these women anyway once they left their abuser, whether or not they went to the shelter to stay. But the study does show a definite association between the degree of exposure to the shelter and the degree of recovery shown on the reported measures, and this finding is a major step forward in the existing research base.

Given that shelters are the front-line resource for many battered women, and given the lack of studies on their social and psychological effects, this project offers valuable information on this subject.

Notes

1. These percentages probably overestimate the percentage of women who return to their abusers, since it is more difficult, when doing a follow-up, to track down those who do *not* return, and such women are more often "lost" to the study, decreasing the sample in a biased direction.

2. Not without good reason, to be sure. No ethical researcher deliberately establishes an *un*sheltered control group by denying shelter to those who seek it, and naturally occurring unsheltered women who are comparable to the shelter residents in all conceivably important respects are difficult (if not impossible) to identify and study.

3. This design is the Separate Sample Pretest-Posttest design discussed by Campbell and Stanley (1963).

4. Strictly speaking, these results emerged from an analysis of covariance, using number of children as a covariate. Women with more children were more depressed on the CES-D (r = .552, p = .012) and less hopeful on the Beck (r = –.574, p = .008). At the same time the number of children was unrelated to a woman's pretest-posttest group assignment (p = .652). Removing some of the extraneous variability in CES-D (or Beck) scores—namely, that due to the effects of number of children—increases the chances of observing small but systematic variations associated with pretest-posttest group status.

5. Here again the number of children in the woman's custody proved to be a useful covariate since, independent of her pretest-posttest status, the more children she had the more likely she perceived her return to be (r = .666, p = .005).

References

Campbell D. T. & Stanley J. C. (1963). *Experimental and quasi-experimental designs for research.* Chicago: Rand McNally.

Colorado Association for Aid to Battered Women. (1979). *A monograph on services to battered women.* U.S. Department of Health and Human Services. DHHS Publication No. (OHDS) 79-05708. Washington, DC: Government Printing Office.

Doherty, D. (1981). Salvation Army study of battered women clients. *Response to Violence in the Family, 4*(4), 5.

Labell, L. S. (1979). Wife abuse: A sociological study of battered women and their mates. *Victimology, 4*, 258-267.

Menzies K. S. (1978). The road to independence: The role of a refuge. *Victimology, 3*, 141-148.

Ridington, J. (1977-1978). The transition process: A feminist environment as reconstitutive milieu. *Victimology, 2*, 563-575.

Seward, R. G. (1980, February). *Shelters for battered women and their children.* Testimony before the subcommittee on Child and Human Development of the Committee on Labor and Human Resources. Domestic Violence Prevention and Services Act, 1980. (United States Senate, 96th Congress, second session on S. 1843.) Washington, DC: Government Printing Office.

Snyder D. K., & Scheer N. S. (1980, September). *Predicting adjustment following brief residence at a shelter for battered women.* Paper presented at the Annual Meeting of the American Psychological Association, Montréal, Canada.

Vaughan, S. R. (1979). The last refuge: Shelter for battered women. *Victimology, 4*, 113-150.

Walker, L. E. (1978). Treatment alternatives for battered women. In J. R. Chapman & M. Gates (Eds.), *The victimization of women.* Beverly Hills, CA: Sage.

8

How Some Men Stop Their Abuse: An Exploratory Program Evaluation

Edward W. Gondolf

There is increasing attention being given to developing programs for men who batter their wives (see Roy, 1982). A diverse range of philosophies and formats has emerged, including mental health, family service, women's shelter adjunct, self-help, and antisexist men's movement programs (Mettger, 1982; Roberts, 1984). The tendency appears to be toward professionalizing the services and incorporating them into ongoing mental health programs and family services based on conventional psychotherapy (Heppner, 1981; Weitzman & Dreem, 1982). This trend is not, however, without question and opposition (Morrison, 1982).

Some agreement on basic treatment modalities has also been established. There is wide use of cognitive restructuring, emotional awareness, stress management, and communication skills as a means of anger control (Edleson, 1984; Gondolf, 1985a; Purdy & Nickle, 1981; Saunders, 1984; Star, 1983). Also, a supervised group discussion process is recommended for abuser programs (Adams & McCormick, 1982; Gondolf, 1985b). These common practices, unfortunately, are based largely on untested theoretical and ideological positions or evaluations of a highly elusive clientele. It may therefore be useful to assess the perceptions of the men who batter as to what "works" for them. What stopping strategies do the men in fact adopt from the present range of treatment modalities? And, do their preferences

AUTHOR'S NOTE: This research was made possible through a fellowship from the Institute for Public Policy Studies, Center for Community Affairs, Indiana University of Pennsylvania. David Russell, Director of the Second Step Program; Jack Smith, research assistant and interviewer; and Lee Bowker, Dean of the Graduate School and Research at IUP, also made invaluable contributions to the project.

support the direction of programs for men who batter?

In response to these concerns, I conducted an exploratory study of participants in a structured group program for men who batter and of nonparticipants who contacted the program but never joined. Three major questions guided the research. One, do any significant differences appear between the participants and the nonparticipants in terms of their reported violence and stopping strategies? Two, is there any clearly preferred "stopping strategy," and what is the role of the program format in sustaining it? Three, what makes for nonviolence; that is, what strategies, if any, correlate with the reported nonviolence?

Methodology

Subjects. The subjects for this study were drawn from the Second Step program for abusers in Pittsburgh. The Second Step program offered a suitable source of subjects for a number of reasons. Founded in 1979, it is one of the longer running programs for men who batter and has drawn a wide range of clients. Furthermore, it was initiated by an antisexist men's movement collective as an extension of their campaign for social change, much as the mainstay organizations, RAVEN and EMERGE. The program, therefore, incorporates the anger control techniques prominent in the mental health-oriented programs and also emphasized resocialization from sex-role stereotypes and sexist behavior.

Second Step was, at the time of this study, structured as follows. A full-time director and two part-time staff maintained a hot line that received 8-10 inquiries weekly about the program from apparent batterers. After an initial interview for assessment and orientation, those who joined the program attended weekly one of the three two-hour group sessions of 4 to 10 participants. The group sessions followed a theme-centered group process led by the staff. That is, each session incorporated instruction, exercises, and discussion on a set topic. The eight themes address lack of self-awareness, denial, isolation, stress, rigid sex-role expectations, devaluing of the feminine, low self-esteem, and avoidance of conflict.

In January 1984, two samples were drawn from the men who had previously contacted the Second Step program. One, a sample of program participants included the 51 men who had attended two or more sessions of the Second Step program since its founding in 1979. Two, a control group of nonparticipants was composed of 54 men who contacted the program but did not participate. This second sample was drawn randomly from the 157 calls from nonparticipating batterers logged since the program's beginning.

The respondents can be characterized further by the following background information. Half of both samples found out about the program through their wives or women's shelters. The program participants attended an average of 11 sessions (s.d. = 6) with a range of from 3 to 25 sessions. Between 1 and 36 months had elapsed since their initial contact with the program (average = 14 months, s.d. = 10). The nonparticipants, of course, had not attended any sessions and had a lower range of time since program contact—3 to 18 months (average = 10). (The time since program contact was lower for the nonparticipants in part because the phone log of the program was not complete in the initial year of the program.) The age of the participants ranged from 22 to 60 with a mean of 35 (s.d. = 9.5). Five were 50 years old or over. An equal number (12, or 36%) were in white collar jobs and blue collar jobs, with four in other kinds of employment and five unemployed.

Interviews. A telephone interview of open-ended questions was administered to those who could be contacted within the three-week period of interviewing. Each man was told that a follow-up study of men who had contacted the Second Step program was being conducted and since they, according to the records, had contacted the program, we would like to ask them a few questions about their situation. The men were then asked a series of mostly open-ended questions about their perceptions of the program, the nature and duration of their abuse (specifically whether they had been physically violent since their initial contact with the program), and their strategies for stopping their abuse. The questions were designed to solicit the men's "definition of the situation," however, a series of probes were necessary in many cases to reduce evasiveness and obtain concrete replies to as many questions as possible.[1]

The nonparticipants proved to be much more evasive and less available than the participants were. For instance, the interviews ranged from 10 minutes to one and a half hours in both samples, but on the average, the participant interviews were 15 minutes longer and more comprehensive. About two-thirds of the nonparticipants did not complete all of the background questions. Furthermore, 31 (64%) of the participant sample were reached and responded, while only 23 (42%) of the nonparticipant sample was interviewed. Although the two groups have similar refusal rates, 23 (43%) of the nonparticipants had disconnected telephones and no new phone number available from directory assistance; whereas, only 6 (12%) of the participants had disconnected phones (see Table 8.1).

Analysis. The transcribed responses were categorized into a series of ordinal categories for each of 25 variables (as indicated in the accompanying tables). For instance, the scales for severity of prior abuse and recent abuse span from the least physically severe abuse to the most severe, that is, verbal abuse to physical injury. Also, the scale for stopping strategies ranges from joining the program to using control techniques, and finally to leaving the women. This range reflects greater to lesser programmatic reliance. First

TABLE 8.1
Participant and Nonparticipant Samples

	Sample Response		
	Participants/%	Nonparticipants/%	Combined/%
Respondents	33/65	23/43	56/53
Disconnected	6/12	23/43	29/28
Not available	7/14	0/0	7/7
Refused	5/10	8/15	13/12
Total	51/100	54/100	105/100
	Currently Residing with a Woman		
	Participants/%	Nonparticipants/%	Combined/%
Yes	20/63	17/74	37/35
No	12/37	6/26	18/17
Total	22/100	23/100	55/100

NOTE: Both the participant and nonparticipant samples each had three members living with a different woman than when they contacted the program.

mentions, the total number of different subcategories mentioned (A, B, C, and so on), and the range of mentions in different primary categories (I, II, III, and so on) were tabulated for the description of abuse and stopping strategies. Frequency distributions and bivariate correlations (tau b; $p < .05$ to .001) were used as the basis of the analysis of the primarily ordinal level data (bivariate correlations are contained in Table 8.5).

As will be discussed, the reported severity of prior abuse was comparable between the two samples. A total of 70% reported striking their wives. Moreover, the program participants' frequency of abuse prior to program contact ranged from once (2) or yearly (4) to monthly (9) or weekly (2). Overall, 63% of the participants and 74% of the nonparticipants reported that they were currently living with a woman (three in each sample were living with a different woman than when they contacted the program). Given these circumstances, the reported nonviolence (about 60% of each group of respondents) is substantial evidence that men who batter can change their behavior.

Participants Versus Nonparticipants

The participant and nonparticipant respondents, as mentioned, reported similar levels of violence. This offers a convenient constant for other comparisons but most likely does not reflect the actual abuse present in the different samples. Other indications, especially in stopping strategies, suggest that the two groups are very different populations.

Reported abuse. The participants and nonparticipant respondents are on the surface similar in the nature and duration of their reported violence (see Table 8.2). About 60% of each group reported not being physically violent since they contacted the program. In comparing the most severe abuse prior to contacting the program, 76% of the participants reported striking their wives with a fist or hard slap; whereas 67% of the nonparticipants admitted to some kind of striking. Similarly, the nonparticipants, on average, mentioned fewer kinds of abuse and a smaller range of abuse, when they described their previous abuse. Also, the differences between the samples in the reporting of recent abuse (since program contact) were similar. The severity of the recent abuse remained about the same as severity of the previous abuse.

These comparable levels of reported abuse, of course, do not suggest that the nonparticipants in general are less abusive than the participants are, or that the program fails to reduce appreciably the violence. Many of the phone disconnections among the nonparticipants may have resulted from the separation of the battering man and his battered wife, and therefore might reflect continued violence or abuse since the program contact. Were this to be the case, the nonparticipants could be as much as twice as violent as the participants since their program contact. If the presence of a disconnected phone is used simply as an indicator of residential stability, the nonparticipants appear to be nearly four times as transient as the participant sample.

Moreover, the participants and nonparticipants appear to have very different conceptions of their abuse. In their descriptions of their prior abuse, the participants cited many more kinds of abuse than did the nonparticipants. Several offered details of how they attacked their wives and the consequences of it. The inference may be that the participants are more aware of their violence and less apt to deny it—an important precondition for changing behavior. This may be further reflected in that 10% more of the nonparticipants than the participants were rated evasive, resistant or hostile during the interview.

Stopping strategies. A comparison of participants and nonparticipants on their reported stopping strategies reveals a more explicit difference between the two groups (see Table 8.3). More than three-fourths of the participants first mentioned that they used and/or would recommend programmatic measures to stop their violence; whereas the nonparticipants first cited nonprogrammatic strategies. For instance, in a tabulation of all the strategies mentioned by each sample, 28 (85%) participants mentioned joining a group program as one of their strategies; whereas only 6 (26%) nonparticipants mentioned joining a program. Nearly one-half (16) of the

TABLE 8.2
Reported Violence

Physically Violent Since Program Contact

	Participants/%	Nonparticipants/%	Combined/%
Yes	12/39	9/43	21/40
No	19/61	12/57	31/60
Total	31/100	21/100	52/100

Overall Total Mentions of Prior Abuse

	Participants/%	Nonparticipants/%	Combined/%
Verbal	17/20	7/26	24/21
Name calling	11	3	14
Yelling 2	4	6	
Objects	10/12	1/4	11/10
Break things	6	0	6
Throw things	4	1	5
Push/grab	22/26	4/15	26/23
Push/shove	16	3	19
Grab	6	1	7
Strike	30/36	15/56	45/40
Slap/punch	24	12	36
Severe injury	5	3	8
Other	4/5	0/0	4/4
Total mentions	83/100	30/100	113/100

Most Severe Abuse Prior to Program Contact

	Participants/%	Nonparticipants/%	Combined/%
Verbal	1/3	2/10	3/6
Break/throw	1/3	1/5	2/4
Push/grab	6/18	4/19	10/19
Strike	25/76	14/67	39/72
(severe injury)	(5)	(3)	(8)
Total	33/100	21/100	54/100
Average	5.8	5.4	5.6
	(based on 8-point scale)		

Kinds of Prior Abuse per Person

	Participants/%	Nonparticipants/%	Combined/%
1 Kind	6/18	15/71	21/39
2 Kinds	10/30	5/22	15/28
3+ Kinds	17/52	1/4	18/33
Total	33/100	21/100	54/100
Average	2.3	1.3	1.9

(*continued*)

TABLE 8.2 (continued)

	Categories of Prior Abuse		
	Participants/%	Nonparticipants/%	Combined/%
1 Category	6/18	18/86	24/44
2 Categories	16/48	3/14	19/35
3 Categories	11/33	0/0	11/20
Total	33/100	21/100	54/100
Average	2.2	1.1	1.8

participants first mentioned control techniques, as opposed to only 14% (2) of the nonparticipants. The participants also mentioned more different strategies and a greater category range per person than did the nonparticipants. On the average, the participants mentioned 3.1 different strategies as opposed to 1.7 of the nonparticipants.

At the other extreme, only 4 (12%) participants specifically mentioned the strategy of "help yourself" versus 8 (25%) of the nonparticipants. Furthermore, 72% of the responding nonparticipants noted that they did not join the program because they, in some way, took care of the problem themselves. (At least 3 remarked that they did not join the program because they did not want anything to do with a group.) A total of 16 (70%) nonparticipants, as opposed to 3 (9%) participants, recommended leaving the women entirely as a way to stop the violence. The majority of these respondents supporting the nonprogrammatic strategies tended to blame the victim for the abuse. (A total of 6, or 11%, of all respondents mentioned "turning to God" as a strategy, two mentioned lifting weights, and three mentioned AA.)

In sum, the participants reported having different stopping strategies and more extensive repertoires of strategies than did the nonparticipants. They obviously have taken much of the program's training and counseling to heart. But the difference in approaches to stopping violence may be, as well, a reflection of the two very different populations. The nonparticipants, as discussed, seem openly less aware and less willing to admit to their violence, more transient and less conciliatory, and more evasive and resistant to getting help. They appear to hold more tenaciously to the masculine "I'd rather do it myself" attitude. This difference may also reflect differing appraisals of their relationships. The nonparticipants may be less motivated to join a program because they have less regard for their spouses and/or less desire to maintain the relationship.

TABLE 8.3
Stopping Strategies

Overall Total Stopping Strategies

		Participants/%		Nonparticipants/%		Combined/%
Join program		26/28		2/6		28/21
Self awareness		17/18		0/0		17/14
Insight	8		0		8	
Feelings	9		0		0	
Control techniques		30/32		6/19		36/29
Think	15		2		17	
Time out	15		4		19	
Nonprogram		19/21		24/75		43/35
Individual counseling	2		7		9	
Talk to friend	5		1		6	
Leave woman	3		5		8	
Help self	4		8		12	
Other (God, weights, A.A.)	5		3		8	
Total mentions		92/100		32/100		124/100

First Mentioned Stopping Strategy

	Participants/%	Nonparticipants/%	Combined/%
Join program	5/15	0/0	5/9
Self aware	6/18	1/5	7/13
Control Techniques	16/49	3/14	19/35
Other	6/18	17/81	23/43
Total	33/100	21/100	54/100

Kinds of Stopping Strategies per Person

	Participants/%	Nonparticipants/%	Combined/%
1 Kind	2/6	12/60	14/26
2 Kinds	7/21	4/20	11/21
3 Kinds	13/39	3/15	16/30
4 Kinds	7/21	1/5	8/15
5+ Kinds	4/12	0/0	4/8
Total	33/100	20/100	53/100
Average	3.1	1.7	2.6

Categories of Stopping Strategies per Person

	Participants/%	Nonparticipants/%	Combined/%
1 Category	4/12	14/70	18/34
2 Categories	10/30	5/25	15/28
3 Categories	15/46	1/5	16/30
4 Categories	4/12	0/0	4/8
Total	33/100	20/100	53/100
Average	2.6	1.4	2.1

The Preferred Stopping Strategies

The group dimension of the program is highly valued by the participants. It is unclear, however, what motivates the men to adopt the strategies that they do.

Correlates to stopping strategies. The kind, amount, and range of strategies do not appear to correspond to the number of sessions one attends, or whether or not one is living with a woman. In other words, there is no evidence that stopping strategies reflect more the program's instruction over time or become more complex to meet the pressures of living with a woman. The stopping strategies do not appear related to other background variables like age, occupation, or time since program contact.

The amount of time spent in the program also does not in itself appear to reduce violence. The number of sessions does, however, correlate with age (tau b = .40, p > .001). That is, the younger men tend to drop out of the program sooner than the older men. (Occupation may also be related to session attendance with white collar workers staying longer in the program [tau b = –.21, p > .08].) These particular findings may suggest that learning how to stop violence is likely related to motivational factors outside the program.

Program evaluation. The group program nonetheless is very useful to the participants (see Table 8.4). A total of 79% of the participants mentioned joining the group program as one of the ways to stop abuse and 15% cited it first among their stopping strategies. On an earlier question in the interview about the most useful aspects of the program, 60% of the total mentions referred to social aspects of the program (sharing opinions and emotions, making friendships, and talking with others in a similar situation), compared to 25% of the mentions that referred to psychological aspects (learning to communicate feelings, gaining self-awareness, and developing greater self-control). Some 63% of the participants, in fact, mentioned the social aspect first in their response.

Moreover, most of the participants valued the program enough to complete the required eight sessions and express interest in a follow-up program. Specifically, 52% were either still in the program or had completed a full cycle. (Overall, 29% reported leaving the program because of problems with transportation, finances, or schedule, and 19% left because they had "solved" their problem or separated from their wives.) Of the former participants, 82% expressed an interest in joining a follow-up group (15% very much so, 9% maybe).

Social support. Suggestions for improving the program reflected the emphasis on the group dimension of the program among the majority of participants. Some 79% of the participants offered suggestions for

TABLE 8.4
Usefulness of Program to Participants

Overall Mentioned Uses of Program

		Participants/%
Social aspects		44/60
Sharing	21	
Friendship	4	
Talk	19	
Psychological aspects		18/25
Learn feelings	4	
Gain awareness	8	
Self control techniques	6	
Other		11/15
Help self	2	
Program counselor	4	
Other	5	
Total mentions		73/100

First Mentioned Usefulness of Program

	Participants/%
Social	21/64
Psychological	9/27
Other	3/9
Total	33/100

Kinds of Uses Per Person

	Participants/%
1 Kind	9/27
2 Kinds	13/39
3 Kinds	9/27
4 Kinds	1/3
5 Kinds	1/3
Total	33/100

Categories of Uses Per Person

	Participants/%
1 Category	18/55
2 Categories	12/36
3 Categories	3/9
Total	33/100

improvements, and 70% of their suggestions centered on expanding the group in some way. The participants recommended more advertising and promotion, more localities and different times for the sessions, extending the required term of the program and the number of required sessions each week, including spouses in at least one session, and dividing groups into personality types or married and unmarried men.

The remaining suggestions (28%) focused on program content. They included recommendations to offer personal counseling and psychiatric consultation, set specific objectives for individuals, deal more with child abuse, instruct more about stress, and include the Bible in the program.

The social support of the group apparently is vital to the men and should be considered as an essential component to abuser programs. The men who batter rely heavily on anger control to stop their abuse. However, an overemphasis on control techniques may be at the expense of more substantial strategies. Those who first mentioned control techniques cited fewer stopping strategies in all (tau b = –.28; $p < .03$).

In this regard, some glaring omissions exist in the respondents' preferred strategies. Only two respondents referred to the need to genuinely change themselves, as well as control their behavior. None of the respondents, however, made reference to the sex-role issues or societal sources of the abuse. These topics were emphasized by the program staff and are found in the wife-abuse literature (Pagelow, 1981; Dobash & Dobash, 1979). There was no mention, for instance, of learning to share power or of changing one's appraisal of women.

Correlates of Reported Nonviolence

This research offers no evidence of any one "successful" stopping strategy or array of strategies, nor does it reveal any other decisive factors in ending the violence. The only implicit contributor to nonviolence is the "woman factor"—that is, the urging or insistence from the battered woman that her spouse seek help.

Background and abuse correlates. The various background variables, including age and occupation, do not show any significant correlation to the reported violence. In this regard, the duration since contacting the program does not appear to influence the reported violence, as common sense might suggest. That is, the likelihood of violence does not increase with more time to be abusive. The severity of abuse is modestly correlated with the reported violence (tau b = .21; $p < .05$), suggesting, logically, that it is easier to stop the milder forms of abuse.

Although the stopping strategies are uncorrelated with nonviolence, they are strongly associated with aspects of the previous abuse. The first mentioned stopping strategy, the total number of strategies, and the range of categories of these strategies show correlations with the total number (tau b = –.36, .41, .40; $p < .001$ in each case) and range of abuses (tau b = –.38, .45, .49; $p < .001$, in each case). The more program oriented the strategy is, the less the number and range of prior abuse. The number of strategies and range of strategies are similarly associated with the number of kinds and categories of reported abuse. (Furthermore, a slight correlation is present between the time since program contact and the range of stopping strategies [tau b = .24; $p < .04$], suggesting that over time the men learn and try a greater array of strategies; see Table 8.5.)

There are at least two possible explanations for the relationship between the stopping strategies and the prior abuse. One, the participants may feel that their more diversified abuse warrants the broader scope of the more programmatic strategies. Similarly, their diverse abuse warrants a diverse and more complex strategy, reflected in the total number and range of strategies mentioned. Two, the men who mention the more diverse strategies may be more sensitized to their abuse and therefore describe more of it. They may be more self-reflective and talkative, in part because of the program. However, the indicators for stopping strategy and prior abuse did not correlate with a subjective five-level rating of the respondents' cooperation in answering questions on the interview. Also, the correlation with the specific "first mention" appears independent of any talkative factor.

The woman factor. As mentioned, the only hint of a "success indicator" lies in the "woman factor." Not living with a woman in itself does not appear to decisively reduce violence. (A larger sample may indicate a statistically significant but slight correlation for residence with a woman, given the coefficient in this analysis—tau b = .20; $p < .078$.) In short, separation from one's spouse is not a substantial deterrent, even though eight (14%) of the respondents mentioned separating from the woman as the best way to stop the violence. This finding is, no doubt, a reflection of the lack of validity in the "residence with a woman" variable. Many men who do not live with their wives may regularly visit them or other women—and continue to abuse them.

The "woman factor" may be more accurately represented by the battered woman's insistence that her husband seek help. As mentioned, 50% of both samples found out about the program from their wives, so many of the men are led to seek help by their wives, as many clinicians observe. Furthermore, a modest correlation exists between how the men found out about the

TABLE 8.5
Bivariate Relationships of Important Study Variables

Strategy first mentioned with abuse kinds	tau b = –.36; $p < .001$
Strategy first mentioned with abuse categories	tau b = .38; $p < .001$
Strategy first mentioned with woman residing (P)	tau b = .24; NS
Strategy kinds with abuse kinds	tau b = .41; $p < .001$
Strategy kinds with abuse categories	tau b = .45; $p < .001$
Strategy kinds with found out	tau b = .21; $p < .05$
Strategy kinds with occupation (P)	tau b = .30; $p < .05$
Strategy categories with abuse kinds	tau b = .40; $p < .001$
Strategy categories with abuse categories	tau b = .49; $p < .001$
Strategy categories with time since contact	tau b = .24; $p < .05$
Violence since program with found out	tau b = .31; $p < .05$
Violence since program with abuse severity	tau b = .21; NS
Violence since program with woman residing	tau b = –.20; NS
Violence . . . with usefulness first mentioned (P)	tau b = –.36; $p < .05$
Recent abuse kinds with woman residing	tau b = –.23; $p < .05$
Recent abuse categories with woman residing	tau b = –.25; $p < .05$
Sessions attended with age (P)	tau b = .40; $p < .001$
Sessions attended with occupation (P)	tau b = –.21; NS
Usefulness first mentioned and age (P)	tau b = –.46; $p < .01$

(P = participant sample only)

program and their reported violence (tau b = +.31, $p < .02$). The men who found out about the program through their wives and the shelters were more likely to report nonviolence than were the men who found out through advertisement or referral. Similarly, a modest correlation exists between how men learned about the program and their total stopping strategies. The men appear to learn more or try harder with the women's urging. In short, women motivate men to get help and stop their violence.

This speculation about the woman's influence conforms to the findings of a substantial study of formerly abused women. Bowker (1983) recently conducted a study of women who succeeded in stopping their husbands' violence—of women who "beat wife beating." His findings suggest that the woman's success in stopping the violence was related to their persistence and range of efforts in convincing their husbands of their unwillingness to tolerate further abuse.

Summary. The findings of the study in themselves raise some important considerations for further research into this relatively unchartered area. They also pose some important implications for the emerging abuser programs.

The interview data suggest that the program participants hold very different ideas from nonparticipants about how to stop violence, even when comparable in levels of reported violence and residence with a woman. The participants endorsed the programmatic strategies, while the nonparticipants strongly recommended nonprogrammatic strategies. The participants notably emphasized the usefulness of the social aspects of the program. The value placed on the group sharing, interaction, and friendship may be a counter to the social isolation noted in many of the characterizations of men who batter (see Coleman, 1980). Ironically, the nonparticipants appeared to be more transient, resistant to help, and more evasive—factors that further isolate them.

The men, on the whole, rely on willful self-restraint to stop their violence, rather than on personal and social change. The most often cited strategies for dealing with violence are anger control techniques, including taking a time out when angry, self-talk about restraint, recalling the consequences of violence, and visualizing the other participants in the program. There is no evidence, however, that the anger control is more successful in stopping the violence than any other strategy. It may in fact divert abusers from developing more substantial stopping strategies.

There was minimal mention of substantial self-searching. Several men were regretful and even remorseful; however, no specific mention was made of the need for deeper personal change and a reappraisal of one's relationship to women. An acknowledgment of this need may be implicit in the great emphasis that participants placed on the group process. The group interaction does offer an alternative model for male relations. The masculine tendencies of withholding, competing, and belittling are minimized in the group interactions. The reliance and trust placed on others in the group represents a substantial departure from the do-it-yourself attitude of the nonparticipants.

Battered women may play the most prominent role in the cessation of violence. Insistence that their spouses get help appears to influence the men to try harder to stop abusing. The amount of time in the program and the time since contact with the program, contrarily, do not appear related to stopping the violence. Programs for men who batter, therefore, may do well to work with the women and build a strong alliance with the services for battered women.

Discussion

Qualifications. The findings of this exploratory study are of course tentative in light of the small sample, low response rate, and unverified self-reports. Much more research needs to be done on the men who batter and how they stop their abuse. Some of the shortcomings of this study, as well as its findings, may be instructive in this regard.

Further research might refine the assessment of nonparticipant batterers, the nature of the abuse, and the men's relationship to the battered women. First, there is an obvious need to include men who have not been in a program. Most batterers who have been studied are self- or court-referred, and they represent less than 1% of the batterer population as a whole. This study suggests that those who do not seek program help may be a very different population in attitude and living pattern—and a very difficult set of subjects to access.

Second, the means of measuring wife abuse need to be refined. The instruments need to be more sensitive to the nature, frequency, and severity, yet penetrate the denial of many men who batter. Also, verification from the battered woman and consideration of her subjective experience is essential in establishing a more meaningful assessment of abuse. Many of the men in this study may have stopped their physical violence, but still torment their wives through other unreported means.

Three, more attention needs to be given to the role women play in motivating men to seek and respond to help. In this process, other motivators, like police intervention, might be sought that relieve women from the responsibility for initiating change. A more precise determination of the batterer's contact with his spouse is warranted. Also, a better appraisal of the men's reaction to the women's tactics and men's initiative are needed, given the woman's influence suggested in this study.

In conclusion, more attention needs to be given to the substantial resistance and elusiveness of the nonparticipants, the vital role of group counseling in programs for men, and the way that battered women help motivate men to stop their abuse. There is however no magic formula for stopping the violence.

Note

1. The security of the spouses or female partners of the interviewees was addressed in the following manner: First, the interviewees were informed at the outset about the topics of the interview and asked if they were willing to participate. Those who might have been irritated by the interview were likely to have refused it. Second, each of those men who were interviewed were offered a follow-up group program. Also, several interviewees expressed their appreciation for the contact. They wanted to call the program for quite some time but had not gotten around to it. Third, respondents specifically mentioned that they needed help from the program director who was informed accordingly. Fourth, the interviewers used counseling techniques to debrief the interviewees after the questioning. Each interviewer probed personal concerns of the interviewee to "cool out" any hints of anger. (One interview with a man who appeared in an emotional depression lasted nearly two hours.) No one reported being presently involved in violence; those who suggested recent violence were encouraged to get

help and were referred to the program. Fifth, the shelters in the area were alerted to the project but did not report any calls from women related to our project. As mentioned in the findings, a substantial portion of the interviewees were already separated from their abused spouses or were presently nonviolent with their current spouses.

References

Adams, D., & McCormick, A. (1982). Men unlearning violence: A group approach based on the collective model. In M. Roy (Ed.), *The abusive partner.* New York: Van Nostrand Reinhold.

Bowker, L. (1983). *Beating wife beating.* Lexington, MA: Lexington Books.

Coleman, K. (1980, April). Conjugal violence: What 33 men report. *Journal of Marriage and Family Counseling,* pp. 207-213.

Dobash, E., & Dobash, R. (1979). *Violence against wives: A case against the patriarchy.* New York: Free Press.

Edleson, J. (1984, May-June). Working with men who batter. *Social Work,* pp. 234-242.

Gondolf, E. (1985a). *Men who batter: An integrated approach to stopping wife abuse.* Holmes Beach, FL: Learning Publications.

Gondolf, E. (1985b). Fighting for control: A clinical assessment of men who batter. *Social Casework, 66*(1), 48-54.

Heppner, P. (1981). A holistic approach to the treatment of violent families. *Social Casework, 62,* 594-600.

Mettger, Z. (1982). Help for men who batter: An overview of issues and programs. *Response, 5*(6), 1-2, 7-8, 23.

Morrison, M. (1982). Seem angry? I am angry! *Aegis, 36,* 17-25.

Pagelow, M. D. (1981). *Woman battering: Victims and their experiences.* Beverly Hills, CA: Sage.

Purdy, F., & Nickle, N. (1981). Practice principles for working with groups of men who batter. *Social Work with Groups, 4,* 111-122.

Roberts, A. (1984). Intervention with the abusive partner. In A. Roberts (Ed.), *Battered women and their families.* New York: Van Nostrand Reinhold.

Roy, M. (Ed.) (1982). *The abusive partner.* New York: Van Nostrand Reinhold.

Star, B. (1983, June). *Helping the abuser.* New York: Family Service Association.

Saunders, D. (1984). Helping husbands who batter. *Social Casework,* pp. 347-353.

Weitzman, J., & Dreen, K. (1982, May). Wife beating: A view of the marital dyad. *Social Casework,* pp. 259-265.

9

Issues in Conducting Treatment Research with Men Who Batter

Daniel G. Saunders

Following the establishment of shelter services for battered women in many communities, a number of intervention programs were developed for their partners. Unfortunately, outcome evaluations of these programs have rarely been conducted. Evaluation research is needed because the impressions of service providers and clients regarding treatment outcome may not match the actual outcome of treatment, and battered women may remain in dangerous relationships in the hope that treatment will end the violence.

Information about the effectiveness of interventions can be used to guide the decision making of service providers, clients, policy makers, and funding sources. In addition to answering the question, "How successful is this program?" research can answer a number of other questions: "What are the social and psychological characteristics of abusers in treatment? How effective is one method compared with another, for example, cognitive-behavioral versus self-help? What is the relative effectiveness of each treatment component of a larger treatment "package," for example assertiveness training versus relaxation training? What treatment works best with what types of clients? Offenders with alcoholism problems or overcontrolled hostility, for example, may respond better to one type of treatment than to another. As in most psychotherapy outcome research, the more fruitful line of inquiry is to not ask simply "What works?" but, "What works with what type of client, under what conditions, with what type of provider?"

AUTHOR'S NOTE: The writing of this chapter was supported in part by NIMH Grant MH-17139-01 while I was a postdoctoral research fellow. I would like to thank Sharon Berlin and Alan Gurman for their helpful comments on an earlier version of the manuscript.

The researcher who attempts to answer these questions is faced with an array of ethical and practical issues and dilemmas. As in all treatment research, the potential risks to human subjects need to be balanced by the potential loss of knowledge about effective treatment (see O'Leary & Borkovec, 1978). In this chapter, I will discuss some of these issues and dilemmas and make some recommendations for conducting outcome evaluations. Two major areas of the research process will be discussed: design and measurement.

Design Issues

Experimental designs. Because dangerous behavior is being treated, it seems impossible to justify ethically the random assignment of clients to a no-treatment control group, as in the classical experimental design. Even when the control group is a minimal treatment group, the ethics of this design are very questionable (Kaslow & Gurman, 1985). A situation may arise, however, in which there is a naturally occurring waiting list, thus ethically allowing random assignment to a "waiting list control group." Couples who are waiting need to be informed of available crisis services and if these services are needed repeatedly, data from these cases can be analyzed separately (see Gurman, 1979).

Random assignment to two different forms of treatment, a comparison group design, is more ethically acceptable than random assignment to a no-treatment or minimal treatment control condition. A practical limitation with random assignment in some programs is the small number of men who enroll in groups, making it difficult to have enough men in each treatment condition.

Random assignment sometimes meets with resistance within one's agency, with other community agencies, and with clients. Providers of service or referral sources may feel invested psychologically and programmatically in one treatment condition, especially if the treatment has been used for a while prior to the experiment. Clients may be generally wary of experiments or feel dissatisfied if, for experimental reasons, the description of treatment prior to random assignment is vague.

The concerns of each group need to be met with the explanation that experimentation is the only way that effective treatments will be discovered. A procedure that is accepted more readily is to offer the alternative treatment to each group after the random assignment experiment. This procedure's major disadvantage is that it precludes long-term follow-up, which is an important aspect of the treatment evaluation of men who batter. Because of these concerns, some programs have made good use of quasi-experimental designs, for example the nontreatment "control group" may be composed of group noncompleters, those not referred by probation officers, or a matched group of untreated arrestees (e.g., Dutton, 1986).

Voluntary participation. When clients are referred from the criminal justice system, the use of experimental designs may be restricted. Contracts with human subjects are not valid if they involve coercion, duress, or subjects judged "incompetent." From a legal standpoint, the presentation of options, even if punishment is one of them, does not qualify as "coercion" (Wexler, 1976). However, one of the options needs to be the chance to improve behavior so that prosecution may be avoided. Treatment programs for men who batter provide the chance for improvement of behavior. To minimize the coercion to become an experimental subject, criminal justice clients are typically given the choice between the "standard" treatment or participation in a random-assignment experiment.

The question of who is the primary client is an important one. The abuser usually wants the violence to stop less than those who are most affected—the women and children in the family. In this sense, the woman is the primary client and should give informed consent before her partner participates in an experiment (Hart, 1987).

"Duress" may be a factor making it difficult for some victims and abusers to make rational decisions about participation in research projects. Many abusers and victims suffer severe stress reactions and may try to please the researcher, especially if separated from their partners and their only goal is reunion with them. To mitigate against the factor of duress, the contract can be reviewed in more than a single session and the client can be advised to consult an attorney.

Long-term follow-up. There are two major reasons to try to conduct long-term follow-up evaluations: (a) the base rate of violent behavior may be relatively low (once or twice a year), making recidivism a low probability a year after treatment whether or not treatment was given, and (b) the man may be without an intimate partner during and after treatment. Many of the men are violent only in an intimate relationship, yet treatment often coincides with divorce or separation. An adequate test of treatment would need to wait until the man becomes involved with a woman after treatment to the same extent as before treatment. This reinvolvement may take several years. A follow-up period of two to five years seems adequate. One alternative is to analyze data from men who have frequent base rates and/or remain with their partners (e.g., Edleson, Miller, Stone, & Chapman, 1985). Naturally, sample size and sample characteristics are restricted with this alternative.

A major ethical concern with follow-up studies is the maintenance of confidentiality. Not only must names be kept through the follow-up period but also records of criminal, violent behavior. Clients have not complained about the intrusiveness of the follow-up contacts from our program, perhaps because both partners give permission to the follow-up calls prior to treatment.

A practical problem, of course, is locating the men or their partners during the follow-up phase. Battered women no longer living with their partners often relocate suddenly or get unpublished telephone numbers in order to escape harassment. In some cases it has helped for us to request at intake the name of a friend or relative who will be expected to know the battered woman's whereabouts.

Pre-post measurement. Measures taken immediately before and after treatment do not have the ethical and practical problems of long-term follow-up. The major drawback here is the inability to assess adequately a change in abusive behavior. It is possible to measure some correlates of abusive behavior in relatively unbiased ways. Some of these measurement techniques will be described later.

Single-subject designs. Because they do not involve random assignment of clients, single subject designs are generally more acceptable to practitioners (Berliner & Conte, 1984). Assessment with single-subject designs is usually restricted to cases with a high base rate of behavior. Otherwise they have the same practical and ethical problems as long-term follow-up. The need for a high base rate is especially important if an actual rather than a retrospective baseline is measured. Edleson et al. (1984), for example, using a multiple baseline design, had the men give weekly reports of their violence during the assessment, treatment, and follow-up phases. Many of the men reported no violence during the assessment phase, thus their data were not analyzed. Alternatively, a retrospective baseline may be both more reliable and more ethical for the measurement of violent behavior (for discussion of retrospective baselines, see Houtler & Rosenberg, 1985).

What works with whom? All forms of treatment may be less effective with particular types of clients; but also, some treatments may be less effective with particular types of clients. Brisson (1981), for example, speculates that abusers who are violent only at home rather than generally violent may benefit more from traditional psychotherapy, whereas the generally aggressive abuser may benefit more from the application of external controls, such as probation. Designs that tackle this question may develop knowledge for constructing more specialized interventions and also raise less evaluation anxiety for service providers.

If a single group, pre-post design is used, then the change scores can become the dependent variable in a multiple regression equation and client characteristics become the independent variables (e.g., severity of abuse, alcoholism, criminal record). Frequently, however, multiple regression is not suitable because there are too many independent variables to make a stable equation or provide adequate statistical power (see Cohen & Cohen, 1975, regarding power analysis).

Therefore the t-test can be used with the change score as the dependent variable and client characteristics as independent variables. Better yet, to reduce the unreliability of two measurements (pre- & post-), analysis of covariance is suggested rather than the t-test, with the pretest as the covariate.

A simpler procedure is to dichotomize the sample using a median split of the change scores or a predetermined criteria of success. The chi-square statistic, t-test, or a discriminant analysis can be used to analyze the data. Discriminant analysis, like multiple regression analysis, however, is often not suited for small samples or when independent variables are highly correlated.

Who drops out? There are a number of reasons to study the characteristics of those who drop out of treatment. First, when we speak about treatment effects, we will know to which types of clients we can generalize. Second, if the drop-out rate is high, then characteristics associated with high motivation rather than treatment may be the primary cause of change. Third, making statistical predictions of those who are likely to drop out will help in devising pretreatment motivational programs.

There are various points at which attrition can occur and these need to be defined and analyzed separately. For example, service may be requested but there is no client follow-through; some or all of the assessment may be completed with no treatment; and some but not all of the treatment may be completed. Those who complete follow-up evaluations comprise yet another group. The evaluation report also needs to indicate the type of contract made with clients, for example, was there a contract to drop clients from treatment if they missed a set number of sessions? (for discussion see Eufemia, Colvin, Seaman, & Wesolowski, 1984).

Measurement Issues

Violence: What to measure? One of the most important tests of treatment effectiveness is the impact it has on violent behavior. A number of ethical issues are involved in measuring violence, securing confidentiality being a major one. Records must be kept on criminal behavior with names attached and these records may be subpoenaed into court if privileged communication or special federal research provisions are not available. Obtaining information about violence has not been as emotionally upsetting to respondents as many researchers anticipated. Individual rather than conjoint interviews should be able to keep the procedure at the "minimal risk" required for ethical research (Back, 1984).

The simplest measure is to find out the percentage of men who are violent at some point in time after treatment. A much better procedure is to gather baseline and follow-up data on the severity and frequency of violence. With a baseline comparison, one can tell if the treatment is "on the right track" because decreases in the levels of violence will be known. Therefore a post hoc baseline or actual baseline reporting will detect changes in frequency; similarly, a scale of severity will detect changes on that dimension. Many treatment programs are using modifications of Straus's (1979) Conflict Tactics Scales, a measure of frequency and severity of verbal and physical aggression in marriage. One of its advantages is the progression it makes from positive behavior to aggressive behavior of increasing severity. The version used at our counseling program has added several items (e.g., "driving reckless in order to frighten"; "physically force sex"). We try to obtain rates of psychological and physical abuse for each year for the previous two years of the relationship.

Clinicians and researchers are becoming increasingly aware of the need to measure psychological abuse in addition to physical abuse. Several studies indicate that the majority of men can stop their physical abuse but there seems to be little progress made in stopping psychological abuse (e.g., Edleson & Grusznski, in press; Dutton, 1986). Fortunately, researchers are responding by developing measures of psychological abuse (e.g., O'Leary & Curley, 1986; Tolman, in press).

Violence: Who should report? Ideally, reports of violence should be obtained in separate assessment interviews with both partners. Reports from the victim, however, should be relied on more heavily because the offender is more likely to underreport the severity of violence (e.g., Browning & Dutton, 1986; Szinovacz, 1983), especially at the point of intake. There is evidence that the couple's reports become more congruent after treatment (Edleson & Brygger, 1986).

While the victim is generally seen as having fewer motives for distorting her reports of violence, evaluators need to be aware of possible underreporting from her fear of retaliation or blocking of unpleasant memories; or overreporting from the overestimation of the frequency of painful events. A confounding factor from the standpoint of evaluation is that more accurate recall may occur after a period of treatment (see Berliner & Conte, 1984).

One advantage of having reports from both partners is that signs of underreporting from the man can be used by practitioners to indicate low motivation or high levels of denial. Normally, pretreatment reports of violence from one partner are not shared with the other. This confidentiality probably improves the validity of reports and protects the partner from retaliation.

One dilemma for programs is whether to share reports of the violence among staff during and after treatment. If reports are shared (from the victim, to her counselor, to the offender's counselor, to the offender), there are two problems: There is the ethical problem that the sharing may trigger violence, and the methodological problem that both offender and victim will minimize the extent of abuse. On the other hand, if reports are not shared, the man cannot be confronted with his continuing abuse. A middle position is that only the counselor working with each partner, and not the man, know about the woman's reports.

One study relied on estimates of recidivism made by program directors (Pirog-Good & Stets, 1986). The authors make conclusions about treatment effectiveness that are unwarranted because of the bias that is likely to occur when directors rate the success of their programs. The authors also made the mistake of combining data from a large number of diverse programs and performing data analysis with too many variables (for a critique, see Saunders, in press).

The following section suggests measures that are possible substitutes for the measure of violence. Some variables are correlates of violence but the specific measures need further validation as predictors of wife abuse.

Physiological anger arousal. High levels of anger arousal are often associated with aggressive behavior (Novaco, 1978). Anger arousal can be measured with blood pressure readings following a stress role-play. Novaco (1976) found that blood pressure readings correlated more highly with self-reported anger arousal than galvanic skin resistance readings and were not correlated with social desirability response bias. The average of readings after several different role-plays would of course give more reliable results than a single role-play. Measurement can be made before and after treatment and at follow-up.

Behavioral role-play tests. As with physiological measures, role-play measures are difficult to fake, especially if one is trying to assess the presence of behaviors like assertiveness that are substitutes for aggressiveness. No role-play tests have yet been developed for assessing treatments for men who batter but several are available from other treatment applications (e.g., Haynes & Wilson, 1979). Both standard situations and those unique to the man could be used. Standard situations allow comparisons between subjects and unique situations add relevancy.

A trained partner surrogate can play the part of the wife. The role-play of a neutral or pleasant situation at the end of the sessions helps to diffuse the anger. Having the actual partner role-play the situation adds to its realism but ethically is more questionable because of the risks of violence.

There is the possibility that the couple will leave in an angry mood and that violence will ensue (see Kaslow & Gurman, 1985).

Self-reports of correlates of violence. Recent studies are uncovering correlates of abuse that have implications for treatment programs (for a recent comprehensive review of these studies see Hotaling & Sugarman, 1986). The studies point to a number of characteristics of men who batter, including nonassertiveness, exposure to violence in the family of origin, and norms supportive of violence. Many of these correlates can be assessed with self-report measures. A major advantage of self-report measures is their ease of administration. Very little staff time is involved. Computerized scoring and interpretation are now available for a variety of measures and some agencies are also using computerized intake interview procedures.

A major disadvantage of self-report measures is their susceptibility to response bias. On attitude scales, some respondents may fake their responses in a direction that would gain social approval. On measures of psychological health, respondents may try to appear healthier or sicker than they actually are.

Some measures, the Millon Clinical Multiaxial Inventory, for example, have built-in validity scales. Other measures, such as the Marlowe-Crowne Social Desirability Scale (Crowne & Marlowe, 1964) can be added to a collection of instruments and titled the "Personal Reaction Inventory" to disguise its purpose.

One way to treat response bias is to exclude from analysis those cases that score the highest on response bias. A more sophisticated method that makes use of all of the cases, is to adjust scores to remove the bias prior to analysis (for example, see Saunders & Hanusa, 1986). First, simple regression is used in order to find the unstandardized regression coefficient in predicting the unadjusted score from the Marlowe-Crowne Scale. Second, to find the adjusted score, the unstandardized regression coefficient (the correction factor) is multiplied by each person's Marlow-Crowne score and subtracted from his or her unadjusted score on the variable needing adjustment.

There are a number of behavioral, attitude, and personality measures that measure correlates of wife abuse and that can be used as pre-post measures of treatment. Among the several assertiveness measures available, the Interpersonal Behavior Survey (Mauger, Adkinson, & Simpson, 1979) is probably most appropriate because it has several subscales of aggressiveness in addition to assertiveness.

Measures of couple's conflict resolution and decision power (e.g., Blood & Wolfe, 1960) need to be checked for their sensitivity to measuring change during the period of treatment. Neidig (1986) found positive changes on the Dyadic Adjustment Scale (Spanier, 1976) for men who completed cognitive-behavioral couples counseling. Similarly, Myers (1983) found positive changes on the Marital Satisfaction Scale (Snyder, 1979) in a treatment package that combined psychotherapy and skills training. She also used the Child Abuse Potential Inventory (Milner, 1980), child abuse being a strong risk factor for men who batter (Hotaling & Sugarman, 1986).

Attitude measures may cover attitudes about violence, sex roles and other issues. General measures of the justifiability of violence are available (Blumenthal, Kahn, Andrews, & Head, 1972), as well as scales specific to woman abuse (Saunders, Lynch, Grayson, & Linz, 1987). Scales that include a variety of abuse consequences and a variety of situations are likely to obtain a larger variance in responses (Saunders, 1980), than those using a single, mild form of violence (Straus, Gelles, & Steinmetz, 1980). A commonly used measure of attitudes about sex roles is the Attitudes About Women Scale (Spence & Helmreich, 1978). A more subtle, less cognitive measure is the Male Threat From Competence Scale (Pleck, 1976). It is a sentence completion task with stems such as the following: "When Ellen began to do the job, Chuck. . . ." Responses are scored as positive, neutral, or threatened.

A large variety of personality measures can be used as outcome measures, providing they are sensitive to change resulting from therapy. Among the more commonly used for this population are the Millon Clinical Multiaxial Inventory (Millon, 1980) and the Minnesota Multiphasic Personality Inventory. However, not surprisingly there is evidence that such measures are not sensitive to change from short-term treatment (Hamberger & Hastings, 1988). Measures of internal-external locus of control (e.g., Nowicki & Stricklund, 1973), jealousy (e.g., White, 1976), and self-esteem are being used fairly often and show more sensitivity to change than the personality measures (e.g., Neidig, 1986; Saunders & Hanusa, 1986).

Client feedback. The most subjective forms of evaluation are ratings of client satisfaction and helpfulness. In our program, these ratings are made after weekly group sessions. These ratings may not be related to changes in behavior, attitude, and personality but they provide indicators of the attractiveness of the methods and of the group. If several treatment methods are used, each at a distinct phase over the course of a group, the ratings for each method can be averaged and compared with each other.

Summary

This chapter describes some of the ethical and practical dilemmas encountered when conducting treatment outcome research on programs for men who batter. Often an ideal design, such as random assignment to a no-treatment control group, is not ethically or practically feasible. Compromises with an ideal design or an ideal measure can be made. However, the pros and cons of these compromises need to be carefully considered. Multiple designs and multiple measures will be needed to make conclusions about the effects of the various treatment formats, methods, settings, and client types. It is only through such carefully conducted research that effective solutions for ending woman abuse will be found.

References

Back, S. M. (1984). *Ethical issues in family violence research.* Paper presented at the Second National Conference for Family Violence Researchers, University of New Hampshire.

Berliner, L., & Conte, J. (1984). *Practice and research integration: An ongoing tension.* Paper presented at the Second National Conference for Family Violence Researchers, University of New Hampshire.

Blood, R. O., & Wolfe, D. M. (1960). *Husbands and wives.* Glencoe, IL: Free Press.

Blumenthal, M. D., Kahn, R. L., Andrews, F. M., & Head, K. B. (1972). *Justifying violence: Attitudes of American men.* Ann Arbor: University of Michigan Press.

Brisson, N. (1981). Battering husbands. *Victimology, 6*(1-4), pp. 338-344.

Browning, J., & Dutton, D. (1986). Assessment of wife assault with the Conflict Tactics Scale: Using couple data to quantify the differential reporting effect. *Journal of Marriage and the Family, 48,* 375-379.

Cohen, J., & Cohen, P. (1975). *Applied multiple regression/correlation for the behavioral sciences.* Hillsdale, NJ: Lawrence Erlbaum.

Crowne, D. P., & Marlowe, D. (1964). *The approval motive: Studies in evaluative dependence.* New York: John Wiley.

Dutton, D. (1986). The outcome of court-mandated treatment for wife assault: A quasi-experimental evaluation. *Violence and Victims, 1*(3), 163-176.

Edleson, J. L., Miller, D. M., Stone, G. W., & Chapman, D. G. (1985). Group treatment for men who batter: A multiple-baseline evaluation. *Social Work Research and Abstracts, 21*(3), 18-21.

Edleson, J. L., & Brygger, M. P. (1986). Gender differences in reporting of battering incidences. *Family Relations, 35,* 377-382.

Edleson, Jeffrey L., & Grusznski, R. J. (in press). Treating men who batter: Four years of outcome data from the Domestic Abuse Project. *Journal of Social Service Research.*

Eufemia, R. L., Colvin, R. H., Seaman, J. E., & Wesolowski, M. D. (1984). Some modest guidelines for reporting attrition from treatment in weight reduction programs. *Behavior Therapist, 7*(2), 27-28.

Gurman, A. S. (1979). Family therapy research in community clinics. *American Journal of Family Therapy, 7*(2), 9-11.

Hamberger, L. K., & Hastings, J. H. (1988). Skills training for treatment of spouse abuse: An outcome study. *Journal of Family Violence, 3*(2), 121-130.

Hart, B. J. (1987). *Ethical principles for woman abuse research.* Paper presented at the Third National Conference for Family Violence Researchers, University of New Hampshire.

Haynes, S. N., & Wilson, C. C. (1979). *Behavioral assessment.* San Francisco: Jossey-Bass.

Hotaling, G. T., & Sugarman, D. B. (1986). An analysis of risk markers in husband to wife violence: The current state of knowledge. *Violence and Victims, 1*(2), 101-124.

Houtler, B. D., & Rosenberg, H. (1985). The retrospective baseline in single case experiments. *Behavior Therapist, 8*(5), 97-99.

Kaslow, N. J., & Gurman, A. S. (1985). Ethical considerations in family therapy research. *Counseling and Values, 30,* 47-61.

Mauger, P. A., Adkinson, D. R., & Simpson, D. G. (1979). *The Interpersonal Behavior Survey Manual.* Los Angeles: Western Psychological Services.

Milner, J. S. (1980). *The Child Abuse Potential Inventory Manual.* Webster, NC: Psytec Corp.

Millon, T. (1980). *Millon Clinical Multiaxial Inventory.* Minneapolis: Interpretive Scoring Systems.

Myers, C. (1983). *Some preliminary data on a treatment program for spouse abuse.* Paper presented at the Second National Conference for Family Violence Researchers, University of New Hampshire.

Neidig, P. H. (1986). The development and evaluation of a spouse abuse treatment program in a military setting. *Evaluation and Program Planning, 9,* 275-280.

Novaco, R. W. (1976). *Anger control: The development and evaluation of an experimental treatment.* Lexington, MA: Lexington Books.

Novaco, R. W. (1978). Anger and coping with stress: Cognitive behavioral interventions. In J. P. Foreyt & D. P. Rathjen (Eds.), *Cognitive behavior therapy: Research and applications.* New York: Plenum.

Nowicki, S., & Strickland, B. R. (1973). A locus of control scale for children. *Journal of Consulting and Clinical Psychology, 40,* 148-154.

O'Leary, K. D., & Borkovec, T. D. (1978). Conceptual, methodological, and ethical problems of placebo groups in psychotherapy research. *American Psychologist, 33,* 821-830.

O'Leary, K. D., & Curley, A. D. (1986). Assertion and family violence: Correlates of spouse abuse. *Journal of Marital and Family Therapy, 12*(3), 284-289.

Pirog-Good, M. A., & Stets, J. (1986). Recidivism in programs for abusers. *Victimology: An International Journal.*

Pleck, J. H. (1976). Male threat from female competence. *Journal of Consulting and Clinical Psychology, 44*(4), 608-613.

Saunders, D. G. (1980). *The police response to battered women: Predictors of officers' use of arrest, counseling, and minimal action.* (Doctoral dissertation, University of Wisconsin-Madison, 1979). *Dissertation Abstracts International, 40,* 6446A. (University Microfilms No. 80-08, 840)

Saunders, D. G., & Hanusa, D. R. (1986). Cognitive-behavioral treatment of men who batter: The short-term effects of group therapy. *Journal of Family Violence, 1*(4), 357-372.

Saunders, D. G., Lynch, A. E., Grayson, M., & Linz, D. (1987). The inventory of beliefs about wife beating. *Violence and Victims, 2*(1), 39-57.

Saunders, D. G. (in press). What do we know about abuser recidivism? A critique of "Recidivism in Programs for Abusers." *Victimology: An International Journal.*

Snyder, D. K. (1979). Multidimensional assessment of marital satisfaction. *Journal of Marriage and the Family, 41*(4), 813-822.

Spanier, G. B. (1976). Measuring dyadic adjustment: New scales for assessing the quality of marriage and similar dyads. *Journal of Marriage and the Family, 38,* 15-28.

Spence, J. T., & Helmreich, R. L. (1978). *Masculinity and femininity: Their psychological dimensions, correlates and antecedents.* Austin: University of Texas Press.

Straus, M. A. (1979). Measuring intrafamily conflict and violence: The Conflict Tactics (CT) Scales. *Journal of Marriage and the Family, 41*(1), 75-88.

Straus, M. A., Gelles, R. J., & Steinmetz, S. K. (1980). *Behind closed doors: Violence in the American family.* Garden City, NY: Anchor/Doubleday.

Szinovacz, M. E. (1983). Using couple data as a methodological tool: The case of marital violence. *Journal of Marriage and the Family, 45,* 633-644.

Tolman, R. M. (in press). The development and validation of a non-physical abuse scale. *Violence and Victims.*

Wexler, D. B. (1976). *Criminal commitments and dangerous mental patients.* (DHEW) Washington, DC: Government Printing Office.

White, G. L. (1976). *The social psychology of romantic jealousy.* (University Microfilms International, No. 77-7700.) *Dissertation Abstracts International, 37*(10), 5449-B. (Doctoral Dissertation, University of California, Los Angeles).

PART IV

The Response of the Criminal Justice System

10

An Empirical Analysis of Police Responses to Incidents of Wife Battery

Richard A. Berk
Sarah Fenstermaker
Phyllis J. Newton

Most of the literature describing police responses to incidents of wife battery is rather critical of police practice. In particular, there is a widespread view that police officers are, for a variety of reasons, reluctant to arrest batterers (Field & Field, 1973; Martin, 1976; Woods, 1978; Dobash & Dobash, 1979; Patterson, 1979). Yet, the criticism of police work is seldom based on strong multivariate analyses in which wife battery incidents are compared to other kinds of person crimes, or the behavior of police is subjected to rigorous empirical scrutiny.

On the other hand, there are two recent studies of police responses to wife battery incidents that explicitly make police behavior an empirical question (Berk & Loseke, 1981; Worden & Pollitz, 1984). These studies build on the perspective that police work involves gaining control over environments that are sometimes ambiguous, unpredictable, and dangerous (Wilson, 1968; Bittner, 1967a, 1967b, 1970, 1974), and conclude that the key to understanding police responses to wife battery lies in the features of the immediate circumstances that police face. An arrest, therefore, is but one means of "handling the situation."[1]

From this situated perspective, criticisms of police practice can take at least three forms, each involving normative judgments concerning the

AUTHORS' NOTE: This research was supported by a grant from the Center for the Study of Violence and Antisocial Behavior, NIMH (Grant No. 2 RO1 MH34616-04). We are also indebted to Elizabeth Kirton, Martha Fredrick, Jannalee Smithey, and Gayle Gubman for their help in data collection.

relevance of different influences on police actions. To begin, one can argue that in "handling the situation," police officers are sometimes influenced by factors that should be irrelevant to police work. For example, Berk and Loseke find that police are less likely to make an arrest if it is the victim who calls the police. They speculate that when the victim calls, the incident has not come to the attention of neighbors and other outsiders and, consequently, it is seen as less serious by the police. That is, the problem involves the immediate parties to the dispute and not a larger set of concerned citizens. On a normative basis, one might decide that such considerations should not affect how police respond to wife battery incidents.

Second, it can be argued, there are factors influencing police that, on a normative basis, should be irrelevant, and as a practical matter, when they are not irrelevant, they are counterproductive. For example, in one of their models, Worden and Pollitz find that police are less likely to make an arrest if the offender and victim are married. This, in turn, may encourage future violence by communicating that husbands are within their rights (and the law) when they assault their wives.

Finally, not only may there be factors influencing police that should be irrelevant, but the fact that they are relevant to the police raises fundamental questions of "equal protection." Thus had either of the two studies found that police were less likely to arrest white offenders, there would have been evidence of racial discrimination. Few would dispute that such influences should have no role in police work.

Taking the statistically significant findings in *both* the Berk-Loseke and Worden-Pollitz studies, police decisions in wife battery incidents are dominated by what seem to be relevant and appropriate variables: whether the victim initiates a citizen's arrest, whether the victim alleges that violence has occurred, and whether the offender had been drinking. However, when each study is considered separately, there is some evidence that less desirable influences may also be at work. That is, both studies hinted that extralegal factors mattered, but different factors surfaced in the two studies. This lack of correspondence between the studies makes any findings for extralegal variables unconvincing.

With these and other shortcomings in mind, this chapter will enlarge on prior studies and examine what police do in response to wife battery incidents. However, whereas the Berk-Loseke and Worden-Pollitz studies focused solely on the decision to arrest, we will consider three options available to police: arresting the offender, ordering the offender from the premises, and a mix of other actions including warnings and dispute mediation. If one is concerned with how police handle wife battery situations, our analysis should better reflect the range of actions police can take.

In addition, the Berk-Loseke data come from police records, which in principle are the most germane; in that analysis it is the decisions of police that is of interest. Nevertheless, one should always remain a bit skeptical of the veracity of police reports. The Worden-Pollitz data come from field notes taken by observers. Such data are often extremely rich, but it is difficult to know what is overlooked and whether what observers record is necessarily relevant to (or even known by) the actors at the scene. One should also be uneasy unless observer data are checked for reliability. Our data come from interviews with female battery victims assaulted by husbands or lovers, and these data certainly have their own flaws. Still, using a different data source we hope to replicate the findings of the two earlier studies as well as examine the role of influences that the police may have failed to record or that observers may have overlooked. In this way, we hope to confirm and extend the earlier research.

Finally, both Berk and Loseke, and Worden and Pollitz, failed to consider the impact of sample selection bias (Heckman, 1979; Berk, 1983), which could result from working with only those incidents in which the police were involved. As a result, both external *and* internal validity are threatened. In this chapter, we attempt to correct for the sample selection bias stemming from the process by which the police are summoned to some incidents and not others. Thus by controlling for one important source of sample selection bias we hope to reduce internal and external validity of problems.

Data, Model Specification and Statistical Issues

Our data come from face-to-face interviews with 237 female victims of wife battery, recruited in Santa Barbara County, California, from local shelters, a victim/witness assistance program in the county district attorney's office, or recruited from some other public agency. This is hardly an ideal sample. It is not drawn by probability procedures from any known population, but reflects the practical and economic constraints associated with the collection of interview data on *serious* wife battery incidents. The data may also be colored by particular features of the local law enforcement scene.

While our sample is not random, it still reflects a diverse set of individuals and households, consistent with the spousal violence literature (Walker, 1979; Straus, Gelles, & Steinmetz, 1980). Details can be found elsewhere (Berk, Berk, & Newton, 1984), but for example, about half the offenders are white, nearly 15% have a college degree, and over 10% are found in professional or technical occupations. Even in our sample of rather serious incidents, wife battery knows no racial or class bounds.

In short, our data provide the opportunity to undertake falsification tests with a heterogeneous sample. Thus we are in a reasonable position to evaluate previous research findings. An important caveat, however, is the need to adjust for sample selection bias. Recall, that nonprobability samples can introduce internal validity biases into one's results *even if one is prepared to interpret these results conditional upon the data set on hand.*

There is little we can do about the winnowing process from all households to those in which women are battered by their husbands or lovers. The Berk-Loseke and Worden-Pollitz studies are similarly vulnerable. However, we can respond to the winnowing process by which only some battery incidents come to the attention of the police. In brief, we can apply the two-step procedures developed by Heckman (1979) to get at least a rough fix on the bias.[2] In the first step, we model within a probit formulation the process by which police are summoned. In the second step, we construct the hazard function from this model and insert it as a control variable in any multivariate analyses with the subset of incidents in which the police become involved. Consistent parameter estimates should follow.

The first step results are discussed at length elsewhere (Berk et al., 1984). Suffice it to say that a number of factors affect whether the police are called as well as who calls them (e.g., the victim or a bystander). For example, while bystanders are more inclined to call the police when the victim is injured, they are, other things being equal, less inclined to call the police if the victim and offender are married. More important for our purposes, we were able to construct a hazard function that was unlikely to be highly collinear when used in the second step.

With the sampling issues behind us, the next concern is how best to formulate the endogenous variable. Recall that we are focusing on three outcomes: whether the offender is arrested, whether the offender is ordered from the premises, and whether the offender and/or victim experience some other form of intervention such as a warning. If one treats these actions as nominal, a multinomia logit approach naturally follows (Maddala, 1983, pp. 34-37). However, if one views the outcomes in terms of punitiveness, the outcomes can be ranked. An arrest is the most punitive. An ordered separation is the next most punitive. And warnings, advice, or mediation are the least punitive. From this perspective, the multinomial logit framework becomes an ordinal logit framework and, in the process, more information is brought to bear on the estimation procedures (Maddala, 1983, pp. 46-49). That is, the ordinality is taken into account. In short, we employ ordinal logit estimation procedures.

Finally, we turn to specification issues. By and large, we will attempt to replicate Berk and Loseke and Worden and Pollitz, in terms of their substantive models, insofar as we have the data. Thus we will include two categories of causal (predetermined) variables: variables characterizing the immediate features of the situation police have been summoned to handle and variables characterizing the actors and setting more generally. The former will be formulated as interaction effects with whether both the victim and offender are present when the police arrive. Unless both parties are present, the situation has in an important sense already been resolved; the violence has ended, at least for the time being. For example, one such interaction variable will be whether both parties are present and the offender has been drinking. On the other hand, variables describing actor or setting characteristics will be formulated as main effects. For example, we will consider the role of race, and whether the victim and offender are married.

Results

Our endogenous variable takes on three ordinal levels with 44% of the offenders arrested, 7% of the offenders ordered from the premises, and 49% of the offenders receiving a mix of less punitive interventions. We should stress, however, that only the perceptions of the victim are reflected, and it is conceivable that some forced separations were confused with arrests and the reverse. Likewise, it is not clear than when a respondent claimed that she signed a citizen's arrest, she actually did. In any case, it seems that among serious wife battery incidents coming to public attention in Santa Barbara County, separation is the least used police response of the three we have considered. Perhaps more interesting, arrests are made in only about half the incidents despite the fact that according to interview data from the victim, injuries were the result in 80% of the cases. Unfortunately, we cannot determine how these figures compare to *other* kinds of battery.

Table 10.1 shows the results for the ordinal logistic analysis.[3] Each coefficient can be interpreted as the change in the log of the odds of moving up one step in the ordinal scale (any step) for a unit change in the regressor. It is also possible to transform these coefficients into a more convenient form reflecting the change in the *probability* of moving up one step in the ordinal scale for a unit change in the regressor (Maddala, 1983, pp. 23). However, since that change in the probability depends on where the marginal effect (i.e. slope) is evaluated, there is no single translation. We will evaluate the slope at the 50-50 tipping point, where the result is most similar to coefficients produced by the more common linear probability model.

TABLE 10.1
Ordinal Logit Results For Police Actions
(N = 84)

Variable	Mean	Coefficient	Chi-Square	*P*
Intercept 1	—	0.38	0.19	.66
Intercept 2	—	–0.06	0.01	.94
Hazard rate	.61	–1.22	1.80	.09
Citizen arrest	.32	2.66	13.73	.0001
Offender does damage X both present	.31	–0.23	0.12	.36
Any injuries X both present	.60	0.79	1.96	.08
Offender drinking X both present	.38	1.17	3.80	.03
Mixed marriage X both present	.15	–1.35	3.06	.04
Victim called the police	.44	–0.56	0.99	.16
Couple married	.52	–0.64	1.40	.12

NOTE: model chi-square = 38.12; p = .0001; df = 8; fraction of concordant pairs = .83; rank correlation = .67.

The significance tests reported in Table 10.1 also need a bit of explanation. Since we are building on two earlier studies, all of our tests for the logit coefficients (but not the intercepts) will be one-tailed using the .10 level of statistical significance. In other words, we decided to be a little more tolerant of Type I errors.

Turning to the results, it is clear from the information provided at the bottom of the table that the model fits the data reasonably well. The chi-square for the model as a whole is statistically significant, the rank correlation between the predicted probabilities and the observed response is .67 (roughly comparable to a multiple correlation coefficient), and over 82% of all pairs of responses are concordant with their predicted probabilities.[4]

Perhaps more important, our findings are at least consistent with the two earlier studies. We too find that when the victim signs a citizen's arrest, police are very likely to be more punitive. Indeed, the probability is increased by nearly 67% (p = .0001). Given California state law, this is perhaps not surprising; it would have been quite disconcerting had no such effects appeared. On the other hand, one must keep in mind that our data come solely from victims who cannot be assumed to be seeing the situation in the same manner as police officers or trained observers.

We also find that police will be more punitive if the offender has been drinking and both parties are present when the police arrive. Presumably, intoxicated offenders are viewed by police as needing somewhat more coercion.

Unfortunately, we cannot distinguish between allegations of injuries and actual injuries, and so cannot literally replicate the earlier studies. However, we find that when victims told our interviewers that someone (almost always the victim) was injured in the incident, police are nearly 20% more likely to be more punitive ($p = .08$). This is at least consistent with the earlier findings on victims' allegations.

Finally, the Berk-Loseke and Worden-Pollitz studies found no effect for property damage when both parties were present. We also cannot reject the null hypothesis of no effect. In short, we replicate the general finding that many immediate features of the situation affect police actions, and that at least some of these seem consonant with expected police practice.

Other effects reported in Table 10.1 are a bit more difficult to fit into the previous work. In contrast to the Berk-Loseke and Worden-Pollitz efforts, we find clear evidence of racial effects. When the victim and offender are of different ethnic backgrounds (primarily white and Hispanic), the police are 68% *less* likely to take a punitive stance ($p = .04$). Since the majority of these relationships involve Hispanic males and Caucasian females, some police may believe that the victim is getting what she deserves.[5]

The finding for mixed marriages seemed so at variance with Berk and Loseke, and Worden and Pollitz that we tried introducing several control variables into the equation. When the ethnicity of the offender was *added*, the impact of mixed marriages remained and no new effects emerged. The same pattern followed when instead of the offender's ethnicity, the victim's ethnicity was added. When the variable for mixed marriages was *replaced* by the offender's ethnicity, white males were *more* likely to face punitive police action. Since this seemed less plausible than the mixed-marriage effect (and can be explained by the relationship between the offender's ethnicity and the victim's ethnicity), we stayed with the specification reported in Table 10.1.

Like Worden and Pollitz, and unlike Berk and Loseke, we do *not* find a statistically significant effect for whether or not it was the victim who called the police. However, the sign is in the proper direction, the logit coefficient is nontrivial, and the p-value for the chi-square is "close." In Santa Barbara County, at least, we are inclined to reject the null hypothesis, especially given Berk and Loseke's findings. One must keep in mind that our sample is modest and we are a bit short on statistical power.

Like Berk and Loseke, and unlike Worden and Pollitz, we find no effect for whether the victim and offender are married (nor for whether they live together). However, consistent with Worden and Pollitz, the sign is negative: Police are less likely to be punitive if the couple is married. And much as for the variable "who called," the p-value is "close." Keeping in mind the constraints noted immediately above, we are inclined to reject the null hypothesis. Finally, we find evidence of sample selection bias, presumably corrected by the inclusion of the hazard rate.[6] The negative coefficient ($p = .09$) indicates that cases more likely to be excluded from the sample of 85 are less likely to be treated punitively. This makes sense because it is just these cases that are less likely to be seen as police business by victims or bystanders. For example, such cases are often less serious.

In summary, by and large we manage to replicate Berk and Loseke and Worden and Pollitz when we find that several immediate features of the wife battery situation sensibly and appropriately affect what actions police take: whether the victim seeks a citizens arrest, whether when both parties are present the offender has been drinking, and whether when both parties are present, the victim alleges injuries. In addition, there is in our results some evidence that inappropriate factors influence the actions taken by police officers in wife battery incidents: whether the victim and offender have different racial backgrounds, whether it is the victim who calls, and whether the couple is married. It cannot be overemphasized, however, that in no instance is the case for these effects overwhelming.

Conclusions

Stepping back from the details, five conclusions can be drawn. First, we have shown how ordinal endogenous variables may be properly analyzed. Ordinal endogenous variables are endemic in studies using survey data, and there is no longer any reason why one should risk biased estimates through the application of ordinary least squares. Second, we have shown how one can correct for sample selection bias when one has a nonprobability sample of police-citizen encounters. One risks a distorted set of findings unless such corrections are made (Heckman, 1979; Berk, 1983).

Third, we are encouraged by the fact that much the same story surfaces whether the data come from police officers, trained observers or wife battery victims. The results of all three studies are enhanced because the overall story does not seem to be data dependent.

Fourth, despite a modest sample and data only from victim interviews, we have replicated the findings of both Berk and Loseke and Worden and Pollitz. In a general sense, we find that the immediate features of the wife battery situations are vital in determining how police respond. In addition, the central factors surfacing in these earlier studies surface in our analysis.

Finally, there is a suggestion in our results that irrelevant or inappropriate features of the situation also influence police actions. This is *not* to say that wife battery incidents are unique in the role that such factors play. Indeed, it is likely that all sorts of questionable features affect police responses to situations needing "handling." However, it may well be that at least some of the *particular* and questionable features important in wife battery incidents are distinctive. It is hard to imagine, for example, other kinds of encounters between police officers and citizens in which the (shared) marital status of the victim and offender matter.

On the other hand, there is good reason to suspect that police respond differently in a variety of situations—depending on whether the victim and offender have the same ethnic background. Likewise, it may often make a difference whose call brings police to the scene. In short, it is virtually certain that questionable factors influence police actions in a wide variety of settings. That comes with the territory; as long as the police officer's task is to take control and bring order, extralegal situational features will always be important. The important issues are, therefore, which of these influences should be singled out for special concern and remediation and which are distinctive to wife battery incidents.

Notes

1. The Worden and Pollitz paper is an explicit effort to first replicate and then expand the earlier work of Berk and Loseke. In other words, while for our purposes the two papers are put on equal footing, the basic conceptualization and initial findings appear in Berk and Loseke.

2. The approach is only an approximation because we are violating one of the underlying assumptions of Heckman's formulation. He assumes, among other things, that all disturbance terms in any equations estimated behave as if drawn from a multivariate normal distribution. This will not be true for the procedures we will be using. However, while we do not assume normality, we will be assuming that the disturbances behave as if drawn from the logistic density, which is very close to the normal. We suspect, therefore, that no serious distortions are produced. Similarly, we are not correcting for heteroskedastic disturbances associated with the Heckman approach (because we see no ready way to do that within the techniques we will be applying). But what experience exists (Berk, 1983; Marini, 1984) indicates that no serious problems will result.

3. Basically, what the procedure does is estimate a binary logit equation for each step in the ordinal scale. However, all of the logit coefficients (but not the intercepts) are constrained to be the same for each equation (Maddala, 1983, pp. 46-49). Hence, one can interpret the logit coefficients just as one does in the binary case as long as one understands that they apply to the log-odds of moving to the next level in the ordinal scale, *whatever the level happens to be*. One happy consequence is greater statistical efficiency than could be obtained if the set of binary

logistic equations were estimated one at a time. And that efficiency is vital here, given the modest sample size.

4. Imagine an ordinal variable and an outcome for person A and an outcome for person B. Assume that A's outcome ranks higher than B's. The pair is concordant if the predicted value from the ordinal logistic regression also ranks A higher than B. The fraction of concordant pairs is calculated by dividing the total number of concordant pairs by the sum of concordant and discordant pairs (throwing out ties). In this process, each outcome is compared (and ranked) to all other outcomes.

5. Note that the mixed-marriage variable is formulated as an interaction effect with "both present." We used the interaction form because it was not clear how the police would know the ethnic backgrounds of the victim and offender unless both were present when they arrived.

6. Recall, that we are not meeting all the assumptions that these corrections require. However, we are probably not being led seriously astray.

References

Berk, R. A. (1983). An introduction to sample selection bias in sociological data. *American Sociological Review, 48,* 386.

Berk, S. F., & Loseke, D. R. (1981). Handling family violence: Situational determinants of police arrest in domestic disturbances. *Law and Society Review, 15,* 317.

Berk, R. A., Berk, S. F., & Newton, P. J. (1984). Cops on call: Summoning the police to incidents of spousal violence. *Law and Society Review, 18,* 479.

Bittner, E. (1967a). The police on skid row: A study of peace keeping. *American Sociological Review, 32,* 193.

Bittner, E. (1967b). Police discretion in emergency apprehension of mentally ill persons. *Social Problems, 14,* 699.

Bittner, E. (1970). *The functions of police in modern society.* Maryland: National Institutes of Mental Health.

Bittner, E. (1974). Florence nightingale in pursuit of Willie Sutton: A theory of the police. In H. Jacob (Ed.), *The potential reform of criminal justice.* Beverly Hills, CA: Sage.

Dobash, R. E., & Dobash, R. (1979). *Violence against wives: A case against patriarchy.* New York: Free Press.

Field, M. H., & Field, H. F. (1973). Marital violence and the criminal process: Neither justice nor peace. *Social Service Review, 47,* 221.

Heckman, J. J. (1979). Sample selection bias as a specification error. *Econometrica, 45,* 153.

Maddala, G. S. (1983). *Limited-dependent and qualitative variables in econometrics.* Cambridge: Cambridge University Press.

Marini, M. M. (1984). *Women's educational attainment and the timing of entry into parenthood.* Department of Sociology, Vanderbilt University.

Martin, D. (1976). *Battered wives.* San Francisco: Glide.

Patterson, E. J. (1979). How the legal system responds to battered women. In D. M. Moore (Ed.), *Battered women.* Beverly Hills, CA: Sage.

Straus, M. A., Gelles, R. J., & Steinmetz, S. (1980). *Behind closed doors: Violence in the American family.* Garden City, NY: Anchor/Doubleday.

Walker, L. J. (1979). *The battered woman.* New York: Harper & Row.

Wilson, J. Q. (1968). *Varieties of police behavior: The management of law and order in eight communities.* Cambridge, MA: Harvard University Press.

Woods, L. (1978). Litigation on behalf of battered women. *Women's Rights Law Reporter, 5*, 1.

Worden, R. E., & Pollitz, A. A. (1984). Police arrests in domestic disturbances: A further look. *Law and Society Review, 18*, 105.

11

Explaining Variations in Police Response to Domestic Violence: A Case Study in Detroit and New England

Eve Buzawa

This chapter will seek to examine and contrast current police officer attitudes toward domestic violence in Detroit, Michigan, a major urban police department, and in nine small to medium size New England police departments.

This study has several goals. First, the study of police attitudes toward domestic violence remains a major issue for those concerned with domestic violence research. In the last 10 years, 47 states and the District of Columbia have enacted legislation designed to modify societal responses to the problem of domestic violence (Lerman & Livingston, 1983). Such legislation has markedly changed the underlying legal philosophy toward the problem of domestic violence.

Before the new legislation, few states separately dealt with the problems of the government's response to domestic violence. The new legislation changed this orientation and instead identified the problem of the neglect of government institutions to prevent or ameliorate domestic violence. Such changes have included increasing law enforcement's powers to arrest offending individuals. Unfortunately, it is difficult to determine what actual attitudinal or behavioral changes have occurred on the part of law enforcement officers in recent years. The outcome of intervention in this area is subject to the responding officer's discretion, the exercise of which may not be easily observable by traditional measures of output—arrests, for example. This study tentatively will report whether there appears to be any change in the previously reported, largely negative police attitudes toward domestic violence intervention.

Second, previous research has customarily studied domestic violence attitudes or practices in one or two large urban police departments and has generalized such findings to the "police" in general. It is the author's purpose to discover whether this is an appropriate model for predicting officer attitudes in the broad spectrum of the nation's numerous smaller police departments.

The study of such practices in smaller police departments is itself quite significant since there are thousands of police units in the United States, the vast majority of whom have less than 50 officers. Further, domestic violence victims in such locations are often even more dependent upon police assistance than are their more urban counterparts because fewer alternatives or supplementary support services are available. The different problems of these departments would therefore appear to intrinsically warrant serious attention.

Third, the author has identified four major frameworks or models in which research in police attitudes and behavior has been presented. The author will review the applicability of these models to future research in the area of domestic violence in light of the tentative results reported herein.

Past Literature

Research on the development of police conduct in general has pursued four broad models. First, certain research views police behavior as being primarily reflective of the normative values achieved during the process of occupational socialization or the norms of police behavior (Niederhoffer, 1967; Westley, 1970; Van Maanen, 1973, 1974, 1975; Skolnick, 1975). This approach focuses upon similarities of police attitudes and behavior, and often explicitly or implicitly generalizes such findings to the "police" in general. There is no emphasis on the existence or explanation of variance therein.

Most studies of police behavior in the area of the response to domestic violence have been of this type. One Police Foundation study on domestic violence in Kansas City and Detroit between 1971 and 1973 reported that the police were called to the location of a single previous domestic assault or homicide in 85% of the cases, and to the location of four or more incidents in 50% of the cases (Wilt & Bannon, 1977). Other studies have found that police intervention has tended to be limited to briefly separating the assailant from the abused party and sternly warning both that society doesn't tolerate "disturbances of the peace" (Parnas, 1967) or that "call screening" has resulted in far less effective police response (Bannon, 1975). Arrests were also reported as being an infrequent occurrence, estimated at between 3% (Langley & Levy, 1978) and 10% of the total reported cases of domestic violence (Roy, 1977).

The second type of police research consists of studies emphasizing and explaining differences in attitudes as a function of different police departments (between group variance). These studies typically find that organizational factors such as the professionalism of command officials or the existence of a departmental orientation toward service calls are most predictive of an individual officer's attitudes and performance. Research adopting this model focuses upon the causes of organizational differences, often specifying political variables (Manning, 1979; Swanson, 1978), community characteristics (Wilson, 1968; Mastrofski, 1981), methods of police organization (Sherman, Milton, & Kelly, 1973; Gay, Day, & Woodward, 1977) and administrative style (Wilson, 1968).

To the author's knowledge, little empirical research in the field of domestic violence has focused upon the extent of interdepartmental variance in the police response to domestic violence. This may be a particularly significant omission. Extremely great organizational variation has been found in the provision of service type functions (see especially Wilson, 1968) detailing characteristics of three departmental models: watchman, legalistic, and service. In addition, studies of differences in smaller police departments may be fruitful because past research typically has focused upon major urban departments and findings therefrom were implicitly generalized to smaller departments. This is not a valid assumption because smaller police organizational units have been found to vary dramatically from their larger counterparts and from each other in salient characteristics including responding to unpopular Supreme Court decisions, an area directly analogous to the response to legislative fiats in the area of domestic violence (Wasby, 1976).

In addition, research has also suggested that laws or court decisions have been inadequately communicated in many departments (Milner, 1970, Wasby, 1976). This is directly applicable to the police response to domestic violence. The author's previous research indicated that many officers were unfamiliar with the relatively new domestic violence legislation (Buzawa, 1982). Furthermore, many departments did not have policies concerning such legislation, or if there were policies, did not adequately communicate them to the officers. This factor had been found to account for a significant portion of the variance in responses (Buzawa, 1982).

Third, research has reviewed the extent and causation of within group variance in police units. These studies typically find significant attitudinal and behavioral differences among officers in the same department and seek to explain such differences by reference either to fixed demographic variables or to such changeable characteristics as the officer's training in the particular subject area and general educational level. Examples include age (Cohen & Chaiken, 1973); length of service (Friedrich, 1977; Forst, Lucianovich, & Cox, 1977); and sex of officer (Bloch & Anderson, 1974; Bayley & Mendelsohn, 1969; Chevigny, 1969; Lefkowitz, 1971).

Little empirical research has attempted to explain variance in the police response to domestic violence as a function of identifiable sociodemographic variables. Most studies either have been descriptive in nature or, if empirical, had too small a sample size to attempt such a detailed analysis, apart from largely anecdotal observations.

It is unclear whether such analysis will be found to explain significant variance. The author in previously conducted research on attitudes of officers in the Detroit Police Department (Buzawa, 1982) reported that relatively few significant differences appeared to be related to any identifiable officer characteristics.

Fourth, certain studies have found that the primary determinants of police behavior are the structural attributes of the police citizen encounter. For example, if the police enter the police-citizen encounter on their own initiative (proactively), they may perceive themselves as having somewhat less legitimacy than when called by the citizens (see especially Black, 1971) resulting in greater police-citizen antagonism (Reiss, 1971), and somewhat greater police harshness toward suspects (Friedrich, 1977; Reiss, 1971) and a higher likelihood of police arrests (Reiss, 1971). In addition, race of the citizen may effect the police encounter with suspects (Black & Reiss, 1976) and the degree of coercion applied to settling of social disputes (Black, 1976). Similarly, suspect demeanor and complainant characteristics have been held to be important in the decision to arrest (see studies cited in Sherman, 1980), and whether the police have actually witnessed the incident dramatically effects police behavior (Black, 1971).

This model has been used in several studies of police behavior in the context of domestic violence. Berk and Loseke (1981) found that the determinants of police response to domestic violence were primarily situational factors such as the source of the complaint and the presence of both parties. Similarly, Donald Black (1971) reported that social class, household status, age, and the relationship of disputants explained how the police responded to domestic disputes, although it should be noted he did not distinguish "violence" from "dispute" calls.

Closely related to other situational factors is the severity of the offense being handled by the officer. Some research has suggested that the legal characterization of offense severity outweighs all other explanations of police attitudes and behavior (Sykes, Fox, & Clark, 1976). For example, offense seriousness has been found to effect the likelihood of arrest (Black & Reiss, 1970, Black, 1971; Friedrich, 1977), with police being more likely to take a crime report (Black, 1970) and to treat suspects more harshly when a felony rather than a misdemeanor has occurred (Friedrich, 1977).

Although there has been no research on this point in the field of police response to domestic violence, police usually are called to the scene of a domestic dispute to handle a simple assault, or the threat thereof. Some of the apparent police disinterest in such cases could be attributable to this typology rather than factors customarily cited. If this is true, then the recent laws increasing the status of such offenses should of themselves cause a more positive police response.

Research Design and Instruments

Two primary research instruments were adopted: structured interviews of command officials and a questionnaire administered to their subordinates. First, structured interviews were conducted with the Detroit Police Department's director of the Metropolitan Police Academy and commanders of each of the precincts studied as well as most of the frontline supervisory staff. These interviews were designed to evaluate knowledge of domestic violence statutes, attitudes toward the police role therein, and methods to communicate these attitudes to their subordinates.

In New Hampshire, nine of the largest police departments in the state were selected for examination. Because of the increased importance of examining the attitudes of command officials in relatively small departments, the author and her assistants conducted even more extensive structured interviews with police command officials there than she did in Detroit. The interviews stressed the attitudes of the official toward the police role in domestic violence, their knowledge of the recent New Hampshire statute on domestic violence, actions taken to adopt policies to comply with the new statute and to train their officers on domestic violence and similar questions to ascertain the officials' knowledge and commitment to the police role in domestic violence.

The author then constructed a questionnaire containing 23 substantive questions on issues related to the police role in handling domestic violence. It also requested the officer to report his or her demographic characteristics including age, race, sex, marital status, years in policing, level of education and college major, and whether the officer had completed, in Michigan, the Detroit Police Department's Domestic Violence Training Program and, in New Hampshire, the New Hampshire Standards and Training Program on domestic violence.

Substantive questions primarily used a forced-choice format supplemented by opportunities in several questions for nondirective supplementary information. The data analysis included frequency determination and cross-tabular analysis between demographic and substantive variables.

Sample selection was undertaken as follows. In Detroit, after obtaining approval from the office of the Chief of Police, the precincts in which high percentages of the officers had attended the Domestic Violence Training Program were isolated and their commanders contacted. Various shifts were contacted and the questionnaires distributed to 250 officers. Owing in large part to resentment over imminent layoffs, 116 officers refused to respond, leaving a Detroit sample of 134 officers. According to officers familiar with department personnel, the officers to be terminated constituted almost the entire group of officers declining participation.

Sample characteristics were representative of patrol officers in the Detroit Police Department (prior to layoffs). However, because of affirmative action and high educational requirements in the Detroit Police Department, this group had a far higher proportion of minorities, women, highly educated, and younger officers than other studies have suggested are representative of "typical" police departments.

New Hampshire officers were administered the questionnaire just discussed and 169 responses or a response rate of 89% resulted. The percentage of respondents varied significantly by department, depending primarily upon whether a police command official stressed the importance of the questionnaire or if, instead, the officers were handed the instrument and told to fill them out on their own time or at a later date.

Data Analysis

(1) Command Officer Interviews

The author reached the following conclusions from the structured interviews. First, command officers in the Detroit Police Department could no longer be termed as being unaware of or indifferent toward the problem of domestic violence. Knowledge of the statute among command officers was very high. Precinct captains and the actual trainers had an extremely thorough understanding of the provisions of the statute including the statutory goal of increasing police response to domestic violence and the broadening of police arrest powers designed to accomplish this goal. (For a more detailed analysis of the statute, see Buzawa & Buzawa, 1979). The attitudes toward the police role were extremely positive. The executive deputy chief had previously published a Police Foundation study in the area of domestic violence and was the author of numerous articles and speeches exhorting increased police response to domestic violence.

Finally, there were multiple mechanisms by which the knowledge and positive attitudes of command officials would reach patrol officers. Training bulletins on the Michigan legislation and preferred methods of handling domestic violence were issued to all officers. Short briefings and summaries of desirable arrest policies were instituted on a regular basis. The board of police commissioners adopted a formal task force to implement changes to domestic violence responses. In addition,"911" operators and dispatchers were given increased training to prevent the former practice of call screening. Finally, in-depth training in handling family disputes was given to several hundred officers within one year of the enactment of the statute.

In contrast, the level of knowledge of the domestic violence statute by the New Hampshire police chiefs varied considerably. Several chiefs were extremely well versed in the contents of the statute, the Protection of Persons from Domestic Violence Act Chapter 173-B NH R.S.A. The majority knew of its existence but their comments suggested that they were unfamiliar with its provisions.

This level of variance was reflected by their attitudes toward the proper police role in domestic assaults. At one extreme was a chief of a major New Hampshire city who could not recall a "genuine" call for domestic violence in his numerous years as an administrator, and who therefore did not highly value the role of police intervention in this area. This was highly unlikely, given the author's own observations of the extensive nature of domestic violence in rural communities, acquired as a member of the New Hampshire Domestic Violence Evaluation and Treatment Board. At the other extreme, one chief required his officers to always make arrests in cases of domestic assault, despite victim acquiescence, because he believed the problem could be ameliorated only by prompt effective police action. Finally, the mechanisms by which in-service training and the dissemination of knowledge on domestic violence varied greatly. Enrollment in the voluntary state-administered training programs reflected the chief's concern with the issue, with several departments rarely or never showing enrollment, and others encouraging their officers to attend regularly. Finally, some departments had no written policies, others had written policies that were not distributed to officers (primarily as a device to protect the department in civil suits and not actually to change behavior), and still others wrote summaries of domestic violence statutes and actively disseminated such summaries to their patrol officers.

(2) Responses to Officer Questionnaires

Overall police attitudes toward domestic violence. Officers in Detroit do not appear to fit the previously reported stereotype of denigrating the importance of domestic violence and their role in its prevention or treatment. Responses to a series of questions show a much more activist approach. For example, past studies have shown that officers rarely made arrests when domestic violence was threatened but had not occurred, and only rarely made such arrests even when violence occurred in their presence (Langley & Levy, 1978, Roy, 1977). Based on officers' perceptions, at least, it is clear this pattern has changed. Although 90% of officers never or rarely make arrests when violence was threatened but had not yet occurred, the result was markedly different when violence had actually occurred. Under those circumstances, 19% stated that they would make arrests "50% of the time," 15% would "usually make arrests," and 2% "always make arrests." When the act of violence occurred in the officer's presence (and therefore could be easily proven in court), the results were even more positive. 17% of the officers would make arrests "50% of the time," 30% "would usually make arrests" and 11% would "always make arrests."

Similarly, the Detroit study found that officers as a group were quite willing to intervene in domestic disputes. In cases in which violence had been threatened but had not yet occurred, only 25% believe that they should not respond, compared to 35% who would respond primarily by referring to outside agencies, and 40% who would respond and attempt counseling or other action (including making arrests). When violence had occurred but not in the officer's presence, the number believing they should not respond decreased to 15%, while those preferring primarily a referral type response increased to 39%, and those desiring counseling or other more active alternatives increased to 46%. Finally, when violence actually occurred in the officer's presence, few would not desire to intervene: 26% would respond by making referrals, while fully 60% would respond by counseling or taking more aggressive action.

The response in the various New Hampshire departments also demonstrates that officers appear to be somewhat more likely to make arrests than previously assumed in existing literature, although not to the degree shown in Detroit. When domestic violence was threatened but had not yet occurred, 23% would never arrest, 64% would rarely arrest, 8% would arrest approximately 50% of the time, while only 1% would usually arrest, and no one would always arrest. (The totals do not equal 100% because not everyone responded.) When violence occurred prior to the officer's arrival, 4% would never arrest, 44% would rarely arrest, 28% would arrest approximately 50% of the time, 15% would usually arrest and 1% would always arrest. Finally, when the act of domestic violence occurred in their presence, most officers would make arrests. Only 1% would never arrest, 8% would rarely arrest, 17% would arrest approximately 50% of the time,

47% would usually arrest, and 19% would always arrest.

It appeared that New Hampshire officers were as willing to intervene in domestic violence as were their Detroit counterparts. In response to a question requesting their preference of police actions upon an allegation of domestic violence placed on a telephone, fewer than 3% believed they should not send a unit while the remainder believed that, at a minimum, a police unit should be sent. Further, although the questionnaires were not strictly equivalent to reflect differences in the applicable governing statutes, it appears that over 50% of the New Hampshire officers believe that police should refer or counsel in situations involving threats of domestic violence as well as domestic violence occurring both before and during their intervention.

This data does not support traditional research findings reporting highly negative police attitudes and response toward domestic violence. It appears that such attitudes, if they previously were applicable, have changed. The nature and extent of such changes would appear to be a fruitful area for future empirical research, and will be actively studied in future research by the author.

Interdepartmental variations. The author believes that it would not be fruitful to empirically explore differences between Detroit and the various New Hampshire departments because of dissimilarities in police structure and sizes of the departments. Therefore, the following analysis will focus instead upon descriptive observations of interdepartmental differences among the New Hampshire police departments studied. Because of the small sample sizes for each of the New Hampshire departments (the total sample size being 169 for all 9 departments), it proved impossible to obtain statistically significant differences in the responses to particular questions. Despite this, the author believes that the data does indicate the potential of dramatic attitudinal differences in the departments studied.

These differences may be illustrated by the responses to several questions. Officers were asked their opinions of the value of responding to domestic violence requests. They were to indicate whether they thought such services were: completely or usually a waste of time, sometimes helpful, or usually or very helpful. There was considerable variation in the responses to this question. Only 10% of the 169 officers thought the responses were customarily a waste of time, 50% thought they were sometimes helpful, and 40% thought they were often helpful. However, there were obvious differences between departments. In 3 of the 9 departments, 70% or more of the officers thought they were usually helpful, whereas in four other departments, fewer than one-third of the officers took this position. In the latter departments, a significant percentage, 20% to 35%, of officers believed that their response was usually a waste of time, compared to virtually no officers in the other departments.

Similarly, on the issue of whether the police department should send a unit to all domestic violence calls, 82% of the 169 responding officers stated that such units should always be sent, compared to only 18% that believe such units should only sometimes be sent. However, these figures concealed apparently material differences between departments. In several departments, between 20% to 35% would only sometimes send units, whereas in the majority of the departments fewer than 5% of respondents would take this position.

Finally, there appeared to be dramatic differences in the number of arrests made by officers in domestic violence cases in the various departments. The 9 New Hampshire departments studied (39%) reported no arrests made in domestic violence incidents in the past year, compared to 38% making 1 to 4 arrests and 24% making 5 or more arrests. However, the incidence of arrests among various departments varied considerably. On one extreme, in 3 departments, over 50% of the officers reported making no domestic violence arrests, while in another department 37% of the officers made 5 or more arrests, and in another department 67% of the officers made 5 or more arrests. Although a large portion of the variance may be explainable by differences in the community served, from the author's experiences as a member of the New Hampshire Domestic Violence and Evaluation Board, these percentages do not appear to coincide with actual incidents of domestic violence.

It is naturally difficult to account for interdepartmental variance. The author, however, can advance the following observations. First, she found that officers in the police departments headed by chiefs that were not as cognizant or supportive of police efforts in domestic violence, appeared to be far less likely to desire intervention. This may be especially true in smaller police units since such departments tend to use their own highly personal screening mechanisms for hiring and promotion without the encumbrance of civil service examinations. As a result, senior commanders positions may influence officer attitudes in some departments more than in others. In addition, officers in such departments are not as likely to be exposed to formal training as they would be in a larger department such as Detroit, thereby making departmental attitudes more polarized.

Sociodemographic and other individual variables. The author found that in Detroit relatively few identifiable sociodemographic characteristics affected officer attitudes to any significant degree. Specifically, race, education, marital status, officer sex, military service, years in policing, and college major did not statistically affect the responses to any material questions. However, age of the officer did appear to affect one aspect of attitudes: Older officers appeared more willing to intervene actively.

By far, the major significant predictor of responses to domestic violence situations appeared to be exposure to advanced training in domestic violence (see Buzawa, 1982 for a more detailed analysis). Results were statistically significant in willingness to make arrests. In the case of a threat of violence, 21% of the trained officers would arrest 50% or more of the time, compared to only 2% of untrained officers (significant at .004). In cases in which violence occurred prior to intervention, 51% of the trained officers would arrest compared to only 23% of the untrained officers (significant at .006) and in cases in which the violence occurred in the presence of the officers, 71% of the trained officers, compared to 45% of the untrained officers, would make arrests (significant at .01). Similar statistically significant differences were found between trained and untrained officers in their attitudes toward domestic violence training and their confidence in handling domestic violence situations.

The results in New Hampshire were dramatically different in several regards. First, 56% of the older officers made no domestic violence arrests in the past year, compared to 31% of their younger colleagues (significant at .05). This indicates either an apparent generational change in attitudes toward domestic violence or a socialization change into preferring not to respond to such calls.

Second, and more important, attendance at New Hampshire's voluntary training program on domestic violence did not appear to relate to any significant attitudinal change on the part of attendees. It is unclear why this did not happen since it is in stark contrast to the results in Detroit. However, although not empirically demonstrable, the author has attended the New Hampshire program in the past and found that it was much shorter than the Detroit program and not as sophisticated. Also, it did not use expert trainers but instead relied on older officers, judges, and prosecutors who often did not appear to be very committed to an active police involvement in domestic violence.

Therefore, this study can suggest only that such sociodemographic variables may prove to be differentially relevant in various departments, for example, factors salient in one organization may not be in another. It appears that future research must examine the organizational context of such sociodemographic variables being studied and forego attempts to make more generalized conclusions.

Situational factors affecting domestic violence response. The relevance of this model will be explored in future research. However, the author has several observations from the data collected. First, as stated earlier, domestic violence occurring in the presence of officers is far more likely to result in an arrest or more active police action than are acts of domestic violence that have occurred prior to the officer's intervention. The officers, when asked to explain this difference, usually expound on the rational problem of proof of an assault when there are no corroborating witnesses. However, it is also possible that an assault that occurs in the presence of an officer becomes the assailant's symbolic challenge to the officer's authority and control of the situation, a highly situational variable. This factor may be very relevant, given that virtually all domestic violence occurs prior to the officer's arrival.

Second, the victim's preference regarding arrest or nonarrest appears to be an extremely important factor in the officer's subsequent decision as to whether to arrest.

Third, when the officer indicates that he is confident of how to handle domestic violence situations, he appears to be far more likely to be willing to counsel or make arrests than are his less confident colleagues. This is important because it suggests that training that increases such confidence may increase the likelihood of arrest or other intervention by such officers.

Fourth, officers have clearly changed attitudes from the earlier negative attitudes reported in previous research. Therefore, although these observations are extremely tentative, they are suggestive of the possible role of including such factors in attempting to explain police attitudes and behavior in this area.

Conclusion

To summarize the goals of this work, it appears that police attitudes toward their role in domestic violence is not as negative as most existing research has reported. Second, there do appear to be significant differences in attitudes in different police departments, thereby warranting future cross-departmental studies with sample sizes large enough to test significance of such differences. In addition, there is some tentative evidence for believing that small departments may be somewhat more likely to exhibit greater uniformity of attitudes than are their more diverse larger counterparts. Third, it appears that all four of the generally used models for examining police attitudes and behavior have applicability in the study of the police reaction to domestic violence.

References

Bannon, J. (1975, August). *Law enforcement problems with intrafamily violence.* Paper presented at the annual meeting of the American Bar Association, Montreal, Canada.

Bayley, D., & Mendelsohn, H. (1969). *Minorities and the police.* New York: Free Press.

Berk, S. F., & Loseke, D. R. (1981). Handling family violence: Situational determinants of police arrest in domestic disturbances. *Law and Society Review, 15,* 315-346.

Black, D. (1970). Production of crime rates. *American Sociological Review, 35,* 733-748.

Black, D. (1971). The social organization of arrest. *Stanford Law Review, 23,* 1087-1111.

Black, D. (1976). *The behavior of law.* New York: Academic Press.

Black, D., & Reiss, A. J. (1976). *Studies in law enforcement in major metropolitan areas* (Field survey 3). Washington, DC: Government Printing Office.

Black, D., & Reiss, A. J. (1970). Police control of juveniles. *American Sociological Review 35,* 66-77.

Bloch, P. B., & Anderson, D. (1974). *Policewomen on patrol: A final report.* Washington, DC: Government Printing Office.

Buzawa, E. (1982). Police officer response to domestic violence legislation in Michigan. *Journal of Police Science and Administration, 10*(1).

Buzawa, E., & Buzawa, C. (1979). Legislative responses to the problem of domestic violence in Michigan. *Wayne Law Review, 25,* 859-881.

Chevigny, P. (1969). *Police power: Police abuses in New York City.* New York: Pantheon.

Cohen, B., & Chaiken, J. J. (1973). *Police background characteristics and performance.* Lexington, MA: Lexington Books.

Forst, B., Lucianovic, J., & Cox, S. (1977). *What happens after arrest?* Washington, DC: Institute for Law and Social Research.

Friedrich, R. J. (1977). The impact of organizational and situational factors on police behavior. (Doctoral Dissertation, University of Michigan). *Dissertation Abstracts International.*

Gay, W., Day, H. T., & Woodward, J. P. (1977). *Neighborhood team policing.* Washington, DC: Institute of Law Enforcement and Criminal Justice.

Langley, R., & Levy, R. (1978). Wife abuse and the police response. *FBI Law Enforcement Bulletin, 47*(5), 4-9.

Lefkowitz, J. (1971). *Job attitudes of police.* Washington, DC: National Institute of Law Enforcement and Criminal Justice.

Lerman, L. G., & Livingston, F. (1983). State legislation on domestic violence. *Response to Violence in the Family and Sexual Assault, 6*(5), 1-28.

Manning, P. K. (1979). *The social organization of policing.* Cambridge: MIT Press.

Mastrofski, S. (1981). Surveying clients to assess police performance focusing on the police-citizen encounter. *Evaluation Review, 5*(3), 397-408.

Milner, N. (1970). Comparative analysis of patterns of compliance with Supreme Court decisions: Miranda and the police in four communities. *Law and Society Review, 4,* 119-134.

Niederhoffer, A. (1967). *Behind the shield: The police in urban society.* Garden City, NY: Anchor.

Parnas, R. (1967). The police response to the domestic disturbance. *Wisconsin Law Review,* 914-960.

Reiss, A. J. (1971). *The police and the public.* New Haven, CT: Yale University Press.

Roy, M. (1977). *Battered women.* New York: Van Nostrand Reinhold.

Sherman, L. W. (1980). Causes of police behavior: The current state of quantitative research. *Journal of Research on crime and Delinquency, 17,* 69-100.

Sherman, L. W., & Berk, R. (1984). The specific deterrent effects of arrests for domestic assault. *American Sociological Review, 49,* 261-272.

Sherman, L. W., Milton, C. H., & Kelly, T. V. (1973). *Team policing: Seven case studies.* Washington, DC: Police Foundation.

Skolnick, J. H. (1975). *Justice without trial* (2nd ed.). New York: John Wiley.

Swanson, C. (1978). A comparison of organizational and environmental influences on arrest policies. In F. Meyer & R. Baker (Eds.), *Determinants of law enforcement policies.* Toronto: D.C. Heath.

Sykes, R. E., Clark, J. P., & Fox, J. (1976). A socio-legal theory of police discretion. In A. Neiderhoffer & A. Blumberg (Eds.), *The ambivalent force: Perspectives on the police* (2nd ed.). Hinsdale, IL: Dryden.

Van Maanen, J. (1973). Observations on the making of policemen. *Human Organization, 32,* 407-418.

Van Maanen, J. (1974). Working the street: A developmental view of police behavior. In H. Jacob (Ed.), *The potential for reform of criminal justice* (pp. 83-130). Beverly Hills, CA: Sage.

Van Maanen, J. (1975). Police socialization: A longitudinal examination of job attitudes in an urban police department. *Administrative Science Quarterly, 20,* 207-228.

Wasby, S. (1976). *Small town police and the Supreme Court.* Lexington, MA: Lexington Books.

Westley, W. A. (1970). *Violence and the police: A sociological study of law, custom and morality.* Cambridge: MIT Press.

Wilson, J. Q. (1968). *Varieties of police behavior.* Cambridge, MA: Harvard University Press.

Wilt, M., & Bannon, J. (1977). *Domestic violence and the police: Studies in Detroit and Kansas City.* Washington, DC: Police Foundation.

12

Victims Who Know Their Assailants: Their Satisfaction with the Criminal Court's Response

Barbara E. Smith

The criminal justice system is increasingly being employed to adjudicate personal and property disputes between family members, friends, neighbors, and other acquaintances. Yet the ability of criminal courts to effectively resolve interpersonal disputes has been seriously challenged by legal and social scientists. This chapter is based upon a study that explored the adequacy of various courts' responses, from the victim's perspective. The research, funded by the National Institute of Justice (see author's note), examined the outcomes of nonstranger violence cases and victims' satisfaction with those outcomes in three court systems—Charlotte, North Carolina; Los Angeles, California; and Minneapolis, Minnesota. The data presented here are based upon interviews with 125 victims of nonstranger violence whose cases went to criminal court and 75 such victims whose cases were diverted to mediation programs.

Previous Research

Violence between those who know each other has been well documented in previous studies. In a national victimization survey in 1975, it was found that in one out of every five violent crimes in the United States the victim

AUTHOR'S NOTE: Points of view are the author's and do not necessarily represent the viewpoints of the National Institute of Justice.

and assailant were acquainted with each other (U.S. Department of Justice, 1975). Interpersonal disputes also constitute the single largest category of calls received by most police departments in the country (Wilt, Bannon, & Breedlove, 1977; Parnas, 1967: Breslin, 1978).

When not successfully resolved, such incidents can eventually result in serious injury or death. According to a recent National Crime Survey Study (Gaguin, 1977-1978) and the Uniform Crime Reports for 1975, one-quarter of all homicides were committed by a member of the victim's family, and about half involved spouse killing spouse. Wolfgang (1958) found that over a six-year period 11% of all male homicide victims were killed by their wives, whereas 41% of all female homicide victims were slain by their husbands. A Kansas City study of victims of domestic homicide (Wilt et al., 1977) suggested a pattern of repeated, escalating violence. The study showed that in the two years preceding a homicide, the police had been at the address of the incident for disturbance calls at least once in 85% of the cases and at least five times in about 50% of the cases.

Several studies conducted by staff of the Vera Institute's Victim/ Witness Assistance Project (now the New York City Victim Services Agency) have explored the complexities of relationship cases presented to the court and their long-term outcomes. In Brooklyn Criminal Court, the appearance records and case dispositions of 315 complaining witnesses were studied. In addition, witnesses were interviewed twice, once prior to the entrance of their cases into the court system and again after their cases were disposed (Davis, Russell, & Kunreuther, 1980). As anticipated, complainants in relationship cases were initially less likely than were victims of stranger-to-stranger crimes to want to press charges. Further, even when complainants in relationship cases initially did want to prosecute, they were more likely to change their minds prior to the disposition of their cases than were complainants in stranger-to-stranger cases. Contrary to expectations, however, the study found that complainants in relationship cases attended their court dates *more* reliably than did victims of stranger-to-stranger crimes. This finding was corroborated on a sample of complainants in Suffolk County, New York (Smith, 1979).

These findings are comprehensible in light of initial differences that were found by Davis, Russell, and Kunreuther (1980) in stranger-to-stranger cases in reactions to victimization and demands of the criminal justice system. Complainants in relationship cases suffered greater emotional stress as a result of the crime. They were angrier, more afraid, more confused, more likely to receive threats from the defendants, and more likely to oppose their pretrial release. In short, they appeared to have a greater emotional stake in their cases; victimization for them was not a discrete experience bound in space and time, but a source of continuing stress each time they encountered (or feared they might encounter) the defendants. However, complainants in relationship cases were less likely to seek punishment of the defendants than were complainants in stranger-to-stranger cases. Rather, their primary concern was that the criminal justice system protect them from the defendants. Often, the victim may have felt that his or her aim was met just by the defendant's arrest and the threat of sanctions that existed during the period that the case was active in the court. In other words, the importance of the case to victims more often motivated them to go to court, but once in court, they were less willing to aid in convicting and punishing the defendants.

Recognizing the complexities and problems relationship cases frequently pose for traditional adjudication, court officials are increasingly exploring ways to divert these cases to alternative dispute resolution mechanisms. Mediation and neighborhood justice centers have been established in numerous jurisdictions to address the underlying problems precipitating property disputes and violent acts between those who know each other. Several research studies have found such alternatives are generally more satisfying to disputants than traditional court adjudication (Davis, Tichane, & Grayson, 1980; Cook, Roehl, & Sheppard, 1980). In addition, preliminary studies suggest that alternative programs can be just as effective as courts in deterring future hostilities between the parties (Felstiner & Williams, 1980; Cook, Roehl, & Sheppard, 1980). A study by the Vera Institute and the Victim Services Agency (Davis, Tichane, & Grayson, 1980) addressed the questions of (a) what happens after intervention of the criminal justice system in crimes between acquaintances, and (b) whether mediation is (as many persons have suggested) a more effective means of resolving interpersonal cases than prosecution. In that study, a sample of 465 felony interpersonal cases that entered Brooklyn Criminal Court between September 1 and December 23, 1977 were randomly assigned to one of two conditions. In one condition, cases were processed in the traditional way in criminal court; in the other condition, cases were diverted from the court to a mediation program run by the Institute for Mediation and Conflict Resolution. Victims were interviewed, and data on new arrests of either party for a crime against the other were collected from records for four months following termination of their cases in both settings.

The study found that, regardless of which condition cases had been assigned to, the rate of recidivism over four months was surprisingly low: continued interpersonal problems with the defendant were reported by 19% of victims whose cases were diverted to mediation and 28% of victims whose cases were prosecuted; calls to the police were made by 12% of victims whose cases were diverted to mediation and 13% of victims whose cases were prosecuted; and subsequent arrests of one of the parties for a crime against the other occurred in 4% of cases prosecuted (none of the differences between cases referred to mediation, and cases prosecuted approached statistical significance).

Analysis of the data revealed that the low rate of recidivism resulted from the fact that disputants' interaction with each other was greatly reduced subsequent to their court involvement. Over all cases, 67% of disputants reported less interaction with the other party, and 41% of respondents reported no contact at all subsequent to the defendant's arrest. Among disputants who did maintain contact, 57% reported an improvement in the relationship.

These results suggest that recidivism in cases between acquaintances may not be as widespread as is often assumed because many disputants have little desire to continue a relationship that has become destructive. In other words, most dispute cases do not seem to return to the criminal justice system again and again, nor do such cases seem to escalate into more serious violent incidents. Because of the relatively short duration of the follow-up period, this finding must be viewed as tentative and in need of further confirmation.

But, although the recidivism rate in the Davis, Tichane, and Grayson sample was generally low, the study was able to isolate one group of cases that were at relatively high risk of recurrence of interpersonal hostilities. These were cases in which police had been called upon to intervene previously and in which disputants had strong interpersonal ties (i.e., nuclear family members or lovers). In such cases (regardless of whether they were diverted to mediation or prosecuted), disputants were far more likely to report continuing problems, to summon police again, and to be rearrested for a crime against the other, compared to cases that lacked these characteristics. These seem to be the sorts of cases that have been found by Wilt et al. (1977), to escalate into even more serious violence. It may be that for successful resolution of these "high risk" cases, a more sustained form of intervention than they normally receive either in criminal courts or mediation programs is necessary.

We now turn to the results of our nonstranger violence study.

Profile of Cases and Courts

All the cases in our sample involved misdemeanor assaults. Over two-thirds of the victims sustained injuries, with a full quarter requiring medical attention. In the majority of cases, the assault was carried out by using fists or bodily force, but over one-quarter of the assaults involved guns, knives, bludgeons, or other weapons. Victims reported many problems resulting from the assault. Especially common were problems associated with increased nervousness. The nervousness often extended beyond the circumstances of the actual assault and individual perpetrator into their daily lives, thus creating an environment of general vulnerability and fear.

The size and complexity of the court systems varied considerably among our sites. In Charlotte, cases are processed rapidly and traditionally. Cases are automatically dismissed by the prosecutor if the victim fails to appear on the second court date. A domestic relations court handles domestic violence cases; it carries a lighter caseload and cases are given more time and attention than in the general misdemeanor court. No alternative dispute resolution programs are available. In contrast, a mediation program exists in Minneapolis that handles a sizable proportion of all nonstranger cases. Those that remain in the court system are processed in courtrooms with light caseloads and more time and attention are given to individual cases than in the crowded Charlotte courtrooms. Los Angeles represents our largest and most complex system in terms of jurisdictional boundaries and specialization of courtrooms within the system. A domestic violence program designed to train prosecutors to prosecute cases successfully and a hearing officer program for mediation are available. Courtrooms are formal and quick paced.

The Court's Response and Its Immediate Impact on the Victim

Nonstranger violence cases—the findings. We asked victims in our court and mediation samples about their experiences and satisfaction with legal officials and the process. Most victims were satisfied with the police, especially those in the court sample. Victims were satisfied with the police more often than with court/mediation officials. Prosecutors spoke with victims in approximately one-half of the cases and slightly over one-half of the victims were satisfied with the prosecutors. Judges spoke with victims in only one-fourth of the cases. Three-fifths of the victims thought the judge was concerned with their interests and were satisfied with the judge; similar rates were found for the mediators. Only the victims in the mediation sample frequently felt that they had a chance to tell their side of the story and that they exerted an influence on the final outcome. Court victims typically reported that they had little opportunity to participate in the process. Overall, three-fifths of the victims in both the court and mediation samples felt they were well treated while in court or at the mediation session.

One-half of the cases resulted in a guilty plea or verdict; the other half were dismissed. Jail sentences were imposed in one-third of the cases; most defendants were incarcerated for very short periods (less than 30 days).

Victims in the mediated sample were satisfied with the outcome of their cases slightly more often than were those in the court sample, but the differences were not large or statistically significant. Victims in the court and mediation sample were satisfied slightly more than one-half the time. Satisfaction levels were not correlated with the disposition of the case in the court sample. Whether the case resulted in a guilty plea or verdict or a dismissal, victims reported similar rates of satisfaction. During the interview we asked victims *why* they were satisfied or dissatisfied with the outcome and discovered that the disposition is frequently less important than (a) the victim's perception of how the disposition affected the defendant's behavior toward him or her *after* the case or (b) the victim's assessment of the appropriateness of the sentence. In other words, it is not the disposition itself that generally counts, but whether or not victims believe that the court's action stopped the physical abuse and/or the defendant received the appropriate punishment or treatment.

Generally, we found more similarities than differences in the experiences of the victims among our sites. The major difference among the sites was in case outcomes. The majority of the cases in Charlotte were dismissed as were one-half of the Los Angeles cases, but less than one-tenth of the Minneapolis cases. Sentences among the sites also varied with jail being imposed much more often in Los Angeles than elsewhere, although the incarceration frequently involved very small periods of time. Jail sentences for extended periods (30, 60, 90 days) were handed out in few Los Angeles cases, at rates similar to those in Charlotte and Minneapolis.

Some site differences in victims' satisfaction with legal officials and the process emerged among the court sample. Although the rates of satisfaction with the police and prosecutors were similar everywhere, Charlotte victims tended to perceive judges as concerned with their interests more often than those in Minneapolis and Los Angeles, and were also more satisfied with the judge. Overall, Charlotte and Minneapolis court victims felt they were treated better than did those in Los Angeles.

Nonstranger violence cases—a discussion of the findings. Victims in the court and mediation samples reported similar rates of satisfaction with officials and the process. As we might expect, victims whose cases were mediated reported higher rates of participation in the process than did those who went to court. Although not statistically significant, mediated victims also reported higher rates of satisfaction with their treatment and the mediators than did court victims, but the differences were not large. While it is important to note that at least one-half of the victims were satisfied with legal officials, the court or mediation process, their overall treatment, and case outcomes, we should not lose sight of the significant proportion—one-quarter to one-half of the sample in some instances—

who were dissatisfied. It is reassuring that at least one-half of the victims were satisfied with the system's response, but for a sizable minority of the victims there clearly is room for improvement. What improvements can be made? We look to some of the differences among our sites for the answer.

Charlotte victims thought the judge was more often concerned with their interests and were also more satisfied with the judge than were those elsewhere. Overall, Charlotte and Minneapolis victims felt they were treated better than did Los Angeles victims. What can be learned from this? From our observations and conversations with victims, two related phenomena appear to be operating. First, the interactive style of the judge may influence the victim's satisfaction and may ultimately affect the cessation or resumption of violence. Second, the courtroom atmosphere and the speed with which cases are adjudicated may make a difference in how well victims feel they are treated.

Victims were exposed to very different courtroom environments in Charlotte, Los Angeles, and Minneapolis. The greater satisfaction with the judge and their overall treatment expressed by Charlotte victims seems to result from the specialized courtroom developed to handle domestic violence cases—the domestic relations courtroom. The establishment of a separate courtroom to handle domestic assaults has potential for discrimination and inferior treatment *if* these cases are removed from the traditional courtrooms because they are seen as less important than "real" assaults or less worthy of the court's time. However, quite the opposite appears to be true in Charlotte. Because these cases are consolidated in one courtroom, legal officials are immediately "flagged" when the case is called that this involves a domestic assault, frequently with complexities that extend beyond the single incident. Consequently, they are immediately aware of the problems often associated with such an incident, and the potential for renewed hostilities. Of course, simply being aware is not enough; officials must also make an effort to grapple with the complexity of the cases and forestall further violence. It appears such an attitude existed in the two judges who presided over the domestic relations courtroom during our observations and data collection period. These judges specifically volunteered for this assignment and presided over the courtroom for periods of several months. From what we observed and what victims reported, these judges were especially careful, professional, and courteous in their treatment of victims and their cases. They also verbally warned or lectured defendants about the consequences of their actions and the possibility of harsher punishment if they were violent in the future. Even when victims stepped forward only to drop charges, the judge frequently expressed concern about the incident and counseled the victim. Therefore, it is little wonder that Charlotte victims reported the highest rates of satisfaction with the judge and believed that judicial concern was shown for their interests. In some cases they also believed that the judge's warning was effective, that is, that the abuse stopped because the defendant had been warned. We will return to this point later.

The courtroom atmosphere and speed of the disposition may also affect victims' satisfaction. Overall, Charlotte and Minneapolis victims felt they were better treated than did Los Angeles victims. We have already discussed the specialized Charlotte courtroom where judges tended to spend time with victims. This also occurred in Minneapolis courtrooms, but it was not so much the interactive style (indeed, many different judges handled the cases in our sample, each with different styles) as the clarity of the formal proceedings that seemed to make a difference. Among our courts, Minneapolis had the lightest caseload, which helps to account for the higher rate of satisfaction felt by Minneapolis victims than by Los Angeles victims. Light caseloads allowed the judge to spend more time explaining the procedures and to handle each case distinctly. Also, light caseloads meant that victims did not have to spend several hours waiting for their cases, a common complaint among our Los Angeles victims who not only had to wait for prolonged periods, but also were subjected to a busy chaotic atmosphere where numerous cases were being considered almost simultaneously. Picture the difference between Minneapolis victims who sat for brief moments in small courtrooms, carpeted on the floor and walls for improved acoustics, where cases were considered for several minutes, in contrast to Los Angeles victims who sat for long periods in large courtrooms where numerous prosecutors and defense attorneys mingled in front of the rail while two or more cases were being presented and considered in rapid succession. Is it any wonder that more Minneapolis victims stated that they understood the proceedings and were satisfied with their overall treatment?

Although case outcomes were significantly different among the sites, victims' satisfaction with the outcome was similar because satisfaction was not correlated with the outcome. Rather, victims tended to be satisfied if the violence stopped and dissatisfied if it did not, regardless of the outcome.

The Long-Term Impact of the Court's Response on the Victims and Renewed Violence

We examined the frequency of renewed violence between the parties several weeks after the incidents in Charlotte, Los Angeles, and Minneapolis. We found that for a significant minority of victims, problems, sometimes violent ones, continue long after the case has been closed by the criminal justice system.

Long-term problems—the findings. Two to three months after the case was closed, 22% of the nonstranger victims in Los Angeles, Minneapolis, and Charlotte reported renewed problems with the other party in the court sample, whereas 15% in the mediation sample reported problems. The rate of renewed problems was slightly higher for those victims involved in intimate or close relationships with the other party—24%. More Charlotte victims were experiencing problems than were those in Los Angeles or Minneapolis. A majority of those victims who were experiencing such problems reported previous violence in the relationship. For these victims, a pattern of violence had been established that was not broken by the intervention of the criminal justice system.

How did the criminal courts' response affect the likelihood of renewed problems? Of the 75 nonstranger cases we interviewed, 31% of the victims whose cases were dismissed reported new problems with the other party, compared with 15% of the victims whose cases resulted in a guilty plea or verdict, but the difference was not statistically significant. We did, however, ask victims whether they believed the court system's response was helpful in resolving their relationship with the other party. Even for those victims who reported problems several months after the case was disposed, many believed that the court's treatment, including the decision to divert the case to mediation, was helpful or at least somewhat helpful in improving their relationship with the other party. Thus even when the court's treatment is not entirely effective in deterring problems, it may lessen the frequency or seriousness of recurring problems.

The courts' impact—a discussion of the findings. In the long-term follow-up in Charlotte, Los Angeles, and Minneapolis, we found that the continuation of hostilities between disputants is the exception rather than the rule, regardless of whether cases are referred to mediation or to court. We also found that renewed problems were slightly more prevalent in cases that had been resolved with a guilty plea rather than a dismissal, but even cases that were dismissed resulted in renewed problems infrequently. This suggests that dismissals may not be "failures" of the system but may help many victims to resolve their problems. Some commentators have suggested that victims who call the police but fail to follow through with the prosecution are using the court system frivolously and inappropriately. On the contrary, we found that victims called the police and wanted arrests because they felt seriously threatened by the defendants in their cases. Even though some of these victims subsequently requested that charges be withdrawn, it does not mean that the victim should not have brought the case to the attention of the system in the first place or that the court had been misused and served no useful purpose. The informal resolutions that may have been reached outside of the courtroom and the cessation of the violence in many cases may have been possible *because* the victim communicated the message to the abuser that "things have gone too far." Especially for the first time offender, the prospect of prosecution may be sufficiently frightening to alter his conduct toward the victim; particularly for those defendants who were warned by the judge about consequences of any future assaults. This, at least, is what many victims told us. This is not to suggest that dismissals are appropriate responses in all cases, nor that how the courts respond makes no difference. Some defendants do continue their violent behavior against those they know and against strangers. Clearly, for these defendants, a simple warning is unlikely to have much impact, especially if the warning is never carried out.

Although only a minority of victims reported problems, these victims represent an important minority because, for them, the violence continues for months, even years after the case is closed. For these cases, it appears that greater attention and intervention is needed than is normally received either in mediation or in court.

References

Breslin, W. (1978). Police intervention in domestic confrontation. *Journal of Police Science and Administration, 6,* 293.

Cook, R., Roehl, J., & Sheppard, D. (1980, February). *Neighborhood justice center field test: Final evaluation report.* Washington, DC: Government Printing Office.

Davis, R., Russell, V., & Kunreuther, F. (1980a, July). *The role of the complaining witness in an urban court.* Vera Institute of Justice.

Davis, R., Tichane, M., & Grayson, D. (1980b, March). *Mediation and arbitration as alternative prosecution in felony arrest cases: An evaluation of the Brooklyn Dispute Resolution Center (first year).* New York: Vera Institute of Justice.

Felstiner, W., & Williams, L. (1980). *Community mediation in Dorchester, Massachusetts.* Washington, DC: Government Printing Office.

Gaguin, D. (1977-1978). Spouse abuse: Data from the National Crime Survey. *Victimology, 2,* 632.

Parnas, R. (1967). The police response to the domestic disturbance. *Wisconsin Law Review,* 914.

Smith, B. (1979). *The prosecutor's witness: An urban/suburban comparison.* Unpublished doctoral dissertation.

Wilt, G., Bannon, J., & Breedlove, R. (1977). *Domestic violence and the police: Studies in Detroit and Kansas City.* Washington, DC: Police Foundation.

Wolfgang, M. (1958). *Patterns in criminal homicide.* Philadelphia: University of Pennsylvania Press.

13

Coordinated Police, Judicial, and Social Service Response to Woman Battering: A Multiple-Baseline Evaluation Across Three Communities

Denise J. Gamache
Jeffrey L. Edleson
Michael D. Schock

A large variety of interventions for aiding female victims of battering have been developed over the past decade. Among the more widely applied interventions are safe home networks, battered women's shelters, and counseling programs for men who batter.

More recently, interventions coordinating the responses of the police, the judiciary, and social services have been developed (e.g. Pence, 1983; Soler & Martin, 1983). Such interventions have developed out of a recognition that the police and courts have, in the past, not responded adequately in aiding victims of battering.

Specifically, several studies have reported that from one-third (Gayford, 1975) to over one-half (Fagan et al., 1983; Gaquin, 1977; Saunders & Size, 1980) of women who have been battered had at some point called local police to intervene. The typical response of police officers, however, has been governed by formal or informal policies of "nonintervention." In few cases are men arrested, and women are often discouraged from asking for arrest (Saunders & Size, 1980). Substantially fewer cases are ever prosecuted by the judicial system (Ford, 1983).

The lack of police and judicial system response may lead men who batter to believe that community institutions will do little to stop their behavior and that they will experience few negative consequences as a result of their violence. In a widely publicized study, Sherman and Berk (1984) experimentally compared three police responses to domestic violence; arrest, advice, and ordering the man to leave for eight hours. The researchers found significantly less subsequent violence resulting from arrests, compared to the other two police responses.

All of the above findings point to the need for new police, judicial, and social service system responses to woman battering. As innovative interventions develop it also becomes necessary to systematically evaluate them.

This chapter presents such an evaluation. It presents an experimentally controlled study of coordinated police, judicial, and social service interventions in three suburban communities over a two year period. These community intervention projects represent the first of seven such projects so far created by the Domestic Abuse Project of Minneapolis. Before presenting the specifics of the evaluation carried out, however, it is critical that the assumptions underlying the community intervention projects be made explicit.

Beliefs and Values Explicit in Project Designs

Explicit in the design of the intervention projects to be described are several beliefs and values about the causes of woman battering and what types of intervention goals should be pursued in response to such events. These values lay the foundation upon which concrete intervention programs are built.

One core value or belief is that neither men nor women have a right to use violence except in self-defense against a physical assault. It follows, therefore, that the use of physical violence to maintain power, to control others, to punish, or to obtain one's desires should be confronted and stopped wherever it occurs—even in the privacy of the home.

Another belief is that "domestic" violence is rooted in a societal norm that males, as a class, have the right to resort to violence in order to maintain their power and control in the family. Thus any attempt to effectively address the issue of woman battering must explicitly challenge this norm. The reluctance of our social systems to do so, their failure to intervene on behalf of battered women and the resulting inconsistent social responses are believed to contribute directly to the perpetuation of such violence.

This then leads to a third belief: If woman battering is rooted in societal norms, then social systems must bear the responsibility for confronting men who batter and maximizing the protection of victims. To address effectively the issue of woman battering, efforts must include interventions aimed at changing the responses of our social systems.

These three beliefs lead to a set of guidelines that influence decisions about policy development, project procedures, and individual case management. The guidelines include: (1) a primary intervention goal of ending the violence; (2) that to achieve this goal, social systems must confront the person responsible for the violent behavior (the assailant) and impose existing sanctions to deter further abuse; (3) that the community should remove the responsibility for confronting the assailant as much as possible from the victim who currently is often left to bear this burden alone; (4) that the social systems should apply the same existing sanctions in dealing with woman battering as they do in other assault cases (failure to treat these cases equally conveys the message to both the victim and the assailant that the system views this behavior as different from other forms of violence); (5) that social systems should strive to maximize the protection available to victims and that intervention efforts should be evaluated in terms of their potential for further endangering or victimizing the victim or her children; (6) that the responses of social systems should be scrutinized for biases or discriminatory practices against persons because of their race, sex, ethnic origin, sexual preference, or age and interventional efforts should attempt to eliminate discrimination at every level of the social systems' responses; and (7) that intervention efforts should strive to coordinate various social systems that respond to woman battering in order to communicate consistently to both the victim and the assailant a social norm that violent behavior is not acceptable.

These seven guidelines were developed specifically in work with the criminal justice and social service systems. They are, however, directly applicable in the analysis of other social system interventions and in the evaluation of each intervention's ability to respond consistently and effectively to woman battering.

Now that these guidelines and their underlying beliefs have been made explicit it seems appropriate to describe the community intervention projects and the results of a multiple-baseline evaluation across the first three communities in which interventions were initiated.

Method

Participating Communities

Three suburban Minnesota communities are the subject of this evaluation. The communities range from just over 15,000 to almost 36,000 residents and all three are racially homogeneous (97% white). Median household incomes reflect middle-income levels (from $17,000 to $27,500) with only about 2% of the population in each community receiving public assistance payments. In all three communities the great majority (70% to 80%) of employed residents work in white-collar positions.

Community Intervention Projects

As stated earlier, community intervention projects (CIPs) are designed to coordinate community responses to domestic violence that are immediate, consistent, and effective in preventing continued woman battering. Each project, therefore, focuses upon changes in and coordination between three separate systems in each targeted community; (1) law enforcement, (2) criminal justice and (3) social service systems. The CIPs assist police departments in implementing "probable cause" arrest policies and criminal justice systems in providing prompt prosecution. They actively advocate mandated batterers' counseling for the assailants and help to develop such counseling programs in target communities.

As pointed out in the beginning of this chapter, seldom do the police, judicial, and social service systems respond to woman battering in this manner. Furthermore, certain traditional responses, for example, police mediation, may contribute to the continuation of woman battering. The net result is to place total responsibility for initiating action onto the victim, the one person most vulnerable to future assaults. By maximizing the use of its interventive powers, the community is able to remove this burden from the victim, confront men who batter, and impose sanctions to control the violence until the men learn nonviolent alternatives to their use of violent behavior.

The CIP in each community operates as a coordinated set of intervention components. In each suburban community the Domestic Abuse Project and a local battered women's shelter (either Sojourner Shelter or B. Robert Lewis House) jointly coordinate CIP activities. Each such project requires one and a half full-time equivalents of staff to coordinate the various intervention components. Staff coordinators maintain communication among the participating agencies, oversee the flow of cases through the project, collect data and evaluate project outcomes, provide necessary training or community education, and both recruit and supervise volunteers. The following subsections describe the various component interventions that are the subject of coordination.

Police intervention. In each community, the police administration has adopted departmental policies requiring that officers make, whenever possible, a "probable cause" arrest in domestic assault situations. Until

June of 1983 an officer was permitted to arrest without a warrant even if he or she did not witness the battering. All that was required was probable cause that the person to be arrested had in the past four hours assaulted "his spouse or other person with whom he resides" and that the officer observed "recent physical injury to or impairment of condition of the alleged victim" (Minnesota Statute 629.341). This statute was amended so that observation of injury or impairment is no longer required. At present, an officer may arrest without a warrant if he or she has probable cause to believe that "the person within the preceding four hours has assaulted, threatened with a dangerous weapon, or placed in fear of immediate bodily harm his spouse, former spouse, or other person with whom he resides or has formerly resided" (Minnesota Statute 629.341).

As part of a CIP, the police department immediately notifies the local battered women's shelter that an arrest has been made. The assailant is moved from the home to the police station for booking and may be held until arraignment the next morning. Copies of arrest reports as well as reports on nonarrest domestic cases are supplied to the CIP.

Advocate intervention. Upon notification of an arrest by the police department the local shelter immediately dispatches volunteer advocates through the use of an electronic beeper system. Trained volunteer advocates are "on call" for visits to both the victim and the assailant. A male advocate, some being former batterers, visits the assailant in jail, provides support and encouragement to face his violent behavior problem directly and discusses the range of treatment options available to the man. Women's advocates are simultaneously visiting the victim in her home to provide support, information about subsequent court proceedings, and other available remedies. If requested, the women's advocates also transport the woman and her children to the local shelter. Both men's and women's advocates submit a written report to CIP staff describing their meetings with the victim and assailant.

Advocates not only work with cases when arrests take place. They also attempt intervention when arrests are not made. Advocates and CIP staff telephone or write to the battered woman to provide information about local shelter and counseling resources. In one community the batterer is also contacted.

Criminal justice intervention. The city attorneys in each community aggressively pursue the prosecution of these cases in court. CIP staff assist by maintaining contact with the victim to encourage her to cooperate in the prosecution and by providing support and advocacy for her throughout the prosecution process. As a result of such victim assistance, CIP staff are involved in contacting witnesses, gathering other evidence, and attempting to obtain disposition and sentencing outcomes that provide the opportunity for long-term resolution of the individual situation. In many cases the long-term resolution of the situation depends upon the male assailant being mandated to complete a batterer's counseling program as part of his sentence.

Upon entry of a guilty plea or finding, the judge or referee orders a presentence investigation by a probation officer. Probation officers cooperate by including CIP staff and information regarding the battered woman's wishes in developing their recommendation to the court.

In CIP cases, the judges or referees are asked to pronounce a sentence that includes imprisonment (in Minnesota the maximum for a misdemeanor is 90 days) and then to stay part or all of the sentence pending successful completion of a batterers' counseling program as a condition of probation. CIP staff link assailants with such counseling programs, monitor each man's compliance with probation conditions, and regularly report on progress. If another assault occurs or the probation agreement is violated, the CIP staff notify the probation officer. The case is then returned to court for revocation and the judge is requested to impose the stayed prison sentence.

Social service intervention. The Domestic Abuse Project and three other participating batterer's treatment programs give first priority to serving men referred by CIPs. The man's treatment counselors report to CIP staff regarding compliance with the conditions of probation set by the court. Groups for battered women are also available through both the therapy and support programs at D.A.P., the local shelters and cooperating social services.

Shelter or CIP advocates also assist women who wish to secure orders for protection, a temporary restraining order that can exclude the abuser from the couple's residence for periods of up to a year. In crisis situations, the cooperating shelters also provide emergency housing to the woman and her children.

Evaluation Procedures

The development in recent years of research designs that require few subjects but provide experimental controls (see Bloom & Fischer, 1982; Hersen & Barlow, 1976; Kratochwill, 1978) enabled a systematic evaluation of program impact. Phased establishment of the CIPs in the three communities allowed the application of a single-system research design without requiring alterations in the operating procedures of the CIPs.

A multiple-baseline design across subjects (communities) was used to evaluate the impact of the CIPs. Using a multiple-baseline design requires repeated measurements prior to intervention (baseline) and during intervention. Archival data on frequency of domestic calls to the police, arrests of assailants on those calls, and judicial system outcomes related to the arrests were collected for a 22-month period beginning in May 1982, and ending in February 1984.

By lagging the introduction of the intervention, a multiple-baseline evaluation is able to rule out most changes caused by other intervening variables. Thus, as will be seen in the figures below, the intervention in the third community was begun three months following its introduction in the second community and six months after its introduction in the first community. Through this lagging procedure, one can rule out intervening variables such as historical events other than the CIPs as being responsible for visible changes. As such, if the data show desired changes concurrent with the onset of intervention in all three communities one can presume a causal linkage between the independent and dependent variables. While visual analysis of plotted data will often indicate clear changes between baseline and intervention data, several statistical procedures have been developed to analyze differences between baseline and intervention data. In two out of three communities fewer than 10 baseline measurements were gathered necessitating the use of Shewart Charts (see Gingerich, 1983; Gottman & Leiblum, 1974; Shewart, 1931) to evaluate changes. Essentially, Shewart Chart analyses require the plotting of a zone two standard deviations above and below the mean of the baseline. If two successive points during the intervention phase fall outside of this zone one can conclude that there has been a statistically significant change with only a 5% (.05) likelihood of this occurring by chance.

Results

The archival data collected on changes in police and court responses to woman battering are presented next. Two types of data are presented in two different ways. Data on the raw frequencies of arrests made, on convictions, and on men mandated to batterers' counseling are presented. Data is also presented on arrests as a percentage of total male-female domestic violence calls to the police and on the percentage of those arrested who are eventually convicted and mandated by the courts to batterers' counseling.

Percentages are presented in order to show changes in police and court response relative to the total number of "opportunities for change" with which each system was presented. For example, two men arrested out of a total of two male-female domestic violence calls represents quite a different response than two men arrested out of a total of 100 calls. It seems important, therefore, to inspect both raw frequency and relative percentage data.

It should also be noted here that out of a total of 98 arrests for domestic violence between men and women, only four arrests of women were made by the three police departments. In two of these four cases both the man and the woman were arrested. Arrested women were also the subject of intervention but because they represent such a small percentage of the total population they have been excluded from the figures shown next.

Police Response

In looking at changes resulting from a CIP, police are the first point of system contact for the men who batter and for their female victims. Therefore, an examination of arrest data is a logical starting point. In Figure 13.1, the number of arrests per month both before intervention (baseline) and during intervention are presented for each of the three communities. The broken line down the middle of the charts divides baseline periods on the left from intervention periods on the right.

By visually evaluating changes from baseline to intervention, definite trends toward increased numbers of arrests by police in all three communities are seen. These visual trends are backed up by statistical analyses in two of the three communities. Using Shewart Charts, changes in the first and third community reflect statistically significant ($p < .05$) differences between baseline and intervention in the desired direction. Changes from baseline to intervention in the second community, though not yet statistically significant, also tend to point strongly in the desired direction.

Figure 13.2 presents the number of monthly arrests as a percentage of the total number of domestic male-female violence calls received by each community. Even more so than the raw arrest data, these figures show a definite and general move by the three police departments toward increased use of the arrest response. When statistically analyzing the increase of arrests relative to calls, changes from baseline to intervention are significant ($p < .05$) in all three communities.

When examining Figure 13.2 it should be noted that in the second community in July of 1983 and in the third community in June, July, September, and November of 1983 there were no domestic calls received. Therefore, a zero percentage of arrests to calls for those months in those communities does not necessarily represent a negative finding.

Criminal Justice Response

Once arrested, men who batter begin contact with the criminal justice system. From the point of view of the CIPs, the desired outcomes of the

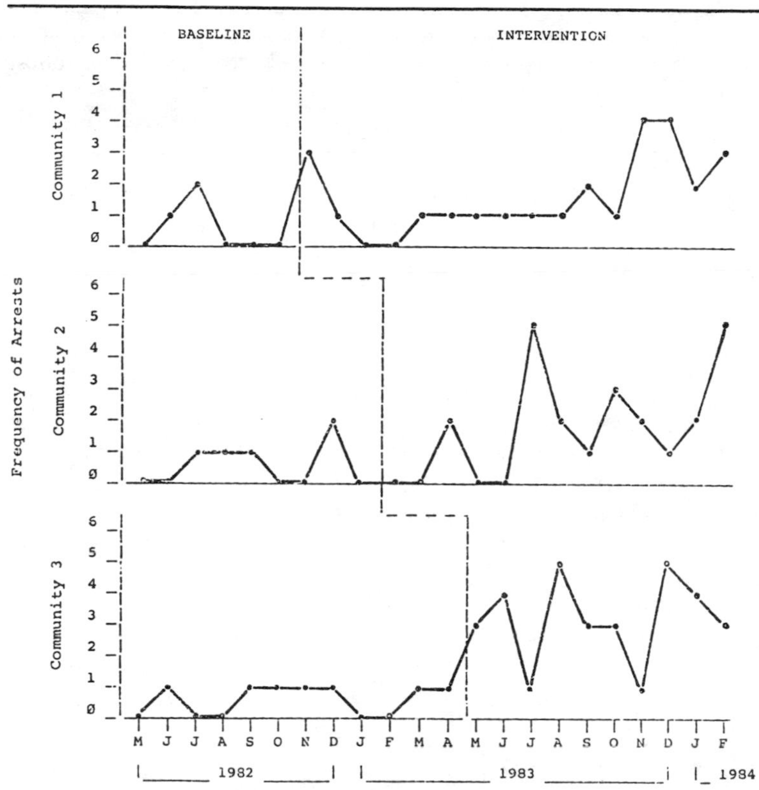

Figure 13.1 Frequency of arrests by month from May 1982 to February 1984, across three target communities.

court process are successful prosecution of each abuser and some form of mandated batterers' counseling for him. Data on both prosecutions and on men mandated to counseling are again presented here as both raw frequencies and percentages of arrests.

Successful prosecutions include guilty pleas by the abuser that are accepted by the court as well as convictions after a plea of not guilty. Figure 13.3 presents the raw frequencies of successful prosecutions of men who batter. As can be seen in the figure, only one man was prosecuted successfully prior to intervention. This changed during intervention, especially in the third community, and represented statistically significant ($p < .05$) changes in all three localities.

Taking into account the opportunity to prosecute in each community, that is, men arrested and arraigned, there were dramatic changes in court response as interventions continued. Figure 13.4 presents successful

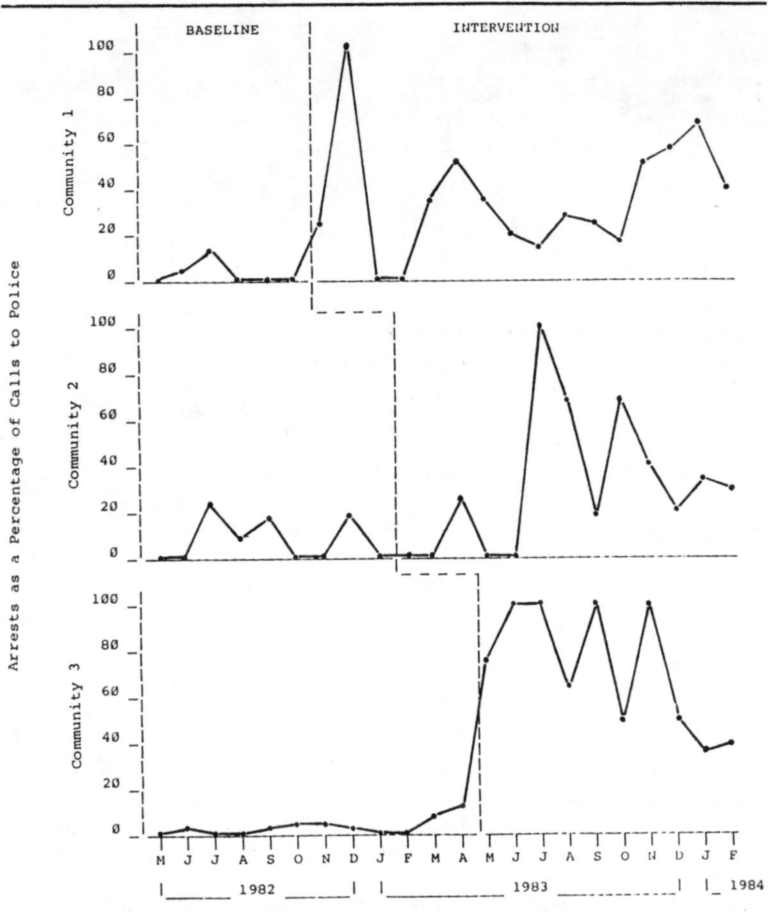

Figure 13.2 **Arrests as a percentage of the total number of male-female domestic violence calls received each month by police from May 1982 to February 1984, across three target communities.**

prosecutions as a percentage of arrests thus adjusting the data to account for the number of opportunities the criminal justice systems had to prosecute abusers. Both visually and statistically ($p < .05$), these data showed dramatically different criminal justice responding during intervention when compared to baseline. Again, as in Figure 13.2, one must consider those months in which there were no arrests, therefore, no opportunity to prosecute men. In those months a zero percent prosecution rate may be a result only of there being no opportunities to prosecute the men.

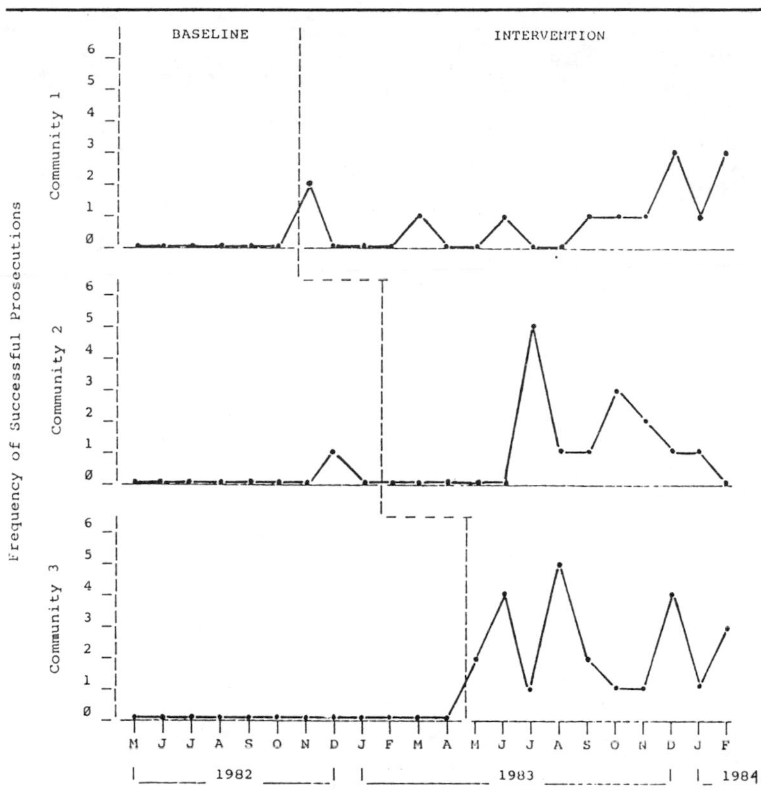

Figure 13.3 **Monthly frequency of successful prosecutions of men who batter, across three target communities from May 1982 to February 1984.**

Both Figures 13.3 and 13.4 present data that are conservative. There are a number of cases that are still pending prosecution in all three communities. On the one hand, if swift prosecution is a goal then these cases do not represent clear success. They may, however, eventually be successfully prosecuted. The totals presented in Figures 13.3 and 13.4 may, therefore, still increase as these cases are prosecuted. Specifically, in the first community two cases are still pending, one from December 1983, and the other from January 1984. In the second community, there are three cases pending, one each from May and October of 1983 and another from January 1984. Three cases are also pending in the third community, one from August 1983, and two from February 1984. As these cases are tried, the successful prosecution rates and percentages for these months may increase.

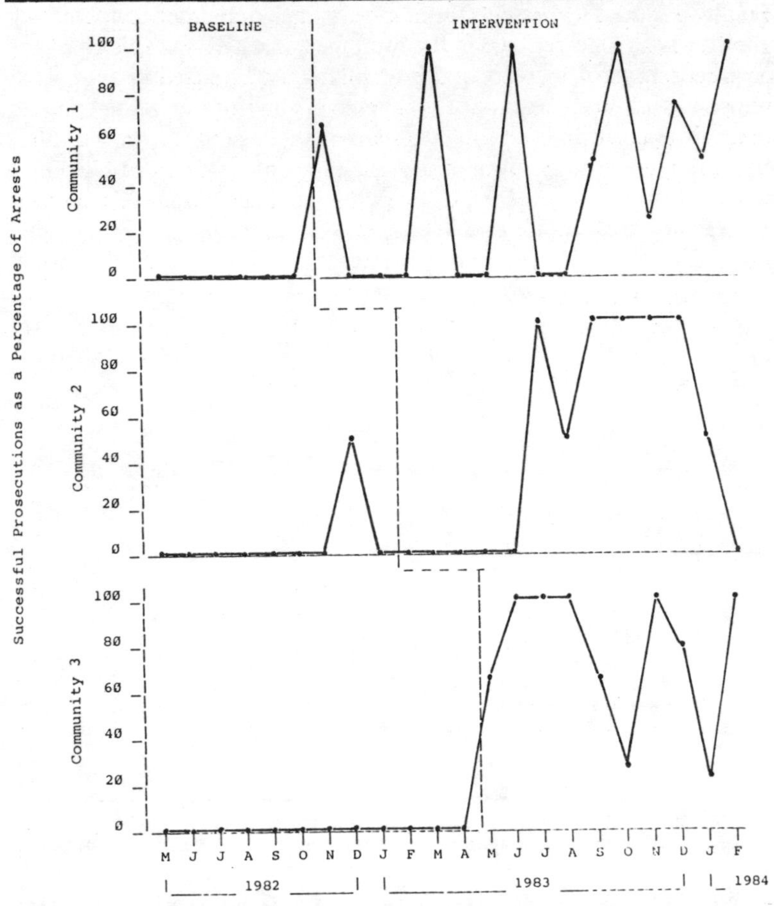

Figure 13.4 Successful prosecutions as a percentage of total number of monthly arrests, across three target communities from May 1982 to February 1984.

One desired outcome of successful prosecution is that each abuser will be mandated to counseling. Looking at the raw number of men mandated to batterers' counseling in Figure 13.5, it can be seen that there is again a general trend toward increased use of mandated counseling by the courts after intervention took place in the three communities. Again, using Shewart Charts, intervention in all three communities resulted in statistically significant ($p < .05$) changes in court response from baseline to intervention.

Finally, Figure 13.6 presents the number of men mandated to counseling by the courts as a percentage of the total men arrested. On this chart the same trends toward increasing use of mandated counseling as a court response is seen and these data presented in this format also represent statistically significant ($p < .05$) changes in desired directions after intervention in all three communities. When examining Figure 13.6, as in Figures 13.2 and 13.4, one should be careful to realize that in some months there were no arrests made and, therefore, a zero percentage of mandated counseling may not in itself represent a negative finding. Thus one should consult Figure 13.1 to determine the months in which there were no arrests in each community. Both Figures 13.5 and 13.6 will also be affected when cases still pending prosecution are concluded. It is likely that some of these eight men will be mandated to counseling if convicted.

Discussion

The results of intervention through police departments and the judicial system are encouraging. Both visually and statistically, the CIPs have had a significant impact upon both police and judicial responses to woman battering.

Each type of data collected reflect how, over time, a CIP can have an impact upon law enforcement and criminal justice system response. The data also show, however, that this can be a slow process. Arrests have been gradually increasing as a percentage of calls. Successful prosecutions as well as men mandated to counseling also have been gradually increasing as a percentage of total men arrested.

Coordinated interventions such as these take a great deal of effort. System responses reflect only the aggregate change by the individual police officers, prosecutors, referees, and judges. Depending upon the size of the systems involved, such changes may take a significant length of time to stabilize. For example, the community that appears at the top of each figure is part of a large urbanized county court system. There are five judges and 18 referees who rotate through that court to rule on cases from this community. As can be seen in Figure 13.4, successful prosecutions of those men arrested began to stabilize at a high rate a full 11 months after the intervention project began. It required that length of time to work with the many judges and referees and bring about a somewhat consistent response from them.

These projects take a great deal of staff effort in order to bring about change. Staff are not just coordinating these systems. They are also monitoring them. The existence of CIPs create accountability where it did not previously exist.

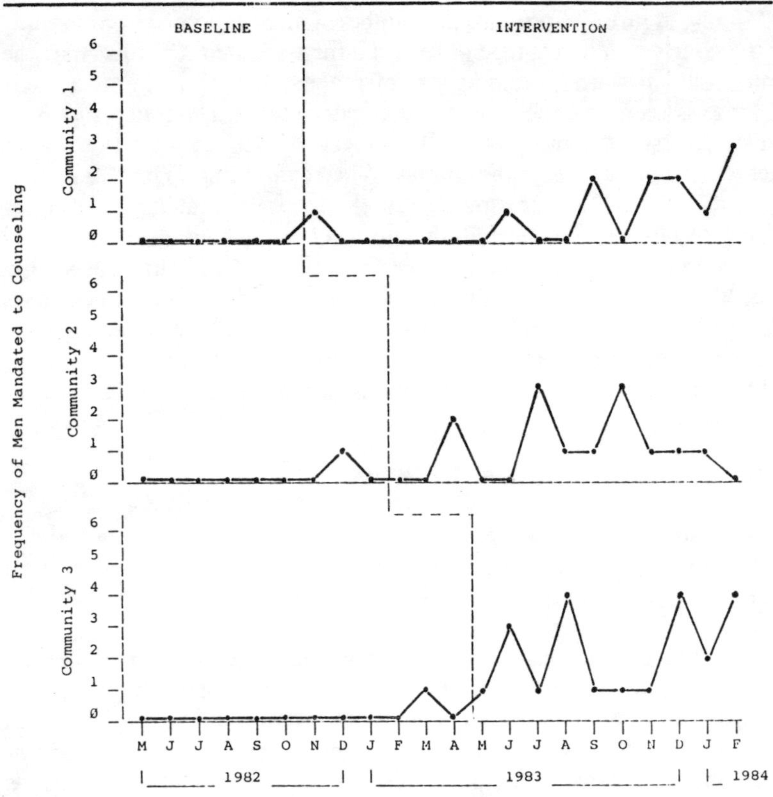

Figure 13.5 **Monthly frequency of men mandated to batterers' counseling by courts from May 1982 to Feburary 1984, across three target communities.**

Beyond creating accountability, however, there is another factor that creates success in system changes. Those in the police and judicial systems cooperate more fully as they begin to see their own role in the CIPs as helping to carry out the law to the fullest extent. By creating this shared goal, many in participating police departments and judicial systems begin to see themselves as partial owners of CIPs and begin to invest in their success.

While the results of this study are promising, there are several questions left unanswered. To date, there have not been replications of the Sherman and Berk (1984) study of police responses. Does the imposition of community sanctions alone lead to changed behavior and altered perceptions about community norms by the assailant?

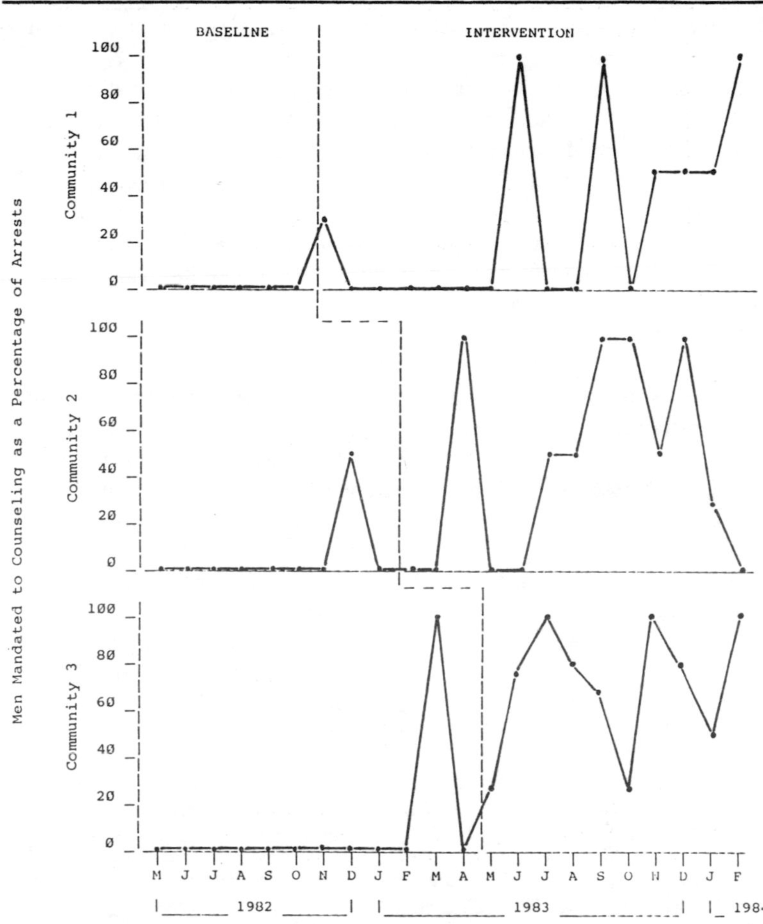

Figure 13.6 Mandated counseling as a percentage of the total number of arrested assailants each month from May 1982 to February 1984, across three target communities.

There is also no research on the impact of various forms of court response. In fact, while this study has presented data on men mandated into counseling, judges mandate counseling in many different ways. For example, some men are convicted and given prison terms, which are suspended if the man completes counseling, whereas other men's cases are dismissed if they complete recommended counseling. The result is that some men are convicted and others are not. At present, it is unclear what impact these various judicial approaches have upon a man's violence. Also, do all of these changed responses result in eliminating assaults by those receiving the changed community response? The CIPs currently assume that by altering police and judicial responding and by coordinating a "referral channel" to batterers' counseling programs the men will eventually either learn to control their own violence or experience consequences that will impose violence control externally. These changes may take place. It remains, however, an unanswered empirical question whether, in fact, they do. To date, there is not a single published evaluation of the effectiveness of court mandated counseling for men who batter. Social service agencies offering such programs may be collecting effectiveness data but such information has yet to be widely disseminated. (Only now are evaluations of the success of programs for voluntary clients being published.)

Other questions about the ways that men are mandated to counseling have also arisen. Do counseling programs for men who are mandated by the courts in different ways require different approaches by the participating social service systems? Can it be determined early which men are likely to succeed in counseling and which ones might not be appropriate for a mandated program?

The results of this study do show how a coordinated community intervention effort can dramatically alter the traditional modes of responding to woman battering by the law enforcement and criminal justice systems. It also raises a wide range of questions that will require a broad spectrum of formative research. Such research is needed in guiding existing community interventions and the design of future ones.

References

Bloom, M., & Fischer, J. (1982). *Evaluating practice: Guidelines for the accountable professional.* Englewood Cliffs, NJ: Prentice-Hall.

Fagan, J. A., Stewart, D. K., & Hansen, K. V. (1983). Violent men or violent husbands? In D. Finkelhor, R. Gelles, G. T. Hotaling and M. A. Straus (Eds.), *The dark side of families: Current family violence research.* Beverly Hills, CA: Sage.

Ford, D. A. (1983). Wife battery and criminal justice: A study of victim decision making. *Family Relations, 32,* 463-475.

Gaquin, D. A. (1977). Spouse abuse: Data from the National Crime Survey. *Victimology, 2* 632-643.

Gayford, J. J. (1975). Wife battering: A Preliminary survey of 100 cases. *British Medical Journal, 1,* 194-197.

Gingerich, W. J. (1983). Significance testing in single-case research. In A. Rosenblatt and D. Waldfogel (Eds.), *Handbook of clinical social work.* San Francisco: Jossey-Bass.

Gottman, J. M., & Leiblum, S. R. (1974). *How to do psychotherapy and how to evaluate it.* New York: Holt, Rinehart & Winston.

Hersen, M., & Barlow, D. H. (1976). *Single case experimental designs.* New York: Pergamon.

Kratochwill, T. R. (1978). *Single subject research.* New York: Academic Press.

Pence, E. (1983). The Duluth domestic abuse intervention project. *Hamline Law Review, 6,* 247-275.

Saunders, D. G., & Size, P. B. (1980). *Marital violence and the police: A survey of officers, victims and victim advocates.* Madison: Wisconsin Council on Criminal Justice.

Sherman, L. W., & Berk, R. A. (1984). The specific deterrent effects of arrest for domestic assault. *American Sociological Review, 49,* 261-272.

Shewart, W. A. (1931). *Economic control of quality of manufactured product.* New York: Van Nostrand Reinhold.

Soler, E., & Martin, S. (1983). *Domestic violence is a crime.* San Francisco: Family Violence Project.

PART V

The Response of Medical and Mental Health Services

14

Child Abuse Incidence and Reporting by Hospitals: Significance of Severity, Class, and Race

Robert L. Hampton
Eli H. Newberger

The visibility of child maltreatment, as reflected in case reports to state welfare agencies has been rising over the past decade. In 1981, according to the National Center on Child Abuse and Neglect, over 850,000 reports were received. This represented more than a tenfold increase in the course of a decade. Estimates of severe inflicted injuries to children deriving not from case reports but from household surveys, range from one to four million incidents per year. The true prevalence of child maltreatment is unknown.

Hospitals and medical personnel have played important roles in the diagnosis, reporting, and treatment of child abuse and neglect. This chapter examines the attributes that are associated with the diagnosis of child maltreatment seen in hospitals and its subsequent reporting to Child Protective Service agencies.

Materials and Methods

Data for this analysis were drawn from the National Study of the Incidence and Severity of Child Abuse and Neglect (NIS). The methodology and overall research design of the NIS have been described elsewhere. Briefly, this study was conducted in a stratified random sample of 26 counties clustered within 10 states: Arizona, California, Georgia, Illinois, Kansas, Missouri, New Hampshire, New York, Ohio, and South Carolina.

Overall the sample contained 10 urban, 6 suburban, and 10 rural counties. Each county had a known probability of selection, which provided the basis for computing national estimates. Data were collected on case reports received between May 1, 1979 and April 30, 1980.

National estimates were produced by attaching various sampling weights to the data collected. The estimation weight for hospital cases consisted of the product of three components: the "county selection weight"; the "hospital selection weight," adjusted for nonparticipation of several hospitals; and an "annualization weight."

The specific secondary analyses reported herein were based on data collected in the hospital sample. In most counties, all short-stay general hospitals containing an emergency room and/or a pediatric department (unit or ward) were included in the study design and asked to participate in the study. An initial list of such hospitals was prepared from directory information contained in the *American Hospital Association Guide to the Hospital Care Field* (1975 edition). This list was modified, as necessary, based on information obtained by the research director. In all, 70 of the 92 eligible hospitals (76%) participated in the study.

A total of 805 actual cases of child abuse and neglect came to the attention of the hospitals in the study during the year of examination. A projected estimate of 77,380 cases of abuse and neglect suspected by hospital professionals was derived from this number by the weighting procedures described above. The study was unique in its ability to measure which cases were selected for reporting to Child Protection Service agencies (CPS). Never before had a systematic effort been made to identify cases before reports were made and to ascertain the differences between cases that were reported and those that were not.

Two modes of data collection were available to all hospital reporters: a data form and a WATS line. Each respondent was given the option to use whichever reporting mechanism he or she preferred. In all instances, the respondent was required to provide some basic nonidentifying information on the child and family involved in the maltreatment incident and an account of what happened. To ensure maximum respondent participation, the study staff took a variety of steps to safeguard the identities of participating agencies and professional staff as well as the families and children involved. Reporting incidents to the study did not constitute an official report of abuse or neglect and data forms were made available neither to the local CPS unit, nor to anyone else at the local, state, or federal level. In addition, all participants were assured that the study's published findings would not present detailed county or state results—only national level findings.

Any particular child may have been reported to CPS more than once during the study year or may have been described to the study by any number or combination of sources. However, enough identifying data were collected to permit a reliable determination of whether or not any two data forms were describing the same child. Duplicate records were purged from the analysis file so that the case could be counted only once. Whenever a particular child was identified to the study by a hospital, or when another non-CPS source also appeared in the CPS file, the CPS record was retained. In effect, non-CPS respondents were given credit only for children who had not been reported to CPS—by the respondent or by anyone else.

Within hospitals, respondents included all professional staff in each of the following areas: emergency rooms, pediatric departments, pediatric outpatient departments, social service departments, and any professionals who might be attached to a child abuse team or program, if the hospital had one.

For the purposes of this study a child maltreatment situation was defined as

> one where, through purposive acts or marked inattention to a child's basic needs, behavior of a parent/substitute or other adult caretaker caused foreseeable and avoidable injury or impairment to a child, or materially contributed to unreasonable prolongation or worsening of an existing injury or impairment.

In implementing the general study definition, seven more specific criteria were established, all of which had to be met in order for a child to be considered within the scope of the study.

Nationally, approximately 652,000 children are estimated to have met the operational definitions of abuse and neglect during the study year, of whom 212,400 would have been known to the local child protective service agencies.

Hospitals identified many more cases of physical abuse than did other agencies. (The proportion of cases in this category alone exceeded the proportion of physical, sexual, and emotional abuse cases recognized by all the other agencies; over half the hospital cases were in one or another category of abuse.)

Compared to other agencies in the sample, hospital reports identified children who were younger and who had younger parents, and contained relatively higher proportions of families in urban areas (65.8% versus 42.1%) and who were black (25% versus 16%). There were no major differences between the hospital and other agencies with respect to income, mode of medical payment (public or private), proportion of single parent families, sex of the child, and other demographic factors.

Results

As can be seen in Table 14.1, there are several important differences between cases reported to CPS and nonreported cases. Black and Hispanic families were more likely to be reported to CPS than were white families. Whereas 60% of white families were reported to CPS, 74% of black and 91% of Hispanic families allegedly involved in child maltreatment were reported.

A similar pattern is found when one looks at the relationship between reporting and family income. Families with incomes in the lower two categories had the highest reporting rates. Approximately 80% of families in the lowest income categories were reported to CPS. Families with annual incomes of $25,000 or more had better than a two-to-one chance of having their recognized child maltreatment go unreported. The sample contained a relatively high proportion of young children. The proportion reported to CPS was also quite high. Children 5 years of age and younger constituted 55% of our sample. A total of 72% of these cases were reported. Adolescents were less likely to be reported. Some 57% of the adolescents in the sample were not reported. This was consistent with the overall NIS finding that older children were less likely to be reported.

Surprisingly, notwithstanding the fact that hospitals identify more serious cases of child abuse and neglect than do other agencies, serious injuries were often unreported. Serious injuries account for only 28% of the reported cases and 40% of the unreported cases. On closer examination the data reveal 53% of the maltreatment cases rated as serious were not reported to CPS.

The data indicated that mothers were the alleged perpetrators in approximately one-half of the cases and were not involved in slightly more than a third of the cases. A case report was more likely to be filed when a mother was not the alleged perpetrator than in cases in which she was the alleged perpetrator. Among nonreported cases mothers were the alleged perpetrators in 76% of the cases.

Physical abuse cases were more likely to be reported than unreported. Emotional abuse and neglect cases tend to be underreported. The latter finding is consistent with the expectation that in the absence of concrete evidence of injury, as frequently occurs in emotional maltreatment, professionals may tend not to report.

Multivariate Analyses

Multivariate analyses (Table 14.2) of all cases seen by hospitals yield a more detailed understanding of the differences between reported and

TABLE 14.1
Reporting of Hospital Maltreatment Cases

Attribute	Prevalence (%) in Sample	Reported	Not Reported	Total %
Race				
white	(66.7)	60.5	39.5	100
black	(25.7)	74.3	25.7	100
Hispanic	(7.6)	91.2	8.8	100
Income				
less than $7000	(49.3)	77.7	22.3	100
7000-14,900	(36.8)	80.0	20.0	100
15,000-24,999	(9.1)	70.2	29.8	100
25,000+	(4.8)	36.7	63.3	100
Severity of Injury Impairment				
fatal	(.3)	100.0	—	100
serious	(33.2)	46.8	53.2	100
moderate	(35.7)	55.2	47.8	100
probable	(30.8)	63.9	36.1	100
Child's Age				
0-5	(54.9)	72.0	28.0	100
6-12	(28.9)	70.8	29.2	100
13-17	(16.0)	42.5	57.5	100
Sex of Child				
male	51.6	65.3	34.7	100
female	48.3	68.0	32.0	100
Role of Mother				
maltreator	(49.6)	48.7	51.3	100
permitted	(8.3)	71.3	28.7	100
not involved	(34.5)	93.5	6.5	100
don't know	(7.5)	56.6	43.4	100
Father in Household				
biological father	(43.4)	64.2	35.8	100
father substitute	(12.7)	74.4	25.6	100
no father in house	(44.1)	66.9	33.1	100
Mother's Age				
19 or less	(10.8)	70.9	29.2	100
20-24	(21.4)	83.0	17.0	100
25-29	(15.5)	76.9	23.1	100
30-35	(18.1)	80.1	19.9	100

TABLE 14.1 (continued)

Attribute	Prevalence (%) in Sample	Reported	Not Reported	Total %
36+	(14.1)	71.0	29.0	100
don't know	(20.0)	28.5	71.5	100
Allegation				
physical abuse	(35.5)	75.6	24.4	100
sexual abuse	(9.4)	80.8	19.2	100
emotional abuse	(5.7)	36.1	63.9	100
physical neglect	(26.3)	65.8	34.2	100
educational neglect	(1.4)	5.5	94.5	100
emotional neglect	(13.7)	42.6	57.4	100
miscellaneous maltreatment	(7.8)	85.4	14.6	100
Urbanicity				
SMSA over 200,000	(65.8)	68.2	31.8	100
other SMSA	(18.7)	70.5	29.5	100
non-SMSA	(15.5)	55.3	44.7	100
Total		66.6	33.4	100

NOTE: Unweighted N = 805; weighted N = 77379.

unreported cases. A stepwise discriminant function procedure was used to select variables for inclusion. The variables in Table 14.2 appear in the order of their selection. In our analysis, the following factors appeared most powerfully to affect case reporting: income, the role of the mother in maltreatment, emotional abuse, race, the employment of the mother, sexual abuse, number of victims, and the education of the mother. Disproportionate numbers of unreported cases involved victims of emotional abuse, families of higher income, mothers who were alleged to be responsible for the injuries, and those who were white.

These findings suggest that for the hospital sample, class and race are the more important factors defining the gradient between reported and unreported cases. The relative discriminating power of severity attains the levels of statistical significance only when income is excluded from the analyses.

Discussion

A major goal of this study has been to gain a better understanding of child maltreatment cases seen in hospitals and to assess the differences

TABLE 14.2
Standardized Canonical Discriminant Function Coefficients and Summary Statistics for Hospital Reporting

Variable	Coefficient	Reported Cases Mean	Reported Cases S.D.	Unreported Cases Mean	Unreported Cases S.D.
Emotional abuse	.65	.04	.21	.38	.48
Role of mother	–.45	.42	.49	.83	.37
Income	.58	1.59	.76	2.08	1.07
Race	–.30	.57	.49	.85	.35
Emotional neglect	.22	.10	.26	.18	.39
Mother employed	.26	.23	.49	.24	.51
Sexual abuse	.24	.08	.23	.08	.27
Number of victims	–.22	1.66	1.13	1.64	1.02
Mother's education	–.20	2.25	.75	2.29	.83
Urbanicity	–.15	1.52	.72	1.65	.82
Sex of child	–.13	.48	.49	.48	.49
Physical abuse	.10	.36	.42	.18	.48
	Canonical R = .602				

NOTE: When emotional abuse is excluded from the analysis, Mother's Role in Maltreatment and Family Income remain the most important discriminators. The relative contributions of Physical Abuse, Physical Neglect, and Ethnicity also increase.

between reported and unreported cases. Analyses of these data support our original hypothesis that within the population of maltreated children, hospitals are more likely to see a higher proportion of moderately to seriously injured children than are other study agencies. However, children identified with serious injuries in hospital settings are often unreported to child protective service.

Although hospitals reported cases within the scope of the study definitions more frequently than did other agencies, they failed to report large numbers of the cases that should have been reported. This is, in part, related to the fact that child abuse is neither theoretically nor clinically well defined. This definitional ambiguity increases the likelihood of subjective professional evaluation. Cases of physical and sexual child abuse may require less subjectivity. Consequently a higher proportion of such cases may be reported. Emotional abuse, on the other hand, requires more subjectivity and may be reported less.

Social distance is inherent to the provider-patient relationship. The provider (e.g., physician, nurse) is always in a superordinate position because of his or her expertise. Sociological labeling theory posits that the greater the social distance between the typer and the person singled out for typing, the broader the type, and the more quickly it may be applied. The label of child maltreater may be likely to be fixed if the diagnostician and possible abuser share similar characteristics, especially socioeconomic status, particularly when the injury is not serious or manifestly a consequence of maltreatment. Although professional practice claims to be value-free, personal prejudices and judgments may affect individuals who are defined as deviant.

Previous research in which physicians were presented with case vignettes in which class and ethnic variables were manipulated suggests that physicians' judgments of possible child abuse are affected by socioeconomic and ethnic status. Socially marginal families may be victimized by a process in which their personal characteristics rather than their behavior defines them as deviant. With respect to child abuse, physicians' preconceptions of an "abuser" stereotype may govern the choice of who among parents presenting an injured child will be seen as a possible abuser.

Families with greater means may have a higher probability of avoiding the abuser label. This discrimination not only subjects lower socioeconomic and ethnic minority families to the stigma of being labeled as abusive, but may also subject them to interventions that may be both intrusive and punitive. The same process discriminates in favor of white and high socioeconomic status families. A latent consequence of this biased reporting may be a failure to address the needs of the many children in middle class families whom surveys suggest are at risk of maltreatment.

It has been proposed that the CPS classification of cases into substantiated or not substantiated categories is a more accurate assessment of whether maltreatment occurred than is the suspicion of someone reporting the case to the system. This proposition rests on the assumption that the reporting process represents a screening test and the CPS investigation represents a "determinant test," or an appropriate measure of whether the abuse indeed occurred. Our data suggest that biases at the point of recognition and reporting play a major role in determining which cases are channeled into the protective services system for investigation. Case substantiation, therefore, may not merely define a function of whether the case exceeds a certain threshold of validity, but may also be affected by a function of the reporting process. Unreported cases are by definition unsubstantiatable.

This formulation is supported by the study of Carr and Gelles (1978), who, in a review of case reports to the Florida central registry, found that the principal determinant of case substantiation was the professional status of the reporter. Physicians' and hospitals' reports were far more likely to be screened in as valid, irrespective of clinical severity.

Conclusion

We perceive from these data a need to sensitize medical professionals to the social dimensions of family violence, and, through theory-building and training, to change the orientation of medical workers and medical institutions from simple, manifestational conceptions of symptoms, causes, and treatments to richer etiologic understandings and actions on social problems expressed at all levels. One desirable outcome of this training and study would be a reduction in the number of cases that are unnecessarily reported and investigated, and there might also follow an increase in the reporting of serious cases of maltreatment. This research suggests that an alarming number of serious cases of recognized maltreatment go unreported.

Definitions of child abuse vary from Henry Kempe and his colleagues' "battered child syndrome," which identifies injuries inflicted by caregivers, to the current Health and Human Services model reporting statutes. In a period of shifting fiscal resources at state and local levels, there is a danger of narrowing the definitions of child maltreatment to exclude many situations currently viewed as placing children at risk. More enlightened formulations of child maltreatment should include considerations of such factors as chronicity of injury and age of child as well as the type and severity of injury. Broad concepts of child maltreatment run the risk of exposing many families to unnecessary intrusions and may deny many families with the greatest needs the resources that might alleviate the problems that threaten the well being of their children. On the other hand, too narrow a notion of child maltreatment will deny families and children opportunities to achieve a level of functioning that would allow minimal levels of growth and survival.

If child abuse reporting is as biased by class and race as these data suggest, then there is clearly a need for a critical review of the *system* as well as the *process* of reporting.

To the extent that we selectively invoke agents of the state to police the lives of poor and nonwhite families, we may be inappropriately—and unfairly—condemning them as evil. They may serve as scapegoats to relieve our community responsibility for violence toward children.

References

American Humane Association (1981). *Highlights of official child neglect and abuse reporting* (Annual Report). Denver: Author.

Carr, A., & Gelles, R. J. (1978). *Reporting child maltreatment in Florida: The operation of public child protective service systems.* (Report submitted to the National Center on Child Abuse and Neglect).

Department of Health and Human Services (1981). *Study findings: National study of the incidence and severity of child abuse and neglect.* (DHHS Publication No. 81-30325). Washington, DC: Government Printing Office.

Department of Health and Human Services (1981). *Study methodology: National study of the incidence and severity of child abuse and neglect.* (DHHS Publication No. 81-30326). Washington, DC: Government Printing Office.

Gelles, R. J. (1982, November). Applying research on family violence to clinical practice. *Journal of Marriage and Family,* pp. 873-885.

Gibbons, D. C. (1970). *Delinquent behavior.* Englewood Cliffs, NJ: Prentice Hall.

Hampton, R. L., & Newberger, E. H. (1983). *Hospitals as gatekeepers: Recognition and reporting in the national incidence study of child abuse and neglect.* Report to the National Center on Child Abuse and Neglect.

Jason, J., Andereck, N. D., Marks, J., & Tyler, T. W., Jr. (1982). Child abuse in Georgia: A method to evaluate risk factors and reporting bias. *American Journal of Public Health, 72,* 1353-1358.

Kempe, C. H., Silverman, F. N., Steele, B. F., et al. (1962). The battered child syndrome. *Journal of the American Medical Association, 181,* 17.

Newberger, E. H., & Bourne, R. (1975). The medicalization and legalization of child abuse. *American Journal of Orthopsychiatry, 48*(4), 593-607.

O'Toole, R., Turbett, P., & Nalepka, C. (1983). Theories, professional knowledge, and diagnosis of child abuse. In D. Finkelhor, R. Gelles, G. T. Hotaling, & M. A. Straus (Eds.), *The dark side of families: Current family violence research* (pp. 349-362). Beverly Hills, CA: Sage.

Pfohl, S. (1977). The discovery of child abuse. *Social Problems, 24,* 310-323.

Schur, E. (1971). *Labeling deviant behavior.* New York: Harper & Row.

Snyder, J., Bowles, R. T., & Newberger, E. H. (1982). Improving research and practice on family violence: Potential of a hospital based training program. *Urban Social Change Review, 15,* 3-7.

Straus, M. A., Gelles, R. J., & Steinmetz, S. K. (1980). *Behind closed doors: Violence in the American family.* Garden City, NY: Anchor/Doubleday.

PART VI

The Response of Protective Services

15

Foster Care for Child Maltreatment: Impact on Delinquent Behavior

Desmond K. Runyan
Carolyn L. Gould

More than 1,400,000 documented allegations of child abuse or neglect were received by state or local welfare authorities in 1982 (American Humane Association, 1984). These data, from the most recent national summary, may underestimate the true magnitude of the problem. Extrapolation of data from other sources puts the actual incidence at well over one million cases a year or more than 10.5 cases per 1,000 children per year (Gelles, 1978; National Center on Child Abuse and Neglect, 1981). The societal response to the abused or neglected child varies widely but approximately 15% of confirmed maltreatment victims are placed in an unrelated family foster home (American Humane Association, 1979; Runyan, Gould, Trost, & Loda, 1981). The apparent sequelae of abuse or neglect have been well described (Elmer & Gregg, 1967; Morse, Sabler, & Friedman, 1970; Elmer, 1977; Martin, & Breezley, 1977; Kinard, 1978). However, many of the landmark cohort studies have

AUTHORS' NOTE: We are grateful for support from the Edna McConnell Clark Foundation and the Robert Wood Johnson Clinical Scholars Program at the University of North Carolina. Drs. Earl Siegel, Frank Loda, Robert Fletcher, Dale Williams, and Carol Runyan have contributed valuable advice to the project. Sue Glassby, Page Hudson, and Larry Sage from the North Carolina Department of Human Resources; G. Styron, V. Bissett, M. Exkels, E. Inman, E. Chapin, and T. Ward from the County Departments of Social Services; Judges D. Carter, S. Peel, G. Bason, J. Allen, M. Read, Jr., and W. Jones from the District Courts involved in the study; and many individual social workers all contributed to the successful completion of data collection. Research assistants for the project were Leandrus Christian, Jean Forster, Mary Lee Roberts, Mary Renkens, Clark Charlton, and Ann Woodward. Ellyn Harris assisted in the preparation of the manuscript.

This chapter is reproduced by permission of *Pediatrics*, volume 75, page 562, copyright 1985.

given little or no attention to the possible modifying or confounding effects of intervening treatments. A number of experts are alarmed that one type of service, foster care, is seldom done well and may itself be harmful to the maltreated child (Shor, 1982; Kadushin, 1978; Governor's Advocacy Council on Children and Youth, 1978; Fanshel, 1981).

This historical cohort study was undertaken to examine the impact of foster care on the maltreated child and thereby allow more careful consideration of the sequelae of maltreatment.

Beginning as early as 1950, published reports have linked harsh physical punishment with juvenile delinquency (Glueck & Glueck, 1950). More recent retrospective work found that the vast majority of juvenile delinquents in one setting had a history of child abuse and neglect early in childhood. A cohort study of children abused or neglected in the early 1950s in eight New York counties found that 19% had been found to be delinquent or in need of supervision after a dozen or more years (Alfaro, 1976). In studies of incarcerated juvenile delinquents, children with a history of either violent crimes or crimes against persons are more likely to have been abused compared to children guilty of either crimes against property or less violent crimes (Rodgers & Leunes, 1979; Lewis, Shanok, Pincus, & Glaser, 1979). Analysis of the data from Lewis et al. reveal an estimated relative risk ratio of 2.9 for a child abuse history in the medical record of incarcerated delinquents compared to delinquents who had not been incarcerated (Lewis, Shanok, & Balla, 1979). When delinquent children were compared to a community sample of nondelinquent children of the same age, the odds ratio for history of abuse was 8.8 (95% CI; 2.78-23.4)[1]; suggesting that abused children are at 8.8 times higher risk of subsequent delinquency than are their nonabused peers (Lewis & Shanok, 1979; Kleinbaum, Kupper, & Morgenstern, 1982; Cornfield, 1951). In this study juvenile delinquency has been used as a potential marker for "iatrogenic" damage done to the child victim. No other studies have similarly attempted to use delinquency in such a manner. Although delinquency is a limited behavioral phenomenon that does not encompass the variety of potential harms of child abuse or neglect, it appears to be useful as one indicator in an overall evaluation of the impact of services.

Methods

This study used a matched historical cohort design. We compared the rate of subsequent juvenile delinquency between current foster children who had been maltreated and maltreated children who had been left in their own homes. Maltreated children in six central North Carolina counties were eligible for the study. Maltreatment was determined by the presence of a confirmed report of neglect or abuse by a parent or guardian in the cumulative social service record. Restriction by age was used to limit the study group to children old enough to be at risk for juvenile delinquency, the outcome of interest.

The "treatment" cohort was formed by including all children presently in unrelated family foster care who had been in care for at least three continuous years. Adolescents who had been in family homes for at least three years but who were now hospitalized, incarcerated, or in group homes were still considered part of this cohort.

The comparison cohort was formed by systematically searching county department of social service records for a maltreated child who was the closest match for the date of report, the same age, confirmed as maltreated the same year, maltreated by a parent or guardian, and provided services in the home. Children whose cumulative file suggested that they had moved from the county or were later placed in foster care were excluded. When more than one potential match was found within the same year, the control child that most closely matched the foster child by race and/or sex was selected. Earlier work in North Carolina had found that the type of severity of maltreatment bore little relationship to the decision to place a child in care; the decision to place a child in foster care appeared to be most directly affected by the source of referral (i.e., courts or police, the particular agency responsible for the investigation, or the particular court jurisdiction in which the case was decided [Runyan, Gould, Trost, & Loda, 1981]). Because the type of maltreatment and severity were so unimportant in the earlier analysis, and many of these children were originally placed in care during the same time period, we made no attempt to match by maltreatment type.

Informed consent and permission for access to records were obtained from the State Department of Human Resources, the county social services departments, the county school systems, the appropriate district court judges, and the parents of all children in parental legal custody. The data were collected by abstracting the cumulative folders maintained by the social service agencies, the juvenile court records in each county, and the cumulative school record of each child.

Specific information sought in the review of records included the following:

(1) type of maltreatment(s) and age of the child at occurrence,
(2) type of social services provided by county agencies,
(3) type, duration, and number of foster home placements for each child,
(4) race, education, occupation, and marital status of natural parent(s),
(5) observations of behavior by social services agency employees,
(6) nature, date, and outcome of all juvenile court hearings, and
(7) evidence of severe mental retardation.

Children whose social services or school records indicated either severe mental retardation or an IQ score of less than 50 on either the Stanford-Binet or WISC-R intelligence tests were excluded from the analysis because of the presumed decreased likelihood of their being able to become involved in criminal activity.

The data were collected by trained research assistants or the authors directly at the site that the records were located. Because of the necessity of probing legal access to records at each site by presentation of a signed release, it was not possible to blind the research assistants to the foster or home care status of the children. The estimate of risk for delinquency was calculated for both the foster and home groups using an incidence-density measure (Kleinbaum, Kupper, & Morgenstern, 1982). The risk of delinquency per year at risk after the eleventh birthday was chosen as the measure of interest in order to adjust the risk estimate to include the shortened time period of risk for the younger children in the sample. Restricting the risk period to time after the eleventh birthday served both to assure that the crime reports followed the maltreatment reports temporally and to eliminate those years of life when the risk of ratio was used to measure the relative risk of juvenile delinquency among foster children compared to their peers in home care (Kleinbaum, Kupper, & Morgenstern, 1982). Statistical tests of significance included student's t-test, Fisher's Exact Test, and the Mantel-Haenzel chi-square test. Risk ratio confidence intervals were calculated using a test-based method (Kleinbaum, Kupper, & Morgenstern, 1982). Logistic regression was used to confirm the simpler analyses (Kleinbaum, Kupper, & Morgenstern, 1982; Cornfield, 1951; Miettenen, 1976; Mantel & Haenzel, 1959).

Results

A total of 114 foster children who met the study criteria were found in the six counties. A group of 106 children were identified as controls: 69 children matched a foster child by age at report, year of report, sex, and race; 19 controls were identified after allowing the sex and/or race to vary between cases and controls; 19 additional control children were selected by allowing the year of report to vary while maintaining a match for the current age. Eight foster care children could not be matched because county records for the years surrounding an early report were inadequate to locate children served in the home during that time period.

The baseline demographic data for the children in the home and foster care groups are compared in Table 15.1. A few significant "pretreatment" differences are notable between the two cohorts: maternal education,

TABLE 15.1
Description of Study Groups

	Foster Care (N = 114)	Home Care (N = 106)
Age at time of study	14.09 years	14.07 years
Race	66% black	55% black
Gender	48% female	54% female
Mother's age	29.5 years	29.1 years
Maternal education*	8.8 years	10.2 years
Parental alcohol abuse	48%	34%
Type of maltreatment*	9% physical abuse	22% physical abuse
History of prior maltreatments*	25%	9%

* significant at $p < .05$ (student's t-test, uncorrected for multiple comparisons).

history of prior maltreatment, and percentage of children physically abused at the time of the index report. These differences contrast with the findings of earlier research that suggested that there were few differences between children selected for foster care and children left in the home (Maden, 1980). The discrepancies most likely result from the selection of only those children in care for three years or longer as the foster care group.

The foster care children averaged 2.6 foster homes during a mean of 8.6 years since the initial report. The median number of foster home placements was 2; 36 children (32%) remained in the foster home in which they were first placed; 23 (20%) had been in four or more foster homes. Two children in the sample had each experienced 9 foster homes and one child had been in 11 homes. The mean duration of the first home placement was 3.6 years.

Social Service records were not always adequate to determine length, duration, and type of services provided to children in home care. Among the 77 children with adequate records for home services, the average number of visits in the first two months was 5.3. The mean number of visits by six months was 8.25. The mean number of months that home services were provided, among those 60 children with records detailed enough to assess duration of service, was 22 months. Longitudinal information that adequately addressed the issue of psychological development was not available in any of the social service agency records examined. Behavioral difficulties, such as stealing, fighting, lying, or running away, were reported in the social service record in 45 of the 114 foster care children (39%) at some time after the report that resulted in foster care placement. Stealing was the most commonly reported phenomenon; 13 children were said by social workers or foster parents to have taken private property. Among the children in home care, 13 (12%) were reported to have had subsequent behavior problems. The usefulness of recorded behavior problems as a marker of subsequent development is limited because the bias of increased observation of children in foster care by foster parents and social workers. The rate of reported maltreatment subsequent to the index report that initiated services is one measure of the success of protective services. Among the 106 home care children, 27, or 25% were subsequently confirmed as victims of repeated maltreatment. Of the 114 foster care children, 12 were also confirmed as having been victims of repeated maltreatment (half at the hands of foster parents and half by natural parents on home visits). The overall relative risk of all subsequent confirmed reabuse for home care children compared to foster care children is 2.42 (95% CI: 1.33, 4.39). If the reabuse by natural parents of foster care children is excluded, the relative risk of subsequent reabuse is 4.84 for home children compared to foster children. In addition to the confirmed reports, there were 18 unsubstantiated reports of maltreatment among the 220 study subjects: 7 among foster children and 11 among home care children.

Only 93 foster care children were available for follow-up with court records; 12 had been placed in care outside of the study counties and 9 were excluded because of severe or moderate mental retardation. In all, 83 home care children were available for follow-up through court records. A total of 20 home care children had moved out of the study counties and 3 children were excluded because of mental retardation. Comparison of the remaining study subjects and the children who had moved revealed no significant differences in age, race, sex, or maternal education.

Overall, 28 crimes were found from among the sample of 176 maltreatment victims. Ten foster care children committed 14 crimes after the age of 11; 8 home care children also committed a total of 14 crimes. The overall rate of .053 crimes/child/person year after age 11 did not differ statistically by group membership. The nature of crimes committed did differ; 5 charges of assault were made against children in foster care, while no assault charges were lodged against children in home care (Table 15.2). This result was at the $p < .05$ level of significance.

There was a significant correlation of 0.578 ($p = .001$) between number of foster home placements and convictions for criminal activity among all foster children. Children who experienced a higher number of placements were more likely to have also been involved in criminal activity. This relationship is shown graphically in Table 15.3. The estimated relative risk for delinquency climbs from 0.20 for delinquency of foster children in their first foster homes (compared to home care children) to 3.77 for children who have been in more than four foster homes.

TABLE 15.2
Crimes Committed Since Maltreatment Report

Home Care Children	(number)	Foster Care	(number)
Vandalism	(2)	Assault	(5)
Breaking and entering	(4)	Breaking and entering	(1)
Shoplifting	(2)	Delinquency	(1)
Larceny	(3)	Drugs	(2)
Theft	(1)	Forgery	(2)
Auto theft	(1)	Possession of stolen goods	(1)
Undisciplined	(1)	Parole violation	(2)

The association between the number of foster home placements and subsequent delinquency does not appear to be causal. A total of 65 children left their first foster homes, 18 of them because their behavior was a problem for their new foster parents; 5 of these latter children were subsequently charged with juvenile delinquency. The children whose own behavior resulted in removal from their first foster homes were 2.36 times as likely to become involved in delinquency as were their foster care peers who were moved for another reason. Among the 42 children who were moved out of their second foster homes, 7 of the 8 children who subsequently got into legal difficulty and had been moved because their behavior was a problem for the foster parents. The early removals for behavior problems appear to be at highest risk of later delinquency.

Discussion

Cohort Differences

Significant discrepancies are apparent between the cohorts with respect to history of prior maltreatment, maternal education, and type oi abuse. The group of children who were in foster care had less educated mothers, a history of more episodes of prior maltreatment and were more likely to have been physically abused than were their home care peers. These differences may represent family differences that influence a decision to place a child in foster care. A history of prior maltreatment in addition to the current report can be viewed as a strong risk factor for subsequent abuse or neglect or represent evidence of reported failure of less dramatic interventions. The significantly lower maternal education, as a proxy for social class, may indicate that the abusing or neglecting family has fewer resources or alternatives. Social service agencies, public hospitals, courts,

TABLE 15.3

Estimated Relative Risk of Delinquency for Foster Children Compared to Home Care Children After Maltreatment (by Number of Foster Homes)

GROUP	N	Years of Risk[a]	Total No. of Crimes	Incidence Density (Crimes/person-year)	Incidence Density Ratio (R.R.)[b]	95%CI[c]
Home	83	254.0	14	.055	—	
In one foster home	34	90.66	1	.011	.20	(N.S.)
In two foster homes	22	36.1	0	.0	.0	(N.S.)
In three foster homes	11	47.5	1	.021	.38	(N.S.)
In four foster homes	9	27.85	2	.072	1.30	(N.S.)
In more than four homes	12	48.08	10	.208	3.77	(1.77—8.02)
All foster care	93	279	14	.050	0.91	(N.S.)

a. Years or age from time of eleventh birthday until date of data collection for group.

b. Incidence density ratio is the estimate for relative risk.

c. Test-based confidence interval, calculated by methods described by Kleinbaum, et al., using Mantel-Haenzel chi-square.

and the other professionals involved with poor families may be more inclined to advocate for a child's removal from a maltreating environment. Neglect may be viewed as inherently more chronic and pervasive than physical abuse and thus physically abused children may be less likely to be placed in foster care than are neglected children. Since known sexual abuse involved only three children from this study (2 foster care children and 1 home care child), the role of this type of abuse in determining foster care placement cannot be ascertained. The differences between cohorts in the proportions of neglect versus abuse may be artifactual. Foster care placement requires an antecedent juvenile court hearing and, in North Carolina, legal charges of child neglect appear to be easier to establish than charges of child abuse (personal communication, Supervisors of Protective Services in Cumberland and Orange Counties, April and May 1981).

Evidence from North Carolina (Runyan, Gould, Trost, & Loda, 1981), and a more recent national study on sexual abuse by Finkelhor (1983), indicate that socioeconomic status and race are not important determinants of foster care for maltreated children. The North Carolina data suggest that the victim's age is relatively unimportant in the placement decision when maltreatment of all forms is considered. The Finkelhor study did find that age is a significant determinant of foster care placement for sexually abused children (Finkelhor, 1983). Age is not an important confounder in this investigation because of its strict control through matching. This study's findings of cohort differences in maternal education may not contradict the studies just cited. The differences may result from the effects of the exclusion of foster care children who were able to return home before a minimum of three years of foster care.

Children from families of lower socioeconomic status, represented by maternal education, may be less likely to be reunited with their own families. Their parents may have difficulty securing release of their children through the courts or be less able to participate in treatment programs that will allow them to resume care of their children. Similarly, children who have been neglected or who experience multiple episodes of maltreatment may be at increased risk of prolonged stay in foster care because their parents may be viewed as more intractable. Better educated families may be more willing or able to modify their behavior and cooperate with a social service agency, thereby permitting earlier reunification of the family.

Two other factors, sex and race, were not statistically significantly different between cohorts, although the foster care group had both more males and more blacks. The sex and race variations between the two groups reflects the difficulty encountered in locating adequate numbers of blacks and males in the social service records who had never been removed from their homes after a report of maltreatment. Regression analyses controlling for the variation between the cohorts in maternal education, race, sex, and type of past maltreatment confirmed the lack of a significant relationship between foster home placement and juvenile delinquency. The regression analyses are not presented here because they do not add to the simpler analyses.

Outcomes

Our data on the process of foster care in North Carolina are similar to experience elsewhere. Over an average of more than eight years in care, the mean number of placements, excluding emergency shelters, was 2.6 homes; 20% had been in four or more homes (Shor, 1982; Kadushin, 1978; Vasaly, 1976). The impact of these serial uprootings with the concomitant interruption of newly formed emotional bonds must be important. This study has attempted to clarify some of the risks and benefits of foster care because the experience has so much theoretical hazard.

The risk of subsequent maltreatment is lower in foster care. Fear of repeated abuse is clearly one factor that prompts an original decision to place a child (Gould & Runyan, 1984). One-quarter of the home care subjects in this study were subsequently rereported for abuse or neglect. This figure may be lower than a random sample of all previously reported children because of our exclusion of children who were subsequently placed in foster care for any period of time less than three years. Any children placed in care for three or more years and still in care would have been a part of the foster care cohort. Six foster children experienced confirmed maltreatment within the foster home. These children were all moved to new homes. Foster care reduces, but does not eliminate the risk of subsequent maltreatment.

The use of juvenile delinquency rates as a measure of the impact of services for maltreated children is a novel approach that is particularly appealing because of its unobtrusive nature. Even more important, it represents an outcome that is of major concern to society and one that has been repeatedly linked with child maltreatment. Insofar as the agencies providing services to the child and agencies responsible for investigation and arrest of delinquents are independent, the outcome is independent of home care or foster care cohort status. Neither the number of children caught nor the number of crimes committed varied significantly by cohort status. The overall rate of crimes committed, .05 crimes per person a year after age 11, multiplies to .367 crimes per child over the seven years of adolescence between ages 11 and 18. This figure, though calculated using an incidence-density estimation of risk, looks remarkably similar to the 30% of a cohort of maltreated children noted to have been subsequently charged with delinquency in a study from New York State (Lewis, Shanok, & Balla, 1979).

Perhaps the most unexpected finding in this study is the difference in numbers of assault charges between the two groups. No home care child was even charged with assault, whereas 5 foster children were convicted of criminal assault. The numbers are too small to have great confidence in this result but the suggestion of difference should be examined in other studies. While the police and courts are generally independent of social services, it may be that foster children are more likely to be charged with assault because of decreased tolerance for violence among foster parents or social workers. The larger number of assault convictions among the foster care cohort may also represent either a real influence of foster care or a basic tendency among more severely maltreated children. Earlier work suggested that crimes against persons were more commonly committed by abused and neglected children (Lewis, Shanok, & Balla, 1979; Lewis & Shanok, 1979). Foster care may exacerbate this response. However, chance alone is one possible explanation for the difference in number of assault charges.

Finally, we attempted to explore the relationship between multiple foster home placements and juvenile delinquency. The positive correlation between number of foster home placements and number of delinquency convictions suggests that multiple foster home placement is related to subsequent juvenile delinquency. However analysis of the reasons behind changes in placement revealed that many of the foster home changes for children subsequently convicted of a crime were motivated by foster parents being unable to tolerate the child's behavior. The multiple home changes were an early marker of behavior that later was manifested as delinquency. Regardless of the causal direction, children who fail in their early foster care arrangements are in need of special services to prevent subsequent juvenile delinquency. These data provide strong evidence for even more widespread adoption of "permanency planning" efforts by social service agencies.

Limitations

The limitations of this study result from three features of the design: nonrandom allocation to foster care, the requirement that eligible foster children have been in care for three or more years, and use of existing social records to document the outcome.

The determinants of foster care have been discussed. In North Carolina, as elsewhere, there are few standardized criteria for determining the need for foster care and the counties vary widely in its use. The inclusion of six different counties in this study ensures that there was some variation in the decision. Our decision to use only children who had been in foster care for three or more years resulted from the need to ensure that sufficient time in foster care has had a significant impact. Data from North Carolina suggest that the median duration of foster care is approximately three years (Governor's Advocacy Council on Children and Youth, 1978); the three year requirement for foster care thus reflects the experience of many children in care. The type of social service records kept by the county agencies meant that only foster children currently in foster care could be identified by length of time in care. We were limited to studying only foster children in care at the time of data collection, a limited sample of all foster children. Social service records proved inadequate to establish either baseline functioning of the children at the time of maltreatment report or subsequent development and behavior. Even simple descriptions of the child's physical appearance, affect, and level of cognitive functioning were present in very few records. The impact of foster care may be quite different for children who are returned home to their parents within three years or for children who are in care for longer than three years but who subsequently return home.

Summary

Foster care placement of maltreated children does not appear to have a clear detrimental effect on the child victims. Children in foster care are not at increased overall risk of juvenile delinquency when compared to peers left in their own homes. Perhaps equally important, there is also little evidence of a therapeutic benefit from foster care. The finding of increased convictions for assault among foster care children may prove to be important, representing a demonstration of lack of therapeutic effect. Regardless of the causal direction, the relationship between number of foster homes and number of crimes after age 11 merits close attention. Whether or not the frequent moves only herald early antisocial behavior or are in part responsible for it, this group of children is in need of special services. Policies must be developed to provide the necessary resources for this subgroup of foster children. Definitive assessments about the effects of foster care on maltreated children will require evaluation of the impact on other measures of function and, ultimately, prospective longitudinal studies.

Note

1. Recalculated by the authors using test-based method of Miettenen and chi-square value supplied by Lewis and others (Lewis & Shanok, 1979; Kleinbaum, Kupper, & Morgenstern, 1982).

References

Alfaro, J. (1976, January). Report of New York State Assembly Select Committee on child abuse. *Child Protection Report, II*(1).

American Humane Association (1979). *National analysis of official neglect and abuse reporting*. Denver: Author.

American Humane Association (1984). *National analysis of official neglect and abuse reporting*. Denver: Author.

Cornfield, J. (1951). A method of estimating comparative rates from clinical data. Applications to cancer of the lung, breast, and cervix. *Journal of the National Cancer Institute, 11,* 1269-1275.

Elmer, E. (1977). A follow-up study of traumatized children. *Pediatrics, 60,* 185-167.

Elmer, E., & Gregg, G. (1967). Developmental characteristics of abused children. *Pediatrics, 40,* 596-602.

Fanshel, D. (1981). Decision making under uncertainty: Foster care for abused or neglected children? *American Journal of Public Health, 71,* 685-686.

Finkelhor, D. (1983). Removing the child—prosecuting the offender in cases of sexual abuse. *Child Abuse and Neglect, 7,* 195-205.

Gelles, R. (1978). Violence toward children in the United States. *American Journal of Orthopsychiatry, 48,* 450-592.

Glueck, S., & Glueck, E. (1950). *Unraveling juvenile delinquency*. Cambridge, MA: Harvard University Press.

Gould, C., & Runyan, D. (1984). Foster care for the maltreated child. In D. Kerns (Ed.), *Child abuse and neglect*. Philadelphia: Saunders.

Governor's Advocacy Council on Children and Youth (1978). *Why can't I have a home?: Foster care and adoption in North Carolina*. Raleigh, NC: Department of Administration.

Kadushin, A. (1978). Children in foster families and institutions. In H. Maas (Ed.), *Social services research: Review of studies*. Washington, DC: National Association of Social Workers.

Kinard, E. (1978). Emotional development in physically abused children: A study of self-concept and aggression. *Dissertation Abstracts International, 39* (6-B), 2964-2965.

Kleinbaum, D., Kupper, L., & Morgenstern, H. (1982). *Epidemiologic research*. Belmont, CA: Lifetime Learning.

Lewis, D., & Shanok, S. (1979). A Comparison of the medical histories of incarcerated delinquent children and a matched sample of non-delinquent children. *Child Psychiatry and Human Development, 9,* 210-214.

Lewis, D., Shanok, S., & Balla, D. (1979). Perinatal difficulties, head and face trauma, and child abuse in the medical histories of seriously delinquent children. *American Journal of Psychiatry, 136,* 419-423.

Lewis, D., Shanok, S., Pincus, J., & Glaser, G. (1979). Violent juvenile delinquents. *Journal of the American Academy of Child Psychiatry, 18,* 307-319.

Maden, M. (1980). *The disposition of reported child abuse.* Saratoga, CA: Century 21.

Mantel, N., & Haenzel, W. (1959). Statistical aspects of the analysis of data from retrospective studies of disease. *Journal of the National Cancer Institute, 22*(4), 719-798.

Martin, H., & Breezley, P. (1977). Behavioral observations of abused children. *Developmental Medicine and Child Neurology, 19*(3), 1373-1378.

Miettenen, O. (1976). Estimability and estimation in case-referent studies. *American Journal of Epidemiology, 103*(2), 226-235.

Morse, C., Sabler, S., & Friedman, S. (1970). A three-year follow-up study of abused and neglected children. *American Journal of Diseases of Children, 120,* 439-446.

National Center on Child Abuse and Neglect (1981). *National Survey of the incidence and severity of child abuse and neglect.* (DSS Publication No. 81-30325). Washington, DC: Government Printing Office.

Rodgers, S., & Leunes, A. (1979). A psychometric and behavioral comparison of delinquents who were abused as children and their non-abused peers. *Journal of Clinical Psychology, 35,* 470-472.

Runyan, D., Gould, C., Trost, D., & Loda, F. (1981). Determinants of foster care for the maltreated child. *American Journal of Public Health, 71,* 706-711.

Shor, E. (1982). The foster care system and health status of foster children. *Pediatrics, 69,* 521-528.

Vasaly, S. (1976). *Foster care in five states.* (DHEW Publication No. OHD 76-30097). Washington, DC: Government Printing Office.

16

Factors Influencing the Response of Child Protective Service Workers to Reports of Abuse and Neglect

Susan J. Wells

Studies of child abuse deaths highlight some of the problems that can occur during protective service intake and investigation and illustrate the most serious consequences of decisions gone awry. An anecdotal study of 13 child abuse deaths in Ontario (Greenland, 1978) found that many workers did not use the central registry to inquire about a possible history of abuse and that after-hours response to reports were often made by untrained or inexperienced workers. Decisions regarding placement in these cases were made without consulting allied agencies and client resistance was not countered with forceful efforts to relocate the client or gain entry to the home.

In a study of child fatalities from 1980, the Mayor's Task Force in New York City found that, of the deaths studied that were associated with abuse or neglect, half had been reported to child protective services on previous occasions (N = 451). There were 18 cases in which the Task Force determined that credible evidence of abuse existed at the time of the report, but that the case had been "unfounded" by the agency. Some reasons given for not substantiating the cases were that the mother promised to do better or showed affection for her children, that the reporting agency did not offer sufficient evidence to support the contention of possible neglect, and that a lawyer had intervened on behalf of the family.

Additional factors found to influence case decisions were the worker's inability to recognize patterns of parental behavior that would indicate risk,

AUTHOR'S NOTE: This research was supported by grant 90-CA-0925 from the Department of Health and Human Services, National Center on Child Abuse and Neglect.

for example, starting fires while intoxicated or incapacity resulting from active psychoses; lack of sufficient medical knowledge; use of voluntary placement in high risk cases; and acceptance of hazardous home conditions. The worker's inaction was explained by lack of training in child and family assessment, lack of sufficient guidelines in custody arrangements, hesitancy to use authority, and lack of coordination and monitoring among agencies.

While these reports are anecdotal and do not consider the numbers of children who are successfully served by the agency, these examples are helpful in determining a course for further study. Factors that influence clinical judgment and attempts at prediction of future client behavior must be examined in order to achieve optimal agency policies and training packages for workers.

Clinical Judgment

Workers are seldom educated in the use of probabilities, base rates, and knowledge about regression principles as they pertain to child welfare judgments. Stein (1974) related these propositions to decision making in child welfare, noting how easily one can miscategorize a client and proceed thereafter, building one misjudgment upon another. In a review of literature on decision making, Stein, Gambrill, & Wiltse (1978) noted that Wolins (1963) found agreement on clinical judgments among caseworkers to be very poor when given entire case records but that it increased measurably when given only the information thought necessary for decision making. In his own dissertation, Stein (1974) found that 78% of the information gathered during the intake interview for potential placements was not related to the placement decision. Golan (1969) also found that workers gathered information that was inconsistent, either including unneeded data or omitting crucial facts. In a related study, Brieland (1959) found that when making judgments about the suitability of applicants as adoptive parents, caseworkers based their judgments on information presented in the first half of a recorded interview, completely ignoring what was included in the second half. Monahan (1981) reported similar findings in studies of decision making among other professionals. For example, in one study of psychologists, respondents were better able to predict student grades with only four items of information than when they were given the original four, plus 18 others (Bartlett & Green, 1966). They were more certain, however, of predictions made with more information. To add to an already dismal picture, Nisbett and Ross (1980) report that clinical predictions of even the most experienced professionals are woefully inaccurate when compared to the performance of statistical formulas:

> Human judges are not merely worse than optimal regression equations: they are worse than almost any regression equation. Even if the weights in the equation are arbitrary, as long as they are nonzero, positive and linear, the equation generally will out-perform human judges (Dawes & Corrigan, 1974). Human judges do not merely apply invalid weights unreliably: a computational model of an individual judge, one which calculates the weights applied by the judge to the first N cases, will out-perform the judge on the next batch of cases because of improved reliability alone. (Nisbett & Ross, 1980)

The authors believe that people commonly make mistakes in judgment and prediction because of perceptual and processing errors. Errors which may influence judgment are the maintenance of incorrect or inaccurate beliefs or schemas about the world and the inaccurate perception or labeling of events and observations.

There are many ways that worker perceptions and information processing can affect clinical practice. Clinical decisions are not only influenced by knowledge about the problem to be considered; they are also subject to personal perceptions; habits of information processing; the context of the problem; and the situation of the decision maker particularly with regard to stress and conflict.

Child Abuse Prediction

Much research has been done to aid the worker in making judgments about the current status and future behavior of parents who are referred to protective service agencies. One line of inquiry has been to further knowledge about the problem by trying to determine the individual and social characteristics that separate abusive from nonabusive parents. While many studies have attempted to find the personal, familial, and ecological correlates of abusive behavior, very few have qualified as more than exploratory attempts to formulate hypotheses. They often lack comparison groups, rely heavily on clinical impression, and lack appropriate statistical analysis (Plotkin, Azar, Twentyman, & Perri, 1981).

Although there are studies that have been done under more controlled circumstances, the state of the art is not yet at a point that would permit unfailing identification of those who are likely to be abusive. To illustrate, Starr (1982) reported on a study in which nine variables, including marital, social, and psychological factors, could be used to achieve 70% correct classification of abusive mothers. He then went on to show that even with an impressive rate of correct classifications, the rate of incorrect classifications in a population with low incidence of "disease" would be very great. In the author's example, if these variables were used to predict abuse in a population of 100,000 families with an incidence rate of 1%, 32,967 would be incorrectly classified as abusive.

In a study of child deaths from abuse and neglect, the Mayor's Task Force (1987) reported similar problems in differentiating children in CPS families who would subsequently die from maltreatment from those who would not. With such a low incidence phenomenon, it was not possible to identify indicators of risk. Further, the task force found that fatal and nonfatal cases are more alike than different. The most striking conclusion of the study, as reported by the authors, is that "the fatal and nonfatal cases belong to a common pool of cases in which fatality is primarily a chance outcome."

In spite of the seemingly apparent obstacles in developing predictive instruments regarding child maltreatment, there have been several attempts to do just that. Although some efforts (such as Polansky's 1972 Childhood Level of Living Scale and Helfer, Schneider, & Hoffmeister's Michigan Screening Profile of Parenting, 1978) have been an aid to worker assessment, they have not been able to systematically differentiate between those who will abuse or neglect and those who will not.

The Child Abuse Potential Inventory, currently under development by Milner and Wimberley (1980) shows some promise of being a more exacting instrument. It measures feelings of distress, rigidity, perceptions of the child as having problems, feelings of unhappiness, loneliness, and negative concepts of oneself and one's child. Although this scale is still in the developmental stages, in one study 96% of 130 matched case and control subjects were correctly classified as abusive or nonabusive.

Rosenberg, Meyers, & Shackleton (1982), attempted to develop an assessment form that would aid in predicting which children, age 2 or under, brought to emergency rooms would be abused. Children who were identified as abused at the time of their first examination or who had a record of being previously abused were omitted from the study. Of 476 children who met this criteria, abuse was later found in 19% of those who were unkempt and in 28% who had abnormal bruises, burns, or bites. Of those who were both unkempt and had abnormal bruises, burns, or bites, 42% were later found to be abused. An unkempt child who had a parent with one or more of the diagnostic features studied had a 30% chance of being abused. The presence of one or more "abnormal features" increased the chance of being abused from 2.5% to 15.2%.

The design of this study is limited by the use of indicators already defined as abusing (e.g., human bites) as a predictor of whether or not a child will be abused. Nevertheless, one can see that when other factors, in addition to severity of injury are considered, one can significantly increase the chances of predicting future abuse.

Prediction and Recidivism

Another approach to enhancing predictive abilities has been to look at recidivism. Monahan (1981) has done a critical review of recidivism studies in the field of criminal justice and concluded that, at best, one could develop an accuracy rate of one in three clinical predictions. Some work with actuarial methods has shown an improvement in these success rates. Using information only on type of crime, nature of institutional behavior, and arrest record before the fifteenth birthday, a State of Michigan study (1978, cited in Monahan, 1981) showed better results. Overall, 40% of those identified as very high risk, 20% at high risk, and 12% at middle risk were recidivists. Of those found to be at very low risk, only 2% were recidivists.

Recidivism studies specific to child welfare have been fewer. Herrenkohl (1978) followed up 328 families that had received protective service and looked for subsequent official reports or similar recorded incidents. Using case records, interviews, and selected birth records, the investigators found that abused children are viewed more negatively by their parents and seen as more difficult than their siblings. The actual characteristics of the child contributed very little to the variance associated with child abuse. Babies of teenage mothers were at higher risk for subsequent abuse. Families in which violence occurred among other adult family members were also at high risk for continuing abuse, as were parents who were resistant to treatment.

Current research in child protective services has focused on "risk assessment," the prediction of future risk to children reported for abuse or neglect. In a recently completed project for the state of Alaska, Baird (1988) developed instruments for assessing risk in cases of abuse and neglect. Applying the abuse scale to incoming reports, Baird found that, in the highest of five levels of risk, 90.7% of these referrals (N = 88) either resulted in removal of the child from the home or subsequent abuse. At the lowest level of risk, 4.8% of cases studied (N = 124) involved placement or subsequent abuse. Application of the neglect scales to neglect reports yielded similar results. While the abuse and neglect scales should be applied separately, there are several items that are common to both scales: number of prior referrals for abuse (or neglect), number of prior placements outside of the family residence, caretaker abused (or neglected) as a child, caretaker history of drug/alcohol abuse, and caretaker primarily involved in negative social relationships. Additional risk assessment studies are underway in various states and at least two others have been funded through the National Center on Child Abuse and Neglect.

The research on characteristics of abusing and neglecting parents and the limited information gathered on recidivism indicate that, while one cannot make positive predictions about future behavior, there are some guidelines for conducting family assessments and determining potential risk.

Studies of Worker Decision Making

Early studies of worker decision making often focused on determinations of placement. Later efforts included examination of substantiation and initial treatment decisions. Although the generalization from these findings is constrained, owing to limitations of sample selection and other design considerations, one can begin to piece together a picture of selected worker practices.

The Decision to Place

Boehm (1962) found that when workers were asked to examine their own cases regarding the decision to place, they tended to compare clients to a model of what a family should be. In order to determine which factors most significantly differentiated placement from nonplacement families, she had workers rate families on 12 dimensions (Boehm, 1967). The factors that differentiated between placement and nonplacement families were maternal behavior, household management, family insight, and the father's affection for the child, with maternal care playing the greatest role.

At about the same time, Briar (1963), using vignettes, tested the hypotheses that workers would recommend institutional placement more often for seriously disturbed children, and that type of foster care recommended would be influenced by the parents' wishes. He found that parental wishes were a definite influence in type of placement recommended and that there were differences in worker assessments of disturbance, prognoses for the children, and recommended placement formulations. No relationships were found between clinical judgments and worker age, sex, marital status, experience, or training.

Fanshel (1963) questioned Briar's findings largely because of the contrived nature of the vignettes that represented limited facets of a complex decision-making process, the lack of real consequences to hypothetical judgments, and the assumptions about accepted practice principles upon which the research was based. His criticisms illustrate the difficulties of researching the complex process of decision making and the elusiveness of practice principles.

In 1970, Roberts sought to improve on the problem of unrealistic vignettes by using four case examples from actual practice. Social workers from different agency settings were asked to rate the cases in terms of perceived risk to the child, assessment of the parents, prognosis for the child, and necessity of placement.

Again, personal characteristics such as age, sex, race, marital status, or social class did not influence worker judgments. Workers with more experience or graduate work tended to be more pessimistic about treatment outcomes and more likely to recommend placement. Workers from protective service, child welfare, family service, and public assistance showed significant levels of agreement ($p < .001$) across agency boundaries on all clinical judgments. In a study of actual practice, Phillips, Shyne, Sherman, & Haring (1971) used specially constructed intake and decision schedules completed by workers from public agencies. They found that placement children came from families with less money and had mothers who were more likely to have a history of mental illness, to appear emotionally disturbed, to have difficulty in holding a job and managing money, and to show a lack of concern for their children. Fathers of placement children were also much more likely to exhibit deviant behavior and placement children were more likely to have behavior disturbances. It is worthwhile to note that the major difference between the groups was that the placement group had requested placement, whereas the nonplacement group did not want any service. There was little evidence that worker characteristics influenced the decision to place.

Although, because of missing data, there were some limitations to conducting a cluster analysis, the authors reported that for mothers living alone, Background Factors (inadequate income, mother wants placement, other child placed), Child Traits (acting out behavior) and General Mother Traits (difficulty holding a job, suspiciousness, withdrawn, depressed) were strongly predictive, while Adequacy of Parental Care or Child's Relationship with Mother were not. With intact families the "single most important criteria" was General Father Traits. To determine on what basis experts would make decisions, three experienced workers were also solicited as judges of the need for placement. They agreed among themselves and the workers less than half of the time. They were most often influenced in their decisions by general adequacy of care, mother's disturbance, mother's attitude toward the problem, and the behavior of the child. Even when in agreement, however, judges often gave different rationales for their decisions.

In a study of case registry data from North Carolina, Runyan, Gould, Trost, & Loda (1981) examined 7,770 first reports of child maltreatment to determine factors that explain the decision to place a child. A total of 250 variables were analyzed. Adjusted odds ratios indicated that characteristics that differentiated placement from nonplacement children included parents who perceived severe punishment as acceptable, parents with substance abuse problems, injuries requiring hospitalization, abandonment of young children, and some types of abuse (e.g., burns and scalds). Additional factors included referral source, geographic location, and court jurisdiction, with court jurisdiction being the single most influential variable. Race, income, and education of parents were not influential in placement decisions, nor was occupation, excepting for those who were in the military. Urban/rural composition, types of industry, and other ecological characteristics also showed no effects but cases reported to law enforcement authorities had higher risk of removal, regardless of severity of abuse. The total variation explained by the model was only 17%, indicating that unknown factors accounted for 83% of the variance.

Workers themselves report guidelines for decision making that are similar to the research findings just noted (Graham, 1978). They indicate that the most important factors in assessing imminent danger are the child's inability to escape serious harm, absence of a caretaker, and necessity of immediate action to prevent harm to the child. The workers reported that the caretaker's willingness to work toward eliminating the problem was most important in deciding to provide in-home services, while seriousness and frequency of past harm to the child were most important in removal of the child from the home.

Decisions in Intake and Investigation

Research studies on decision making during intake and investigation, like those on placement decisions, often yield contradictory results and lack sufficient replication. Nevertheless, there is a growing body of research that describes factors that influence initial case decisions.

Worker response to case vignettes. Case vignettes are used in some inquiries in order to better control the stimulus presented to the respondents. While Fanshel's (1963) comments about the usefulness of hypothetical vignettes are well taken, it may be instructive to examine workers' responses to vignettes taken from actual case material.

In studies that preceded Roberts' work, Billingsley and his associates (Billingsley, 1964; Billingsley, Streskinsky, & Gurin, 1966) found that protective service workers tended to identify abuse as a problem more often than did family service workers and that more workers were willing to intervene in cases of physical abuse than in other types of maltreatment. In addition, younger workers recommended placement more often than older workers did.

Giovannoni and Becerra (1979) reported "virtually no consensus about the seriousness of incidents of mistreatment" among lawyers, pediatricians, social workers, police, and lay people in the community. There were, however, patterns of agreement among professional groups. The police and social workers agreed most often (73% of the time) and generally rated incidents as less serious. On matters of physical care, social workers and police were most often in agreement. Incidents concerning cleanliness and medical care tended to polarize the professions: police and social workers versus pediatricians and lawyers. Incidents concerning nutrition and supervision resulted in agreement among pediatricians, social workers, and police. Lawyers were most different in reactions to failure-to-provide incidents that would probably not meet legal standards of physical harm as a basis for state intervention. While lawyers rated incidents as generally less serious, they agreed with others on the relative seriousness of the incidents.

Including factors such as race and socioeconomic status of the child, O'Toole (1983) studied identification of abuse and neglect by physicians and nurses. He found that both physicians and nurses could identify those "obvious" cases of abuse that resulted in serious injury, but that when the harm incurred was more ambiguous, physicians in particular were more likely to be influenced by such factors as race and socioeconomic status of the patient.

In a study involving 38 protective service workers in five counties, Craft, Epley, & Clarkson (1980) presented case descriptions that manipulated the factors of previous injury, severity of injury, consistency of explanation, and parental reaction to the worker. Workers generally did not recommend court action for the cases described, but often disagreed on their recommendations when presented with cases that had more than one negative factor and some positive factors. Workers more often recommended court action when there were previous reports, a negative reaction by the parent, and when the explanation of the injury was suspect. Seriousness of injury interacted with previous record and parental reaction and explanation to result in more court action.

In order to determine what specific cues influence the workers' judgment of whether abuse has occurred and what type of intervention is desired, Rosen (1981) administered case summaries to 162 workers. She chose six indicators of possible abuse: injury to the child, history of injury, vague explanation for injury, unusual behavior or characteristics of the child, environmental stress, and emotional disturbance of the parent. There were 64 cases that included all possible combinations of presence or absence of a cue, presented in groups of eight to each participant.

Comparisons of the influence of each cue on determination of abuse (from very certain to uncertain) revealed that presence of injury was the most influential variable; followed by history of injury, emotional disturbance of parent, environmental stress, and unusual behavior of the child. The five cues that were significant for determination of abuse were also significant for choice of intervention but there was some difference in the weights of the cues when considering determination of abuse versus choice of treatment. Treatment choices were: extended placement, temporary placement with parental treatment, child at home with parental treatment, monitoring, or no intervention. Presence of injury, history of injury, and emotional disturbance of the parent were the most influential variables. Unusual behavior in the child was more influential in determining intervention than in determining abuse.

When the relationship between determination of abuse and suggested intervention was examined, the author found that almost half of the variance was explained by the influence of cues (r = .70623). She noted, however, that the intensity of treatment responses seemed to be uncorrelated with greater evidence of abuse when combinations of cues were present. For example, a worker could have indicated that a strong intervention was appropriate for a case that was not judged as having a high probability of abuse. Rosen's work is useful not only in getting a sense of the impact of indicators of abuse on worker judgment, but also because of the comparison between judgment pertaining to determination of abuse and intensity of intervention.

In an extension of Craft's approach, Alter (1985) examined factors used by CPS workers to make the substantiation decision when there is an absence of evidence that the child has been seriously harmed. She found that workers then rely on more abstract issues, such as whether the neglect is willful, the parent-child relationship poor, the parents' behavior is socially deviant, and the parents demonstrate a desire to change. When workers were presented with 16 analogues, moderate physical harm alone was not sufficient to substantiate the case. However, willful neglect and a poor parent-child relationship combined with moderate physical harm led to agreement to substantiate among four-fifths of the workers studied (N = 73). When all four variables were present, 97% of the workers agreed to substantiate.

Wolock (1982) used vignettes taken from actual cases to examine the influence of community characteristics on worker judgments. She found that protective agencies in areas that ranked highest on a scale of social and economic problems also had a greater number of severe child maltreatment reports. She also found that workers from agencies with more severe cases tended to judge the case examples as needing less intensive intervention than did workers from agencies with less severe cases. It seems that factors pertaining to severity of caseload (as rated by expert judges) and community problems are influential in worker responses to case material.

Thus far investigations using vignettes have shown that severity and history of injury are fairly consistent indicators of intended intervention but that combinations of case factors may tend to dissolve worker agreement. Additional factors influencing worker judgment may include assessment of parental characteristics, nature of the community, and severity of cases in workers' caseloads.

Studies of case disposition. In an early examination of state registry data, Groeneveld and Giovannoni (1979) looked at substantiation practices and factors related to initial case disposition. The authors observed variation in substantiation owing to type of maltreatment and source of report. They also found that court intervention and placement decisions were not related to type of maltreatment, characteristics of the child and family, or county in which the investigation was done. Emergency placement of the child was the sole factor that was related to both outcomes. The involvement of law enforcement agencies also influenced whether court action would be sought, while number of children in the family was negatively related to the decision to seek placement.

Giovannoni and Becerra (1979) studied 949 randomly selected cases of substantiated abuse from four California counties to determine characteristics associated with substantiation and initial dispositions. In order to determine worker judgments of severity, the workers were given behavioral checklists and asked to check off which behaviors formed the basis for protective intervention. When given the entire list and asked to rate the severity of the incidents described, they had very high agreement on the ratings of seriousness of the incidents.

Of the 949 cases reviewed, 52% received in-home services without court intervention, 5% remained at home under court supervision, 18% were placed under voluntary agreements, and 25% were removed by the court. In counties where the investigation was handled by the protective agency (as opposed to probation workers), only two kinds of mistreatment did not differentiate between court removal and in-home (noncourt) supervision: children's drug use or disordered behavior. More extreme intervention was more likely when more kinds of mistreatment were involved. The kinds of mistreatment that were most significant in predicting outcome were immoral/illegal behavior of the parents, sexual abuse, physical injury, and emotional neglect. When the parents wanted help for emotional problems or when they wanted removal of the child, their wishes influenced the type of disposition made.

DiLeonardi (1980) examined service and disposition decisions by reviewing case records and data collected from the Metropolitan Area Protective Services Project of Chicago. She found that many factors were related to the decision to provide service. Source of referral, age of the child, hospitalization of the child or temporary removal, involvement of more than one child, and the mother as perpetrator were some relevant factors. Type of abuse (fractures, visible sores, failure to thrive, and neglected infants), parental admission of abuse, arrested development, and delay in getting medical care were more likely to result in service provision. In addition, children who were unwanted, premature, or emotionally different were more likely to receive service.

Parental factors that influenced acceptance for service included substance abuse, lack of impulse control, inappropriate expectations of the child, and verbal hostility. Significant but weaker associations were found for inadequate supervision, parental depression, endorsement of physical punishment, and parental mental illness. Home situations that were stressful or "especially poor" were more likely to result in service. In some cases services were recommended by the worker but were not received because parents had moved or refused service and there was insufficient evidence for court action.

The patterns of service provision noted by the author were that workers recommended service based on chronicity of injuries to the child and the parents' receptiveness to help. Cases of physical injury that were supported by medical evidence were more likely to be taken to court if workers met with parental resistance. Those parents who were not receiving public assistance and who refused service were able to maintain their refusal of protective intervention.

In an analysis of 416 referrals for neglect, Foster (1981) found that employment status was the single most important factor in substantiation, with poverty and ethnicity also playing a role. Of worker variables, only age influenced dispositional decisions. Worker sex, ethnicity, education, SES, and work experience were all insignificant.

Lamb (1979) examined the influence of family stress, type of injury, method of abuse, child/family characteristics, and social worker characteristics on case substantiation. She found that type of injury sustained by the child accounted for 32% of the variation in case substantiation. The abuser's relationship to the child interacted with injury to result in more substantiation when there were no parental ties. Abusive method and chronic stress were not good predictors. Of the child and family characteristics examined, only ethnicity of the child and status of the reporter were significant.

Interestingly, none of the personal attributes of workers were associated with outcome, nor were years of professional experience, specialization, or years in protective services. Workers with master's degrees, however, were less likely to judge outcomes severely. This relates to Giovannoni and Becerra's (1979) findings that lay people judge incidents more severely than do professionals. Workers with caseloads of over 30 also judge outcomes less severely than do those with lower caseloads.

Recently, three studies were funded by the National Center on Child Abuse and Neglect to look at the differences between substantiated and unsubstantiated cases. The research questions focused on differences in case characteristics as well as source of report. Using a representative sample from case registry data, Eckenrode and Doris (1987) looked specifically at difference in substantiation rate for reports from professional sources versus nonprofessionals (e.g., relatives and neighbors). They found that when background variables were controlled for by regression analysis, reports from professional sources concerning physical abuse (N = 198) were 23% more likely to be substantiated, those concerning neglect (N = 880) were 26% more likely to be substantiated, and those concerning sexual abuse (N = 796) were 11% more likely to be substantiated. There was, however, a large amount of variation within the study categories. For example, sexual abuse reports made by the mother of a child were as likely to be substantiated as physician's reports. Also, in addition to the influence of case factors such as race and age of child, cases involving court action, those with a higher number of worker contacts with the subject of the report, and those with longer investigations were more likely to be substantiated. In this type of study, one cannot say whether these factors were a result of perceived seriousness or whether increased time led to more certainty regarding substantiation.

Abramczyk and Sweigart (1985) sampled 731 cases from reports made in South Carolina over one year's time, gathering data from intake reports and case records. Relying largely on bivariate analysis, the researchers found that unsubstantiated cases were more likely to involve neglect, mental injury, and physical abuse (as opposed to sexual abuse and educational neglect). They were also more likely to be from the city, reported by nonprofessionals (e.g., relatives, neighbors, noncustodial parents), reported by people who requested anonymity, not clearly involve first-hand information, concern one-parent families, and involve custody or divorce situations. Using stepwise regression, the authors also developed three profiles of substantiated cases. These profiles described source of report, type of allegation, family descriptors, and report characteristics, for example, relationship of source of report to the child. While there were some unique characteristics about each of the profiles, the most striking finding was the similarity between them, for example, two of three included "sexual abuse reported" and "source of report is professional."

In a study on reporting, screening, and substantiation, Giovannoni (1987) used a sample of 975 investigated cases to examine the nature of the report, the source of report, the identity of the perpetrator, and factors relating to the investigation and disposition. For urban reports, substantiation was more likely if the case was rated as more serious, there was more time spent on investigation, address of caretaker was listed, child was seen, report was not physical abuse, perpetrator was contacted, alleged perpetrator did not deny the allegation, and school problems were noted in the investigation. For reports in rural areas, the most influential factors in substantiation were: total number of categories of maltreatment noted along with school problems, time spent on investigation, presence of school problems, lack of supervision, inadequate housing, or child behavior problems, involvement of law enforcement, referral made to an outside agency, and perpetrator being the child's caretaker. Source of report was not a factor in rural or urban counties, nor was kind of maltreatment reported. The major contributions to substantiation were the maltreatment found and maltreatment of a serious nature or multiple kinds of maltreatment.

Agency and community factors that form the ecology of the protective service agency will also influence worker decision making. Using data gathered by Nagi, Gershenson, and Haller (1978) examined the influence of caseload on protective service practices. Because the findings were based on a national probability sample, the authors projected their findings to national figures. They found that agencies with high reporting rates (from 7 to 60 reports per 1,000 children under 18) and moderate or low caseloads (from less than one report per worker per year to 34 reports per worker per year) tended to make home visits within 24 hours, and to place children with relatives instead of in foster care. Placements also seemed to be less common for those with high caseloads and those with a combination of high caseloads and high reporting rates. Rates of court compliance with requests for temporary or permanent placement did not seem to be influenced by any measure of reporting. In looking further at substantiation practices, Trainor (1983) surveyed child welfare administrators in 54 states and territories on their substantiation and screening practices. The author found that even though most (80%) of the responding states (N = 46) have varying degrees of written guidelines for substantiation, these are not always followed in practice. The respondents reported that individual workers or worker/supervisor combinations most often determined whether a case should be substantiated on a case by case basis.

In a recent study of reporting rates and disposition decisions at the county level, the American Humane Association (Trainor, DePanfilies, & Fluke, 1983) found that although reporting rates were related to county budgetary levels, types of dispositions made were most influenced by previous decision making patterns in the county. Surveys of 36 counties, conducted in conjunction with the study, found that counties that have high rates of substantiation per number of reports received were more likely to require prior child protection experience for CPS supervisors, have more decisions made by the worker rather than the worker and supervisor together, more often use multidisciplinary teams, and have a somewhat higher level of community involvement. In addition, those counties also demonstrated a greater intensity in the investigation process, using more collateral contacts, and taking more time to complete the investigation. Their workers tended to have more training, more CPS experience, and were more often satisfied with their jobs. In a study of case re-reporting and factors influencing worker decision making, Wells (1986) found that substantiation practices varied by county in which the report was made, but that demographic characteristics of the counties were not good predictors. In looking for factors that would explain county differences, it was found that the following factors should receive further study: attitudes of administrators toward CPS intervention, use of multidisciplinary teams, use of collaterals in decision making, and worker group cohesion.

The question of training and use of standardized guidelines for worker decision making has been recently addressed by Stein and Rzepnicki (1984). In an experimental study of worker decision making in two states, they found that structured decision making accompanied by intensive training resulted in a significant level of agreement between judges and that standardized instructions for data gathering resulted in time savings for the workers.

In a secondary analysis of the Stein and Rzepnicki data, Gleeson (1987) found that structured decision making was more likely to be used "when the worker was new on the job, did not have previous intake experience, when the case was unfamiliar, and when the client situation was viewed as being of greater risk to the child." Obstacles to using the structured model were related primarily to worker characteristics and the unit in which the worker was employed.

Discussion

The theme that emerges from this review is that certain case factors, such as severity of abuse, type of injury, chronicity, and some parental characteristics are influential in the decision to substantiate a case. While placement decisions and substantiation decisions are not always clearly related and workers express concerns about lack of criteria for decision making, they are able to delineate some practice principles and describe types of incidents that most often influence substantiation and placement decisions. Ecological factors such as county in which the investigation is conducted, court jurisdiction, worker caseload, and severity of caseload may also be important in making judgments about case severity and in determining level of worker intervention.

Worker personal characteristics seem to be less influential than one might have thought, but certain professional indicators, such as a master's degree in social work, may account for some variance in the decision that is made. The influence of additional or specialized training is not clear, but studies indicate that standardization of practices and intensive training can indeed enhance the level of worker performance and consistency of decisions made (Stein, 1984). The survey by Trainor (1983) illustrates, however, that there is a long way to go in developing such standardized practices.

Implications of these findings for future research are many. It is clear that although the development of screening instruments for use in intake and investigation is needed, further work must be done in order to better understand what differentiates those with the potential to abuse or neglect and what factors contribute to creating situations in which that potential can be expressed.

Further work must also be done to determine the effectiveness of intervention and to better understand the decision making process itself. Two lines of inquiry might be followed. Following of unsubstantiated cases within the agency and the community would aid in judging the efficacy of the decisions made in intake. It would also be instructive to determine the characteristics of those cases that are substantiated but not served. Work such as Baird's (1987), using actuarial principles to identify risk for placement and re-abuse, is a critical step. While several risk assessment studies are underway, there is more to be done to aid workers in the decision making process.

Replications across states and counties are needed as are more in-depth studies of actual disposition patterns. Studies that attempt to account for more of the variance observed by including ecological factors are necessary. In addition, studies in which one can examine actual practices of the workers and have input from the workers themselves will prove the most valuable. This may necessitate more intensive studies in smaller geographic areas before more expansive efforts are pursued.

References

Abramczyk, L., & Sweigart, C. (1985). *Child Abuse and Neglect Indicated versus Unfounded Report Characteristics*. Columbia, SC: University of South Carolina, College of Social Work.

Alter, C. (1985). Decision-making factors in cases of child neglect. *Child Welfare, 64*, 99-111.

Baird, C. (1988). *Development of risk assessment indices for Alaska family services* (final report). San Francisco: National Council on Crime and Delinquency.

Bartlett, C., & Green, L. (1966). Clinical prediction: Does one sometimes know too much? *Journal of Counseling Psychology, 13,* 267-270.

Billingsley, A. (1964). *The social worker in a child protective agency.* New York: National Association of Social Workers.

Billingsley, A., Streskinsky, N., & Gurin, V. (1966). *Social work practice in child protective service in public welfare agencies.* Berkeley: University of California Press.

Boehm, B. (1962). An assessment of family adequacy in protective cases. *Child Welfare, 41,* 10-16.

Boehm, B. (1967). Protective services for neglected children in social work practice. *Proceedings of the National Conference on Social Welfare.* New York: Columbia University Press.

Bradford, R. A. (1976). Critical factors that affect the judgements of protective services workers in child abuse situations. Unpublished doctoral dissertation, Catholic University of America, Washington, DC.

Briar, S. (1963). Clinical judgment in foster care placement. *Child Welfare, 42,* 161-168.

Brieland, D. (1959). *An experimental study in the selection of adoptive parents at intake.* New York: Child Welfare League of America.

Craft, J. L., Epley, S. W., & Clarkson, C. D. (1980). Factors influencing legal disposition in child abuse investigations. *Journal of Social Service Research, 4,* 31-47.

Dawes, R. M., & Corrigan, B. (1974). Linear models in decision-making. *Psychological Bulletin, 81,* 95-106.

DiLeonardi, J. (1980). Decision-making in protective services. *Child Welfare, 6,* 356-364.

Eckenrode, J., & Doris, J. (1987). *Unreliable child maltreatment reports: Variations among professional and non-professional reporters* (final report). (Grant 90-CA-1008, Administration for Children, Youth and Families). Ithaca, NY: Family Life Development Center, Department of Human Development and Family Studies.

Fanshel, D. (1963). Commentary on "Clinical Judgment in Foster Care Placement." *Child Welfare, 42,* 169-172.

Foster, D. L. (1981). *Referrals of child neglect to child protective services: Status characteristics associated with disposition.* Unpublished doctoral dissertation, Case Western Reserve University.

Gershenson, H. P., & Haller, R. I. (1978). Rates of reporting, caseloads and levels of work in child protective services. Columbus: Ohio State University, Mershon Center.

Giovannoni, J. M. (1987). *Final report, private individuals' reports of child abuse and neglect.* Los Angeles: University of California, School of Social Welfare.

Giovannoni, J. M., & Becerra, R. M. (1979). *Defining child abuse.* New York: Free Press.

Gleeson, J. (1987). Implementing structured decision-making procedures at child welfare intake. *Child Welfare, 66,* 101-112.

Golan, N. (1969). How caseworkers decide: A study of the association of selected applicant factors with worker decisions in admission services. *Social Service Review, 43,* 286-296.

Graham, F. (1978). *A survey of caseworkers: Criteria for decision-making in abuse and neglect cases.* Trenton, NJ: Division of Youth and Family Services.

Greenland, C. (1978). *Child abuse deaths in Ontario* (Research papers for report of task force on child abuse). Ontario: Ministry of Community and Social Services, Children's Services Division.

Groeneveld, L. P., & Giovannoni, J. M. (1979). Disposition of child abuse and neglect cases. *Social Work Research and Abstracts, 13,* 24-30.

Helfer, R. E., Schneider, C. J., & Hoffmeister, J. K. (1978). *Report on the research using the Michigan Screening Profile of Parenting (MSPP).* Lansing: Michigan State University Press.

Herrenkohl, R. C. (1978). *Recurrence of abuse in child abuse families* (final report). Bethlehem, PA: Lehigh University, Center for Social Research.

Lamb, K. L. (1979). *Outcomes of child abuse complaints: Caseworkers as predictors.* Unpublished doctoral dissertation, University of Arizona.

Mayor's Task Force on Child Abuse and Neglect. (1987). *High risk factors associated with child maltreatment fatalities.* New York: Author.

Mayor's Task Force on Child Abuse and Neglect. (1983). *Report on the preliminary study of child fatalities in New York City.* New York: Author.

Milner, J. S., & Wimberley, R. C. (1980). Prediction and explanation of child abuse. *Journal of Clinical Psychology, 36,* 875-884.

Monahan, J. (1981). *Predicting violent behavior, an assessment of clinical techniques.* Beverly Hills, CA: Sage.

Nisbett, R., & Ross, L. (1980). *Human inference: Strategies and shortcomings of social judgment.* Englewood Cliffs, NJ: Prentice-Hall.

O'Toole, R., Turbett, P., & Nalepka, C. (1983). Theories, professional knowledge, and diagnosis of child abuse. In D. Finkelhor, R. J. Gelles, G. T. Hotaling, and M. A. Straus (eds.), *The dark side of families: Current family violence research.* Beverly Hills, CA: Sage.

Phillips, M. H., Shyne, A. W., Sherman, E. A., & Haring, B. L. (1971). *Factors associated with placement decisions in child welfare.* New York: Child Welfare League of America.

Plotkin, R. C., Azar, S., Twentyman, C. T., & Perri, M. G. (1981). A critical evaluation of the research methodology employed in the investigation of causative factors of child abuse and neglect. *Child Abuse and Neglect, 5,* 449-455.

Polansky, N. A., De Saix, C., & Sharlin, S. A. (1972). *Child neglect: Understanding and reaching the parent.* New York: Child Welfare League of America.

Roberts, R. W. (1970). *A comparative study of social caseworker's judgments of child abuse cases.* Unpublished doctoral dissertation, Columbia University.

Rosen, H. (1981). How workers use cues to determine child abuse. *Social Work Research and Abstracts, 17,* 27-33.

Rosenberg, N., Meyers, S., & Shackleton, N. (1982). Prediction of child abuse in an ambulatory setting. *Pediatrics, 70,* 879-882.

Runyan, D. R., Gould, C. L., Trost, D. C., & Loda, F. A. (1981). Determinants of foster care placement for the maltreated child. *American Journal of Public Health, 71,* 706-711.

Starr, R. H. (1982). A research based approach to the prediction of child abuse. In R. H. Starr (Ed.), *Child abuse prediction: Policy implications.* Cambridge, MA: Ballinger.

State of Michigan. (1978). *Summary of parolee risk study.* Unpublished manuscript, Michigan Department of Corrections.

Stein, T. J. (1974). *A content analysis of social caseworker and client interaction in foster care.* Unpublished doctoral dissertation, University of California, Berkeley.

Stein, T. J., Gambrill, E. D., & Wiltse, R. T. (1978). *Children in foster homes: Achieving continuity of care.* New York: Praeger.

Stein, T. J., & Rzepnicki, T. L. (1984). *Decision-making in child welfare services: Intake and planning.* Boston: Kluwer Nijhoff.

Trainor, C. M. (1983). *National substantiation and screening practices* (draft report). Denver: American Humane Association.

Trainor, C., DePanfilies, D., & Fluke, J. (1983). *Child abuse and neglect reporting and disposition in the State of Virginia* (final report). Denver: American Humane Association.

Wells, S. (1986). *Decision-making in child protective service intake and investigation* (final report). (Grant 90-CA-0925, Administration for Children, Youth and Families) Washington, DC: American Bar Association.

Wolins, M. (1963). *Selecting foster parents*. New York: Columbia University Press.

Wolock, I. (1982). Community characteristics and staff judgments in child abuse and neglect cases. *Social Work Research and Abstracts, 18,* 9-15.

17

Intervention, Outcome, and Elder Abuse

Rosalie S. Wolf
Karl A. Pillemer

Ten years ago Suzanne Steinmetz, testifying on family violence before a House Subcommittee, startled the audience and the nation with a report on "battered parents" (Steinmetz, 1978). Although the initial reaction was disbelief and righteous indignation, studies conducted in the subsequent two years showed that elder abuse was occurring nationwide and that its incidence was rising. Those early research reports produced profiles of the victims, perpetrators, and abuse/neglect situations, but little information about the intervention strategies and results.

Because of the sense of urgency associated with the problem, the Administration on Aging designated elder abuse as one of the priority demonstration areas for funding under its 1980 Model Projects program. Three organizations received three-year grants to demonstrate improved mechanisms for reporting, investigation, treatment, and prevention of elder abuse and neglect. They included the Massachusetts Department of Elder Affairs, which contracted with one of its affiliated home care corporations, Elder Home Care Services of Worcester Area, Inc., to conduct the demonstration; the Metropolitan Commission on Aging of Onondaga County, which contracted with Alliance Division of Catholic Charities of Syracuse; and the Rhode Island Department of Elderly Affairs, which chose to operate the model project from the state office. A grant for evaluating all three projects was given to the University Center on Aging at the University of Massachusetts Medical Center. The adoption of a common set of definitions of abuse and neglect and assessment instruments by the three projects made it possible not only to compare the case loads but also the organizational structure, intervention process, and outcomes.

It is important at this time to emphasize that the primary purpose of the evaluation of the model projects as outlined in the funding application was for program planning and development. A methodology was selected that would be least disruptive to the model projects, that would incorporate forms already part of the day-to-day operation for the agencies and that would involve project personnel in decision making. For all project staff, the tasks required for the evaluation (completing case assessments and reassessment forms, time studies, organizational analyses) were added to their responsibilities as case workers or project directors. Although there were opportunities at joint staff meetings to discuss the assessment forms, the client data from the sites (other than the sociodemographic statistics) reflected the training, experience, and judgment of the respective project workers, rather than the findings of objective researchers. The plan of this chapter is to summarize briefly the literature on intervention strategies and organization related to elder abuse and neglect, to describe the models and the organizational performance, and to analyze the outcome of the three projects.

Selected Literature Review

Despite the attention that elder abuse and neglect have received in the past, particularly from the media, there have been only a handful of studies on the topic, and they have been concerned primarily with defining the problem and its causes. Interest in intervention strategies has focused mainly on clinical aspects with little information in the literature on organizational issues. Lau and Kosberg (1978) in their retrospective study of victims seen by a chronic illness facility outline the steps required to handle a case (establish a positive relationship, engage other relatives or homemakers, provide regular nursing care) but do not suggest a model for delivering these services. In their discussion of intervention strategies based on a survey of professionals, Block and Sinnott (1979) note that action may involve social services, civil sanction, and criminal proceedings, but found that none of the 26 victims of elder abuse reported in their survey had received any assistance at all with the abuse problem. The Massachusetts Survey of professionals and paraprofessionals by the staff of the Legal Research and Services for the Elderly (O'Malley, Segars, Perez, Mitchella, & Knuepal, 1979) was the first to document the type of intervention action that had been taken on behalf of the victims: direct services were provided in 62% of the cases; emergency provisions in 22%; and referral in 48%. Data from 183 cases included a wide variety of interventions, most often consisting of social service, counseling, arrangements of in-home services, and removal of the victim. The researchers raise the question as to whether these responses were appropriate or a function of the availability of services in the area, professional style, or bias.

After surveying direct service providers in Michigan regarding their experience with elder abuse and neglect cases, Douglass, Hickey, and Noel (1980) conclude that the different types of abuse reported by different professional groups may be due to particular settings, training, and perspectives. From the results of their survey of the Detroit area, Sengstock and Liang, 1982) suggest that effectiveness of services seem to be highly dependent on the characteristics of the agency and the worker. In a subsample of that study drawn from the case files of a legal agency that had shown considerable success in working with such problems, Sengstock and Barrett (1982) found that legal agencies may be more likely to act directly on behalf of clients, whereas social service agencies are more inclined to counsel the family or to refer to another agency. These researchers add that legal agencies rarely deal with the family problems that may have generated or contributed to the episodes of maltreatment.

More recent reports in the literature have given somewhat greater attention to the intervention process. Pratt, Kane, and Lloyd (1983) in their study of service workers' response to abuse of the elderly state that it is unlikely that any one individual working with the aged can adequately assist families in alleviating the factors contributing to elder abuse. Such situations require the coordinated effort of a number of professionals and service agencies. Writing on "clinical interventions with abused elders and their families," Humphreys, Campbell, and Barrett (1983) also note that the complex phenomenon of family violence requires the involvement of numerous professionals and a coordinated approach to attain the maximum results from the intervention. The emphasis on coordination is also made in two guides issued for practitioners. Villomare and Bergman (1981) characterize an effective service system as one that has the "capacity for a coordinated, interdisciplinary response" to both chronic and emergency situations. The *National Guide Series on Improving Protective Services* outline a number of coordination methods (Hornby, 1982). While the literature on elderly abuse and neglect has not dealt directly with program models and effectiveness, it has made the point that whether handled by social, legal, or health agencies, a coordinated approach is necessary.

Methodology

As noted earlier, the evaluative research of the three model projects offered an opportunity to move beyond the clinical investigations and to study the organizational models and their performance and outcomes. Several different data collection techniques were employed. In-depth interviews were held with the model project staff, other personnel in the same agency, and selected individuals in community organizations. The status of the abused elders, the abusers, and abuse situation, and the barriers to service delivery were assessed by the project staff on 328 cases at intake and on 309 cases at reassessment, approximately seven months later. A third set of data was obtained from community agencies, first surveyed at the beginning of the grant period and then two years later; approximately 210 agencies were surveyed each time. Chi-square analysis was used to test for significant differences among the sites.

Results

After a short description of the three model projects, three aspects of organization performance will be presented: implementation, coordination, and time analysis. Case resolution, barrier to service delivery, and community agency response have been selected as measures of project outcome.

Characterization of the model projects. Although the projects did show some variation with respect to specific characteristics, the goals, target population, staffing, and definitions of abuse and neglect were alike. All three had the primary purpose of providing casework services to abused and neglected elderly (60 years and over) and members of their families. The goal was to intervene in cases of maltreatment, to introduce services when appropriate, to counsel victims and relatives, and to help resolve conflicts between abuser and abused. In addition to the objective, the model projects were to function as coordinators among other service providers and to serve as a focal point for action by local agencies in behalf of abused clients. Finally, all three projects had the responsibility of educating the community concerning the problems of abuse and neglect.

Another point of similarity was the target population. Only domestic abuse and neglect cases were included; professional, institutional, and self abuse were excluded. Regarding staff support and budget, the projects operated at about the same level. Each employed a director (full- or half-time) and a full-time case worker, although the Rhode Island project did hire an information and referral specialist as a result of the mandatory reporting legislation.

In spite of these similarities, each project represents a specific service approach to elder abuse and neglect. The Worcester Project is located in an agency where the case workers have direct control over a wide range of social services that can be used to help with a case (e.g., homemaker, transportation, chore, friendly visiting, senior companion). In addition to identification and assessment of the victim and the abuse situation, a major function of this model project is to manage and monitor the services that are provided. Two basic components stand out in the Syracuse Project, which is more aptly described as a "coordination model": interagency coordination, highlighted by the convening of a formal service team for most cases, and specially trained aides who work with the most troublesome cases. As the only official unit among the three projects legislated to respond to abuse reports, the Rhode Island Project emerges as a distinct type, a "mandatory reporting" model. It has primarily a short-term focus and relies on other agencies to provide direct services and to monitor the case. The role of the Rhode Island Project is to act as a catalyst for action, to bring together the relevant resources, and to remain in the picture until the abuse situation is alleviated.

Implementation. Generally, the implementation of the three model projects proceeded relatively smoothly. Although the presence of "abuse" workers was seen as an asset in all three sponsoring agencies, defining the workers' roles vis-à-vis those of other workers in the Worcester agency did present a problem. Although having the model project within the agency relieved case managers of difficult cases, some social workers found abuse and neglect cases interesting and satisfying and were less than willing to relinquish them. This situation was at least partially resolved by arranging for the "comanagement" of the case. In such instances, the case manager remained involved, but received advice and direction from the model project staff member.

At the Syracuse Project, no such "turf problems" existed with other workers, since within the home agency (Alliance), there were no other staff members working directly with elders. In Rhode Island, however, it occurred on a small scale in the intake process. The Elder Abuse grant allowed for the hiring of one intake worker for the information and referral unit. When it proved to be extremely difficult to transfer abuse reports to the one person, a decision was made to share elder abuse intake duties among the entire information and referral staff, all of whom were trained to carry out this responsibility.

Regarding interagency implementation, two problems became evident. The first one, shared by all the projects, was that of obtaining clients. By visiting relevant agencies in their areas, arranging for media announcements, and conducting training sessions, the model projects were able to make themselves known and to generate referrals. After these initial attempts, cases came very quickly. In fact, the model project workers found other agencies only too willing to transfer complicated and frustrating abuse cases to them.

A different problem occurred in the Syracuse and Rhode Island sites. At both locations, an Adult Protective Services (APS) unit existed in another agency that legally had overlapping responsibilities with the model project. Both were forced to answer the question: What is special about what you offer? These two projects were able to reach an agreement with the APS units, arguing convincingly that they were free of the stigma associated with the welfare agencies in which both APS programs were located. By maintaining open lines of communication with these APS programs and, in particular, showing a willingness to take over the more troublesome clients, the model projects avoided serious conflict.

Coordination. While the precise extent of elder abuse/neglect is not known, it is clear from the research that such cases are often very complicated and difficult. They generally require the involvement of a number of social service, health, and legal agencies before they are resolved. A critical question for the analysis of the model projects was: How does interagency coordination take place?

Each project was asked to list the agencies with whom they worked most closely. The answers were similar for all three sites. They included a home health agency, a mental health counseling service, and a senior center. Rhode Island and Syracuse added the APS unit in their welfare departments with whom coordination was essential. Rhode Island, unlike the other projects, also listed the Police Department. Because of their increased legal responsibilities under mandatory reporting, the Rhode Island Model had much closer ties to the police than did the other two projects. All three had extensive contact with community agencies, making use of both informal and formal mechanisms to maintain agency linkages.

A major problem in interagency coordination is assigning responsibility for management of the case. Most often among the model projects, the decision was based on the client's primary problem. If it was health related, then the home health agency was likely to take charge, and the model project was called in for consultation. If the case presented itself initially as an abuse case, the model project tended to manage it, and consulted with other agencies as needed. Interagency coordination was found to be more important to the Rhode Island and Syracuse Model Projects than to Worcester. Since the latter controlled many services within its own organization, it required less contact with other agencies, but, conversely, it experienced more intraagency coordination problems.

Syracuse and Rhode Island established special programs to facilitate agency coordination. For every client, the Syracuse staff organized a "team" that at a minimum involved a public health nurse and the APS worker. This team met formally as needed to review the case and followed its progress at other times through telephone contact. Rhode Island made use of "key councils," groups of elder service providers in local communities that met on regular intervals to discuss common cases. A special subcommittee of the Providence Key Council was established to work with the model project.

Of the three abuse programs, the Rhode Island group experienced the greatest difficulty in interagency coordination, which appeared to be attributable to the constraints demanded by mandatory reporting. Because this project received a very large number of referrals, many more than could be handled by the project staff, an attempt was made to transfer control of the cases to other agencies as quickly as possible. Also, Worcester and Syracuse had concrete services to offer, such as home care services and geriatric case aides, while the Rhode Island Project was forced to ask other agencies for help, for which, because of the time constraints, they had less to give in return.

Time analysis. In order to obtain a more complete picture of the staffing pattern, model project personnel were asked to complete daily time sheets for one month, February 1983. Activities were divided into two general types: client-related, which included screening, referral, interviews, case conferences and the like; and nonclient-related, which encompassed such activities as project administration, staff meetings, providing and receiving training, and others. These time sheets were tallied, and a composite picture for each month was developed. The breakdown of time between social workers and directors is broadly similar, in that social workers devoted considerably more time to client-related services than did the project directors. As would be expected, the project directors devoted more time to agency relations, staff meetings, and project administration.

One particularly interesting difference emerged between the three projects. The social worker in Worcester spent a considerably greater percentage of her time in client interviews/home visits (29.6%) than did the workers in the other two projects (5.8%, Syracuse; 5.4%, Rhode Island), probably owing to the case management model, which requires periodic in-person assessment and monitoring. The Worcester social worker spent less time than her colleagues did in the other two projects in case recording/correspondence, in part because the Worcester agency served fewer total clients during the course of the demonstration. Evidence from the time analysis supports the notion that the approach of the Worcester Project involved more intensive and extensive involvement with fewer cases than was the case in the Syracuse or Rhode Island models.

Case comparisons. Before discussing the relationship of outcome to organizational structure, it is important to compare the case loads. Three groups of variables were selected for this purpose: sociodemographic for both the victim and perpetrator; those related to the "causes" of maltreatment (stress, social isolation, dependency, psychopathology of the perpetrator), and type of abuse. To eliminate as much respondent bias as possible in these interproject comparisons, variables that relied on the subjective interpretation of the social workers were eliminated.

As Tables 17.1 and 17.2 indicate, there were no differences among the three groups of victims regarding their age, sex, marital status, and living arrangement, and among the perpetrators, their sex and living arrangements. Only the age of the latter varied, with the Rhode Island case load having a significantly larger percentage (51.3) of abusers under 50 years of age than did Worcester (39.0) or Syracuse (35.7).

There was no difference among the site case loads in the victim's use of the supportive devices and weight change (variables used as proxies for health status) although the Syracuse case workers found their victims to be more a source of stress ("a lot" and "a little," 88.6%) than did Worcester (80.6%) and Rhode Island (76.2%) (Table 17.3). In terms of socialization, (frequency of contacts and attendance at church or clubs) the groups were not alike. Rhode Island reported less frequency of contact for its clients; 33.6% of group had contact with others outside the household monthly or less, compared to 19.2% of the Worcester and 16.5% of the Syracuse abused elders. Attendance at church or club meetings also varied significantly among the sites. Again, Rhode Island reported that 96.1% of their clients did not attend these activities, while Worcester showed 86.2% and Syracuse, 93.1%. Finally, a comparison of the case loads on the basis of the perpetrator's psychological state (history of mental illness and alcohol abuse) showed no significant difference among the three projects (Table 17.2).

On the whole, the case loads of the three sites were remarkably similar. The abused clients differed in the amount of socialization and the perpetrators differed in age. The most critical difference among the sites, however, was the variation in proportion of physical abuse and passive neglect (Table 17.4). Just about half (49.3%) of the Rhode Island cases listed physical abuse as the type that precipitated the report to the agency in contrast to about one-third (35.6%) of the Worcester case load and a little more than one-fourth (28.9%) of the Syracuse case load. On the other hand, almost 1 out of 5 (18.6%) Worcester and Syracuse cases checked "passive neglect" as the precipitant of the report, compared to about 1 in 15 (6.7%) for Rhode Island.

Case resolution. For the purposes of the evaluation, case resolution was defined as the reduction or elimination of the circumstances that had resulted in the abuse or neglect. According to Table 17.5, there was a significant difference in the degree to which the cases were resolved, with the Worcester Project reporting the largest proportion of cases, 35.2%, "not

TABLE 17.1
A Comparison of the Victims of Elder Abuse/Neglect by Site—Sociodemographic Factors

	Worcester		Syracuse		Rhode Island	
	#	%	#	%	#	%
Age	n.s.					
59-64 years	11	(18.6)	15	(11.2)	27	(20.3)
65-74 years	13	(22.0)	35	(26.1)	40	(30.1)
75-84 years	25	(42.4)	47	(35.1)	46	(34.6)
85 years and older	10	(16.9)	37	(27.6)	20	(15.)
no answer	—		1		1	
Sex	n.s.					
male	12	(20.3)	21	(15.6)	27	(20.1)
female	47	(79.7)	114	(84.4)	107	(79.9)
Marital Status	n.s.					
single	7	(12.1)	8	(6.0)	10	(8.0)
married	21	(36.2)	41	(30.8)	38	(30.4)
widowed	26	(44.8)	72	(54.1)	61	(48.8)
divorced/separated	4	(6.9)	12	(9.0)	16	(12.8)
no answer	1		2		9	
Living Arrangements	ns.					
lives alone	9	(13.6)	37	(27.6)	31	(23.3)
lives with others	51	(86.4)	97	(72.4)	106	(76.7)
no answer	—		1		1	

NOTE: n.s. = no significant difference in chi-square analysis.

resolved" or "a little," For the other sites the figures were: Syracuse, 22.9%, and Rhode Island, 26.4%. In all sites, however, at least one-third of the cases were reported as resolved, with Rhode Island showing the highest percentage, 41.5. A fairly large proportion of these cases involved the separation of the abused and abuser. A closer look at case disposition reveals that 29.9% of the Worcester victims were at the time of the case reassessment in new living arrangements; 35.7% for Syracuse and 26.9% for Rhode Island (Table 17.6).

Barriers to service delivery. To provide further information concerning case resolution, the staff were given a list of possible barriers to service delivery and asked to note the degree to which they had hindered the particular case effort: "not at all," "a little," or "a lot." When the three projects were compared on the nine barriers (see Table 17.7), the differences were significant for only four of them. One, the "number of agencies," was

TABLE 17.2
A Comparison of the Perpetrators of Elder Abuse Neglect by Site

	Worcester		Syracuse		Rhode Island	
	#	%	#	%	#	%
Age	p =	.0386				
under 50 years	23	(39.0)	46	(35.7)	61	(51.3)
50 years and over	36	(61.0)	83	(64.3)	58	(48.7)
no answer	—		6		15	
Sex	n.s.					
male	42	(71.2)	78	(58.6)	84	(66.1)
female	17	(28.8)	55	(41.4)	43	(33.9)
no answer	—		2		7	
Perpetrator lives with victim	n.s.					
yes	49	(83.1)	91	(67.9)	100	(76.9)
no	10	(16.9)	43	(32.1)	30	(23.1)
no answer	—		1		4	
History of mental illness	n.s.					
yes	24	(40.7)	48	(38.7)	43	(36.4)
no	35	(59.3)	76	(61.3)	75	(63.6)
no answer	—		11		16	
History of alcohol abuse	n.s.					
yes	21	(35.6)	49	(39.5)	52	(44.1)
no	38	(64.4)	75	(60.5)	66	(55.9)
no answer	—		11		16	

NOTE: n.s. = no significant difference in chi-square analysis.

cited by Worcester as a barrier that hindered services "a lot" in two cases (5.6%) and by Syracuse "a little" in two cases (2.6%), but not at all by Rhode Island. The "receptivity of the abused to help" was recorded as hindering case efforts "a lot" in about one-quarter of the cases in Worcester (26.9%) and in Rhode Island (22.8%), but in less than one-tenth of the Syracuse cases (9.5%). Likewise the "receptivity of the abuser" was found to be a barrier that hindered treatment "a lot" in about two out of five cases in Worcester (41.7%) and in Rhode Island (44.7%), but less than one out of five of the Syracuse group (15.7%). The Worcester staff reported "availability of services" to be a barrier that hindered service delivery "a lot" in 21.2% of the cases while Syracuse noted a similar finding for only 6.5% of their cases and Rhode Island for 4.3% of their cases. The final significant barrier was "lack of protective services," which Rhode Island reported as hindering their efforts "a lot" in 42.1% of their cases, compared to 16.7% for

TABLE 17.3
A Comparison of the Victims of Elder Abuse/Neglect by Site

	Worcester		Syracuse		Rhode Island	
	#	%	#	%	#	%
Victim is source of stress to perpetrator and/or family	p =	.0319				
a lot	24	(66.7)	74	(56.5)	49	(55.7)
a little	5	(13.9)	42	(32.1)	18	(20.5)
not at all	7	(19.4)	15	(11.5)	21	(23.9)
no answer	23		4		46	
Victim requires supportive devices/bedridden	n.s.					
yes	27	(51.9)	78	(59.5)	46	(46.5)
no	25	(48.1)	53	(40.5)	53	(53.5)
no answer	7		4		36	
Victim has had recent weight change	n.s.					
yes	5	(14.7)	4	(7.0)	3	(8.3)
no	29	(85.3)	53	(93.0)	33	(91.7)
no answer	25		78		98	
Number of social contacts other than household members	p =	.005				
none	11	(18.6)	21	(15.0)	36	(28.3)
1-4	44	(74.6)	88	(66.2)	83	(75.4)
5 or more	4	(6.8)	24	(18.8)	8	(6.3)
no answer			2		9	
Frequency of social contacts	p =	0159				
daily	31	(59.6)	85	(63.9)	61	(55.5)
weekly	11	(21.2)	26	(19.5)	12	(10.9)
monthly or less frequently	10	(19.2)	22	(16.5)	37	(33.6)
no answer	7		2		24	
Attendance at clubs/church	p =	.0490				
yes	8	(13.8)	8	(6.9)	5	(3.9)
no	50	(86.2)	108	(93.1)	123	(96.1)
no answer	1		19		6	

NOTE: n.s. = no significant difference in chi-square analysis.

Worcester and 1.5% for Syracuse.

Community agency responses. Another source of information concerning the outcome of the projects was obtained from the survey of

TABLE 17.4

A Comparison of the Type of Abuse/Neglect That Precipitated the Report to the Model Project by Site

	Worcester		Syracuse		Rhode Island	
	#	%	#	%	#	%
Physical Abuse	p =	.0024				
yes	21	(35.6)	39	(28.9)	66	(49.3)
no	38	(64.4)	96	(71.1)	68	(50.7)
Psychological Abuse	n.s.					
yes	11	(18.6)	36	(26.7)	32	(23.9)
no	48	(81.4)	99	(73.3)	102	(76.1)
Material Abuse	n.s.					
yes	13	(22.0)	18	(13.3)	19	(14.2)
no	46	(78.0)	117	(86.7)	115	(85.8)
Active Neglect	n.s.					
yes	3	(5.1)	17	(12.6)	8	(6.0)
no	56	(94.9)	118	(87.4)	126	(94.0)
Passive Neglect	p =	.0092				
yes	11	(18.6)	25	(18.5)	9	(6.7)
no	48	(81.4)	110	(81.5)	125	(93.3)

NOTE: n.s. = no significant difference in chi-square analysis.

TABLE 17.5

Extent to Which Cases of Elder Abuse/Neglect Were Resolved by Site*

	Worcester		Syracuse		Rhode Island	
	#	%	#	%	#	%
Not at all	7	(13.7)	5	(4.6)	18	(17.0)
A little	11	(21.6)	20	(18.3)	10	(9.4)
A lot	14	(27.5)	49	(45.0)	34	(32.1)
Completely	19	(37.3)	35	(32.1)	44	(41.5)
No answer	8		26		28	

*p = .0089

community agencies. A total of 101 agencies in the Worcester area returned the survey form, 52 in Syracuse (Onondaga County) and 60 in Rhode Island (Table 17.8). When asked, "Are you aware that there is a specific

TABLE 17.6
Status of Victim and Perpetrator at Case Reassessment by Site

	Worcester		Syracuse		Rhode Island	
	#	%	#	%	#	%
Victim died			15	(11.9)	8	(6.5)
Victim in nursing home/rest home	7	(12.3)	29	(23.0)	16	(13.0)
Victim in hospital	5	(8.8)	7	(5.6)	4	(3.3)
Victim in new housing arrangement	5	(8.8)	9	(7.1)	13	(10.6)
Perpetrator died/absent	6	(10.5)	11	(8.7)	17	(13.8)
Perpetrator in nursing home	1	(1.8)	1	(0.8)	3	(2.4)
Housing arrangement unchanged	33	(57.9)	72	(56.7)	62	(50.4)
No answer	—		—		2	

NOTE: Total is greater than 100% because of multiple responses.

project in your area dealing with abuse?" more than three-quarters of the agencies replied affirmatively, with the highest percentage registered by the Syracuse area (86.5%). Those agencies responding "yes" were then asked whether they had referred a client to the project. About 45% of the Syracuse agencies said, "yes"; about half of the Worcester group; and two-thirds of the Rhode Island group. The agencies then were asked to rate the response they had received from the model project. At least six out of seven agencies in all sites marked "excellent" or "good."

Of the 39 agencies in the Worcester area answering this question, 36 were very positive. The most common adjective they used was "prompt." Several commented that the service was "excellent," and a few other singled out its "comprehensiveness." The agencies listed a variety of tasks that were performed by the model project, noting especially "follow-up." Among the Rhode Island agencies that completed the questionnaire, 34 added comments about the response they had received from the project. Of these, 30 were favorable; 7 cited the timeliness of the response, and 5 wrote "good" to describe the agency's efforts. Of the 52 agencies returning questionnaires in the Syracuse area, 22 added comments about the response from their Elder Abuse Project. All were positive except for 2; 4 agencies remarked about the "promptness of the response," and several agencies described the model project efforts as "very good." Some agencies also singled out "follow-up" as a particularly commendable aspect of the project's response.

Because of the importance of "coordination" in providing services to abused and neglected elders, the agencies were asked "if involved in cases of abuse, indicate the degree of satisfaction with the extent of cooperation or

TABLE 17.7

Degree of Hindrance of Barriers to Delivery of Services

	Worcester		Syracuse		Rhode Island	
	#	%	#	%	#	%
Availability of services	p =	.0052				
not hindered	22	(66.7)	64	(68.8)	59	(94.3)
hindered a little	4	(12.1)	23	(24.7)	8	(11.4)
hindered a lot	7	(21.2)	6	(6.5)	3	(4.3)
no answer	26		34		55	
Bureaucratic red tape	n.s.					
not hindered	20	(80.0)	28	(73.7)	14	(87.5)
hindered a little	2	(8.0)	6	(15.8)	2	(12.5)
hindered a lot	3	(12.0)	4	(10.5)	—	
no answer	32		91		115	
Coordination of agencies	n.s.					
not hindered	37	(94.9)	74	(90.2)	75	(97.4)
hindered a little	1	(2.6)	8	(9.8)	2	(2.6)
hindered a lot	1	(2.6)			—	
no answer	20		45		48	
Coordination of services	n.s.					
not hindered	32	(86.5)	75	(91.5)	76	(97.4)
hindered a little	3	(8.1)	6	(7.3)	2	(2.6)
hindered a lot	2	(5.4)	1	(1.2)	—	
no answer	20		45		47	
Lack of protective services	p =	.0413				
not hindered	15	(83.3)	62	(95.4)	20	(52.6)
hindered a little	—		2	(3.1)	2	(5.3)
hindered a lot	3	(16.7)	1	(1.5)	16	(42.1)
no answer	39		62		87	
Lack of respite care	n.s.					
not hindered	12	(70.6)	57	(87.7)	50	(71.0)
hindered a little	3	(17.6)	4	(6.2)	6	(19.4)
hindered a lot	2	(11.8)	4	(6.2)	3	(9.7)
no answer	40		60		94	
Lack of support groups/caretakers	n.s.					
not hindered	11	(68.8)	46	(69.7)	25	(78.1)
hindered a little	4	(25.0)	18	(27.3)	5	(15.6)
hindered a lot	1	(6.3)	2	(3.0)	2	(6.3)
no answer	41		61		93	

TABLE 17.7 (continued)

	Worcester		Syracuse		Rhode Island	
	#	%	#	%	#	%
Legal implications of intervention	n.s.					
not hindered	17	(63.0)	60	(75.0)	34	(75.6)
hindered a little	6	(22.2)	12	(15.0)	6	(13.3)
hindered a lot	4	(14.8)	8	(10.0)	5	(11.1)
no answer	50		47		60	
Non-reimbursement for services	n.s.					
not hindered	18	(85.7)	56	(66.7)	17	(100)
hindered a little	1	(4.8)	10	(11.9)	—	
hindered a lot	2	(9.5)	18	(21.4)	—	
no answer	36		43		108	
Number of agencies involved	p =	.0197				
not hindered	33	(94.3)	75	(97.4)	76	(100)
hindered a little	—		2	(2.6)	—	
hindered a lot	2	(5.7)	—		—	
no answer	22		60		59	
Receptivity of abused to help	p =	.0120				
not hindered	24	(46.2)	74	(70.5)	56	(60.9)
hindered a little	(14	(26.9)	21	(20.0)	15	(16.3)
hindered a lot	14	(26.9)	19	(9.5)	21	(22.8)
no answer	5		22		33	
Receptivity of abuser to help	p =	.0000				
not hindered	17	(35.4)	65	(63.7)	45	(47.9)
hindered a little	11	(27.9)	21	(20.6)	7	(7.4)
hindered a lot	20	(41.7)	16	(15.7)	42	(44.7)
no answer	9		25		31	

NOTE: n.s. = no significant difference in chi-square analysis. Because some items not appropriate, data not available on entire caseloads.

coordination of services in your area." Again, the most positive response came from the agencies in the Worcester site, over two-thirds of which (68.9%) marked "very satisfied," and a little over one-quarter (28.9%) "reasonably satisfied." The Syracuse area agencies were almost equally divided with 46.2% saying that they were "very satisfied" and 53.8% "reasonably satisfied." Among the Rhode Island agencies, there were about one-third (35.3%) who were "very satisfied" and almost two-thirds 61.8%, "reasonably satisfied." Only one agency responded "not at all satisfied" in the Worcester and Rhode Island surveys.

TABLE 17.8
Findings from a Survey of Community Agencies

	Worcester		Syracuse		Rhode Island	
	#	%	#	%	#	%
Are you aware that there is a specific project in your area dealing with elder abuse/neglect?						
yes	78	(78.8)	45	(86.5)	43	(75.4)
no	21	(21.2)	7	(13.5)	14	(24.6)
no answer	2		—		3	
If yes to above, indicate whether you have referred a client to the project.						
yes	42	(51.9)	21	(47.7)	31	(64.6)
no	39	(48.1)	23	(52.3)	16	(33.5)
no answer	20		8		13	
If yes to above, rate the response you received from the project.						
excellent	37	(86.1)	13	(56.5)	10	(32.2)
good	4	(9.3)	9	(39.1)	15	(48.4)
fair	2	(4.7)	1	(4.4)	6	(19.4)
poor	—		—		—	
no answer	58		29		29	
If involved in cases of abuse/neglect, indicate satisfaction with extent of cooperation or coordination of services in your area:						
very satisfied	31	(68.9)	12	(46.2)	12	(35.3)
reasonably satisfied	13	(28.9)	14	(53.8)	21	(61.8)
not at all satisfied	1	(2.2)	—		1	(2.9)
no answer	56		26		26	

Discussion

A variety of data has been presented here that involves client characteristics, case resolution, barriers to intervention, and perceptions of other agencies. Among the sites, there were only a few differences found in client characteristics, the most important being the type of abuse/neglect that precipitated the report. Rhode Island had the highest proportion of physical abuse and lowest proportion of passive neglect cases; for Syracuse, this was reversed, while Worcester had the same proportion of passive neglect as Syracuse had, but more physical abuse. Regarding client outcome, each project reported a majority of cases as being resolved at least "a little," or "a lot," or "completely." However, the Worcester group included one-third of its cases in the "not resolved" or resolved "a little" categories compared to about one-quarter for Syracuse and Rhode Island.

Since there seemed to be no systematic relationship between abuse/neglect type and client outcome, the analysis then focused on the impact of the organizational models. Although they were similar in many respects, two differences stood out: The strategies adopted to promote coordination and the extent or degree of staff involvement in direct client services. With respect to coordination effects, there was no difference among the sites in the degree to which "coordination of services" and "coordination of agencies" hindered case management. If, indeed, coordination of services is a key factor in achieving case resolution, then the Worcester Project should have had the best record since the agencies in Worcester were more satisfied with the coordination of services than were those in Syracuse or Rhode Island.

The one important factor that does emerge as a possible explanation for the difference in case resolution among the sites is the extent or degree of involvement in direct client services. The Worcester staff saw a much smaller number of clients over a long period. Their style of practice involved lengthy case work with families, while Rhode Island used a short-term intervention and referral strategy, and Syracuse took a sort of middle road with greater likelihood of relocating clients to new living situations. Rather than leading to a higher degree of case resolution, the Worcester approach apparently made the staff more aware of the dynamics within the family. Because of their deep involvement in these family situations, the Worcester staff seemed to be less willing to label them "resolved." This interpretation may also explain why they found "receptivity of the abused and abuser" to be more of a barrier than either Rhode Island or Syracuse. From a cost benefit perspective, the Worcester Project was the least efficient model. On the other hand, its intensive effort to keep the family intact, including providing services to the perpetrator and other family members, may make it the most acceptable and satisfying approach in the eyes of the victims.

References

Block, M. R. & Sinnott, J. D. (1979). *The battered elder syndrome.* College Park: University of Maryland Center on Aging.

Douglass, R. L., Hickey, T., & Noel, C. (1980). *A study of maltreatment of the elderly and other vulnerable adults.* Ann Arbor, MI: University of Michigan, Institute of Gerontology.

Hornby, H. (1982). *Improving protective services for older Americans: Program development and administration. A National Guide Series* (Vol. 1). Portland: Center for Research and Advanced Study, University of Southern Maine.

Humphreys, J., Campbell, J., & Barrett, S. (1983, November). *Clinical intervention with the abused elderly and their families.* Paper presented at the 36th Annual Scientific Meeting of the Gerontological Society of America, San Francisco.

Lau, E. E., & Kosberg, J. I. (1978, November). *Abuse of the elderly by informal care providers: Practice and research issues.* Paper presented at the 31st Annual Scientific Meeting of the Gerontological Society of America, Dallas.

O'Malley, H., Segars, H., Perez, R., Mitchella, V., & Knuepfel, G. (1979). *Elder abuse in Massachusetts: A survey of professionals and elderly.* Boston: Legal Research and Services for the Elderly.

Pratt, C. C., Koval, J., & Lloyd, S. (1983, March). Service workers' responses to abuse of the elderly. *Social Casework,* pp. 147-153.

Sengstock, M. C., & Barrett, S. (1982, November). *Legal services for aged victims of domestic abuse: The experience of one legal aid agency.* Paper presented at a meeting of the American Society of Criminology, Toronto, Ontario.

Sengstock, M. C., & Liang, J. (1982). *Identifying and characterizing elder abuse.* (Final report submitted to NRTA-AARP Andrus Foundation). Detroit, MI: Wayne State University, Institute of Gerontology.

Steinmetz, S. K. (1978, July-August). Battered parents. *Society,* pp. 54-55.

Villomare, E., & Bergman, J. (1981). *Elder abuse and neglect: A guide for practitioners and policy makers.* (Paper prepared for the Oregon Office of Elderly Affairs). San Francisco: National Paralegal Institute.

18

Child Maltreatment Evaluation Efforts: What Have We Learned?

Deborah Daro
Anne H. Cohn

In 1974, with the passage of the federal Child Abuse and Neglect Treatment Act, policymakers had little basic research and program evaluation information to turn to for guidance. Existing studies suffered from the limitations of small, nonrepresentative samples, an uncertainty over which variables to explore and monitor, and a very narrow range of intervention strategies to apply to what was even then described as a multidimensional social welfare problem. Although research and program evaluation in child maltreatment continues to be plagued with methodological problems and ethical dilemmas endemic to human subject research, the past 14 years have provided policymakers at all levels of government with a rich base of empirical studies and a small but growing number of longitudinal studies upon which to draw in designing their laws and intervention systems. One particularly rich research field has been the multiple site program evaluations funded by the federal government since 1974. Among the largest evaluation contracts awarded during this period are:

- Berkeley Planning Associates' evaluation of the 11 joint OCD/SRS demonstration programs in child abuse and neglect conducted between 1974 and 1977 with a client impact sample of over 1,600 families;
- Abt Associates' evaluation of 20 demonstration and innovative treatment projects funded by the National Center for Child Abuse and Neglect (NCCAN) between 1977 and 1981 with a client impact sample of 488 families;
- E. H. White's evaluation of 29 service improvement grants funded by NCCAN between 1978 and 1981 with a client impact sample of 165 families; and

- Berkeley Planning Associates' evaluation of 19 clinical demonstration projects funded by NCCAN between 1978 and 1982 with a client impact sample of 1,000 families.

Collectively, these four studies represent over a $4 million federal investment in child abuse and neglect program research.[1] Realizing a solid return on this investment is largely contingent upon the careful articulation and dissemination of those findings most likely to enhance treatment performance. While each of these studies explored different aspects within the child maltreatment spectrum[2] and used a variety of methodologies, each generated several consistent findings regarding the relative efficacy of different treatment strategies, and the most effective means of preventing child maltreatment. Common findings include the advantage of including in the treatment package supportive services such as group counseling services and lay therapy; the difficulty in eliminating reincidence and propensity toward future maltreatment with a client population that has experienced severe and longstanding patterns of abuse and neglect; and the need for expanding prevention efforts beyond the traditional "high risk" populations.

This chapter summarizes the key findings of these research efforts and their collective contributions to the fields of child abuse and neglect treatment, prevention, and research. This is the first such effort to do so.

Methodology

A variety of methodological techniques were used by the four evaluations. Qualitative or descriptive approaches, such as case studies and in-depth interviews, were used both to summarize the organizational and service structures of the individual demonstration projects (Berkeley Planning Associates, 1977, Vol. 12, *Historical Case Studies: Eleven Child Abuse and Neglect Projects, 1974-1977;* Berkeley Planning Associates, 1983, Vol. 9, *Historical Case Studies.*) and to highlight the key clinical issues raised in addressing the needs of multiproblem families and individuals (Berkeley Planning Associates, 1983, Vol. 3, *A Qualitative Study of Most Successful and Least Successful Cases;* White, 1981). In addition to assessing the most effective organizational and staffing configurations in working with maltreating families (Berkeley Planning Associates, 1977, Vol. 9, *Project Management and Worker Burnout*), assessments were also conducted on the relative costs of providing various service packages (Berkeley Planning Associates, 1977, Vol. 7, *Cost Report;* Berkeley Planning Associates, 1983, Vol. 6, *Resource Allocation Study*); on the elements of a well-functioning community systems response to maltreatment (Berkeley Planning Associates, 1977, Vol. 5, *Community Systems Impact;* Vol. 10, *Guide for Planning and Implementing Child Abuse and Neglect Programs*); and on the attributes of quality case management (Berkeley Planning Associates, 1977, Vol. 6, *Quality of the Case Management Process*). Specific studies also identified the key issues in addressing child neglect (Berkeley Planning Associates, 1983, Vol. 4, *Child Neglect*) and in providing therapeutic interventions to young children (Berkeley Planning Associates, 1977, Vol. 11, *Child Impact;* Berkeley Planning Associates, 1983, Vol. 5, *Therapeutic Child Care—Approaches to Remediating the Effects of Child Abuse and Neglect*).

Three of the evaluations employed multivariate statistical techniques to identify the specific service and client characteristics that accounted for positive client outcomes. The dependent variables used in the evaluations included reincidence during treatment, future likelihood for maltreatment following termination, progress in overall functioning, and progress in resolving a number of specific behavioral or psychosocial problems exhibited at intake. Using data collection instruments developed by the evaluators, individual project staff provided detailed assessments of their clients at both intake and termination. Each of the evaluations used a multiple comparison group design in which the performance of clients receiving one set of services was compared to the performance of clients receiving a different service package. Multiple regression was used in the analyses, with covariates entered to control for differences in client characteristics and in the types and severity of maltreatment (Abt Associates, 1981, Vol. 2, *Detailed Account of Study Findings, Methods, and Conclusions*; Berkeley Planning Associates, 1977, Vol. 8, *Methodology for Evaluating Child Abuse and Neglect Service Programs*; Berkeley Planning Associates, 1983, Vol. 8, *Final Analysis Plan and Methodology for the Exploration of Client Characteristics, Services and Outcomes;* White, 1981).

Nature of the Maltreating Population

The clients served by these 88 federally funded demonstration projects have represented a broad spectrum of families. Wide variation in the types of maltreatment, household income, household composition, race, and presenting problems were noted by all four evaluation efforts. As summarized in Table 18.1, the four client impact samples represented a wide range of maltreatment.[3] The most notable differences among the four studies were the decrease in the number of "high risk" families included in each sample and the increase in the recorded incidence of sexual abuse.

While approximately one-quarter of the clients included in the initial BPA and Abt evaluations were identified as "high risk," this classification applied to only 5% of the most recent demonstration effort's caseload. Of the substantiated cases served by the projects, the percentage of families who had previously been reported for child maltreatment jumped from 29% in the first BPA sample to over 40% in both the Abt and second BPA samples. Variations in the percentage of sexual abuse cases is partially reflected in the selection criteria NCCAN employed in establishing each demonstration effort.[4] Larger numbers of sexual abuse cases among the more recent demonstration project caseloads, (from 4% of the first BPA study, to 7% of the Abt study, to over 28% of the latest client sample) is also indicative of the growing awareness and thus detection of this particular form of maltreatment.

Despite this diversity in family characteristics and type of maltreatment the major presenting problems of families involved in maltreatment remained remarkably similar across the studies. As summarized in Table 18.2, contextual problems such as financial difficulties or unemployment and interpersonal problems such as marital conflict, social isolation, substance abuse, and spouse abuse, were identified by sizable percentages of clients in each study population. As might be expected, given the shift to serving more severe cases, the frequency of all of these problems showed a dramatic increase over time. For example, financial difficulties jumped from 46% of the client population studied in 1975 to over 80% of the client population studied in 1979-1980. Similarly, employment problems jumped from 18% to 36%. In the most recent evaluation study, these financial and employment difficulties appear to be not only a function of chronic unemployment or poverty but also a reflection of a generally poor economy and the impact poor national economic performance has upon children.

Service Effectiveness for Adults

While the Abt study found no notable correlation between a given set of services and positive client outcomes, and in fact suggested that the more services a family received, the worse the family got, both of the BPA evaluations identified specific services as enhancing client outcomes. The first BPA study concluded that, relative to any other discrete services or combination of services, the receipt of lay services—lay counseling and Parents Anonymous—as part of a treatment package resulted in more positive treatment outcomes. The study also noted that group services, such as group therapy and parent education classes, as supplemental services also produced notable effects, particularly for the physical abuser.

TABLE 18.1
Type of Maltreatment

	BPA 1977 (%)	Abt 1981 (%)	E.H. White 1981 (%)	BPA 1982 (%)
High risk	28	25	42	5
Emotional maltreatment	14			23
Physical neglect	20	26	32	27
Physical abuse	31	28	21	17
Sexual maltreatment	4	5		28
Emotional or sexual maltreatment			7	
Neglect and physical abuse	3	13		
Sexual maltreatment, neglect and/or physical abuse		2		
	(n = 1686)	(n = 488)	(n = 164)	(n = 895)

TABLE 18.2
Major Presenting Problems of Maltreating Families

	BPA 1977 (%)	Abt 1981 (%)	E.H. White 1981 (%)	BPA 1982 (%)
Financial difficulties	46	44	62	80
Employment problems	18	30	n.a.	36
Marital conflict	40	36	40	74
Social isolation	29	23	n.a.	67
Substance abuse	19	24	25	54
Spouse abuse	11	13	n.a.	42
	(n = 1686)	(n = 488)	(n = 164)	(n = 903)

Although the BPA study cautioned that the lay services provided by the projects participating in that study involved intensive on-the-job training and ongoing professional backup and supervision for the lay therapist, the study clearly indicated that expansion beyond a strictly therapeutic or counseling service model was both beneficial to the client and cost-effective for the project (Berkeley Planning Associates, 1977, Vol. 3, *Adult Client Impact Report;* Cohn, 1979).

Similar findings were noted by the most recent BPA evaluation. Again, the provision of group counseling and educational and skill development classes showed a significant relationship to both a client's achievement of overall progress and the elimination of a propensity toward future maltreatment. Holding the initial severity of the case constant as well as a number of descriptive characteristics, adults who received group counseling were 27% less likely than those who did not receive this particular service to demonstrate a continued propensity for future maltreatment. Similarly, those clients who received educational or skill development classes, such as household management, health care, and vocational skills development, were 16% less likely than clients who did not receive this service to demonstrate a continued propensity for future maltreatment. Clients receiving group counseling and educational or skill development classes were also significantly more likely than clients not receiving these services to demonstrate overall progress during treatment (Berkeley Planning Associates, 1983, Vol. 2, *The Exploration of Client Characteristics, Services and Outcomes—Final Report and Summary of Findings*).[5]

The two BPA evaluations noted that clients engaged in treatment for less than six months were less likely to make overall progress in treatment or demonstrate a reduced propensity toward future maltreatment. In addition, the latest BPA study found that clients remaining in treatment over 18 months also performed less well on these indicators, suggesting that an optimal treatment period may be between 7 and 18 months. The latest BPA finding corroborates the Abt finding that the longer services were provided, the worse the family got. Whether this finding is the result of the most difficult cases (and consequently the cases with which one would expect to have the least success) remaining in treatment the longest or if the potential for intervention strategies like those supported by federal demonstration efforts diminish after 18 months are hypotheses worth testing in future evaluative efforts.

On balance, the findings just summarized suggest that successful intervention with maltreating families requires a comprehensive package of services that address both the interpersonal and concrete needs of all family members. Strategies that continue to rely solely upon costly professional therapy, without augmenting their service strategies with group counseling efforts and other supportive or remedial services to children and families, will offer less opportunity for maximizing client gains. Also, projects should be aware of the diminishing rate of return on services over time and invest the most intensive resources during the initial months of treatment in order to engage the family successfully and begin altering behavior as close to the point of initial referral as possible.

Success Rates in Treatment for Adults

Overall, federally funded demonstration projects have had their problems in achieving client success, in terms of both stopping reincidence and reducing the likelihood for further maltreatment. As summarized in Table 18.3, reincidence occurred in 30% to 47% of the cases evaluated by BPA and Abt Associates. While the definition of reincidence varied among the three samples (e.g., the initial BPA study noted only cases involving severe reincidence of neglect or physical abuse, whereas the second BPA study recorded all forms of reincidence), the collective impression of these findings suggests that, in the short run, existing treatment efforts have not been terribly successful in protecting children from further harm.

On the other hand, reincidence in treatment is not, in and of itself, a very good predictor of eventual progress in treatment or in eventually reducing the propensity for future maltreatment. All three studies reported a relatively weak correlation between reincidence in treatment and other client outcome measures such as propensity for future maltreatment and overall progress in resolving a range of personal and family functioning problems. In every respect, the projects most successful in eliminating reincidence were projects that generally separated the child from the abusive parent either by placing the child in temporary foster care or by requiring the maltreating parent to move out of the home.[6] The study findings underscore that greater emphasis on monitoring parent-child interactions is necessary to protect the child against continued maltreatment if out-of-home placement options are not used.

In two of the demonstration efforts, reduced propensity toward future maltreatment was measured. Overall, 42% of the clients served by the initial round of demonstration projects demonstrated a reduced propensity for future maltreatment compared to 80% of the clients included in the Abt client impact evaluation. It should be noted that while these clients were found less likely to maltreat their children in the future than they had been prior to services, the likelihood for future maltreatment continued to exist among many of the clients. In order to identify more clearly the children no longer at risk, the second BPA study asked clinicians to assess the future likelihood for continued maltreatment among their adult client population, not simply their reduced propensity. That study identified 46% of the clients served as being unlikely to maltreat their children in the future.

The latest evaluation also noted a dramatic difference in the performance of clients involved in different types of maltreatment on this indicator. For example, 70% of the clients served by the sexual abuse treatment projects were viewed as being unlikely to further maltreat their children, but only 40% of the adults served by the child neglect projects were viewed in this manner. This solid performance by the sexual abuse treatment projects suggests that, although interventions targeted to sexual abuse are relatively new to the field, greater gains have been made in achieving success with these clients than has been made in the more longstanding, and perhaps more difficult, area of child neglect (Berkeley Planning Associates, 1983, Vol. 2.).[7]

TABLE 18.3
Success Rates

Outcome Measures	BPA, 1977	Abt, 1981	BPA, 1982
Reincidence	30% of all cases severe reincidence	44% reincidence for all cases	47% reincidence for all cases
Future likelihood to maltreat	42% reduced propensity	80% reduced propensity	46% unlikely to abuse in future
Improvement on functional problems adult clients exhibited at intake:			
• percentage of clients demonstrating any progress during treatment	—	33	60
• percentage of problems showing improvement:			
0-33	62		
34-66	18		
67-100	21		
Less than 50			49
50-74			14
7599			7
100			30

Measures of improved adult client functioning in behavior and attitudes associated with abuse were used in three of the evaluation efforts. As summarized in Table 18.3, the latest round of demonstrations projects fared better than both previous demonstration efforts in resolving the key functioning problems of their adult clients. While roughly two-thirds of the adults served by the 11 joint OCD/SRS demonstration projects experienced improvement in only one-third or less of their functioning problems, 51% of the clients served by the latest NCCAN-funded demonstration effort realized improvement on at least half of their problems, with 30% of these clients realizing gains on all of their presenting problems. Similarly, while the Abt study noted that 34% of its client sample achieved overall progress during treatment, over 60% of the adults served by the most recent demonstration projects were identified at termination as having made progress.

It is of interest to note that, while reincidence in treatment continues to be a problem, child abuse and neglect treatment projects have made notable progress in reducing the propensity for future maltreatment and in improving client functioning. This pattern of improvement is even more remarkable when one considers the fact that the caseloads of these projects have included larger percentages of families experiencing severe maltreatment and multiple problems.[8] Expansions in the service package and the better targeting of services to specific child maltreatment subpopulations are among the factors that have most likely contributed to these successes.[9]

Services Effectiveness for Children

In the earliest rounds of demonstration projects, very few children received direct services from child abuse and neglect demonstration projects making the assessment of the impact of such efforts on remediating the physical and emotional effects of maltreatment difficult. For example, only 70 children received direct services during the first federal demonstration effort and the Abt evaluation noted that medical care was the only type of direct assistance offered the children they evaluated. Of the 70 children in the first BPA study who did receive some form of therapy, over 50% demonstrated improvements in those developmental, emotional, or socialization areas noted to be serious problems at the time treatment began.

In contrast to the relatively low number of children provided direct services by these early demonstration efforts, over 1,600 children and adolescents served by the latest demonstration projects were provided a wide range of direct services including individual therapy, group counseling, therapeutic day care, speech and physical therapy, and medical care. This expansion of services was correlated with a higher percentage of children achieving improved functioning while in treatment. In comparison to an approximate 50% improvement rate of children served during the initial round of demonstration projects, over 70% of the young children and adolescents served by those projects specifically focusing on their needs demonstrated gains across all functional areas during treatment.

Conclusions

The collective results of the federally funded research and demonstration efforts provide good cause for celebrating. Specifically, the most heartening findings include:

- greater clarity in differentiating among families experiencing various types of maltreatment;
- expanded intervention models that include direct services to *both* adults and children;
- improved client outcomes, especially in the areas of individual and family functioning with increasingly more severe cases of maltreatment; and
- notable success in eliminating reincidence and future propensity among families involved in sexual abuse.

The studies also provide some cause for concern; treatment efforts in general are still not very successful. Child abuse and neglect continue despite early, thoughtful, and often costly intervention. Treatment programs have made very little consistent progress in reducing reincidence or the future likelihood of maltreating in the most severe cases of physical abuse, chronic neglect, and emotional maltreatment. As just outlined, one-third or more of the parents served by these intensive demonstration efforts maltreated their children while in treatment and over one-half of the families served by the two largest demonstration efforts continued to be judged by staff as likely to mistreat their children following termination.

Assessing the overall success rate one can hope to achieve in working with abusive and neglectful families, Kempe and Kempe (1978) estimate that, regardless of the interventions used, 20% of the parents will be treatment "failures" such that the child will not be returned home; 40% of the parents will grow and develop and eventually permanently change their parenting behaviors; and 40% of the parents will no longer physically abuse or neglect their children but will continue to be emotional maltreaters. While the combination of therapeutic and supportive services such as group and family therapy, educational and skill development classes, in-home lay therapists, and self-help groups have enhanced overall performance with families agreeable to intervention, a sizable core of parents remain unchanged and their children remain at risk. In addition to suggesting clear treatment paths, therefore, the collective findings of these national program evaluations underscore the critical need to increase efforts to identify and implement successful strategies for preventing abuse before it occurs.

Notes

1. Detailed findings and descriptions of the evaluations can be obtained from the National Child Abuse Clearinghouse and the National Technical Information Service in the following sources: Berkeley Planning Associates (1977, 1983); Abt Associates (1981); White (1981).

2. It is of interest to note that the 88 demonstration projects evaluated by the four studies reflect a gradual shifting in the auspices and focus of child abuse and neglect treatment programs. Over the time period spanned by the four evaluations, fewer of the demonstration projects were housed in public, protective service agencies; the client population became more dominated by substantiated rather than "high risk" families; the number and range of services provided by the projects to the children and adolescents in these maltreating families increased; and projects targeted their services to a more limited range of maltreatment behavior. Certain of these shifts reflect changes in the funding criteria used for the most recent demonstration effort (e.g., NCCAN required its last set of demonstration projects to identify a specific child abuse and neglect subpopulation, such as neglect or sexual abuse); other shifts are representative of a broader change in what child maltreatment projects across the country have been attempting to do.

3. Reviewing the demographic descriptions of these families, one would be hard-pressed to isolate patterns of maltreatment to a single socioeconomic class. For example, over 15% of the families served by the 11 joint OCD/SRS demonstration projects had household incomes in excess of $12,000, while over 22% of the families served by the most recent round of NCCAN-funded clinical demonstration projects had incomes in excess of $15,000. In addition, income was found in the most recent BPA study to be highly correlated with the family's primary type of maltreatment: over 37% of the families involved in sexual abuse fell into the highest earnings category, an earnings level noted for only 2% of the families involved in physical neglect. Similar differences by type of maltreatment were also noted in the household composition of the families. Although 61% of the families in both of the evaluations conducted by BPA and in the Abt study included two adults, either natural or adult parent figures, the latest BPA study noted that this type of family constituted 82% of the families involved in sexual abuse but only 24% of the families involved in child neglect.

4. Each project funded under this effort targeted services to one of five subpopulations including sexual abuse, adolescent maltreatment, substance abuse, remedial services for children, and child neglect.

5. Similar findings regarding the efficacy of group therapy and parenting education classes have also been noted in other program evaluations. See Bean (1971), McNeil and McBride (1979), and Moore (1982).

6. For treatment projects committed to working with the entire family and in maintaining the family unit throughout the treatment process, this intervention strategy is less viable. Breaking the cycle of maltreatment is a difficult treatment issue that involves not only breaking

the abusive or neglectful patterns but also cultivating different, more appropriate patterns of interaction and discipline. Prior to the completion of this process, it is likely that parents will fall back into those patterns that are familiar and comfortable. As each of these evaluations has pointed out, reincidence in this context is not solely an outcome indicator, but a continuum along which a family's progress may be monitored.

7. Again, similar findings have been noted by others evaluating sexual abuse interventions. See L. M. Anderson, and G. Shafer (1979).

8. The increased percentage of severe maltreatment cases being served by the demonstration projects has both positive and negative aspects. It is certainly encouraging to see that solid success can be achieved with multi-problem families. Whereas 10 years ago the children in such families might have been automatically removed and parental rights terminated, these families are now viewed as viable candidates for treatment and eventual reunification. On the other hand, the focus on the more severe cases places child abuse and neglect treatment projects in the difficult position of working with families that have fewer and fewer material and personal resources. This increase in caseload severity has been noted by each subsequent federal demonstration effort, not only among its substantiated cases, but also among its "high risk" cases. In the most recent demonstration effort, the "high risk" families were as likely as the substantiated cases to exhibit financial difficulties, physical violence, disruptive conflict between spouses and extended family members and social isolation.

The similarities suggest that child abuse and neglect prevention programs that target their services to "high risk" parents may, in fact, be serving as complex and as difficult a population as those programs targeted toward actual maltreaters. By the time families have moved into a "high risk" classification, they have already established behavior patterns and developed functioning difficulties that make efforts to prevent actual maltreatment extremely difficult. One conclusion from these findings is that the prevention of child abuse requires not only a focus on families considered high risk but also a focus on the range of problems that push a family into a "high risk" situation.

9. Hypotheses regarding subpopulations of maltreatment were supported by all four evaluations. Each identified significant differences in demographic characteristics, presenting problems, and service needs among families and perpetrators involved in different types of maltreatment. Segmenting the population for service purposes along this dimension, however, is problematic. The continued funding of projects to serve only one segment of the maltreatment population may be difficult to justify in light of rising fiscal constraints and service demands. Given decreasing resources, can projects afford to specialize? If a community has funding for only one child abuse and neglect treatment program, can it afford to serve only victims of sexual abuse or neglect? For years, one of the keys to a successful community response to child maltreatment has been to establish a coordination system that includes all professional and voluntary agencies concerned with child health and well-being. In the rush to secure funding, this coordination and mutual cooperation may be compromised, as providers claim one type of maltreatment is more severe or damaging than another type, losing site of the fact that all maltreatment is unacceptable.

References

Abt Associates. (1981, May). *Impact Evaluation of Twenty Demonstration and Innovative Child Abuse and Neglect Treatment Projects.* (2 volumes). (Prepared for the National

Center for Child Abuse and Neglect, Office of Human Development Services, DHHS under Contract HEW 105-77-1047. Available from National Child Abuse Clearinghouse and National Technical Information Service).

Anderson, L. M., & Schafer, G. (1979). The character-disorder family: A community treatment model for family sexual abuse. *American Journal of Orthopsychiatry, 49,* 436-445.

Bean, S. L. (1971). A multiservice approach to the prevention of child abuse. *Child Welfare, 50,* 277-282.

Berkeley Planning Associates. (1977, December). *Evaluation of the Joint OCD/SRS Demonstration Projects in Child Abuse and Neglect.* (12 volumes). (Prepared for the National Center for Health Services Research, Office of Assistant Secretary for Health, DHEW, under Contracts HRA 106-74-120 and HRA 230-76-0076. Available from National Child Abuse Clearinghouse and National Technical Information Service).

Berkeley Planning Associates. (1983, June). *Evaluation of the Clinical Demonstrations of the Treatment of Child Abuse and Neglect.* (9 volumes). (Prepared for the National Center for Child Abuse and Neglect, Office of Human Development Services, DHHS, under Contract HEW 105-78-1108. Available from National Child Abuse Clearinghouse and National Technical Information Service).

Cohn, A. (1979). Effective treatment of child abuse and neglect. *Social Work*, 24, 513-519.

Cohn, A., & DeGraaf, B. (1982). Assessing case management in the field of child abuse. *Journal of Social Service Research, 5,* 29-43.

Kempe, R. S., & Kempe, C. H. (1978). Child abuse. In Bruner, Cole, & Lloyd (Eds.), *The Developing Child Series.* Cambridge, MA: Harvard University Press.

Moore, J. B. (1982). Project Thrive: A supportive treatment approach to parents of children with nonorganic failure to thrive. *Child Welfare*, 1982, 61, 389-398.

McNeil, J. S., & McBride, M. L. (1979). Group therapy with abusive parents. *Social Casework, 60,* 36-42.

White, E. H. (1981, October). *Evaluation of Service Improvements Grants: Analysis of Client Case Reports.* (Prepared for the National Center for Child Abuse and Neglect, Office of Human Development Services, DHHS, under Contract HEW 105-78-1107. Available from National Child Abuse Clearinghouse and National Technical Information Service).

19

Methodological Considerations in Treatment Outcome Research in Child Maltreatment

Sandra T. Azar

It is quite fashionable these days for veterans in any given research area to write on methodological issues, such as I have done in this chapter. Having just come fresh from my first encounter with the beast—a comparative treatment outcome study with 60 maltreating parents (Azar, 1984)—I feel that I have already earned veteran status. So much so, in fact, that my experience tempts me to change the title of this chapter from "Methodological Considerations in Outcome Research" to "Considerations That Should be Accorded the Treatment Outcome Researcher!" The purpose of this chapter is to address major obstacles that hinder outcome research with child maltreaters and attempt to make suggestions as to how they might be alleviated. Empirically based treatment outcome research work is still relatively rare in the literature and will continue to be so unless these problem areas are addressed. In addition, common methodological problems that are evidenced in the outcome studies we have already accumulated will be discussed.

The first and probably biggest obstacle that has hindered good empirical outcome research is the sociopolitical atmosphere that child maltreatment has stimulated. A scientific approach to problem solution requires an unhurried attitude and the slow accumulation of knowledge. For treatment outcome work, this means that a strong emphasis is initially placed on defining a disorder and assessing those afflicted. Homogeneous samples for study can thereby be delineated and relevant deficits requiring intervention uncovered. Unfortunately, the emotional atmosphere that child maltreatment generates and the resulting societal press for action have acted to short-circuit this scientific process (Azar, Fantuzzo, & Twentyman, 1984). Answering society's call for action and perhaps responding to funding priorities, child abuse researchers have rushed in and developed treatment packages without an empirically guided understanding of the phenomenon.

This short-circuiting of the scientific process has resulted in a number of obvious methodological problems. First, we have not developed a diagnostic system to define our samples. Essentially, researchers have accepted the diagnostic system of the legal community and social service agencies. Samples are described as "adjudicated child abusers" or "founded cases of child neglect." These legal definitions are troublesome in that they often refer to intentionality on the parents' part or emphasize consequences of the disorder rather than the characteristics of the deviant behavior itself. Furthermore, the source of the diagnosis is frequently an unknown third party, the reliability and validity of whose judgment has not been documented. Although no practicing clinician would accept the word of an anonymous other as evidence of a disorder's occurrence (Ross, 1983), child maltreatment researchers, not having their own definitions, have been content to accept such determinations.

A second consequence of jumping prematurely to treatment outcome studies is poor specificity of targets for intervention. Because of the lack of a solid assessment literature (Plotkin, Azar, Twentyman, & Perri, 1982), there is little consensus as to where intervention is required. As a result, models used to explain other forms of family dysfunction have been borrowed along with their associated techniques and applied to the problem, making untested assumptions regarding their applicability to the disorder in question.

This lack of specificity has led to what Gambrill (1983) has described as a shotgun approach in the intervention studies undertaken to date. Targets for intervention have included everything from length of tolerance for crying (Sandford & Tustin, 1974) to increasing the parent's free time (Stein & Gambrill, 1976). It has been assumed that such factors differentiate maltreating parents from nonmaltreating ones and that training in such matters will be incompatible with maltreating behavior. However, the relationship with abusive behavior may not exist. For example, a recent study found that "negative affect expression," a common treatment target, did not differentiate maltreating parents from nonperpetrator spouses (Reid, in press). Such results question outcome researchers' assumption that "negative affect expression" is on the same continuum as abusive behavior. We may also find that we have operationalized concepts improperly. A good example is the commonly held belief that child maltreaters have unrealistic expectations of children's behavior. This construct has been operationalized as poor knowledge of child developmental milestones and treatments have, therefore, included education in these matters. However, one study found that knowledge of child developmental milestones did not differentiate between maltreating and closely matched comparison mothers (Azar, Robinson, Hekimian, & Twentyman, 1984), but rather it was judgments pertaining to more complex sequences of child behavior that presented more of a problem for these parents.

A second difficulty that has resulted from a shotgun approach to treatment is delineating the effective component. Even if the researcher utilizes reduction of maltreatment referrals as an outcome measure, it is not clear, given the broadness of the treatments used, what component is responsible for the treatment success found.

In general then, this press for action has led outcome researchers to proceed on very weak ground. We have intervened within poorly defined samples, in undocumented deficit areas, and with borrowed theoretical models and treatment techniques. A step backwards to more basic assessment work is needed if we are to develop truly effective interventions. This work would be focused most fruitfully on developing methods for defining samples more directly or at the very least testing out the reliability and validity of the judgments made by the legal and social service systems. In addition, carefully planned studies are needed examining those characteristics that distinguish the maltreating family from the nonmaltreating one and how these characteristics might best be measured.

As a preliminary step in this assessment work, samples for study might be chosen based on the specific type of maltreatment exhibited (e.g., abuse versus neglect), rather than combining them as has been done previously. A step further would be to specify criteria involving intensity of the deviant parenting behavior, as well as duration of maltreatment. We may find that the neglectful mother who fails to feed her children may exhibit quite different deficit areas than the one who does not provide adequate supervision, and may ultimately require very different types of treatment.

Also, in conducting such basic assessment studies, control groups need to be more carefully matched than has been done to date. Matching solely on demographic characteristics such as socioeconomic status and marital status may be insufficient. Recent studies (Wolfe & Mosk, 1983; Aragona & Eyberg, 1981, for example) have shown that qualities that have been thought to distinguish the maltreating parent did not do so when the comparison group was closely matched on distress level. Support network, stress level, cognitive ability, and mobility may all be important dimensions for matching nonmaltreating control groups. Further, it might be argued that being identified by the social service system in and of itself may carry with it unique deviant qualities that do not relate specifically to maltreating behavior and that perhaps the best comparison groups would, therefore, be composed of nonperpetrators within identified maltreating families. Use of such carefully matched control groups might help us to isolate those qualities that most directly relate to the deviant parenting behavior observed.

Along with a lack of a solid knowledge base for defining samples and determining targets appropriate for intervention, a third major obstacle to conducting outcome research is one inherent in the nature of the problem itself. Child abuse is a low frequency, private event. This fact presents measurement problems as an outcome variable. First, participating in a treatment program clearly increases a family's visibility. This fact makes referral for deviant parenting behavior more likely among treated parents than comparison subjects, thereby stacking the deck against demonstrating treatment effectiveness. Second, given its low frequency of occurrence, longer follow-up periods than are currently employed in most outcome research should be required. Lengthy follow-up periods heighten the cost of conducting such research. Such difficulties have probably discouraged work in the area and, with only a few exceptions, presently available research has not used referrals for maltreatment as an outcome measure.

Even if better sample definitions and a solid assessment literature were available and the luxury of lengthy follow-up periods could be afforded, further and less easily solved obstacles await the treatment outcome researcher. Child maltreaters tend to be poor, less well-educated, highly stressed, and socially isolated individuals. It has been my experience that they do not identify their parenting behavior as a problem area and, therefore, are not motivated to change. These characteristics hinder all aspects of treatment outcome work from eliciting the consent to participate to collecting representative evaluation data.

First, there is the very basic requirement of subjects attending treatment and evaluation sessions. Low socioeconomic status has long been associated with poor compliance with traditional treatment delivery services (Lorion, 1978). My experience with maltreating families is consonant with these findings. They lead chaotic lives and the lack of consistency observed in their parenting pervades all aspects of their behavior. Furthermore, they are more likely to lack their own transportation and a support network to provide babysitting. They meet with continual crises that are more likely to involve survival issues (e.g., problems with their welfare checks, being evicted from their homes, battering by their mates). All of these factors interfere with treatment attendance. They also have poor relationship histories—especially with bureaucratic agencies, our easiest point of access. Another "worker" entering their lives, which is how the outcome researcher is perceived, is just not welcomed. Add to this the fact that child maltreaters are often clients involuntarily and it is easily seen that resistance is inevitable. Even our provisions of bus transportation and babysitting did not ensure attendance, we found. Further special allowances were required. Sessions could not be held on days welfare checks arrived in the mail, since staying home meant the check would be protected from theft. Making initial contacts required much persistence. In some cases we found that it took as many as six scheduled appointments before we would find a parent at home for an evaluation. More often than not, we would arrive at their door and knock, only to hear the television turned down and the parent telling the children to be quiet so we wouldn't hear them. Every manner of excuse was heard to explain missed sessions. My favorite was a crumpled note found on the front door that said, "I am sorry I am not here. I forgot you were coming." Obviously, this resistance adds to the burden of conducting such research.

Their chaotic lifestyles and poor economic state hinders research work in other ways. One family's home in our study did not have electricity and home observation data was collected in part by flashlight. Another family's daughter started a fire that burned down their home and home visits had to take place in emergency housing.

The fact that we are dealing with families in which violence is an intrinsic part of their lives also influences our work. Our study lost one subject because she was murdered. Another mother was jailed for murdering her child's foster parent. More than one client missed evaluation sessions or treatment appointments because they or a close family member was the victim of an assault. One home interview was interrupted by the police arriving at the door. In addition, the areas where families lived were dangerous for data collectors and precluded collection of home observation data during evening hours. Furthermore, this required that data collectors always travel in pairs. All of these factors make research with these families more time consuming and much more difficult to complete.

Client characteristics also interfere with the quality of the data that is collected. For instance, these families have been shown to be quite socially isolated with few contacts with friends and family (Salzinger, Kaplan, & Artemyeff, 1983). This social isolation can act as a confound in the outcome research we produce. Most outcome studies to date have compared the performance of a group of maltreating families receiving a particular brand of treatment with that of a group of families that receive no treatment. When success has been found, treatment X has been lauded as the effective component. Yet, by the very act of studying these families and providing them with social contact, we may have also differentially influenced their level of social support and stress, thus accounting for the results found. In the study I have just completed comparing two very distinct treatments, behavioral versus insight oriented group intervention, little differential treatment results were found, despite the finding of treatment versus no treatment differences. It is our tentative conclusion that the support and stress reduction common to both treatments were responsible for the treatment effects found. Our clients' social isolation was quite apparent, as was our impact on it. For example, data collectors and staff who transported clients to and from evaluation and treatment sessions received Christmas presents from parents. Further, it was often difficult to get clients to leave the treatment room after group sessions ended. While such nonspecific factors are always a methodological problem within treatment outcome research, for this particular set of clients it may be especially troublesome. This possible confound will require future research studies to provide credible placebo control groups that would control for these nonspecific factors of support and contact with others. Only then can we truly test the impact of the interventions we are evaluating. The use of such placebo control groups, however, may be difficult, given that our primary source of subjects is through social service agencies. For example, when we attempted to include such a group in our design, we were blocked from doing so because agency personnel object to clients not receiving actual treatment.

Along with compliance problems, the violent nature of these clients' lives, and the difficulties of controlling for nonspecific factors, the use of traditional evaluation and treatment techniques also present a problem. Traditional parent training techniques have been shown to have only limited effectiveness with low SES clients (Graziano, 1977; O'Dell, 1974). Clients' lower educational status limits the use of training manuals commonly employed in parent treatment programs and the use of questionnaires as assessment devices. In pilot work, we quickly found that many of the parents could not read well. Yet, few would openly acknowledge this fact. Even if questionnaires were read to them, we found they did not understand the use of Likert-type scales and training had to be provided before such scales could be used. Even behavioral techniques, which are characterized by their concreteness, present a problem for these parents. Given the continual upheaval in clients lives, charting of child behaviors, for example, needed to be simplified and our expectations of consistent collection of data lowered. Further, techniques were often misused by clients. For example, we found that "time-out" procedures, such as placing a child in his or her room for misbehavior, had to be carefully reviewed, otherwise parents proceeded to lock children in closets, or worse. "Grandma's rule" (e.g., "If you do X, then Y will happen.") became a new form of parental tyranny unless caution was used in training. Such modifications need to be studied and carefully documented if outcome research is to be replicated and disseminated. The need to complete lengthy pilot work to develop such modifications, however, is a further discouragement to researchers entering into outcome work. To date, treatment programs have not developed techniques tailored to the special needs of this population. An exception to this is a single-case design study by Wolfe et al. (1982) who made use of a "bug-in-the-ear" to train parenting skills with a low functioning mother.

The variability in client behavior also presents a problem. In assessment work, I have found little relationship between laboratory and home observation of parent-child interaction, and even within the lab, behavior changed drastically from task to task (Azar, 1984). This variability makes the selection of assessment settings difficult and argues for the use of multiple settings. Anecdotally, it has been my experience that even small matters, such as the television breaking down, will have a major effect on the quality of the data collected. There seems to be a sensitivity to even minor stressors. Longer baseline periods than are currently used may be needed to arrive at the most accurate picture of parental functioning. Again, however, the collecting of more data points at pre- and postassessments in multiple settings further heightens the cost and effort involved in completing such research.

Mobility of clients also adds to the difficulty in undertaking outcome studies. Clients moved as any as three times between the time of referral for treatment and our first contact with them, a period of only three or four weeks. Tracking them down for even our short two-month follow-up was a major undertaking. Such persistence would not be required with a more middle-class and less mobile client population.

This last limiting factor of client characteristics will probably be a perpetual hindrance in our outcome study attempts. Developing methods to circumvent each of the difficulties I have described might constitute a line of treatment research in and of itself. The networking of outcome researchers would also facilitate the sharing of tips on the pragmatics of working with these clients.

Despite these major limiting factors, a few hardy souls, myself included, have proceeded in attempting to test the effectiveness of treatments with child maltreaters. Although this ground-breaking work has been useful, there already have been common methodological problems in the work produced that limits its generalization. These problems include: (1) selection bias in the subjects employed, (2) limited scope and source of dependent measures, (3) poor treatment specifications, (4) limitations in experimental design, and (5) practical significance.

The first concern involves the samples being used for study. The most easily accessible subject pool has been social service agency referred parents. In many cases, research has centered on cases court ordered into treatment and, in particular, on mothers. The applicability of the data to other subsamples of maltreaters is limited. First, court adjudication has been shown to positively affect successful completion of treatment (Wolfe, Aragona, Kaufman, & Sandler, 1980) and this may bias our understanding of treatment effectiveness. Work with a broader spectrum of referrals is needed. Second, male maltreaters constitute a large proportion of maltreating parents. Present studies do not give us much information as to how we might intervene with this subgroup. Efforts need to be directed at eliciting the participation of male abusers in outcome evaluations, as well as in assessment studies. Third, given the fact that the child's behavior has been hypothesized to play a role in maltreatment, it is striking that no studies have focused on direct intervention with the child. While this type of study might be condemned by some as "blaming the victim," there is no reason for researchers to wear such scientific blinders.

Another sampling issue has been the failure in outcome research to control for the age and birth order of the child within the families studied. Both of these factors can have profound effects upon the behavioral data collected. In addition, studies have not concentrated on infants and toddlers, despite the fact that these are the ages at which most abuse takes place. This may limit the usefulness of the information gained in such studies.

Finally, the small sample sizes currently employed in outcome studies with child maltreaters makes generalization of results difficult. Detailed descriptions of subject characteristics are often lacking, making it impossible to determine the representativeness of the parents studied.

The dependent measures being employed by outcome studies also may be insufficient. Although the issue of lack of demonstrated relationship between outcome measures and referral problem has already been discussed, other problems are present. First, only a narrow band of behavior is measured (e.g., tolerance for crying, child compliance), whereas a much broader range of behavior or sequences of behavior may be involved. Second, outcome is often measured only in one setting, under one set of conditions and from only one perspective. The effectiveness demonstrated may be a result of the setting or source chosen for measurement, not of the treatment. Rarely has client or child satisfaction with treatment been tapped. Caseworkers perspectives at times have been used, but data from my own work suggests that such perspectives do not correlate with actual behavioral observations (Azar, 1984) and is, therefore, suspect as an outcome measure.

The third area of methodological problems, the failure to specify therapeutic procedures in detail, is probably one of the most common and yet most serious problems in psychotherapy research in general. Reviews of parent-training studies with a broad spectrum of populations have indicated that the specific methods used in training the same child management techniques can differentially influence effectiveness (Gordon & Davison, 1981; Graziano, 1977). With this very difficult population specification of methods used is even more crucial. However, few published treatment studies with child maltreaters offer detailed manuals describing their interventions. Moreover, the reports often do not specify the exact nature of treatment presentations. The reader is merely told "behavioral training was given" or "education in child development was provided." This vagueness in specifying interventions makes replication of results difficult.

Further, along with a lack of treatment specification, no studies to my knowledge have included a measure checking that the treatment offered was in fact implemented as planned. Such a measure is essential if one is to state unequivocally that a treatment was effective.

The experimental designs commonly being used in current outcome work are also inadequate. Many of the studies have employed single case designs. While such designs are useful in the exploratory phases of treatment development to provide leads for larger group studies, there is a greater probability of nonspecific factors confounding the results of such work. As noted earlier, even if group designs have been used, studies have not used more than one treatment to compare effectiveness, thus leaving open the question of whether the specific treatment was in fact responsible for any effects found. The results of the comparative treatment study I have just completed clearly raise questions as to the specificity of treatment effects that have already been found.

The last and probably biggest methodological issue is the question of practical significance. In present studies the treatment conditions employed are often unrepresentative of those normally available to such clients. Study therapists tend to be doctoral level psychologists or psychiatrists, whereas in most settings these parents are treated by nurses or social workers with either bachelor's or master's level training. In the long run, those studies that use these more representative professionals will have more utility. In addition, many studies employ treatments that are delivered in the home, an approach that is not practical in most mental health centers or medical settings. Though it might be argued that there is no need for researchers to perpetuate the status quo in searching for successful interventions, funding agencies will need to be convinced that such system changes are necessary. This will require hard empirically derived support. Such empirical support comparing innovative approaches to traditional ones is not available as yet.

The lack of a large literature on outcome in treatment is striking, given the prevalence of the problem of child maltreatment. The limiting factors that have been described, however, may be responsible. Until these obstacles to undertaking outcome studies are addressed, empirically based studies will continue to be rare. Funding agencies must be prevailed upon to acknowledge the greater difficulty in conducting studies with maltreating families by increasing funding to allow for longer follow-up periods, larger staffs, and so on. Networking of research projects might also be fostered. This would allow greater dissemination of pragmatic information regarding undertaking such studies as well as provide larger sample sizes defined by very specific characteristics (e.g., type of maltreatment, sex of parent, age of child). Greater methodological care also needs to be taken to avoid the problems already present in the research we have accumulated.

Child abuse research has left its infancy. In many ways it is similar to the young adolescent who has not clearly defined his or her identity and has prematurely taken on adult activities without an adequate experience base from which to operate. The time has come for us to define our identity more clearly by developing our own definitions of the disorder we are studying and doing the basic homework of gaining an empirically grounded understanding of where we should intervene. A caution must be noted, however, as we proceed. No amount of empirical studies will completely eliminate the obstacles present in working with maltreating populations. These will forever be with us and we need to clearly recognize this fact, otherwise we will have unrealistic expectations of ourselves and our clients.

References

Aragona, J. A., & Eyberg, S. M. (1981). Neglected children: Mothers' report of child behavior problems and observed verbal behavior. *Child Development, 52*, 596-602.

Azar, S. T., Fantuzzo, J. W., & Twentyman, C. T. (1984). An applied behavioral approach to child maltreatment: Back to basics. *Advances in Applied Behavior Therapy and Research, 7,* 3-11.

Azar, S. T., Robinson, D. R., Hekimian, E., & Twentyman, C. T. (1984). Unrealistic expectations and problem solving ability in maltreating and comparison mothers. *Journal of Consulting and Clinical Psychology, 52*(4), 687-691.

Azar, S. T. (1984). *An evaluation of the effectiveness of cognitive behavioral versus insight oriented mothers' groups with child maltreatment cases.* Unpublished doctoral dissertation, University of Rochester.

Gambrill, E. D. (1983). Behavioral intervention with child abuse and neglect. In M. Hersen & P. M. Miller (Eds.), *Progress in behavior modification* (Vol. 17, pp. 1-56). New York: Academic Press.

Gordon, S. B., & Davidson, N. (1981). Behavioral parent training. In A. S. Gurman & D. P. Kniskern (Eds.), *Handbook of family therapy* (pp. 517-555). New York: Bruner/Mazel.

Graziano, A. M. (1977). Parents as behavior therapists. In M. Herson, R. M. Eisler, & P. M. Miller (Eds.), *Progress in behavior modification* (pp. 251-298). New York: Academic Press.

Lorion, R. P. (1978). Research on psychotherapy and behavior change with the disadvantaged. In S. L. Garfield & A. E. Bergin (Eds.), *Handbook of psychotherapy and behavior change: An empirical analysis* (pp. 903-938). New York: John Wiley.

O'Dell, S. (1974). Training parents in behavior modification: A review. *Psychological Bulletin, 81,* 418-433.

Plotkin, R., Azar, S. T., Twentyman, C. T., & Perri, M. P. (1982). A critical evaluation of the research methodology employed in the investigation of causative factors in child abuse and neglect. *Child Abuse and Neglect, 5,* 449-455.

Reid, J. B. (in press). Social-interactional patterns in families of abused and nonabused children. In C. Zahn Waxler, M. Cummings, & M. Radke-Yarrow (Eds.), *Social and biological origins of altruism and aggression.* Cambridge: Cambridge University Press.

Ross, A. O. (1983). *Discussion on symposium on current issues in research and treatment in child abuse and neglect.* Paper presented at the annual conference of the Association for the Advancement of Behavior Therapy, Washington, DC.

Salzinger, S., Kaplan, S., & Artemyeff, C. (1983). Mothers' personal social network and child maltreatment. *Journal of Abnormal Psychology, 92*(1), 68-76.

Sandford, D. A., & Tustin, R. D. (1974). Behavioral treatment of parental assault on a child. *New Zealand Psychologist, 2,* 76-82.

Stein, T. J., & Gambrill, E. D. (1976). Behavioral techniques in foster care. *Social Work, 21,* 34-39.

Wolfe, D. A., Aragona, J., Kaufman, K., & Sandler, J. (1980). The importance of adjudication in the treatment of child abusers: Some preliminary findings. *Child Abuse and Neglect, 4,* 127-135.

Wolfe, D. A., & Mosk, M. D. (1983). Behavioral comparisons of children from abusive and distressed families. *Journal of Consulting and Clinical Psychology, 51,* 702-708.

Wolfe, D. A., St. Lawrence, J., Graves, K., Brethony, D., & Kelly, J. A. (1982). Intensive behavioral parent training for a child abusive mother. *Behavior Therapy, 13,* 438-451.

PART VII

Preventing Violence and Abuse

20

Research on the Prevention of Sexual Abuse of Children

Jon R. Conte

Programs to prevent the sexual victimization of children have recently become available in many communities throughout the United States. Since the information in this chapter was gathered (in August 1984), many of these programs have evaluated their prevention models. Some of these efforts have been carried out with minimal funding and reflect careful attention to methodological issues. This chapter discusses some of the methodological and ethical problems that complicate research on prevention. These problems grow inherently out of the nature of prevention programs and are illustrated by some of the evaluation reports currently available. While this chapter will not resolve these issues, it is hoped that it may become part of a discussion among sexual abuse prevention programs and researchers which may lead to cooperative research efforts.

The Nature of Sexual Abuse Prevention Programs

Programs to prevent the sexual victimization of children may differ along dimensions such as the occupation of the prevention trainer, the age of the child the program is intended to serve, the length of training, the terms used to describe the prevention content, and the curriculum materials used. In spite of these differences, a review of program exemplars (Conte, Rosen, & Saperstein, 1986) has suggested that most programs are based upon a common set of prevention concepts. These concepts include:

- Children have a right to control access to their own bodies and decide who will and will not touch what body part;
- Touching can be thought of as a continuum. Children are taught to discriminate between different types of touching (e.g., good versus bad touches, or OK versus not-OK touches);
- There is a difference between a secret and a surprise. Children shouldn't keep a secret if it involves not telling about being touched in ways that make the child uncomfortable;
- Many programs teach children to "trust their own feelings." Their intuition that something is wrong should be acted upon;
- Children are often taught to say "No" to abuse in assertive ways; and,
- Programs almost always teach children to tell if they are touched in ways that aren't OK and to keep telling if the first person doesn't believe them or doesn't take action.

Most programs describe themselves as focused on teaching concepts which children can use to prevent their own victimization (e.g., what is a not-OK touch) and assertive skills for escaping or resisting sexual abuse (e.g., "If approached by someone who asks you to take off your clothes, say: 'No!' Run and tell."). From a researcher's point of view these concepts and the programs that teach them present a number of methodological and ethical issues. Many of these issues are discussed in the remainder of the chapter.

Methodological Issues

What are the appropriate dependent variables? Most of the research efforts to date have focused on assessing children's knowledge gains as a result of participation in a prevention program. Answer formats vary. For example, Ray (1984) employed a 12-item questionnaire in which children responded "Yes" or "No" to questions about prevention. Plummer (1984) used a Likert scale in a 24-item questionnaire (e.g., "Is it OK to say no to adults?" always, often, sometimes, never). Conte, Rosen, Saperstein, and Shermack (1985) used an open-ended interview format (e.g., "When is it OK to tell a secret?"), and Downer (1984) used a 20-item multiple-choice questionnaire.

Children's knowledge of prevention concepts and skills seems an important and logical first dependent variable to assess in evaluating the effectiveness of prevention efforts. In the few evaluation reports generated to date, knowledge tests have been useful both to the programs themselves and to the field more generally. For example many research efforts have conducted question by question analyses and have identified which specific consent areas the prevention program appears to be unsuccessful in teaching. Programs can then be modified to increase their effectiveness in these specific areas. Additionally, programs should also be aware that evidence from one evaluative effort indicates that prevention content of an abstract nature is significantly more difficult for children to learn than content of a more specific nature (Conte et al., 1985).

With the exception of Downer (1984), none of the questionnaires used to date have been subjected to tests of their psychometric properties. Internal consistency or time stability of these instruments would seem important issues for future evaluation efforts. Also important would seem to be some effort to confirm that the readability level of the questionnaires conforms to the age of subjects.

Tests of skills. Although tests of children's knowledge may be a good place to begin in determining the effects of prevention programs, most prevention programs indicate that increase in children's skills is a second major goal. Prevention programs assume that by teaching children certain concepts (e.g., the difference between "OK" and "not-OK" touching) and assertive skills (e.g., "How to say, 'No!'") children will be able to prevent or escape abuse. While this ability involves cognitive and perceptual skills (e.g., to be able to recognize abusive situations) ultimately, resistance and escape behaviors are necessary. Although there are questions as to whether most existing prevention programs spend enough time training to actually be effective in teaching children prevention skills, most programs still suggest that skill acquisition is a major outcome goal (Conte, Rosen, & Saperstein, 1986).

Few of the prevention research efforts have assessed skill acquisition. Conte, Rosen, Saperstein, and Shermack (1985) devoted 4 out of 13 questionnaire areas to asking children which of 3 possible responses indicates what they would do in certain situations (e.g., "Someone you care about and trust tries to touch you in places you do not want to be touched and tells you to keep it a secret. Would you: (1) let him touch you because you do not want to hurt his feelings; (2) say 'No,' run and tell; or (3) leave but don't tell anyone?"). Downer (1984) employed a 20-minute interview with puppets in which children described what they would do in certain situations. Downer's research illustrates the importance of directly assessing children's skills acquisition. Although 94% of the children in her study were able to define assertiveness after prevention training, only 47% could give an example of an assertive reply to an abuse situation.

Asking children to describe what they would do in abuse situations is generally recognized by most programs as a less than optimal means of assessing skill acquisition since self-report of anticipated behavior is generally viewed as unreliable (Nelson, 1977). However there are several other problems prevention programs and researchers will have to address if better measures of skill acquisition are to be developed.

One of the major issues will involve developing greater clarity on the specific skills and behavior that prevention programs try to teach. Assertiveness involves a complex set of behaviors, only one of which is saying "No." Other skills inherent in assertiveness include: body posture which communicates strength, discriminating situations in which an assertive response is called for, and appropriate responses to continued aggression (Gambrill, 1977). The specific types of child behaviors that are to be taught in prevention problems have not to date been fully identified by most programs so efforts to develop means of measuring their acquisition is difficult. Development of a list of these prevention behaviors and a means of teaching them in the context of prevention programs is needed.

Another problem in assessing prevention skill acquisition concerns how to sample the child's behavior. The closer the sampling situation is to actual abuse situations the more likely the sample of behavior is to approximate what the child will be able to do in a real sexual abuse situation. Creating a test situation similar in important respects to abuse situations is extremely difficult. To begin with very little is known about the actual process used by adults who sexually abuse children to engage children in an abusive relationship and maintain their cooperation with ongoing sexual contact. Without a detailed empirically generated description of this process, prevention programs have developed a prevention model based upon anecdotal clinical information. These ideas may be at variance with the processes actually involved in sexual victimization. To the extent that the program models vary from actual victimization processes, so would any assessment situations based upon these prevention models also vary.

Perhaps more troubling, *in vivo* assessment situations are very difficult to construct without raising major human subject protection issues. Subjecting children to sexual abuse situations to assess what prevention behaviors they exhibit is not likely to be acceptable. Poche, Brouwer, and Swearington (1981) did employ an *in vivo* assessment situation in which adult confederates approached three preschool children on the playground to assess how the children responded to adult lures to leave the playground. This study raises a number of ethical concerns as well as sampling only one of many potential adult behaviors that serve to entrap children in sexual abuse situations. Of particular ethical concern is what effect on future behavior the assessment strategy might have. For example, does the lure desensitize children to adult lures or teach children that adult approach behavior on the playground is in fact safe since during the assessment procedure the lure ended in a nonabuse situation?

Although behavior analogue assessment strategies have been criticized for not accurately describing what subjects actually do under "real" life circumstances, they have received renewed interest, since for many behaviors they represent the only means of estimating the strength of the behavior (McFall, 1977). Prevention researchers are likely to pay increased attention to the development of analogue measures of prevention behaviors. Paper and pencil tests that ask children what they would say and do in certain potential abuse situations are one possible approach. However, such paper and pencil tests do require conceptual and verbal response skills which approximate real life conditions only in part. Role-playing situations in which children act out what they would say and do in certain circumstances more directly assesses children's performance. The puppet role-play situations employed by Downer (1984) are in this vein, although the use of puppets does not assess children's performance as directly as would having the children act out the behavior themselves.

The development of an assessment procedure that would ask children to act out what they would do and say to a series of potential abuse situations in what is clearly a "play," an artificial situation, has a number of advantages for prevention research. It would afford an opportunity to sample children's skill acquisition in a number of different areas. By employing adult actors it may approximate real life abuse situations. Also, when a specific child fails to exhibit the prevention behaviors desired, the situation could be adapted even while being administered to ensure that the child was successful in resisting the abuse. While data might indicate that the child has failed to exhibit the desired behavior (an important evaluation question), the child would be left with a sense of success and competence likely to be important in preventing a real abuse encounter.

Unanticipated consequences. Prevention programs deal with issues that are inherently frightening. Sexual abuse of children, child kidnapping, and child murder are public issues children are exposed to on television and in parent conversations. The prevention program rhetoric is that prevention concepts empower children and reduce fear. To date there is no data describing the effects of prevention training on children's fearfulness nor on other unanticipated consequences. For example, it is not clear how prevention training affects children's understanding of their bodies, family relationships, or sense of security. Altering children's basic understanding of themselves and their world either in positive or negative directions is a major evaluative question for prevention efforts in the near future. Although it is likely that most children are unaffected, recent anecdotal evidence suggests that at least some children in some programs may have at least temporary (if not permanent) negative reactions as a result of prevention. For example, one program reports that a few of their preschool children after exposure to a prevention program have been afraid to ride home from school with anyone but their parents (G. Haynes, training coordinator, Girls Club of Omaha, personal communication, June 14, 1984).

The measurement of unanticipated consequences of prevention training might best be accomplished through a combination of quantitative and qualitative approaches. A behavior checklist quantifying behaviors indicative of fearfulness in young children (e.g., clinging to parents or nightmares) would be helpful. Additionally, attention should be directed to determining how children understand the prevention content. An open-ended interview questionnaire could assess children's understanding of prevention content as it may have become incorrectly associated by the child to various aspects of his or her life. Questions could be targeted at areas likely to be influenced by prevention training such as: the child's personal sense of well-being, safety or security, interpersonal safety, touching the child's body, and other areas in which a child might generalize prevention content beyond what programs intend, or supply their own reasoning to ideas presented during prevention training.

A story is frequently told in prevention circles (whether it is true is not known) about a certain group of children who, having seen a filmstrip about Penelope Mouse who was sexually abused by her uncle, told their trainer after the program that only mice were sexually abused. Unstructured interviews with children exposed to prevention programs could be helpful in determining what sense children make of prevention concepts as they process their learning over the time period after training.

A questionnaire for parents might also be developed that asks parents to note any effects of prevention training they observe in the child while at home. The questionnaire could ask parents to report both what children say and any changes in behavior.

Concern as expressed here with the assessment of unanticipated consequences should not be taken to mean that such effects exist. It is not at all clear that such effects are common. Indeed the more likely concern may be that most programs produce only limited and short-lived effects. However, since the risks of negative effects in terms of increased fearfulness or distraction of children's understanding of their world are present, evidence confirming or rejecting their presence seems important.

Timing of measurement. Plummer (1984) raises major questions about the durability of prevention training effects. At two- and eight-month follow-up contacts, children exhibited a significant reduction in the retention of content they initially had learned. Although this decay in learning varied across questions it does suggest both that prevention programs should experiment with means to increase retention of learning (e.g., through periodic booster training sessions) and that prevention researchers should employ several follow-up contacts to determine the durability of effects.

However, repeated measure designs raise a number of additional problems. For example, they increase the risk that children's performance on subsequent testing will be influenced by having taken the pretest (Campbell & Stanley, 1963). Prevention research efforts to date present conflicting data describing the effects of repeated testing. Plummer (1984) indicates that the pretest experience may have influenced children's performance on eight of the questions used in her study. However, since the study did not involve random assignment to groups, it is not clear whether the posttest-only groups may have been different for some other reason. Ray (1984), in another study employing nonrandom assignment, found that a classroom group exposed to two posttest measurement periods did not significantly increase knowledge of prevention content from the first to second testing periods.

While decisions about the number and spacing of measurement points is integrally related to research design, these preliminary evaluation efforts suggest that the potential effects of testing should receive immediate attention in prevention research. The issue is especially important since Plummer's (1984) data indicates decay in learning over two- and eight-month follow-up contacts. These data when viewed in light of Ray's (1984) findings that a review can significantly increase children's knowledge (even over learning at the end of a prevention program) suggests that measurement of learning and maintenance of learning over time as well as prevention efforts to increase the likelihood of maintenance are important. The effects of repeated measurement on children's learning as separated from repeated prevention efforts (such as periodic booster training sessions) will be important to clarify. Interesting in this regard is the possibility of using subsets of questionnaire items at various follow-up contacts so as not to expose subjects to the entire test at each testing period.

Research design. A number of research design issues need to be addressed by prevention researchers. In part, evidence for the effects of prevention programs will be judged by the power of prevention research designs to isolate the effects of the program from other variables affecting children's knowledge. Many prevention programs are presented to entire classrooms. Research efforts to date have often involved randomly selecting one or more classroom groups to receive training and one or more other classrooms to serve as controls. Since the static group comparison design lacks the power to indicate that intervention is responsible for any observed changes, results developed through the use of these designs are generally of a low confidence level (Campbell & Stanley, 1963).

Practical problems of reducing interaction between control and experimental subjects around prevention content may make true experimental design evaluations in which students in a single classroom are randomly assigned to groups very difficult, at least in educational settings. Time series designs, especially the multiple baseline designs, should be considered as an alternative to true experimental designs (Herson & Barlow, 1976). The multiple baseline design would require a repeated measurement strategy in which children's performance (e.g., knowledge of prevention concepts) was assessed. Children from a number of classrooms could be randomly assigned to three treatment groups. All children would take a knowledge test for several weeks prior to prevention training. The logic of a multiple baseline design involves the sequential introduction of intervention to each of the three groups. Increase in the children's knowledge associated with introduction of the intervention on one of the groups and steady level of performance in the other group(s) is an argument for internal validity. Time series designs offer an alternative to true experimental designs, although many of the single subject designs do assume no effect of repeated testing.

Whether the approach to research design is a single-subject or group design effort, in the future it is likely that research questions raised in prevention efforts will be more complex. Simple questions concerning the effects of prevention over no prevention will lead to more complex questions (e.g., what aspects of prevention produce what effects, or how many sessions are necessary to produce what level of student learning?). The construction of designs to address these more complex evaluative questions will be aided as information is developed about the effects of repeated measurement on children's knowledge. Also important will be evaluators' and prevention programs' efforts to work with agencies hosting the program to arrange the delivery of the program in ways to facilitate design construction. For the time being, the demand for most programs is so great that it should be possible to establish training schedules that make possible various design strategies necessary to answer the more complex evaluative questions and maintain rigor. For example, when an entire school is to receive training, random assignment of children from a number of classrooms to training and wait-list control groups or to different cells of a factorial design should pose no practical problems.

Measuring the independent variable. Whatever research questions are asked in the future, prevention researchers need to develop procedures for ensuring that the prevention program children are exposed to is in fact the model intended. Conte, Rosen, Saperstein, and Shermack (1985) reviewed audio tapes of the prevention program they evaluated and found wide variation in the program delivered to children and the one intended. A. Downer (personal communication, April 1984) speculates that some prevention content areas are more likely to be influenced by preexisting cultural biases than others. For example, in the school-based prevention program developed by the Seattle Committee for Children, Downer believes that the biases of certain teachers (in spite of what the training model specifies) that "strangers are the danger" can be detected in responses of children in those classrooms to specific questions in the questionnaire.

Prevention researchers can provide an important aid to programs and an indispensable research function by developing procedures for assessing trainer compliance with the prevention model. Checklists of topics to be covered, illustrations used, and specific language to be employed could be useful to trainers as a self-monitoring device and to independent observers carrying out *in vivo* or audio or videotape reviews of samples of the prevention program. Without such reviews it is possible that differences in children's knowledge between groups represents unintended differences in what they were exposed to, not differences inherent in the research question upon which the research design is based. Procedures to review the content presented to children can ensure that the experimental variables are as intended. This is both an important evaluation and a quality assurance issue.

Conclusion

In a short period of time, a number of evaluation efforts have been completed that address many of the important preliminary research questions about the effects of programs to prevent the sexual abuse of children. That so many of these studies have been carried out so early is an encouraging statement about how research and evaluation are viewed by prevention programs. Although a number of methodological issues need to be addressed, if current trends continue, it is likely that knowledge about prevention will greatly expand in the immediate future. Communication between prevention evaluators and researchers may even lead to cooperative arrangements in which common measures are developed or similar questions addressed. All such cooperative efforts should be encouraged.

References

Campbell, D., & Stanley, J. (1963). *Experimental and quasi-experimental designs for research.* Chicago: Rand McNally.

Conte, J. R., Rosen, C., Saperstein, L., & Shermack, R. (1985). An evaluation of a program to prevent the sexual victimization of young children. *Child Abuse and Neglect, 9,* 319-328.

Conte, J. R., Rosen, C., & Saperstein, L. (1986). An analysis of programs to prevent the sexual victimization of children. *Journal of Primary Prevention, 6*(3), 141-155 .

Downer, A. (1984). *Development and testing of an evaluation instrument for assessing the effectiveness of a child sexual abuse prevention curriculum.* Unpublished thesis, University of Washington. (Available from Committee for Children, 172 20th Ave., Seattle, WA 98122)

Gambrill, E. (1977). *Behavior modification: Handbook of assessment, intervention, and evaluation,* San Francisco: Jossey-Bass.

Hersen, M., & Barlow, D. (1976). *Single case experimental designs.* New York: Pergamon.

McFall, R. M., (1977). Analogue methods in behavioral assessment: Issues and prospects. In John Cone & Robert Hawkins (Eds.), *Behavioral assessment: New directions in clinical psychology* (pp. 152-177). New York: Brunner/Mazel.

Nelson, R. (1977). Methodological issues in assessment in self-monitoring. In John Cone & Robert Hawkins (Eds.), *Behavioral assessment: New directions in clinical psychology* (pp. 217-248). New York: Brunner/Mazel.

Plummer, C. (1984, April). *Research prevention: What in school programs teach children.* Paper presented at the Third National Conference on Sexual Victimization of Children, Washington, DC. (Available from C. Plummer, P.O. Box 421, Kalamazoo, MI 49005-0421)

Poche, C., Brouwer, R., & Swearingen, M. (1981). Teaching self-protection to young children. *Journal of Applied Behavior Analysis, 14*(2), 169-176.

Ray, J. (1984). *Evaluation of the child sexual abuse prevention program.* (Available from J. Ray, Rape Crisis Network, N1226 Howard, Spokane, WA 99201)

21

Child Homicide in the United States: The Road to Prevention

Katherine K. Christoffel

It has become distressingly clear that homicide is a major threat to the survival of American children. Homicide is the only leading cause of death of children under 15 to have increased in incidence in the last 30 years (U.S. Bureau of the Census, 1982). Of all deaths of persons under 18, 5% are homicides; this is five times the relative frequency of homicide among deaths of persons over 18 (1%) (Office of the Center Director, 1982). The scope of the child homicide problem in the United States is greater than in other developed countries (Christoffel & Liu, 1983).

Prevention of child homicide will require interruption of the chains of events that lead to the inflicted or neglectful deaths. Studies to clarify those chains of events are of two major types, based on differing prevention models as seen in Table 21.1.

If preventive efforts rely on deterring and punishing perpetrators, the social and psychological characteristics of perpetrators are of paramount importance. Studies pursuing this model focus on identifying and describing perpetrators (e.g., d'Orban, 1979; Resnick, 1970; Resnick, 1969). The preventive modalities that can be expected to evolve from this approach include tightened criminal controls and intensive psychiatric and social work with the families of individuals who have characteristics that make them likely perpetrators. The disadvantage of this approach is that it requires a difficult effort: identification and successful treatment of all or most likely and proven perpetrators. Because that effort is so difficult, this is not likely to be an efficient approach to preventing child homicide.

The second preventive model relies not on controlling proven and

TABLE 21.1
Approaches to Preventing Child Homicide

Prevention model	Preventive modes	Disadvantages
deter and treat individual perpetrators	intensive psychiatric and social work; criminal control	must identify and successfully treat all or most likely and proven perpetrators
protect potential victim groups	developmentally specific social interventions	identity of high risk groups not yet clear; no proven prevention methods yet

potential perpetrators but on protecting potential victims. This is a public health—as opposed to a clinical or criminal—approach and has the potential to protect children from unsuspected or unrehabilitated perpetrators. Studies pursuing this model focus on identifying subgroups of children with high homicide rates and describing the situations that make them vulnerable to fatal injury (Christoffel, 1984; Christoffel, Anzinger, & Amari, 1983; Christoffel, Liu, & Stamler, 1981; Jason, 1983a; Jason & Andereck, 1983; Jason, Gilliland, & Tyler, 1983). This approach has not yet generated prevention programs, as identification of the high risk groups is not yet firm. The work is slow, largely because there has not yet been the commitment of social resources that would assure rapid progress in research and program development.

What is known about the characteristics of child homicide victims and their fatal injuries is summarized in Table 21.2. The characteristics cluster along developmental lines.

The highest rates of child homicide are in infancy (Christoffel, 1984; Christoffel & Liu, 1983; Christoffel et al., 1983; Christoffel et al., 1981; Jason, 1983b; Jason & Andereck, 1983; Jason et al., 1983; Office of the Center Director, 1982), including neonatal deaths of the pregnancy-parturition-concealment syndrome (Nixon, Pearn, Wilkey, & Petrie, 1981) and post neonatal deaths with other dynamics. The high infancy rate is all the more striking in view of underreporting due to successfully concealed pregnancies/neonaticides and other factors (Jason, 1983b). It seems reasonable to surmise that the stress of infant parenting, especially when added to other stresses, is the critical factor in infanticide. If this is confirmed by more detailed study, stress-reducing programs of the Family Focus type (Distleheim, 1982) are likely to be successful preventive approaches.

TABLE 21.2
Child Homicide Victims and Their Injuries

	Predominant Perpetrator	Predominant Weapons	Information Needed
Neonates	mother	suffocation, drowning	prevalence
Infants	relatives	bodily force	circumstances
Pre-schoolers	relatives and acquaintances	bodily force	circumstances
Adolescents	acquaintances and strangers	guns, knives, cars	situation, supervision

Preschool homicide victims in general suffer beatings by caretaking adults (Christoffel, 1984; Christoffel et al., 1983; Jason, 1983a; Jason et al., 1983) not all of whom are relatives. This suggests that age-inappropriate expectations by adults lead to dangerously severe punishments of these very young children (Christoffel, 1984; Christoffel et al., 1983; Christoffel et al., 1981). If this is confirmed by closer study, the combination of day care for adult relief and child development education of future parents—in primary and high schools and through the media—may protect preschoolers from fatal attack.

Preadolescent homicide victims die as a result of beatings, hit and runs, arson, gunshots, and stabbings (Christoffel, 1984; Christoffel et al., 1983; Jason, 1983a); most adolescent homicide victims die of gunshot wounds and stabbings (Christoffel, 1984; Jason, 1983a). This evolution suggests that as children go through the school years, they are increasingly placed in situations they are ill-equipped to negotiate. We need to know more about how the older children find their way into the overwhelming situations in which they die, so we can develop ways to protect them and, even more, to help teach them to protect themselves. This may require, at a minimum, increased adult supervision of some children at some times and some places, and school instruction in appropriate survival skills (Committee to Stop the Child Murders, 1981).

Progress in development of approaches for prevention of child homicide requires not only clarification of the circumstances of injury, but several other advances as well, such as those listed in Table 21.3.

For all age ranges little is known about how many child homicide victims die despite involvement of their families with child protection/ child welfare agencies. The reasons that such involvement was not protective

TABLE 21.3
Prevention of Child Homicide: Research Needs

- Clarify circumstances of injury by clinical studies.
- Clarify involvement (if any) of child protection and welfare agencies with victims and their families prior to homicide.
- Analyze meaningful age ranges.
- Identify geographical areas and social groups with high age-specific rates.
- Synthesize data sources: death certificates, child protection agencies, criminal.
- Adequate funding for prospective, controlled studies of existing and new prevention programs.

may be a critical missing piece of the child homicide picture.

Because of the striking relationship of injury type to age, the practice of using all child homicides under 15 or under 18 for analysis does not advance prevention efforts (Jason, 1983a; Jason et al., 1983). Meaningful age ranges must become standard in child homicide research.

Data concerning child homicide come from three distinct and often fairly independent sources: death certificates, child protection agencies, and police reports. The different data sources describe overlapping aspects of the problem. Synthesis of these aspects is needed, and could perhaps be advanced by a public health reporting system. An inclusive definition of suspicious death could be developed for such a system.

Preventive programs are most likely to succeed if targeted to specific needs. Identification of geographic and social groups with high age-specific homicide rates is needed for appropriate tailoring of programs.

Finally, and perhaps most importantly, prospective study of existing and new prevention efforts must become a national priority, with its importance reflected in substantial funding.

Child homicide has unfortunately made it into the ranks of major child health problems. Its conquest, like that of measles, must now make it onto our national agenda.

1987 Reflection

Since the preceding material was presented at the National Conference for Family Violence Research in 1984, increased attention has been turned to child homicide, as reflected in the several publications on the subject published since (Abel, 1986; Bass, Kravath, & Glass, 1986; Blaser, Jason, Wenjer, et al., 1984; Centers for Disease Control, 1986; Christoffel et al., 1987; Copeland, 1985; Etherick, Foster, & Campbell, 1986; Fontana et al.,

1987; Kirschner, Christoffel, Kearns, Roseman, et al., 1987; Krugman, 1983-85; Martinez, 1986; National Committee for the Prevention of Child Abuse, 1987; Nersesian, Petit, Shaper, et al., 1985; Paulson & Rushforth, 1986). These have confirmed the developmental patterns, and have ascertained several demographic risk factors: urban residence, Black race, male gender, poverty, and age under 3 or over 9. The findings are now so well established that design of targeted prevention programs should be possible, aimed at protecting potential victims (often by intervention with potential perpetrators).

In Chicago in July of 1987, the First National Symposium on Fatal Child Abuse, hosted by the National Committee for the Prevention of Child Abuse and Neglect and the Illinois Department of Children and Family Services, brought together investigators, public health officials, and providers of direct services in order to begin to devise ways to protect the youngest homicide victims. Recent studies have clarified the fact that it is often only serendipity that causes an assault or episode of neglect involving a young child to be fatal (a homicide) rather than nonfatal (child abuse or neglect) (Fontana et al., 1987; National Committee for the Prevention of Child Abuse, 1987). Means for prevention of fatal child abuse will therefore need to be, in large measure, means for prevention of all child abuse.

The need for better coordination of diverse data sources and for dedication of national resources to prevent child homicide remains.

References

Abel, E. L. (1986). Childhood homicide in Erie County, New York. *Pediatrics, 75,* 708-713.

Bass, M., Kravath, R. E., Glass, L. (1986). Death scene investigation in sudden infant death. *New England Journal of Medicine, 315,* 100-105.

Blaser, M. J., Jason, J. M., Wenjer, B. G., et al. (1984). Epidemiologic analysis of a cluster of homicides of children in Atlanta. *Journal of the American Medical Association, 251,* 3255-3258.

Centers for Disease Control (1986, November). *Homicide surveillance: High-risk racial and ethnic groups—Blacks and Hispanics, 1970 to 1983.* Atlanta: Centers for Disease Control.

Christoffel, K. K. (1984). Homicide in childhood: A public health problem in need of attention. *American Journal of Public Health, 74,* 68-70.

Christoffel, K. K., Anzinger, N. K., Merrill, D. A. (1987, June). *Child homicide in Cook County, Illinois: 1977-1982.* Final report on HHS Grant #90-CA-1050.

Christoffel, K. K., Jordan, T., Seiden, A., Fitzpatrick, J., White, B., Roseman, M., & The Task Force for the Study of Non-Accidental Injuries and Child Deaths (1987). *Protocol for determining if an injury is the result of child abuse or neglect.* Springfield: Illinois Department of Children and Family Services.

Christoffel, K. K., Anzinger, N. K., & Amari, M. (1983). Homicide in childhood:

Distinguishable patterns of risk related to developmental levels of victim. *American Journal of Forensic Medicine and Pathology, 4*(2), 129-137.

Christoffel, K. K., Liu, K., & Stamler, J. (1981). Epidemiology of fatal child abuse: International mortality data. *Journal of Chronic Diseases, 34,* 57-64.

Christoffel, K. K., & Liu, K. (1983). Homicide death rates in 23 developed countries: U. S. rates atypically high. *Child Abuse and Neglect, 7,* 339-345.

Committee to Stop the Child Murders (1981, April). [Workshop at the fifth National Conference on Child Abuse and Neglect, Milwaukee, WI]

Copeland, A. R. (1985). Homicide in childhood: The Metro-Dade County experience from 1956-1982. *American Journal of Forensic Medicine and Pathology, 6*(1), 21-24.

Distleheim, R. A. (1982). A place to come and talk. *Working Mother, 5,* 45-47.

d'Orban, P. T. (1979). Women who kill their children. *British Journal of Psychiatry, 134,* 560-571.

Etherick, S. J., Foster, L. R., Campbell, D. T. (1986). Risk factors for traumatic infant death in Oregon, 1973 to 1982. *Pediatrics, 77,* 518-522.

Fontana, V. J., et al. (1987, January). *High risk factors associated with child maltreatment fatalities.* Mayor's Task Force on Child Abuse and Neglect, New York City.

Jason, J. (1983a). Child homicide spectrum. *American Journal of Diseases of Children, 137,* 578-581.

Jason, J. (1983b). Underreporting of infant homicide. *American Journal of Public Health, 73,* 195-197.

Jason, J., & Andereck, N. D. (1983). Fatal child abuse in Georgia: The epidemiology of severe physical child abuse. *Child Abuse and Neglect, 7,* 1-9.

Jason, J., Gilliland, J. C., & Tyler, C. W. (1983). Homicide as a cause of pediatric mortality in the United States. *Pediatrics, 72,* 191-197.

Kirschner, R. H., Christoffel, K. K., Kearns, M. L., Rosman, M., and the Task Force for the Study of Non-Accidental Injuries and Child Deaths. (1987). *Protocol for child death autopsies.* Springfield: Illinois Department of Child and Family Services.

Krugman, R. D. (1983-1985). Fatal child abuse: Analysis of 24 cases. *Pediatrician, 11*(1), 68-72.

Martinez, L. (1986, June). *Illinois child fatalities, a three-year statistical profile,* Springfield: Illinois Department of Child and Family Services.

National Committee for the Prevention of Child Abuse (1987, June). [Briefing packet on the First National Symposium on Preventing Child Abuse and Neglect Fatalities, Chicago.] Chicago: Author.

Nersesian, W. S., Petit, M. R., Shaper, R., et al. (1985). Childhood death and poverty: A study of all childhood deaths in Maine, 1976-1980. *Pediatrics, 75,* 41-50.

Nixon, J., Pearn, J., Wilkey, I., & Petrie, G. (1981). Social class and violent child death: An analysis of fatal nonaccidental injury, murder and fatal child neglect. *Child Abuse and Neglect, 5,* 111-116.

Office of the Center Director, Center for Health Promotion and Education, CDC. (1982). Child homicide—United States. *MMWR, 31,* 292-294.

Paulson, J. A., Rushforth, N. B. (1986). Violent death in children in a metropolitan county: Changing patterns of homicide, 1958 to 1982. *Pediatrics, 78,* 1013-1020.

Resnick, P. (1969). Child murder by parents: A psychiatric review of filicide. *American Journal of Psychiatry, 126,* 325-334.

Resnick, P. J. (1970). Murder of the newborn: A psychiatric review of neonaticide. *American Journal of Psychiatry, 126,* 1414-1420.

U.S. Bureau of the Census (1982). *Characteristics of American children and youth: 1980.* (Current Population Reports P-23 No. 114) Washington, DC: Government Printing Office.

About the Authors

SANDRA T. AZAR is Assistant Professor in the Department of Psychology at Clark University. She has researched and written extensively in the area of physical child abuse, especially in the areas of cognitive behavioral theory, treatment outcome studies and the development of screening instruments for unrealistic expectations in parent-child relations.

RICHARD A. BERK is Professor of Sociology at UCLA. He has published widely in a number of social science journals, including *American Sociological Review, Social Science Research, Sociological Methods and Research, Law and Society Review,* and *Law and Policy Quarterly*. He was a coinvestigator with Lawrence Sherman on the Minneapolis Police Study, a project on police response to domestic violence, and is currently involved in several research projects on the criminal justice system and the response of the criminal justice system to domestic violence, where policy concerns are paramount.

MICHELE BOGRAD received her Ph.D. in human development from the University of Chicago. She is a psychologist in private practice in Cambridge, Massachusetts. She is on the faculty at the Kantor Family Institute and the Family Institute of Cambridge, Massachusetts. She is coeditor of a forthcoming book on feminist perspectives on wife abuse.

LEE H. BOWKER received his Ph.D. from Washington State University in 1972. He has since written more than a hundred publications, including 12 books, on program evaluation, crime, corrections, the victimization of women (including wife abuse), gerontology, and higher education. His most recent book is *Beating Wife-Beating* (Lexington Books, 1983).

EVE BUZAWA received her Ph.D. from the School of Criminal Justice at Michigan State University. She is Associate Professor of Criminal Justice at the University of Lowell, Lowell, Massachusetts. She has written and researched extensively on police and legislative responses to domestic violence, as well as on police organizational behavior.

KATHERINE K. CHRISTOFFEL is a university-based General Pediatrician at Children's Memorial Hospital (CMH) in Chicago. She is an active member of the Protective Service Team, and regularly works in the busy emergency room. In both of these areas, she is involved with abused and neglected children and their families. Her research focuses on preventive pediatrics, including prevention of both inflicted and uninflicted injury. In addition to continued investigation of homicide, her current clinical and research work includes investigation of growth disturbances (obesity and malnutrition) consequent to family dysfunction.

ANNE H. COHN, D.P.H., has been the executive director of the National Committee for the Prevention of Child Abuse since October, 1980. In 1979-80 she was a White House Fellow and a special assistant to Patricia Roberts Harris, Secretary of the Department of Health and Human Services (HHS), working on child policy issues. In 1978-79, she was a Congressional Science Fellow, working with U.S. Rep. Albert Gore, Jr. of Tennessee. While an associate of Berkeley Planning Associates, she directed the first national evaluation of child abuse and neglect programs, overseeing all phases of a three-year evaluation of 11 demonstration projects funded by HEW (now HHS).

JON R. CONTE, Ph.D., is Associate Professor at the School of Social Service Administration at the University of Chicago. He is a Clinical Social Worker and Researcher, lecturing widely on the topic of child sexual abuse.

DEBORAH DARO, M.C.P., is the Director of Child Abuse Research for the National Committee for the Prevention of Child Abuse. As a Vice President of Berkeley Planning Associates, she directed the firm's comprehensive evaluation of the 19 clinical demonstration projects for the treatment of child abuse and neglect funded by the National Center on Child Abuse and Neglect. She has also directed a multiyear research and evaluation effort on child abuse prevention at the University of California, Berkeley, School of Social Welfare.

JEFFREY L. EDELSON, Ph.D., is Associate Professor in the School of Social Work at the University of Minnesota and Coordinator of Research and Evaluation for the Domestic Abuse Project, Minneapolis.

SARAH FENSTERMAKER is Associate Professor of Sociology at the University of California, Santa Barbara. Her work has appeared in *Law and Society Review, Sociology of Work and Occupations, Social Science Research,* and *Sociological Methods and Research.* She has also edited the fifth volume of the Sage Yearbooks in Women's Policy Studies, *Women and Household Labor*. She has worked for a number of years on research concerning gender equality.

DAVID FINKELHOR is Associate Director of the Family Research Laboratory at the University of New Hampshire. He has been studying the problem of child sexual abuse since 1977, and has published three books, *Sexually Victimized Children* (Free Press, 1979), *Child Sexual Abuse: New Theory and Research* (Free Press, 1984), and *A Sourcebook on Child Sexual Abuse* (Sage, 1986), and many articles on the subject. He has been the recipient of research grants from the National Institute of Mental Health, the National Center on Child Abuse and Neglect, and the Conrad Hilton Foundation. His other research interests include elder abuse and sexual assaults in marriage.

DENISE J. GAMACHE, M.S.W., is the School Curriculum Project Coordinator for the Minnesota Coalition of Battered Women. She was formerly Director of Community Interventions for the Domestic Abuse Project of Minneapolis.

EDWARD W. GONDOLF is Professor of Sociology at Indiana University of Pennsylvania. He formerly worked as a Counselor and Program Coordinator with RAVEN, one of the founding programs for men who batter. He is also the director of the IUP Domestic Violence Study Center and a Research Fellow in Clinic Services Research at Western Psychiatric Institute and Clinic, University of Pittsburgh. He is the author of the book *Men Who Batter: An Integrated Approach to Stopping Wife Abuse* (Learning Publications, 1984), as well as several articles on the topic. His expertise in community development has taken him to Guatemala, Alaska, and India to conduct field studies and mediation of community conflict.

CAROLYN L. GOULD, M.D., is a member of the Department of Pediatrics at the School of Medicine, University of Maryland, Baltimore. She has written extensively on the issue of foster care and child maltreatment.

ROBERT L. HAMPTON, Ph.D., is Associate Professor of Sociology at Connecticut College in New London, Connecticut. He is a former Fellow of the Family Development Program, Children's Hospital Medical Center, Boston. He has written extensively on the subject of child maltreatment and professional responses to child abuse and neglect. He has also conducted research on race and child abuse, for which he received funding from the National Center on Child Abuse and Neglect (1981).

SHARON D. HERZBERGER is Professor of Psychology at Trinity College, Hartford, Connecticut. She received her Ph.D. from the University of Illinois. Her current research focuses on interpersonal perceptions in abusive families and factors affecting decisions to label acts of family violence as abuse. Related previous work includes the cyclical nature of family violence and coping strategies among abused children.

GERALD T. HOTALING is Assistant Professor in the Department of Criminal Justice at the University of Lowell, Lowell, Massachusetts, and Research Associate of the Family Research Laboratory at the University of New Hampshire. He has edited two books on family violence and has been the recipient of a number of grants on violence and child sexual abuse.

JOHN T. KIRKPATRICK is Associate Dean in the College of Liberal Arts at the University of New Hampshire. He received his doctorate in sociology from the University of New Hampshire in 1983. His research interests include interpersonal violence, gender roles and crime, and the epidemiology of violent crime in the United States.

ELI H. NEWBERGER, M.D., is Director of the Family Development Program at Children's Hospital Medical Center in Boston, Massachusetts and a member of the Department of Pediatrics at Harvard Medical School, Boston, Massachusetts. He is an internationally recognized expert in the area of child maltreatment. He has written, researched, and lectured extensively on the topic and has made important contributions to the knowledge base on child abuse and neglect, especially in the areas of risk factors and the long-term consequences of abuse and neglect.

PHYLLIS J. NEWTON is a Statistical Analyst with the U.S. Sentencing Commission in Washington, D.C., working on sentencing guidelines for the new Federal Penal Code.

LEWIS OKUN, Ph.D., began counseling batterers in nonviolence in the spring of 1979, with the Domestic Violence Project, Inc., of Ann Arbor, Michigan. He is a Member of the Board of Directors of the Domestic Violence Project and continues to practice batterers' counseling for the Livingston Area Council Against Spouse Abuse, Inc., Howell, Michigan. He is also a Staff Clinical Psychologist with Ypsilanti Regional Psychiatric Hospital, Ypsilanti, Michigan.

KARL A. PILLEMER is Assistant Professor in the Department of Sociology and Anthropology and a Research Associate of the Family Research Laboratory at the University of New Hampshire. He has published extensively in the area of elder abuse and neglect including, with Rosalie Wolf, a collection of articles, *Elder Abuse: Conflict in the Family* (Auburn House, 1986).

DESMOND K. RUNYON, M.D., Ph.D., is a member of both the Department of Pediatrics and the Department of Social and Administrative Medicine in the Medical School at the University of North Carolina at Chapel Hill. He has written and researched extensively on child maltreatment, especially on issues of treatment and intervention strategies.

DANIEL G. SAUNDERS is the Program Evaluator at the Program to Prevent Woman Abuse, Family Service, Madison, Wisconsin. He was formerly Director of Professional Services and Director of the Program to Prevent Woman Abuse at Family Service. He was a Postdoctoral Fellow at both the Family Research Laboratory at the University of New Hampshire and in the Department of Psychiatry at the University of Wisconsin. His publications include a dissertation entitled "The Police Response to Battered Women" and a number of articles on counseling men who batter and on value issues in working on the problem of woman abuse.

MICHAEL D. SCHOCK, M.S.W., is a social worker at Family and Children's Service of Minneapolis. He was an intern at the Domestic Abuse Project, Minneapolis.

ANDREA J. SEDLAK is a Senior Research Scientist in the Organizational Research Studies Group at Westat, Inc., Rockville, Maryland. She is a social psychologist whose expertise includes children's social development and family interaction dynamics. She has published a number of articles and presented papers at various conferences on the incidence and prevalence of child maltreatment and adult domestic violence, the evaluation of services of a battered women's shelter, and risk factors and consequences of family violence.

BARBARA E. SMITH received her Ph.D. from the State University of New York at Stony Brook and is a Research Scientist at the Institute of Criminal Law and Procedure at Georgetown Law Center. She has conducted research and published reports on victims and various aspects of the criminal justice system. Her current research focuses on the psychological, social, physical, and financial difficulties faced by crime victims and attempts to identify which victims are most "at risk."

MURRAY A. STRAUS is Professor of Sociology and Director of the Family Research Laboratory at the University of New Hampshire. He has also taught at the following universities: Minnesota, Cornell, Wisconsin, Washington State, York (England), Bombay (India), and Ceylon (Sri Lanka). He is a former President of the National Council on Family Relations, Vice President of the Eastern Sociological Society, and Member of the Council, American Association for the Advancement of Science. In 1977 he was given the Ernest W. Burgess Award of the National Council of Family Relations for outstanding research on the family. He is also the recipient of an American Sociological Association award for contributions to undergraduate teaching. He is the author or coauthor of over 125 articles on the family, research methods, and South Asia; and 10 books including *Intimate Violence,* (1988), *Social Stress in the United States* (1986), *Crime and the Family* (1985), *The Dark Side of Families* (1983), *The Social Causes of Husband-Wife Violence* (1980), *Behind Closed Doors: Violence in the American Family* (1980), *Family Measurement Techniques* (1978), and *Sociological Analysis* (1968).

MICHAEL J STRUBE is Associate Professor of Psychology at Washington University in St. Louis. His interests lie primarily in the areas of social perception, social motivation, and social cognition. Most recently, these interests have focused on the dynamics underlying "maladaptive" decisions including the failure to relinquish control, the decision not to comply with a medical regimen, and the decision to remain in an intimate but abusive relationship. This research has been conducted from the perspective that such decisions are rational when viewed from the perspective of the decision maker, and thus require rational decision making models for their understanding.

HOWARD TENNEN is Associate Professor of Psychiatry and Director of Psychology Training at the University of Connecticut School of Medicine. He received his Ph.D. from the University of Massachusetts. His research has focused on how people cope with victimizing events including serious illness, disability, and, most recently, family violence.

SUSAN J. WELLS is with the National Legal Resource Center for Child Advocacy and Protection of the American Bar Association (ABA). She is the Principal Investigator for the Screening Project, a study funded by the National Center on Child Abuse and Neglect to examine screening and prioritization in child protective services' (CPS) intake and investigation. Prior work includes directing the ABA's Child Abuse Decision Making Project to study substantiation and risk for re-reporting in CPS, consulting with the Navy and Army regarding their programs for responding to abuse and neglect, teaching at the State University of New York at Albany and a postdoctoral fellowship in psychiatric epidemiology at the Johns Hopkins University School of Hygiene and Public Health. She has worked in child protective services and has done extensive training of child welfare workers, supervisors, and administrators.

ROSALIE S. WOLF received her Ph.D. from the Florence Heller School at Brandeis University. She is Associate Director of the University Center on Aging and Assistant Professor in the Department of Medicine and Family and Community Medicine at the University of Massachusetts Medical Center, Worcester. She has directed two Federal projects on elder abuse and neglect and, with Karl Pillemer, has edited *Elder Abuse: Conflict in the Family* (Auburn House, 1986).

NOTES

NOTES

NOTES

NOTES

NOTES